Guns in America

Recent Titles in Contemporary Debates

The Affordable Care Act: Examining the Facts
Purva H. Rawal

Climate Change: Examining the Facts
Daniel Bedford and John Cook

Immigration: Examining the Facts
Cari Lee Skogberg Eastman

Marijuana: Examining the Facts
Karen T. Van Gundy and Michael S. Staunton

Muslims in America: Examining the Facts
Craig Considine

Prisons and Punishment in America: Examining the Facts
Michael O'Hear

American Journalism and "Fake News": Examining the Facts
Seth Ashley, Jessica Roberts, and Adam Maksl

Free Speech and Censorship: Examining the Facts
H. L. Pohlman

Poverty and Welfare in America: Examining the Facts
David Wagner

Voting in America: Examining the Facts
H. L. Pohlman

Race Relations in America: Examining the Facts
Nikki Khanna and Noriko Matsumoto

GUNS IN AMERICA

Examining the Facts

Donald J. Campbell

Contemporary Debates

BLOOMSBURY ACADEMIC
NEW YORK • LONDON • OXFORD • NEW DELHI • SYDNEY

BLOOMSBURY ACADEMIC
Bloomsbury Publishing Inc
1385 Broadway, New York, NY 10018, USA
50 Bedford Square, London, WC1B 3DP, UK
29 Earlsfort Terrace, Dublin 2, Ireland

BLOOMSBURY, BLOOMSBURY ACADEMIC and the Diana logo
are trademarks of Bloomsbury Publishing Plc

First published in the United States of America by ABC-CLIO 2021
Paperback edition published by Bloomsbury Academic 2024

Copyright © Bloomsbury Publishing Inc, 2024

Cove photo: Handguns on display in a store.
(Matthew Richardson/Alamy Stock Photo)

All rights reserved. No part of this publication may be reproduced or
transmitted in any form or by any means, electronic or mechanical,
including photocopying, recording, or any information storage or retrieval
system, without prior permission in writing from the publishers.

Bloomsbury Publishing Inc does not have any control over, or responsibility for,
any third-party websites referred to or in this book. All internet addresses given
in this book were correct at the time of going to press. The author and publisher
regret any inconvenience caused if addresses have changed or sites have
ceased to exist, but can accept no responsibility for any such changes.

Library of Congress Cataloging-in-Publication Data
Names: Campbell, Donald J., 1948– author.
Title: Guns in America : examining the facts / Donald J. Campbell.
Description: Santa Barbara, California : ABC-CLIO, [2021] | Series:
Contemporary debates | Includes bibliographical references and index.
Identifiers: LCCN 2021003789 (print) | LCCN 2021003790 (ebook) |
ISBN 9781440870583 (cloth) | ISBN 9781440870590 (ebook)
Subjects: LCSH: Firearms—Law and legislation—United States. |
Gun control—United States. | Firearms and crime—United States. |
Firearms—Social aspects—United States. | Firearms ownership—Social aspects—United States.
Classification: LCC KF3941 .C36 2021 (print) |
LCC KF3941 (ebook) | DDC 363.330973—dc23
LC record available at https://lccn.loc.gov/2021003789
LC ebook record available at https://lccn.loc.gov/2021003790

ISBN: HB: 978-1-4408-7058-3
PB: 979-8-7651-3281-4
ePDF: 978-1-4408-7059-0
eBook: 979-8-2160-9352-7

Series: Contemporary Debates

To find out more about our authors and books visit www.bloomsbury.com
and sign up for our newsletters.

For
DAC & AGC
and
KMC
With love.

Contents

How to Use This Book   xi

Introduction   xiii

1   Guns, Crime, and Crime Prevention   1
    Q1. Does violent gun crime increase with increases in the availability of firearms?   2
    Q2. Do criminals have a preference for certain firearms over others?   7
    Q3. Does the "gun show loophole" substantially contribute to violent crime?   13
    Q4. Do current gun registration laws reduce violent crime and help apprehend violent criminals?   19
    Q5. Do ballistic fingerprinting and microstamping techniques currently in use help police solve gun crimes?   25
    Q6. Would a ban on "assault-style" rifles help prevent or reduce violent crime?   32

2   Guns and Personal Safety   41
    Q7. Does gun ownership and having a gun in the home increase personal safety?   42
    Q8. Does mandatory gun safety training reduce gun accidents and suicides?   48

	Q9. Do mandatory safe storage laws reduce accidental shootings and suicides?	54
	Q10. Do "stand your ground" laws increase an individual's personal safety?	60
	Q11. Do "red flag laws"/extreme risk orders increase domestic and family safety?	66
3	**Guns and Societal Safety**	**73**
	Q12. Is gun violence increasing in America?	74
	Q13. Are the police in favor of armed citizens?	79
	Q14. Can implementing "smart gun" technology make society safer?	86
	Q15. Would banning "bump" stocks and large-capacity magazines (LCMs) reduce shooting casualties?	92
	Q16. Can a comprehensive database on gun sales reduce gun violence?	98
	Q17. Would mandatory gun liability insurance decrease gun violence?	104
	Q18. Do gun control regulations increase the safety of minority group communities?	110
4	**Guns and School Safety**	**117**
	Q19. Are school shootings increasing in America?	119
	Q20. Does intensive media coverage inspire school shootings?	124
	Q21. Does allowing guns on college campuses increase campus gun violence?	130
	Q22. Are current gun regulations effective in preventing school shootings?	136
	Q23. Does designating schools as "gun free" zones increase school safety?	142
	Q24. Does arming willing teachers and school staff increase school safety?	148
5	**Guns and the Law**	**155**
	Q25. Are American gun laws laxly enforced?	156
	Q26. Do harsher sentencing penalties reduce gun violence?	162
	Q27. Does the *Heller* interpretation of the Second Amendment make the country less safe?	168
	Q28. Does allowing "watch list" individuals to buy guns reduce general safety?	174

	Q29. Does the Second Amendment Sanctuary movement increase gun violence?	179
6	**Guns, Drugs, and Mental Illness**	**187**
	Q30. Would relaxing current drug laws reduce gang-related gun violence?	189
	Q31. Do psychotropic drugs increase the likelihood of gun violence?	195
	Q32. Would prohibiting the mentally ill from owning guns reduce gun violence?	201
	Q33. Do purchase waiting periods reduce gun suicides and impulse killings?	207
7	**Guns and Civil Societies: Acceptable Social Contracts**	**215**
	Q34. Do Western democracies with strict gun control regulations have less violent crime?	216
	Q35. Does modern entertainment contribute to societal gun violence?	223
	Q36. Do political, racial, and ethnic extremists contribute disproportionately to gun violence?	230
	Q37. Is modern America more violent than America in past years?	237
Index		243

How to Use This Book

Guns in America: Examining the Facts is part of ABC-CLIO's Contemporary Debates reference series. Each title in this series, which is intended for use by high school and undergraduate students as well as members of the general public, examines the veracity of controversial claims or beliefs surrounding a major political/cultural issue in the United States. The purpose of this series is to give readers a clear and unbiased understanding of current issues by informing them about falsehoods, half-truths, and misconceptions—and confirming the factual validity of other assertions—that have gained traction in America's political and cultural discourse. Ultimately, this series has been crafted to give readers the tools for a fuller understanding of controversial issues, policies, and laws that occupy center stage in American life and politics.

Each volume in this series identifies 30 to 40 questions swirling about the larger topic under discussion. These questions are examined in individualized entries, which are in turn arranged in broad subject chapters that cover certain aspects of the issue being examined, for example, history of concern about the issue, potential economic or social impact, or findings of latest scholarly research.

Each chapter features 4 to 10 individual entries. Each entry begins by stating an important and/or well-known **Question** about the issue being studied—for example, "Do Western democracies with strict gun control regulations have less violent crime?"

The entry then provides a concise and objective one- or two-paragraph **Answer** to the featured question, followed by a more comprehensive, detailed explanation of **The Facts**. This latter portion of each entry uses quantifiable, evidence-based information from respected sources to fully address each question and provide readers with the information they need to be informed citizens. Importantly, entries will also acknowledge instances in which conflicting data exists or data is incomplete. Finally, each entry concludes with a **Further Reading** section, providing users with information on other important and/or influential resources.

The ultimate purpose of every book in the Contemporary Debates series is to reject "false equivalence," in which demonstrably false beliefs or statements are given the same exposure and credence as the facts; to puncture myths that diminish our understanding of important policies and positions; to provide needed context for misleading statements and claims; and to confirm the factual accuracy of other assertions. In other words, volumes in this series are being crafted to clear the air surrounding some of the most contentious and misunderstood issues or our time—not just add another layer of obfuscation and uncertainty to the debate.

Introduction

Few things divide modern American society as thoroughly as firearms. Once a time-honored symbol of American spirit and American values, the gun defined the rugged individuals—the pioneers, the frontiersmen, the cowboys, and the soldiers—whose efforts and achievements helped to shape a young nation into a dominant world power. For well over a century, acquiring a first gun was a badge of honor and a rite of passage into responsible adulthood for many individuals; and for the typical American, the prevalence of firearms in their midst raised scarce qualms or questions. But in the early part of the 20th century, America's love affair with guns noticeably began to fade. Limited attempts at controlling guns certainly had appeared at various earlier times in the country's history, but the 20th century marked the real birth of America's gun control movement, starting with the passage of New York City's Sullivan Law in 1911, and cresting with major federal legislation in the 1930s, '60s, and '80s.

What happened? After an epoch of championing firearms, after elevating the gun to iconic stature, what prompted a sizable portion of America to question the gun's continued prominence in society, and even reject its continued utility outright? What social difficulties and shifting sentiments could so tarnish firearms that substantial numbers of Americans would challenge this remarkable historical orientation toward guns, and provoke a prominent legislator to call not just for gun controls but for actual bans on some firearms such as the AR-15 semiautomatic rifle: "If I could have gotten 51 votes . . . for an outright ban . . . I would have done it. . . ." (Feinstein, 1995)?

Answering this question—by examining the issues and the arguments that lie beneath the contemporary division in America's attitudes toward guns—is the aim of this book. Demands for the regulation and control of guns have traditionally rested on four related justifications: crime prevention; general societal safety; individual personal safety; and the belief that guns no longer have a legitimate place in civilized society (Campbell, 2019). Each of these justifications involves a multitude of complex considerations. These range from determining the proper weight to place on complicated empirical evidence, to determining the most suitable values for guiding America into the future. In making such determinations, gun control activists and gun rights activists reach radically divergent conclusions about the nature of evidence, the importance of specific pieces of evidence, and the social values the nation should endorse. Because these determinations truly are intricate and the evidence supporting most conclusions is ambiguous and open to interpretation, partisans of one view or the other can advocate for their preferred position quite convincingly. But for individuals uncommitted to either perspective, for individuals who just want to understand the debate that has so inflamed both camps, these advocacy assessments are confusing and frustrating. Regardless of how convincingly the two camps present the evidence, clearly they both cannot be absolutely accurate or correct. After all, the debate typically entails contradictory and mutually exclusive positions.

Rather than examine the effectiveness or ineffectiveness of gun regulation generally—impossible to do without simultaneously accepting a large measure of subjective evaluation—this assessment instead examines 37 highly specific questions associated with America's gun debate. This more concrete focus offers the possibility of reaching conclusions actually supported by objective evidence or, alternatively, showing why an evidence-based conclusion is not yet possible. While the questions themselves are distinctive and highly specific, the chapters of the book cluster broadly related items together in an attempt to present a more expansive view of the issue. Each of the chapters concentrates on questions relevant to one of the major justifications for regulating firearms (crime prevention, safety, and societal values), but because some topics have multiple dimensions and are particularly important to the gun debate, the book devotes more than one chapter to questions in those areas.

Selection of the questions themselves warrants some explanation. When it comes to the closely intertwined subjects of gun rights and gun control, the pool of possible questions worth examining is large. Nonetheless, not all questions are created equal; some are simply more important than others. In the case of gun control, the important questions are those that can highlight measures likely to be effective in reducing gun violence, and those likely to be ineffective. As Leah Libresco, a statistician and past news writer at the data journalism site FiveThirtyEight.com, observed, suicides comprise two-thirds of the gun deaths in the United States, and homicides among young men aged 15 to 34 account for the next largest number of gun deaths. These deaths far exceed the numbers killed in mass shootings, yet only a few of commonly touted gun control policies address these populations. She concludes that, rather than focus on sweeping gun bans, the country might save lives by finding more limited gun control measures tailored to specific at-risk populations (Libresco, 2017). Believing that Libresco's point is a valid one, the book favored questions that had the most potential to address the effectiveness of particular gun control measures.

The second criteria for selection was whether the available evidence was likely to provide a factually defensible answer to the question posed. The gold standard for drawing strong inferences about the impact of one factor on another—true experimental manipulation, with random group assignments and appropriate controls—is not possible when examining gun control questions. For example, assume we are interested in whether the presence of a firearm in a household increases or decreases homeowner safety. Ideally, we might choose a random neighborhood, provide firearms to some randomly chosen households in that neighborhood while removing and withholding guns from other, randomly chosen households, wait an appropriate length of time, and then compare the two sets of households on whatever safety measures we used. Although ideal, this approach clearly is not feasible for practical and ethical reasons.

However, a seemingly similar approach is available: identify a set of households that already contain a firearm, find parallel households that are gun-free, and compare them on the various safety measures. While this approach will certainly provide an answer to the question, the answer provided is unlikely to be conclusive. Without random selection and assignment of households, it is possible that preexisting differences in the households themselves—law-abiding homeowners in one set relative to borderline criminals in the other, for example—account for any safety measure differences, rather than just the presence of a firearm itself. Further, this type of inherent ambiguity is commonplace in examining most gun control issues. The relevant data generally suggest an answer to the question posed, but one that is usually open to alternative interpretations. Thus, the reader might keep in mind that "factually defensible" is a term that typically involves at least some subjective assessment.

Further, because of these interpretation difficulties, it is typical for researchers to rely on the "weight of the evidence" to draw conclusions about contradictory empirical findings. For example, when confronting multiple studies by different investigators that have produced conflicting results, reviewers will examine the *overall* pattern of findings in reaching a considered judgment about the issue in question. Since complex research questions often stimulate a significant number of studies, this weight-of-the-evidence approach offers a way to reach empirically supported conclusions even when particular studies disagree.

The last criterion for selection was the significance of the issue explored by the question and how integral it has been to discussions of gun control and gun rights in America. Debates about gun regulation have surfaced periodically over the past hundred years, and similar issues about firearms often reappear and get repeated from one discussion cycle to the next. Presumably, these reoccurring concerns—"Is gun violence reaching unprecedented levels in the United States?" "Can we reduce gun violence by banning certain types of firearms?" and so forth—are particularly important issues in the debate. Thus, the book's coverage is tilted to explore possible answers to these and other vital questions.

FURTHER READING

Campbell, Donald, 2019. *America's Gun Wars: A Cultural History of Gun Control in the United States.* Santa Barbara, CA: Praeger.

Feinstein, Dianne, 1995. "Feinstein in 1995: 'Mr. and Mrs. America, Turn Them All In . . .'" https://www.youtube.com/watch?v=ffl-tWh37UY

Libresco, Leah, 2017. "I Used to Think Gun Control Was the Answer. My Research Told Me Otherwise." *Washington Post*, October 3. https://www.washingtonpost.com/opinions/i-used-to-think-gun-control-was-the-answer-my-research-told-me-otherwise/2017/10/03/d33edca6-a851-11e7-92d1-58c702d2d975_story.html

1

Guns, Crime, and Crime Prevention

Despite the many contributions that firearms have rendered to the founding and development of the nation, Americans have often regarded the guns in their midst as a mixed blessing. Typically touted by gun enthusiasts as valuable and sometimes essential survival tools, as well as enjoyable recreational objects for fostering comradery and friendships, gun control advocates nonetheless note that guns also have a less positive, more disturbing side to them. Because of their inherent lethality, any misuse of firearms can pose potentially dire consequences for a society's peaceable, law-abiding individuals, and for society generally. While guns certainly can save innocent lives, they also can take innocent lives, facilitate illegal activity, escalate violent encounters, and magnify the impact of unbalanced individuals intent on mass murder.

This chapter explores this Janus-sided aspect of guns, focusing specifically on connections between the prevalence of guns and the associated effects on violent crime. The chapter first examines the growth and prevalence of firearms in American society with the frequency and prevalence of violent crime, determining how closely these two elements track each other. It then examines the nature of firearms used in crime, addressing the issue of whether criminals have a general preference for certain types of firearms over others. Next, the chapter investigates whether (or to what degree) the secondary market for guns—private gun sales or the "gun-show loophole"—contributes to gun crime and violence.

Turning to crime prevention, the chapter looks at whether universal gun registration would reduce violent crime and aid in apprehending lawbreakers; and then assesses the effectiveness of several specific gun control measures in reducing violent gun crime. These measures include determining if gun cartridge microstamping and ballistic fingerprinting techniques are useful in helping police solve gun crimes and reduce gun violence; and whether a ban on certain military-style rifles would prevent or reduce crime.

Q1: DOES VIOLENT GUN CRIME INCREASE WITH INCREASES IN THE AVAILABILITY OF FIREARMS?

Answer: The findings are inconclusive, varying from study to study. Findings differ depending on the investigation's measure of "violent crime"—what the definition includes or excludes—and on how the study estimated growth in firearms availability. Because of these differences in measures and estimates, some studies have found a positive increase between the two variables, others have found a negative relationship, and still others have found no relationship. Further, because the data is typically correlational, it is not possible to determine the implications of a positive or negative relationship, even if one is assumed. For example, a positive relationship might mean that an increasing number of firearms in society results in more violent crime, but it might equally indicate that increases in violent crime result in the acquisition of more guns. Similarly, a negative relationship might mean that more guns in society deter violent crime, but it might equally indicate that some third factor—a strongly improving economy, for example—has impacted both, reducing crime and freeing funds for additional recreational gun purchases.

The Facts: Interest in the relationship between gun prevalence and violent crime dates back to at least the late 1970s and early 1980s. Philip Cook, a noted political scientist, published an early influential analysis of the impact of gun availability on violent crime in 1983. He concluded that a reduction in gun availability would likely have little impact on overall robbery and assault rates, because criminals engaging in these types of crimes would simply substitute less lethal weapons when carrying out illegal activities. However, he hypothesized that the use of less lethal weapons by criminals—the substitution effect—would likely result in a reduction in homicide rates.

Although this reasoning makes logical sense, empirical studies have not convincingly confirmed Cook's speculation. For example, the National

Research Council (NCR) concluded in 2004 that limitations in the methodologies and data of existing research investigations make it impossible to show a causal connection between the prevalence of firearms and the prevalence of violent crime (Karimov, 2018). Further, a follow-up analysis reviewing the research area from 2005 to 2016 noted that little had changed in the subsequent 12 years. This analysis identified six new studies specifically designed to estimate the causal effects of gun prevalence on violent crime and concluded that, nonetheless, significant methodological limitations still precluded drawing strong inferences about a causal relationship between gun availability and violent crime.

Further, the specific empirical findings also varied across the six studies. Two of the studies found a positive association between the prevalence of firearms and increases in both the total number of homicides and the number of firearms-related homicides. A third study found a positive connection between the availability of firearms and the number of firearm homicides among Hispanics, but not among Caucasians or Blacks. While a fourth study linked gun prevalence with the number of homicides committed by youths, a fifth study showed a *negative* connection between gun availability and the number of total and firearms-related homicides. Finally, the last study uncovered no relationship between gun availability and the number of intimate partner homicides (Karimov, 2018).

The lack of a direct measure of gun prevalence is a major problem for these studies, and may partially account for their disparate findings. The six studies all inferred the availability of guns using a proxy estimate: the number of firearms suicides over the total number of suicides (FS/S) in the investigated populations. This proportion is commonly used in gun prevalence studies, but since the actual number of guns is obviously unknown, determining whether the proportion is a reasonably valid estimate in any specific study is impossible. For example, two published studies that used this approach to determine gun prevalence in Hawaii and Mississippi reached dramatically different conclusions. Hawaii's prevalence rate was estimated at 25.8 percent in one study but 45 percent in the other. Similarly, Mississippi had a gun prevalence rate of 76.8 percent in one study but a 42.8 percent in the other. As the researcher noted, at least one of the studies (if not both) must have an inaccurate prevalence rate (Campbell, 2018). Other methodological issues with the studies center on the potential impact of missing or misclassified data, for example, classifying justifiable homicides by police officers or civilians in the study's measure of violent crime (Karimov, 2018).

Gary Kleck, a criminologist and gun violence expert at Florida State University, reached similar conclusions in a 2015 research review. His analysis focused on the methodological soundness of 41 studies testing the hypothesis that higher gun prevalence levels cause higher crime rates, particularly increased homicide rates. He examined the methodology of each study along three dimensions: whether the study used a validated measure of gun prevalence; whether it controlled for likely confounding influences; and whether it used appropriate causal ordering procedures to eliminate the possibility that crime rates affect gun rates, rather than the reverse. He found that most of the studies failed to address *any* of the three methodological concerns; and of the 90 distinct analyses generated in the 41 studies, only four addressed all three concerns—and these four analyses failed to support the hypothesis that more guns result in more homicides. Kleck concluded that, overall, while technically weak research offers some support for the hypothesis, strong research does not.

Many gun control proponents find arguments about the various weaknesses and limitations of gun violence research disingenuous. They assert that, if this is actually the case, gun rights advocates are substantially responsible for the problem. They specifically point to the Dickey Amendment—an NRA-backed provision proposed by U.S. representative Jay Dickey and inserted into the federal government's annual omnibus spending bill since 1996. The provision banned the Centers for Disease Control and Prevention (CDC) from funding research used to "advocate or promote gun control." While the amendment did not explicitly prohibit the CDC from financing gun violence research, the organization nonetheless shied away from funding such studies, fearing budget repercussions should Congress find that a CDC-supported study "advocated" for gun control. Congress clarified the provision in 2018, allowing for gun violence research.

Still other investigators have taken a broader approach to investigating connections between gun prevalence and violent crime. These analysts compare trends in the growth of firearms sales or production in the United States with the level of violent crime (using statistics reported by the FBI and Department of Justice) during the same period. For example, John Malcolm and Amy Swearer, analysts for the conservative-leaning Heritage Foundation, noted in 2018 that violent crime in America has been trending downward for decades, while the rate of firearms ownership has increased. They argued that the objective data indicate that higher rates of gun ownership are *not* associated with higher rates of violent crime. More generally, they assert that the available evidence shows no clear relationship between strict gun control legislation and violent crime rates or the number of homicides.

Another analyst, Mike Weisser, noted in the liberal-leaning Huffington Post in 2017 that the widely held belief (at least among many gun control advocates) that more guns lead to more violent crime seems, on the surface, unfounded. He writes, "How do we explain that the number of guns owned by Americans keeps increasing at a rather remarkable rate, yet violent gun crimes have been fairly level since 2000 even though gun sales exploded between 2008 and 2016? . . . . Since 2008, arrests for murder have decreased by nearly 20 percent. Meanwhile, over the same period, more than 75 million guns were added to the civilian arsenal. . . ."

To explain this perceived contradiction, Weisser cites the reasoning of noted University of California at Berkeley law professor and acknowledged gun violence expert Franklin Zimring. Emphasizing that various polls and surveys show a decline in the number of American households owning guns, Zimring argues that that the average number of guns in each *gun-owning* household must therefore be increasing. Thus, if prior gun-owning households are absorbing the additional firearms—if individual or household gun ownership has not grown—there is no reason to expect a major increase in gun-related violence in spite of increased gun sales. Weisser dismisses an alternative possibility famously advanced by the prominent but controversial gun violence researcher John Lott (2010)—that more guns lead to less crime because lawbreakers are more cautious about engaging in crime—claiming Lott's work has serious methodological and statistical flaws (Weisser, 2017). Other gun control advocates and journalists exploring gun issues have also been critical, both of the quality and integrity of Lott's work and of Lott's personal ethics (DeFilippis & Hughes, 2016; Moskowitz, 2018; Winkler, 2011). However, gun rights proponents (e.g., Firearms Owners Against Crime, 2016) and Lott himself (2015) have rejected these allegations, and his findings have long been central to many gun rights arguments.

Another gun violence commentator, University of Houston professor Larry Bell (2013) writing for *Forbes*, also remarked on the inverse relationship between increasing gun sales and decreasing gun crime rates. He was more willing to consider Lott's contention that more guns result in less crime. Bell cites Department of Justice statistics showing that over the course of 18 years (1993–2011), gun-related homicides in the United States decreased 39 percent (from 18,253 to 11,101), and nonfatal gun crimes dropped even more: 69 percent. Further, Pew Research, using data from both the Department of Justice and the Centers for Disease Control and Prevention, found a similar but even larger decline in gun homicides: a 49 percent decrease over the same period. At the same time, gun purchases (as reflected in background checks) were steadily increasing. Citing Lott, Bell attributes diminishing gun violence to the rapid growth of gun ownership and armed citizens. As more states adopted "shall issue" gun-permitting laws (where the issuing authority has no discretion in awarding concealed carry gun permits, and must issue a license to an applicant if that individual meets the law's stated criteria), Bell suggests it is reasonable to expect violent crime to decrease because criminals are deterred by the risk of attacking an armed target.

Malcolm and Swearer (2018) offer some support for Bell's speculation, noting that between 2007 and 2015, the number of adults with concealed carry gun permits increased by 190 percent, while violent crime rates dropped 18 percent and murder rates dropped 16 percent. They further note that, within this population, the proliferation of guns apparently did not lead to increased gun violence. They maintain that concealed carry permit holders are among the most law-abiding individuals in the country, with a crime rate—including gun crimes—between one-sixth and one-tenth that of law enforcement officers, who themselves have a much lower rate than the general population. Nonetheless, not all investigators accept the arguments put forth by Bell and by Malcolm and Swearer. For example, a comprehensive literature review conducted by the National Academy of Sciences in 2004 concluded that, based on the available evidence, it was impossible to determine whether concealed carry increases or reduces violent crime, since some studies found a reduction but others found an increase (Wellford, Pepper, & Petrie, 2005).

Overall, given the wide disparity in empirical results across different investigations and the serious methodological limitations that plague this research area, "inconclusive" remains the most defensible answer to the question of whether more guns increase violent crime.

FURTHER READING

Bell, Larry, 2013. "Disarming Realities: As Gun Sales Soar, Gun Crimes Plummet." *Forbes*, May 14. https://www.forbes.com/sites/larrybell/2013/05/14/disarming-realities-as-gun-sales-soar-gun-crimes-plummet/#873b04c3f7c7

Campbell, BJ, 2018. "Everybody's Lying about the Link between Gun Ownership and Homicide." Medium, March 13. https://medium.com/handwaving-freakoutery/everybodys-lying-about-the-link-between-gun-ownership-and-homicide-1108ed400be5

Cook, Philip, 1983. "The Influence of Gun Availability on Violent Crime Patterns." *Crime and Justice*, 4, 49–89.

DeFilippis, Evan, & Hughes, Devin, 2016. "The GOP's Favorite Gun 'Academic' Is a Fraud." ThinkProgress, August 12. https://archive.thinkprogress.org/debunking-john-lott-5456e83cf326/

Firearms Owners Against Crime, 2016. "John Lott Exposes Critics Lies: Response to Evan DeFilippis and Devin Hughes' Newest Claims at ThinkProgress: 08/19/2016." https://foac-pac.org/John-Lott-Exposes-Critics-Lies:-Response-To-Evan-Defilippis-And-Devin-Hughes-Newest-Claims-At-Thinkprogress/News-Item/5385

Karimov, Rousian, 2018. "The Relationship between Firearm Prevalence and Violent Crime." RAND Corporation: Gun Policy in America, March 2. https://www.rand.org./research/gun-policy/analysis/supplementary/firearm-prevalence-violent-crime.html

Kleck, Gary, 2015. "The Impact of Gun Ownership Rates on Crime Rates: A Methodological Review of the Evidence." *Journal of Criminal Justice*, 43(1), 40–48.

Lott, John, 2010. *More Guns, Less Crime*. Chicago: University of Chicago Press.

Lott, John, 2015. "Response to Evan DeFilippis and Devin Hughes' Claims at 'Armed with Reason' about My Research." John Lott's Website, June 23. johnrlott.blogspot.com/2015/06/response-to-evan-defilippis-and-devin_23.html

Malcolm, John, & Swearer, Amy, 2018. "Here Are 8 Stubborn Facts on Gun Violence in America." Heritage Foundation, March 14. https://www.heritage.org/crime-and-justice/commentary/here-are-8-stubborn-facts-gun-violence-america

Weisser, Mike, 2017. "How Do We Reconcile a Drop in Violent Crime with an Explosion in Gun Sales?" Huffington Post, April 6. https://www.huffingtonpost.com/entry/how-do-we-reconcile-a-drop-in-violent-crime-with-an-explosion-in-gun-sales_us_58e6702de4b0773c0d3edfb4

Wellford, Charles, Pepper, John, & Petrie, Carol (eds.), 2005. "Right to Carry Laws." In *Firearms and Violence: A Critical Review*, Chapter 6, Washington, DC: National Academies Press, pp. 120–151.

Zimring, Franklin, 2017. "Firearms and Violence in American Law." UC Berkeley Public Law Research Paper No. 2939902. March 25. https://www.papers.ssrn.com/sol3/papers.cfm?abstract_id=293902

Q2: DO CRIMINALS HAVE A PREFERENCE FOR CERTAIN FIREARMS OVER OTHERS?

Answer: Yes. Surveys of incarcerated felons spanning a 40-year period, from the 1980s to the present, offer a clear and straightforward answer to the question. Criminals *do* have a preference for certain firearms, overwhelmingly favoring easily concealable, high-caliber, quality handguns over rifles, shotguns, and other types of firearms (Alper & Glaze, 2019; Wright & Rosssi, 1986; Zawitz, 1995). In this regard, criminal gun preferences mirror the gun preferences of law-abiding citizens, who also gravitate to handguns. The compactness and ease of use of such firearms make them a practical carry weapon both for legitimate self-defense and for violent crime.

The Facts: In 1986, James Wright and Peter Rossi conducted one of the earliest studies investigating firearms preferences among criminals. Interested in generating information that might inform social policies aimed at minimizing gun violence, Wright and Rossi observed that such policies typically reflected two general approaches. One focuses on deterring individuals from *using* firearms in criminal activity (usually through severe penalties), while the other focuses on preventing criminally inclined individuals from *acquiring* firearms. The researchers recognized that the success of this latter approach depended on having some understanding of the types of firearms criminals prefer. Such insight could allow society to tailor specific policies narrowly aimed at these types of firearms; and gun-oriented individuals might more readily accept such narrow policies (Wright & Rossi, 1986: 8–12).

Consequently, Wright and Rossi undertook a survey of 1,874 felons incarcerated in prisons across 10 states: Arizona, Florida, Georgia, Maryland, Massachusetts, Michigan, Minnesota, Missouri, Nevada, and Oklahoma. This landmark investigation found that about 60 percent of the felons used some type of weapon in carrying out their illegal activities, and a firearm was their weapon of choice 83 percent of the time. Handguns were the felons' predominant firearm, outnumbering shotguns and rifles by more than a three-to-one margin. Contrary to conventional wisdom suggesting that criminals gravitate to Saturday night specials (small, cheap, unreliable guns), they found that accuracy, untraceability, and quality construction were the handgun characteristics most valued by felons (Wright & Rossi, 1986: 15). Of course, while felons might *value* such traits, circumstances of acquisition (if the handgun was stolen or borrowed) or pragmatic cost considerations (if the gun was purchased) might also determine the actual characteristics of felons' handguns. While noting these possibilities, Wright and Rossi concluded that the correspondence between criminals' preferred and actual handgun characteristics was nonetheless likely to be high, especially among felons habitually engaging in handgun crimes. Such individuals would over time eventually come into possession of a handgun that matched their ideal preferences. In contrast, a preference for small, cheap handguns (Saturday night specials) was highest among felons who had never owned a gun, or never committed a crime with one (Wright & Rossi, 1986: 166–167, 169–170).

In terms of firearm brands apparently favored by armed criminals, Wright and Rossi found that 36 percent carried handguns manufactured by Smith & Wesson, with another 16 percent carrying a Colt, and 5 percent carrying a Ruger (1986: 171). Another 30 percent of the sample could not identify the brand of their most recent handgun.

Of course, since Wright and Rossi obtained these results in the 1980s, Glock and several other manufacturers have entered the gun market, and current preferences would reflect these developments. For example, one study published in 2016 carried out an analysis of the make, model, and caliber of all the crime guns (4,505) that the Chicago Police Department had collected and inventoried in 2014. Five manufacturers dominated the list, and accounted for 33 percent (1,483) of all the guns collected: Smith & Wesson (520), Glock (343), Hi Point (240), Sturm, Ruger & Co. (233), and Taurus (147). Colt (59) was a distant sixth (Kollmorgen, 2016).

Similarly, while the 1986 data showed armed criminals gravitating to .38- and .357-caliber handguns (49 percent), this information predates the general availability and rise in popularity of the 9 mm pistol. For example, while the 2016 study found that .38/.357-caliber handguns represented 21 percent of the 1,483 guns within the top five manufacturing brands (25 percent if Colt is included), it also showed that the popularity of 9 mm pistols, at 46 percent, was almost double, suggesting that Chicago's criminals appear to prefer semiautomatic pistols to revolvers (Kollmorgen, 2016). Since these data are specific to Chicago, and use an entirely different methodology for determining criminals' gun preferences, comparisons to the 1986 data require caution. Nonetheless, while the research indicates that the firearms preferences of lawbreakers have apparently evolved since the 1986 data, the findings remain consistent with Wright and Rossi's conclusion that criminals overwhelmingly prefer handguns.

A 1995 analysis of crime statistics also confirmed many of the Wright and Rossi findings. For example, in examining 1993 National Crime Victimization Survey responses, Marianne Zawitz, a researcher at the Bureau of Justice Statistics, found that of the roughly 4.4 million violent crimes occurring that year (defined as robberies, aggravated assaults, rapes, and sexual assaults), the criminal possessed a firearm in 29 percent of the cases (i.e., about 1.3 million occurrences). Further, that firearm was a handgun about 85 percent of the time (i.e., in about 1.1 million of the 1.3 million cases). This percentage of handgun use was virtually identical to the percentage of handgun use (86 percent) in *all* instances of firearm-linked crime captured by the survey. Additionally, statistics from the FBI's

Supplemental Homicide Reports also demonstrated a criminal preference for handguns, indicating that 57 percent of murders committed in 1993 involved that type of firearm, with only 5 percent attributable to shotguns, and just 3 percent attributable to rifles (Zawitz, 1995). More generally, Bureau of Justice statistics showed that, over a period of 28 years in the United States (1980–2008), handguns were at least three times as likely to be involved in homicides than any other type of gun (see Cooper & Smith, 2011: 27, Table 42).

A 2019 survey of both state and federal prison inmates found that 21 percent of prisoners had carried a firearm during the offense for which they were imprisoned, and that firearm was a handgun in 88 percent of the cases. Criminals carried a rifle in only about 6 percent of the cases, and a shotgun in about 7 percent. Of those state prisoners carrying a firearm during their crime, males were more than twice as likely (22 percent) than females (9.5 percent) to be armed. Blacks were more likely to be armed (29 percent) than Caucasians (12 percent) or Hispanics (21.5 percent). Similarly, younger criminals (less than 35 years old) were more likely to be armed (about 27 percent) than those older than 35 years (about 16.5 percent) (Alper & Glaze, 2019).

While the above studies consistently confirm a handgun preference among criminals, a related piece of information would significantly enhance its usefulness for shaping effective gun policies: information regarding the particular sources criminals typically rely on to obtain their preferred firearms. Based on the survey data they examined, Mariel Alper and Lauren Glaze (2019) identified five main gun supply sources: from the off-the-street underground market (43 percent); borrowed from acquaintances, such as friends or family members (25 percent); taken from the crime victim or found at the crime scene (17 percent); purchased from a retail source, such as a gun store, pawnshop, or gun show (10 percent); or stolen in burglaries, or from family, friends, and retail outlets (6 percent).

Comparisons of these findings with the results obtained by Wright and Rossi three decades earlier show notable similarities. For example, in that earlier investigation, black-market sources accounted for 41 percent of felon-possessed handguns, versus 43 percent in the 2019 study. Similarly, felons obtained their handguns from friends and relatives about 35 percent of the time in the earlier research versus 25 percent in the later study. Further, both investigations indicate that retail sources (such as gun shops and gun shows) are relatively minor sources for criminal guns, accounting for only 16 percent in the Wright and Rossi study and even less (10 percent) in the later study. From a regulatory perspective, these data suggest that any point-of-sale retail focus will clearly not capture the vast majority of criminal handgun transactions (Alper & Glaze, 2019; Wright & Rossi, 1986).

Overall, this type of information has substantial value for policy making. For example, because gun-wielding criminals employ handguns significantly more frequently than rifles in carrying out illegal activities, gun control measures aimed at regulating assault-style rifles would only impact a very small percentage of overall gun violence. Kollmorgen (2016) observed that it was "notable" that only three assault rifles appeared in her data. Despite the rifle's prominence in mass shootings, the firearm plays only a minor role in criminal incidents. Thus, critics assert that from a policy perspective, focusing much regulatory effort on the rifle would not make sense, since even a ban could not significantly reduce general gun violence (Jacobs, 2018). One critic of such proposals asserted that it would likely save fewer than 10 mass shootings victims annually (Gius, 2017).

Conversely, these data also give insight into potential policy efforts more likely to impact gun violence. Since handguns are responsible for the vast majority of gun crimes and homicides (Larsen, 2018; Yellin, n.d. based on 2011 FBI statistics), a regulatory focus on handguns would seem promising. Indeed, many early gun control advocacy groups, such as Handgun Control, Inc., began with precisely such a focus. However, endeavors to severely restrict handguns proved quite unpopular—many law-abiding citizens valued these firearms for self-defense—and the political and legislative realities of American gun politics doomed these efforts. Ironically, it was these failures that eventually led gun control strategists to characterize the popular AR-15 semiautomatic rifle (with its military-style features) as an "assault weapon," and to select this rifle as an easier—if less effective—target than handguns for a regulatory ban (see Blake, 2013; NRA-ILA, 2019; Sugarmann, 1988).

In a similar vein, information about how criminals obtain their preferred firearms is also potentially valuable for policy making. As the research findings above have shown, most criminals do not obtain their guns from legitimate sources. Instead, crime guns are typically acquired from the underground market, from friends and relatives, or from burglaries and thefts. As Ingraham (2016) and others (Wright & Rossi, 1986: 229) have suggested, the policy implication of these findings is that additional regulations focused on gun purchases and gun ownership can do little to combat gun violence: legal gun owners are not the individuals engaging in the violence. Instead, Ingraham (2016) has suggested that the Bureau of Alcohol, Tobacco, and Firearms concentrate on identifying and shutting down the small number of gun dealers whose guns appear disproportionately in crime guns traces. Such targeted dealers, however, would undoubtedly object that additional law enforcement scrutiny based on such subjective and merely suggestive evidence is unfair and discriminatory. For example, more successful gun stores by definition sell more guns, and thus guns from these shops have a greater chance of showing up in gun crime trace analyses. Whether the actual number of guns found from such shops is "disproportionate" to a particular expected number normally involves interpretation and judgment. In any case, as a practical strategy for reducing gun violence, implementing this approach has often proved difficult (Becker, 2015).

The general conclusion suggested by all this is somewhat disappointing. The complexity of gun politics typically makes likely effective solutions to gun violence politically unacceptable; while politically acceptable solutions often have little practical effect. As Wright and Rossi wryly noted back in the mid-1980s, gun violence research is usually quite good in illuminating the problems, but quite poor in suggesting workable solutions (Wright & Rossi, 1986; 228).

FURTHER READING

Alper, Mariel, & Glaze, Lauren, 2019. "Source and Use of Firearms Involved in Crimes: Survey of Prison Inmates, 2016." Bureau of Justice Statistics, January 9. https://www.bjs.gov/index.cfm?ty=pbdetail&iid=6486

Becker, Olivia, 2015. "The Violent History of Chicago's Most Notorious Gun Shop." The Trace, June 26. https://www.thetrace.org/2015/06/the-violent-history-of-chicagos-most-notorious-gun-shop/

Blake, Aaron, 2013. "Is It Fair to Call Them 'Assault Weapons'?" *Washington Post*, January 17. https://www.washingtonpost.com/news/the-fix/wp/2013/01/17/is-it-fair-to-call-them-assault-weapons/

Cooper, Alexia, & Smith, Erica, 2011. "Homicide Trends in the United States, 1980–2008." Bureau of Justice Statistics, November. https://www.bjs.gov/content/pub/pdf/htus8008.pdf

Gius, Mark, 2017. "The Effects of State and Federal Gun Control Laws on School Shootings." *Applied Economic Letters*, 25(5), 317–320.

Ingraham, Christopher, 2016. "Gun Control: What Works, What Doesn't and What Remains Open for Debate." *Washington Post*, March 7. https://washingtonpost.com/news/wonk/wp/2016/03/07gun-control-what-works-what-doesnt-and-what-remains-open-for-debate/

Jacobs, Tom, 2018. "Here's More Evidence That an Assault Weapons Ban Would Decrease School-Shooting Deaths." Pacific Standard, February 27. https://psmag.com/news/assault-weapons-ban-decreases-school-shooting-deaths

Kollmorgen, Sarah, 2016. "Chicago's Criminals' Favorite Gunmakers: A Visual Ranking." The Trace, January 6. https://www.thetrace.org/2016/01/chicago-crime-guns-chart/

Larsen, Emily, 2018. "Fact Check: Are Most Gun Crimes Committed with Handguns?" Daily Signal, February 22. https://www.dailysignal.com/2018/02/22/fact-check-are-most-gun-crimes-committed-with-handguns/

NRA-ILA (National Rifle Association Institute for Legislative Action), 2019. "Background Checks for Guns." NICS NRA-ILA, January 7. https://www.nraila.org/get-the-facts/background-checks-nics/#_edn43

Sugarmann, Josh, 1988. *Assault Weapons and Accessories in America.* Violence Policy Center. https://www.vpc.org/studies/awacont.htm

Wright, James, & Rossi, Peter, 1986. *Armed and Considered Dangerous: A Survey of Felons and Their Firearms.* Hawthorne, NY: Aldine de Gruyter.

Yellin, Tal, n.d. "Handgun Homicides in the United States." *CNN Money.* https://money.cnn.com/interactive/news/handgun-homicides/

Zawitz, Marianne, 1995. "Guns Used in Crime." Bureau of Justice Statistics Selected Findings, July. https://www.bjs.gov/index.cfm?ty=pbdetail&iid=947

Q3: DOES THE "GUN SHOW LOOPHOLE" SUBSTANTIALLY CONTRIBUTE TO VIOLENT CRIME?

Answer: The "gun show loophole" refers to the right of private individuals to sell firearms to other private individuals without a background check. Two major factors influence the impact of this unregulated market on America's violent crime problem: the size of the unregulated market and its popularity among criminals for sourcing crime guns. The most recent research data indicate that the unregulated market accounts for about 13 to 15 percent of total gun sales (Alper & Glaze, 2019; Miller, Hepburn, & Azrael, 2017; see also Kertscher, 2018; Sherman, 2016).

With gun sales averaging about 14.3 million firearms annually (Trotta, 2019), this indicates that as many as two million guns may flow through the unregulated market. This is a substantial number, but the figure represents *all* transfers and sales, including the presumed majority of transfers, which would have passed background checks, had checks been required. Further, multiple surveys of incarcerated felons indicate that about 10 (NRA-ILA, 2019) to 16 percent (Wright & Rossi, 1986) of these criminals obtained their firearms through private gun transactions with legal firearms owners. For gun shows specifically, the figure is less than one percent (Alper & Glaze, 2019, Table 5).

Drawing inferences from these two sets of figures must be done cautiously, but the data appear to justify two conclusions. First, the unregulated gun market may offer prohibited individuals 200,000 to 300,000 firearms annually. Second, only a small minority of criminals appear to use this market to secure their crime guns. Research indicates that criminals predominantly rely on the black market, family and friends, thefts, and illegal "straw purchases," i.e., retail purchases made by individuals who can pass a background check and thus legally buy a firearm, but who then illegally pass the gun to a prohibited person (Alper & Glaze, 2019; NRA-ILA, 2019).

Thus, overall, while the unregulated gun market can serve as a potent source for crime guns and can clearly contribute to violent crime, gun transactions among private individuals are not the predominant means by which criminals obtain firearms.

The Facts: The Gun Control Act (GCA) of 1968 mandated that individuals engaged in the "business" of manufacturing, importing, or dealing in firearms obtain a federal firearms license (FFL). The Act also required such licensed vendors (i.e., FFL dealers) to screen gun buyers, and barred them from knowingly selling firearms to certain classes of "prohibited persons"—minors, felons, mental defectives, and drug addicts (Zimring, 1975). However, this screening requirement applied only to FFL dealers, not to private individuals making occasional firearm sales from their gun collection to other private individuals. With the passage of the Firearm Owners Protection Act (FOPA) in 1986, Congress maintained this regulatory approach. FOPA loosened GCA restrictions on FFL dealers by permitting them to sell firearms at gun shows (the GCA had restricted dealers to selling firearms only at the site listed on their license), but it still barred them from knowingly selling firearms to disqualified classes of individuals, even at gun shows. Further, FOPA explicitly distinguished between commercial and private sales, exempting private sales from the act's dealer obligations: "[dealer requirements] shall not include a person who makes occasional sales, exchanges, or purchases of firearms for the enhancement of a personal collection or for a hobby, or who sells all or part of his personal collection of firearms."

In this sense, discussions of a "gun show loophole" are misleading: federal laws always expected FFL dealers to screen gun buyers, and barred them from knowingly making commercial gun sales to prohibited individuals, regardless of where the sale took place. The "gun show loophole" is more accurately characterized as a "private seller loophole" in that federal law does not require private sellers—unlicensed individuals not engaged in the *business* of selling firearms commercially—to conduct any type of screening or background check when selling or trading to another private individual, at gun shows or elsewhere. Further, the "gun show loophole," by placing focus on *where* these private gun transactions usually take place (rather than on *why* such private sales are treated differently than commercial gun sales) have allowed gun rights advocates to deny that a "gun show loophole" even exists (see Sherman, 2016; NRA-ILA, 2019).

Gary Kleck, a criminologist at Florida State University, has further suggested that even the use of the term "loophole" in these discussions is misleading, in that it implies that the exemption was an inadvertent oversight of lawmakers, and that the law really did not intend to exempt private sellers (see Sherman, 2016). In actuality, the private seller exemption was quite deliberate. This is seen both in FOPA, where Congress clearly and intentionally excludes private gun sales from FOPA's regulatory requirements, and in the earlier GCA, whose preamble similarly indicates a desire to avoid imposing "any undue or unnecessary federal restrictions or burdens on law abiding citizens" (ATF, 2014).

Gun control proponents are dismissive of these arguments. They emphasize that prosecutions for even egregious dealer violations are rare, in large part because of the significant limitations in relying on the almost-impossible-to-prove-or-enforce dealer prohibition against "knowingly" selling firearms to disqualified individuals (Zimring, 1975). Gun control proponents have periodically advocated for more stringent regulations to beef up a provision that they see as essentially meaningless. Thus, in 1994, Congress passed the Brady Handgun Violence Prevention Act (Brady Bill), which imposed a five-day waiting period before a purchaser could collect his firearm, to allow state and local law enforcement officials to conduct background checks on all firearms purchased commercially from FFLs (ATF, 2017). The waiting period requirement was to expire in 1998, when the National Instant Criminal Background Check (NICS) system became operational.

During this interim period, gun policy experts Philip Cook and Jens Ludwig (1997) released a publication that suggested that about 40 percent of gun acquisitions in the United States took place without a background check. They derived this estimate from a telephone survey conducted in 1994, shortly after the Brady Bill became effective. Based on a small subsample of 251 people who had responded to the relevant survey questions (Cook & Ludwig, 1997; Qiu, 2015), the estimate was additionally limited because the data were collected before the implementation of NICS. While this figure was the best estimate at the time, the small sample and the timing of data collection made long-term reliance on this statistic questionable.

Nonetheless, many political figures and commentators continued to cite this figure decades later in discussions and debates. For example, Senator Timothy Kaine cited the 40 percent figure during a Senate speech commemorating the eighth anniversary of the Virginia Tech shooting (Gorman, 2015a); Senator Bernie Sanders of Vermont cited the statistic after the Parkland Florida school shooting during an interview on NBC's "Meet the Press" (Kertscher, 2018); and Governor Terry McAuliffe of Virginia mentioned the figure when he signed an executive order banning firearms from most state buildings (Gorman, 2015b). Similarly, Mark Kelly, husband of former congresswoman and gunshot victim Gabby Giffords, cited the figure during a CNN's State of the Union broadcast (Qiu, 2015); and presidential candidate Hillary Clinton at a campaign rally noted that gun shows and on-line sales accounted for 40 percent of guns sold in America (Masters & Beckett, 2017).

This percentage suggests that unregulated firearm purchases are a substantial source of potential crime guns, alarms the public, and buttresses demands for more stringent regulation. For gun control proponents, the figure is an especially powerful argument in their calls for legislation mandating universal background checks (Gorman, 2015b). Gun rights proponents have typically rejected the notion that private sellers contribute substantially to crime firearms (see NRA-ILA, 2008), and they have suggested that the imprecise nature of "gun show loophole" arguments simply add confusion to the public's understanding of the issue. They see such arguments as no more than a political ploy to justify requiring background checks even on private sales, which would in effect establish a background check system covering virtually all firearm transactions in the United States. Gun rights activists are adamantly opposed to such a universal system. They insist that virtually no evidence exists indicating that private seller background checks are likely to reduce gun violence, and that such checks are unenforceable without a national registry of firearms (Cox, 2019). Such a registry is anathema to most gun owners (see NRA-ILA, 2019), despite claims that a registry might help in the retrieval of firearms from gun owners no longer legally allowed to possess firearms or help the police identify the source of firearms found at crime scenes (Giffords Law Center, undated).

Within this context, the research by Alper and Glaze (2019) and by Miller, Hepburn, and Azrael (2017) updating the percentage of gun transactions occurring in the secondary market (i.e., 13 to 15 percent) has been seized on by gun rights activists to refute calls for additional gun control regulation. For example, gun control advocate Shannon Watts (2016) asserted that "the single most important thing we can do to reduce gun violence is to require a criminal background check for every gun sale," a sentiment echoed by congressional gun control proponents (Speier, 2015). The National Rifle Association (NRA) has vigorously attacked these assertions. The organization has rejected the outdated "40 percent" statistical claim, and asserted that background checks on private sales would have stopped none of the mass shootings referenced by President Barack Obama in a January 2016 White House speech, nor any of the multiple-victim shootings (i.e., those with 10 or more fatalities) that occurred since the speech (NRA-ILA, 2019). The organization maintains that demands for a universal background check system is simply the current manifestation of a long-term, enduring goal of gun control activists: enrolling all gun owners in a federal database in anticipation of ultimately criminalizing and confiscating privately possessed handguns (NRA-ILA, 2019). Gun control advocates reject this claim, maintaining that the only purpose of a universal background check system is to keep guns out of the hands of prohibited individuals.

Although speculations about the usefulness of private seller background checks for controlling violent crime are heavily enmeshed in gun politics, a recent RAND Corporation study offers some empirical evidence on the effectiveness of such checks. The research analyzed data from *states* that required private seller checks. The analysis identified eight studies conducted between 2003 and 2016, and tested for associations between the checks, violent crime and total homicides. The analyses indicated that dealer checks appeared to reduce firearm homicides, but private-seller checks had ambiguous effects on such homicides and were simply inconclusive (Gresenz, 2018). The various limitations in study methodologies and comprehensiveness make these findings only suggestive, but they also appear to justify a conclusion that the private seller loophole in background checks is not likely to contribute substantially to violent crime—a conclusion that even some gun control supporters have reluctantly acknowledged (see Lopez, 2019).

FURTHER READING

Alper, Mariel, & Glaze, Lauren, 2019. "Source and Use of Firearms Involved in Crimes: Survey of Prison Inmates, 2016." Bureau of Justice Statistics, January. https://www.bjs.gov/index.cfm?ty=pbdetail&iid=6486

ATF, 2014. *Federal Firearms Regulations Reference Guide.* https://www.atf.gov/firearms/docs/guide/federal-firearms-regulations-reference-guide-2014-edition-atf-p-53004

ATF, 2017. "Brady Law." Last reviewed April 28. https://www.atf.gov/rules-and-regulations/brady-law

Cook, Philip, & Ludwig, Jens, 1997. "Guns in America: National Survey on Private Ownership and Use of Firearms." National Institute of Justice Research in Brief, May. https://www.ncjrs.gov/pdffiles/165476.pdf

Cox, Chris, 2019. "What Lurks behind 'Universal' Background Checks." NRA-ILA, February 22. https://www.nraila.org/articles/ 201900222/what-lurks-behind-universal-background-checks

Giffords Law Center, n.d. "Registration." https://lawcenter.giffords.org/gun-laws/policy-areas/gun-owner-responsibilities/registration/

Gorman, Sean, 2015a. "Kaine Says 40 Percent of Gun Sales Estimated to Escape Background Checks." PolitiFact Virginia, April 28. https://politifact.com/virginia/statements/2015/apr/28/tim-kaine/kaine-says-40-percent-gun-sales-estimated-escape-/

Gorman, Sean, 2015b. "McAuliffe Says 40 Percent of U.S. Gun Sales Escape Background Checks." PolitiFact Virginia, November 2. https://politifact.com/virginia/statements/2015/nov/02/terry-mcauliffe/mcauliffe-says-40-percent-gun-sales-estimated-escape-backgro/

Gresenz, Carole, 2018. "Effects of Background Checks on Violent Crime." RAND Corporation, March 2. Updated April 22, 2020. https://www.rand.org/research/gun-policy/analysis/background-checks/violent-crime.html

Kertscher, Tom, 2018. "What Percentage of Gun Sales Are Done without a Background Check?" PolitiFact Wisconsin, March 16. https://www.politifact.com/wisconsin/statements/2018/mar/16/steve-bullock/what-percentage-gun-salesare-done-without-backgro/

Lopez, German, 2019. "Democrats Need to Think Way Bigger on Guns." Vox, February 6. https://www.vox.com/future-perfect/2019/1/9/18171909/universal-background-checks-hr-8-gun-violence-democrats

Masters, Kate, & Beckett, Lois, 2017. "Just One in Five Americans Obtains Gun without Background Check, Survey Finds." *The Guardian*, January 2. https://www.theguardian.com/us-news/2017/jan/02/guns-state-background-checks-study

Miller, Matthew, Hepburn, Lisa, & Azrael, Deborah, 2017. "Firearm Acquisition without Background Checks: Results of a National Survey." *Annals of Internal Medicine*, 166(4), 233–239. https://annals.org/aim/fullarticle/2595892/firearm-acquisition-without-background-checks-results-national-survey

NRA-ILA (National Rifle Association Institute for Legislative Action), 2008. "The Gun Show Myth." NRA-ILA, November 7. https://www.nraila.org/articles/20081107/the-gun-show-myth

NRA-ILA (National Rifle Association Institute for Legislative Action), 2019. "Background Checks." NICS NRA-ILA, January 7. https://www.nraila.org/get-the-facts/background-checks-nics/#_edn43

Qiu, Linda, 2015. "Out-of-Date Gun Background Check Statistic Gets New Life after Oregon Shooting." Punditfact, October 4. https://www.politifact.com/factchecks/2015/oct/04/mark-kelly/out-date-gun-background-check-statistic-gets-new-l/

Sherman, Amy, 2016. "3 Things to Know about the 'Gun Show Loophole.'" PolitiFact, January 7. https://www.politifact.com/truth-o-meter/article/2016/jan/07/politifact-sheet-3-things-know-about-gun-show-loop/

Speier, Jackie, 2015. "An Evening to Stop Gun Violence" with Congresswoman Jackie Speier #enough. November 21. https://act.myngp.com/jackiespeier/enough?midqs=1384856885416427520

Trotta, Daniel, 2019. "U.S. Gun Sales Down 6.1 Percent in 2018, Extending 'Trump Slump.'" Reuters, January 29. https://www.reuters.com/article/us-usa-gun-sales-idUSKCN1PN346

Watts, Shannon, 2016. "Moms Demand Action: How a Facebook Group Started a Movement to Change Our Nation's Gun Laws." *Harvard Law & Policy Review*, December 15. https://harvardlpr.com/2016/12/15/moms-demand-action-how-a-facebook-group-started-a-movement-to-change-our-nations-gun-laws/

Zimring, Franklin, 1975. "Firearms and Federal Law: The Gun Control Act of 1968." *Journal of Legal Studies*, 4(1), 133–198. https://www.jstor.org/stable/724104

Q4: DO CURRENT GUN REGISTRATION LAWS REDUCE VIOLENT CRIME AND HELP APPREHEND VIOLENT CRIMINALS?

Answer: Gun registration typically mandates that all firearm sellers and buyers report specific information—for example, gun make and model; serial number and caliber; purchaser's name and address—to an appropriate law enforcement agency for every firearm bought, sold, or transferred. While registration certainly appears to have the potential to reduce violent crime and aid in the apprehension of violent criminals, the actual effectiveness of current registration laws alone (in the absence of more comprehensive gun control measures) in accomplishing these goals is questionable.

Gary Kleck, professor of criminology at Florida State University, investigated the relationship between 19 major types of gun control laws and violent crime in every U.S. city with a population of at least 25,000 (n = 1,078) in 1990. (The city-level suicide data from 2000 and 2010 were no longer publicly available, and such data were essential for calculating the gun-level proxy measure.) He found no relationship between registration and homicide or assault rates—registration did not appear to decrease this type of violence—and it was associated *positively* with robbery rates: that is, registration was associated with an increase in robbery rates (Kleck, Kovandzic, & Bellows, 2016). While we can dismiss this counterintuitive relationship as a random chance statistical artifact, the overall pattern of results in that study indicated that gun registration played no role in reducing violent crime. Similarly, research examining the relationship between criminal gun availability and gun registration found that registration alone was substantially less effective in keeping criminals from getting guns than registration and licensing together (Webster, Vernick, & Hepburn, 2001).

Still other researchers (e.g., Hahn et al., 2005) have concluded that insufficient evidence exists to determine the effectiveness of firearm registration on violent crime—a conclusion also reached by the National Research Council (2004). Further, in an analysis of the practical difficulties associated with even a well-functioning gun registration system, James Jacobs, professor of law and director of the Center for Research in Crime and Justice at New York University, determined that gun registration would likely have little impact on the apprehension of violent criminals since these individuals would not comply with the law—doing so would typically require them to admit to felony possession of a firearm (Jacobs, 2002: 150). Thus, the weight of the evidence, albeit from older research, indicates that as stand-alone measures, typical gun registration regulations currently in place are not effective either in reducing violent crime or in apprehending violent criminals.

The Facts: Proponents of registration have argued that registration has three societal benefits. First, registration facilitates the retrieval of firearms from individuals who can no longer legally possess firearms. Second, registration aids law enforcement in identifying the source of firearms recovered at crime scenes. Third, registration reduces illegal gun sales and transfers by increasing a sense of accountability in firearm owners (see Giffords Law Center, n.d.a). While these are worthwhile goals, their efficacy in directly preventing gun violence is limited. For example, a RAND

Corporation analysis uncovered three relevant studies that examined the impact of retrieving firearms from prohibited possessors (Karimov, 2018). Although one study (Raissian, 2016) found that removing firearms from prohibited individuals appeared to decrease intimate partner and family homicides, the other two studies found no such effects. One study was a state-level analysis of intimate partner homicide rates from 1982 to 2002. The researchers uncovered no evidence that gun confiscation policies had any impact on this homicide rate; and unclear effects on stranger homicides, rapes, and robberies (Vigdor & Mercy, 2006). Similarly, researchers who analyzed data from 46 cities between 1979 and 2003 found no evidence to indicate that confiscating firearms after a domestic violence incident impacted rates of intimate partner homicide (Zeoli & Webster, 2010). Taking the mixed findings of these three studies together, RAND determined that the effects of removing firearms from prohibited individuals on violent crime were inconclusive (Karimov, 2018).

Practical shortcomings also hamper registration's second assumed benefit: the usefulness of gun tracing for reducing crime. While registration does allow police to trace guns and identify owners of firearms recovered at a crime scene, such guns are usually "recovered" by apprehending the lawbreakers at the scene, thus making a trace unnecessary. Further, when criminals successfully flee the crime scene, their firearms generally are never recovered (Jacobs, 2002: 148). Even for guns actually left at the crime scene and traced, the trace often identifies an owner who lost the gun or had it stolen in a break-in or robbery. On the other hand, gun tracing can sometimes help law enforcement deter gun trafficking. For example, the Office of the Mayor of Chicago has used firearm trace data to identify gun shop dealers supplying a disproportionate number of firearms recovered at Chicago crime scenes. Between 2013 and 2016, Chicago police established that about 40 percent of crime guns recovered in Chicago originated from gun dealers located outside Chicago, in suburban Cook County. Just two gun shops were the retail source of over 10 percent of these traced crime guns (Gun Trace Reports, 2017).

Registration's third assumed benefit—increasing a sense of personal accountability in law-abiding gun owners, potentially reducing temptations to engage in questionable gun sales and transfers—also encounters practical limitations in its ability to reduce gun crime. Research indicates that violent criminals identified legal firearms owners as the source of their crime guns less than 10 percent of the time (see NRA-ILA, 2019).

While registration alone is unlikely to reduce violent crime, it is possible that registration, in conjunction with other complementary gun control measures (such as licensing), might have greater violent-crime-reducing impact. The federal government does not mandate licensing of gun owners or purchasers, but state governments have implemented four general types of licensing schemes: permits to *purchase* firearms; licenses to *own* firearms; firearm safety certificates with a licensing component; and registrations with a licensing component (Giffords Law Center, n.d.b). If we overlapped these licensing schemes with registration, might this more comprehensive approach lower violent crime? The Giffords Law Center, in fact, makes such a claim: "Gun licensing has been proven to reduce gun violence and trafficking, and it remains a necessary component to crafting comprehensive gun laws" (Giffords Law Center, n.d.b). To support this claim, the center cites a 2010 report by Mayors Against Illegal Guns that used crime-gun tracing to examine the impact of licensing on crime. This report showed that states implementing licensing laws were the source of substantially fewer crime guns than states without licensing (see Mayors Against Illegal Guns, 2010). Additionally, the center referenced the Webster, Vernick, and Hepburn 2001 study of 25 U.S. cities that also showed the benefits of combining licensing and registration in reducing the prevalence of traced crime guns, and ostensibly of violent crime.

The Kleck study of multiple gun control measures also offers some support for the center's claim. Although gun registration had no impact on violent crime, Kleck's analyses indicated that licensing appeared to have violence-reducing effects on both robbery and homicide (Kleck et al., 2016). Similarly, but approaching the issue from the opposite direction, Webster and his colleagues found that the 2007 repeal of Missouri's permit-to-purchase licensing law resulted in a greater than 25 percent increase in the state's annual firearm homicide rate, with no change in the non-firearm homicide rate (Webster, Crifasi, & Vernick, 2014).

Nonetheless, the strength of support these studies provide for licensing's impact on reducing violent crime is unclear. While Kleck's analysis showed licensing reducing robbery and homicides, it also showed evidence that, in other areas, some forms of licensing increased violence. For example, permit-to-purchase requirements were associated with increased assaults, and registration alone with increased robberies (Kleck et al., 2016). The significance of Webster's Missouri findings is also not clear. As the researchers themselves have noted, implementing permit-to-purchase licensing laws in other states "may not result in as immediate and large a reduction in firearm homicides as occurred in reverse when Missouri's law was repealed" (see Lewis, 2017). This is because other contemporaneous changes in the state may have also impacted homicide rates, thus limiting the lessons that the Missouri findings might have for other states.

A RAND Corporation analysis of licensing's impact on violent crime examined the Webster et al. (2014) study as well as a 2015 study investigating the impact of Connecticut's permit-to-purchase handgun law on homicides. This latter study found a decrease in firearm homicides after the implementation of the law. However, the permit-to-purchase requirement was part of a bundle of other gun control measures, such as raising the minimum age of purchase from 18 to 21, instituting eight hours of gun-safety training, and requiring the purchaser to obtain an in-person eligibility certificate from the local police department. Because of these additional policy changes, and because (as with Missouri) other contemporaneous changes in the state may have impacted homicides, RAND determined that, overall, the evidence was inconclusive regarding the impact of licensing on firearm homicides (RAND, 2018). Another RAND analyst examined an unpublished paper (Luca, Malhotra, & Poliquin, 2016) containing information about the impact of licensing on mass shootings, and reached a similar determination: "inconclusive evidence for the effects of licensing and permitting requirements on mass shootings" (Smart, 2018).

It might be argued that "inconclusive" evidence is exactly that—inconclusive—and such a finding does not justify a determination that gun registration laws are not effective in reducing violent crime or in apprehending violent criminals. Proponents of registration and licensing assert that, to succeed in reducing violent crime, these requirements must be part of a comprehensive package of regulations (see Giffords Law Center, n.d.b), similar to but perhaps even more extensive than those found in the Rudolph et al. 2015 study. With such comprehensive regulation—arguably no more burdensome than that imposed on automobile owners—society can achieve the desired reduction in criminal violence.

James Jacobs, a legal scholar at New York University, has taken issue with this reasoning, however. He asserts that with millions of unregistered firearms now in private hands, individuals intent on criminal violence will still be able to obtain guns. Noting that large numbers of handguns already circulate in the criminal subculture, and that a lawbreaker could use the same unregistered gun throughout his career, he asserted that even a sophisticated and well-executed registration/licensing system would have little impact on the availability of guns for crime. He also claimed that registration/licensing on such a comprehensive scale would require a tremendous amount of societal consensus; and, politically, such consensus simply does not exist (see Jacobs, 2002: 137–152)—a conclusion echoing the assessment of legal scholars decades earlier: "The paradox of handgun regulation is that nothing less than nationwide regulation can possibly be effective, yet federal legislation . . . is perceived as impermissibly intrusive" (Mills, 1983).

FURTHER READING

Giffords Law Center, n.d.a. "Registration." https://giffords.org/lawcenter/gun-laws/policy-areas/owner-responsibilities/registration/

Giffords Law Center, n.d.b. "Licensing." https://giffords.org/lawcenter/gun-laws/policy-areas/owner-responsibilities/licensing/

Gun Trace Report, 2017. City of Chicago, Office of the Mayor, Chicago Police Department. https://chicago.gov/content/dam/city/depts/mayor/Press%20Room/Press%Releases/2017/October/GTR2017.pdf

Hahn, Robert, et al., 2005. "Firearm Laws and the Reduction of Violence: A Systematic Review." *American Journal of Preventive Medicine*, 28(2), 40–71.

Jacobs, James, 2002. *Can Gun Control Work?* New York: Oxford University Press.

Karimov, Rousian, 2018. "Effects of Surrender of Firearms by Prohibited Possessors on Violent Crime." RAND Corporation. https://www.rand.org/research/gun-policy/analysis/prohibited-possessors/violent-crime.html

Kleck, Gary, Kovandzic, Tomislav, & Bellows, Jon, 2016. "Does Gun Control Reduce Violent Crime?" *Criminal Justice Review*, 41(4), 488–513. https://journals.sagepub.com/doi/abs/10.1177/0734016816670457?journalCode=cjra

Lewis, Nicole, 2017. "Do Tougher Gun Laws Lead to Dramatically Lower Rates of Gun Violence?" *Washington Post*, October 17. https://www.washingtonpost.com/news/fact-checker/wp/2017/10/17/do-tougher-gun-laws-lead-to-dramatically-lower-rates-of-gun-violence/

Luca, Michael, Malhotra, Deepak, & Poliquin, Christopher, 2016. "The Impact of Mass Shootings on Gun Policy." Working paper, Harvard Business School.

Mayors Against Illegal Guns, 2010. "Trace the Guns: The Link between Gun Laws and Interstate Gun Trafficking." https://graphics8.nytimes.com/packages/pdf/us/20100927-guns-report.pdf

Mills, Mary, 1983. "Research Report, Licensing and Registration Statutes." In Bijlefeld, Marjolijin (ed.), 1997. *The Gun Control Debate: A Documentary History*. Westport, CT: Greenwood Press, pp. 77–78.

National Research Council, 2004. *Firearms and Violence: A Critical Review.* Washington, DC: National Academies Press.

NRA-ILA (National Rifle Association Institute for Legislative Action), 2019. "Background Checks for Guns." NICS NRA-ILA, January 7. https://www.nraila.org/get-the-facts/background-checks-nics/#_edn43

Raissian, Kerri, 2016. "Hold Your Fire: Did the 1996 Federal Gun Control Act Expansion Reduce Domestic Homicides?" *Journal of Policy Analysis* and Management, 35(1), 67–93. https://ideas.repec.org/a/wly/jpamgt/v35y2016ip67-93.html

RAND Corporation, 2018. "Effects of Firearm Licensing and Permitting Requirements on Violent Crime." RAND Corporation, March 2. Updated April 22, 2020. https://www.rand.org/research/gun-policy/analysis/license-to-own/violent-crime.html

Rudolph, Kara, Stuart, Elizabeth, Vernick, Jon, & Webster, Daniel, 2015. "Association between Connecticut's Permit-to-Purchase Handgun Law and Homicides." *American Journal of Public Health*, 105(8), E49–E54.

Smart, Rosanna, 2018. "Effects of Firearm Licensing and Permitting Requirements on Mass Shootings." RAND Corporation, March 2. Updated April 22, 2020. https://www.rand.org/research/gun-policy/analysis/license-to-own/mass-shootings.html

Vigdor, Elizabeth, & Mercy, James, 2006. "Do Laws Restricting Access to Firearms by Domestic Violence Offenders Prevent Intimate Partner Homicides?" *Evaluation Review*, 30(3), 313–346.

Webster, Daniel, Crifasi, Cassandra, & Vernick, Jon, 2014. "Effects of the Repeal of Missouri's Handgun Purchaser Licensing Law on Homicides." *Journal of Urban Health*, 91(2), 293–302. https://link.springer.com/article/10.1007%2Fs11524-014-9865-8. Also, Erratum to: "Effects of the Repeal of Missouri's Handgun Purchaser Licensing Law on Homicides." *Journal of Urban Health*, 91(3), 589–601.

Webster, Daniel, Vernick, Jon, & Hepburn, Lisa, 2001. "Relationship between Licensing, Registration, and Other Gun Sales Laws and the Source State of Crime Guns." *Injury Prevention*, 7(3), 184–189. https://injuryprevention.bmj.com/content/7/3/184.info

Zeoli, April, & Webster, Daniel, 2010. "Effects of Domestic Violence Policies, Alcohol Taxes, and Police Staffing Levels on Intimate Partner Homicide in Large U.S. Cities." *Injury Prevention*, 16(2), 90–95.

Q5: DO BALLISTIC FINGERPRINTING AND MICROSTAMPING TECHNIQUES CURRENTLY IN USE HELP POLICE SOLVE GUN CRIMES?

Answer: Typically produced by the breech faces, firing pins, and ejectors of semi- and fully automatic weapons, ballistic fingerprints are the markings that a gun leaves on an expelled cartridge case after firing. The markings are assumed to be unique—although this assumption has been questioned by both scientists (e.g., National Research Council, 2008) and defense attorneys (Levinson, 2019). An examination of such marks can sometimes allow forensic experts to link cartridge cases to the specific gun that fired them; and by linking cartridge cases recovered at crime scenes to specific firearms seized from suspected lawbreakers, ballistic fingerprinting can help solve violent crime. Microstamping elaborates on this basic idea, by using lasers to imprint a unique microscopic code on a gun's firing pin and other internal parts. These codes are then entered into a computerized database before the firearm leaves the manufacturer. Police can later run the codes found on recovered crime-scene cartridge cases through the database, identifying the guns—and perhaps the owners—involved. This technology permits crime gun tracings directly through recovered cartridge cases, with no need to recover the gun itself.

Although proponents of these techniques laud their potential for solving gun crimes, the efficacy of both techniques is controversial. Despite the early promise of the National Integrated Ballistics Identification Network (NIBIN) computer system—8,800 ballistic fingerprint matches, linking 17,600 crimes (Boesman & Krouse, 2001)—and the early passage of laws by Maryland and New York requiring ballistic fingerprinting, the actual effectiveness of this method for solving gun crimes has been disappointing. For example, both Maryland and New York later repealed their laws requiring ballistic fingerprinting because the technique had failed to solve a single gun crime in over a decade of use (Associated Press, 2005; Lott, 2015). Other issues center on the fundamental validity of the technique itself. Even with the reduced set of possible cartridge cases identified by the computer, a human expert must make a final match/no-match determination. The human examiner's training and experience influence these judgments, and this subjectivity diminishes the reproducibility of results (see President's Council of Advisors on Science and Technology, 2016). Additionally, concerns exist regarding the precision of the underlying computer algorithms, and their ability to sufficiently curtail the number of matches needing human examination as the ballistic database continually expands (*New York Times* Editorial, 2002).

Critics have also raised questions about the practical usefulness of microstamping technology for solving gun crimes. The National Rifle Association (NRA) has noted that "micro-stamped markings are easily removed, most guns do not automatically eject fired cartridges, only new guns—a small percentage of all guns—would be micro-stamped, . . . and most criminals get guns through channels that would not be affected by a micro-stamping requirement" (NRA-ILA, n.d.). Other gun rights groups have elaborated on these and additional concerns. Proponents of microstamping have vigorously challenged these criticisms. For example, they have argued that, contrary to claims that criminals can easily defeat the technology with household tools, the technology uses redundant markings on the firearm, and an individual would need sophisticated knowledge of both firearms and microstamping (plus appropriate tools) to render the technology ineffective (see CSGV ED, 2013). Nonetheless, the technique remains mired in legal controversy (Egelko, 2018) and has yet to be functionally implemented in any state.

Overall, because both techniques continue to encounter significant practical or legal issues in actual application, neither approach has offered an effective method for helping police solve gun crimes as of 2020.

The Facts: Despite its promising potential for aiding law enforcement "by improving the solve rate of gun related crimes" (Giffords Law Center, n.d.), even proponents of ballistic fingerprinting are cautious in their assessments of its practical effectiveness in reducing gun violence. For example, while the use of NIBIN led to a six-fold increase in ballistic matches for the Boston Police Department (Braga & Pierce, 2004), and by 2005 had produced more than 75,000 crime-gun matches since its inception (U.S. Dept. of Justice, 2005), these results did not "automatically translate into improved crime solving capacity" (Giffords Law Center, n.d.). The center did not attribute this crime-solving failure to problems with the basic concept of ballistic fingerprinting, but rather with the implementation of NIBIN—irregular use, few NIBIN terminals, long processing delays, and lack of resources leading to extensive backlogs. Gun rights advocates, however, have leveled criticisms at the technique itself.

For instance, a report by Gun Owners of America (2009) asserted that, since criminals generally steal their guns, or borrow or rent them from other lawbreakers, ballistic information identifying the crime gun will only rarely connect back to the lawbreaker. The group also insisted that in those cases where a criminal did purchase a firearm from a gun store, the individual is likely to have used a false ID, again limiting the usefulness of the information provided by the ballistic fingerprinting system. Further, the group asserted that, unlike human fingerprints, ballistic fingerprints can change simply through repeated firings of the gun, particularly when the firearm is new. Similarly, a gun owner can deliberately alter the fingerprint of older guns by changing the gun barrel or by replacing or filing the firing pin. Another alternative for lawbreakers wanting to circumvent ballistic fingerprinting is to use a revolver instead of a pistol, or use a brass catcher on a semiautomatic handgun to insure that no casings are left at the crime scene (Gun Owners of America, 2009).

A 2002 report by Fox News also questioned the practical usefulness of the technique. After an extended sniper spree had terrorized Washington,

D.C., the Brady Campaign to Prevent Gun Violence asserted that ballistic fingerprinting would have "solved this crime after the first shooting"; the Coalition to Stop Gun Violence argued that the shootings were "a perfect example of how valuable complete ballistic fingerprinting would be"; and Senator Charles Schumer of New York called for a national ballistic fingerprinting program (Milloy, 2002). Responding to these claims and demands, the Fox report noted that both Maryland and New York already required ballistic fingerprinting, and that neither program helped convict a single criminal (Milloy, 2002).

John Lott (2015), a prominent but controversial gun rights researcher and expert elaborated on the Maryland and New York programs in a later commentary. He noted that in the 15 years it operated, the Maryland program had never solved a single crime after spending $5 million on its computer database. Similarly, the New York program, after 10 years of operation, had never solved a single crime, even after spending about $5 million *per year*—demonstrating that even increased per capita spending could not insure a useful outcome for the technique. Further, he noted that this pessimistic assessment was neither new nor startling: the Maryland State Police in a 2005 report had determined that ballistic fingerprinting was "ineffective and expensive" (Lott, 2015).

The usually gun control–friendly *New York Times* (Editorial, 2002) also had questions about the viability and effectiveness of large-scale ballistic fingerprinting. Noting that the automated searches underlying the technique do not conclusively identify a culprit weapon—they merely narrow the field for a human examiner's final determination—the *Times* wondered if the huge databases used in ballistic fingerprinting would eventually overwhelm the discriminating power of the computer programs involved. As the *Times* pointed out, this was not merely an academic speculation. A California Department of Justice report testing the computer algorithms on cartridges from different manufacturers identified a computer-matching failure rate as high as 62 percent (Tulleners, 2001; see also Gun Owners of America, 2009; Milloy, 2002).

The NRA also dismissed the practical usefulness of ballistic fingerprinting, citing a 2008 National Research Council report. After examining the feasibility, accuracy, and technical capability of a national U.S. ballistic images database, the report recommended against establishing such a database (NRA-ILA, n.d.) because of two significant shortcomings. First, the report concluded that the fundamental assumption of ballistic fingerprinting—that every gun leaves unique microscopic marks that remain the same over repeated firings—had not been fully demonstrated scientifically. Second, the report determined that automated searches of an extensive, large-scale ballistic images database would likely produce too many candidate "matches" to be helpful (National Research Council, 2008).

In a follow-up evaluation of the technique in 2016, investigators were still concerned about its foundational validity. Their assessment noted that casing- and gun-matching judgments remained subjective, and simply reflected a ballistic examiner's determination of "sufficient agreement"—a determination that the items in question were highly unlikely to have different origins. Examiner training and experience impact such judgments, and the investigators concluded that the available evidence did not currently demonstrate that ballistic fingerprinting had reached an appropriate level of objective scientific reproducibility (President's Council of Advisors on Science and Technology, 2016). Despite efforts to make the technology more objective and less reliant on human judgment (see NIST, 2018), uncertainty regarding the reliability of the technique (see Milloy, 2002) and the actual uniqueness of ballistic fingerprints remains (see Levinson, 2019).

As an alternate way to achieve the same goals as ballistic fingerprinting, the National Research Council (2008) recommended that investigators conduct additional research on the viability of microstamping—a procedure for *deliberately* imprinting unique identifying information on guns or ammunition. In October 2007, the governor of California, Arnold Schwarzenegger, signed the first microstamping bill into law, followed by the District of Columbia in January 2009. Skeptics of the technique criticized its likely effectiveness on several grounds. Some criticisms were similar to problems with ballistic fingerprinting: that criminals generally obtain their guns illegally, making microstamping irrelevant; and that criminals could easily defeat microstamping imprints by defacing them with common garage tools. Other criticisms were specific to microstamping: that criminals will "seed" crime scenes with imprinted cartridges pilfered from firing ranges; and that manufacturers' implementation costs, passed on to gun buyers, would raise the price of handguns astronomically (CSGV ED, 2013).

Proponents of the technique have examined these criticisms and rejected them as either incorrect or unlikely. For example, aside from noting that criminals typically do not alter their crime guns, proponents also suggest that attempts to erase or deface the microstamped imprints would require intimate knowledge about microstamping that the common lawbreaker is unlikely to have. Further, the imprints are redundant and located in several areas of the firearm, including the breech face, making defacement (and even swapping out parts) a tedious and difficult procedure. Similarly, the idea of criminals "seeding" a crime scene with pilfered cartridges seems highly unlikely, since few criminals would have the time or the presence of mind to do so following a violent altercation. As for increased manufacturing costs, proponents assert that, in spite of the firearms industry claims to the contrary, the actual cost of implementing microstamping should range between $.50 and $1.00 per handgun, and raise the gun's selling price no more than $3.00 (CSGV ED, 2013).

In practical terms, the contradictory assertions surrounding microstamping represent a largely academic argument, since the technology has never been implemented. Once the 2007 California law took effect in 2013, gun manufacturers such as Smith & Wesson, Ruger, and others stopped selling new handguns in that state. In a press release, Smith & Wesson announced that the firm would not incorporate microstamping in its firearms because "microstamping is unreliable, serves no safety purpose, is cost prohibitive and, most importantly, is not proven to aid in preventing or solving crimes" (NRA-ILA, 2018).

Overall, then, a pessimistic evaluation of the crime-fighting effectiveness of current ballistic fingerprinting and microstamping techniques seems justified. For ballistic fingerprinting, this conclusion reflects the actual long-term failure of the technique to solve gun crimes in several states—in some cases even sparking repeal of the legislation that mandated it. Further, critics contend that continuing questions about ballistic fingerprints' uniqueness, and concerns about the subjectivity of the human judgments involved, imply that the technique's future effectiveness is limited. Similarly, microstamping is also unlikely to help solve gun crimes. Given the general availability of revolvers (which do not eject casings), the reservoir of pistols already manufactured and sold (i.e., prior to any microstamping implementation), the work-arounds that may render such imprints useless, and the gun manufacturers' powerful opposition to its implementation—opting not to market new products in states requiring microstamping—the utility of microstamping for crime solving appears minimal without further significant technological advances and/or substantially increased support from gun enthusiasts, manufacturers, and lawmakers.

FURTHER READING

All4shooters, 2017. "Guns and the Law: Is Microstamping a Good Idea?" All4shooters.com, September 9. https://www.all4shooters.com/en/shooting/law/guns-and-microstamping/

Associated Press, 2005. "National Briefing | Mid-Atlantic: Maryland: Gun Law Faulted." *New York Times*, January 18. https://www.nytimes

.com/2005/01/18/us/national-briefing-midatlantic-maryland-gun-law-faulted.html

Boesman, William, & Krouse, William, 2001. "National Integrated Ballistics Network (NIBIN) for Law Enforcement." CRS Report for Congress, July 3. https://mchenry.house.gov/uploadedfiles/second%20amend%20-%20ballastic%20fingerprinting.pdf

Braga, Anthony, & Pierce, Glenn, 2004. "Linking Crime Guns: The Impact of Ballistics Imaging Technology on the Productivity of the Boston Police Department's Ballistic Unit." *Journal of Forensic Science*, 49(4), 701–706. https://www.researchgate.net/publication/8394737_Linking_Crime_Guns_The_Impact_of_Ballistic_Imaging_Technology_on_the_Productivity_of_the_Boston_Police_Department%27s_Ballistics_Unit

CSGV (The Coalition to Stop Gun Violence), n.d.a. "Microstamping Proves Its Worth . . . Again." https://www.csgv.org/microstamping-proves-worth/

CSGV (The Coalition to Stop Gun Violence), n.d.b. "Microstamping." https://www.csgv.org/issues-archive/microstamping/

CSGV ED (Coalition to Stop Gun Violence and Education Fund to Stop Gun Violence), 2013. "Microstamping Technology: Precise and Proven." June. efsgv.org/wp-content/uploads/2013/06/Microstamping-Technology-Precise-and-Proven-Memo.pdf

Egelko, Bob, 2018. "More than a Decade after It Passed, California Gun Law Still Being Fought in Court." SFGATE, April 4. https://www.sfgate.com/news article/More-than-a-decade-after-it-passed-California-12806379.php

Giffords Law Center, n.d. "Microstamping & Ballistics." https://lawcenter.giffords.org/gun-laws/policy-areas/crime-guns/microstamping-ballistics/

Gun Owners of America, 2009. "Why Ballistic Fingerprinting Is Not an Effective Crime Tool." gunowners.org/fs0203/

Levinson, Jonathan, 2019. "'Ballistic Fingerprint' Database Expands amid Questions about Its Precision." NPR, Oregon Public Broadcasting, January 1. https://www.npr.org/2019/01/01/678408216/ballistic-fingerprint-database-expands-amid-questions-about-its-precision

Lott, John, 2015. "Maryland's Long-Overdue Goodbye to Ballistic Fingerprinting." *Washington Post*, November 13. https://www.washingtonpost.com/opinions/marylands-long-overdue-goodbye-to-ballistic-fingerprinting/2015/11/13/a277d02a-87db-11e5-be39-0034bb576eee_story.html

Milloy, Steven, 2002. "How Reliable Is Ballistic Fingerprinting?" Fox News, October 18. https://www.foxnews.com/story/how-reliable-is-ballistic-fingerprinting

Moskowitz, Peter, 2018. "Inside the Mind of America's Favorite Gun Researcher." Pacific Standard, September 23. https://www.psmag.com/magazine/inside-the-mind-of-americas-favorite-gun-researcher

National Research Council, 2008. *Ballistic Imaging*. Washington, DC: National Academies Press, pp. 3–5.

New York Times Editorial, 2002. "Rethinking Ballistic Fingerprints." *New York Times*, November 11. https://www.nytimes.com/2002/11/11/opinion/rethinking-ballistic-fingerprints.html

NIST (National Institute of Standards and Technology), 2018. "How Good a Match Is It? Putting Statistics into Forensic Firearms Identification." National Institute of Standards and Technology, Department of Commerce, February 8. https://www.nist.gov/news-events/news/2018/02/how-good-match-it-putting-statistics-forensic-firearms-identification

NRA-ILA (National Rifle Association Institute for Legislative Action), n.d. "Micro-Stamping | Ballistic 'Fingerprinting.'" https://www.nraila.org/get-the-facts/micro-stamping-and-ballistic-fingerprinting/

NRA-ILA (National Rifle Association Institute for Legislative Action), 2018. "Mission Impossible: California Court Upholds Microstamping Law." https://www.nraila.org/articles/20180703/mission-impossible-california-court-upholds-microstamping-law

President's Council of Advisors on Science and Technology, 2016. "Forensic Science in Criminal Courts: Ensuring Scientific Validity of Feature-Comparison Methods." Report to the President, September, pp. 104–114. https://obamawhitehouse.archives.gov/sites/default/files/microsites/ostp/PCAST/pcast_forensic_science_report_final.pdf

Tulleners, Frederic, 2001. "Technical Evaluation: Feasibility of a Ballistics Imaging Database for All New Handgun Sales." Bureau of Forensic Services, California Department of Justice, October 5. https://freerepublic.com/focus/news/771039/posts

U.S. Dept. of Justice, 2005. *The Bureau of Alcohol, Tobacco, Firearms, and Explosives' National Integrated Ballistic Information Network Program*. June. https://oig.justice.gov/reports/ATF/a0530/final.pdf

Winkler, Adam, 2011. *Gunfight: The Battle over the Right to Bear Arms in America*. New York: W. W. Norton.

Q6: WOULD A BAN ON "ASSAULT-STYLE" RIFLES HELP PREVENT OR REDUCE VIOLENT CRIME?

Answer: Semiautomatic "assault-style" rifles such as the AR-15, AK-47, and other such arms resemble military-grade automatic rifles (such as the M-16), but, functionally, these firearms are substantially different. While the civilian AR-15 and other such rifles are functionally similar to a traditional hunting rifle (a trigger press fires only one bullet, and the shooter must press the trigger each time the gun is fired), the military M-16 is functionally equivalent to a machine gun, in that the shooter can set the rifle to fire continuously with just a single trigger press. Because of the confusing cosmetic similarity between these two types of rifles, and because deranged individuals have frequently used AR-15 rifles in high-profile mass killings, the rifle has received much attention in news reports and the popular press, and has subsequently acquired a mainstream reputation as a particularly dangerous firearm unsuitable for civilian use. Gun control advocates have argued that a ban on the rifle would curtail violent gun crime, and substantially reduce the lethality of mass shooting incidents.

During the Clinton administration, Congress in fact enacted a 10-year ban on these firearms, from 1994 to 2004. Evaluations of the ban's overall impact on gun crime were mixed. In some localities, the researchers found that the share of gun crimes involving assault weapons (including both rifles and pistols) declined, but this reduction was offset by an increase in other guns equipped with large-capacity magazines. Overall, the ban did not result in a clear reduction in the use of assault rifles, and the investigators concluded that the effects of a new ban on gun violence "are likely to be small at best and perhaps too small for reliable measurement" (Koper, Woods, & Roth, 2004). Nonetheless, despite these findings, and despite research establishing that rifles of any type are rarely used in "normal" gun crimes, gun control advocates continue to call for an assault weapons ban (see French, 2018), presumably because of their lethality—as evidenced by their use in several deadly mass shooting events in America in the late 2010s. However, gun rights proponents contend that no evidence indicates that a new ban would have any greater crime-suppressing success than the old ban. They point to studies that have concluded that banning "assault-style" rifles would not prevent or reduce violent crime (Koper et al., 2004).

The Facts: Although the "AR" in AR-15 is often thought to represent "assault rifle," the letters actually stand for Armalite Rifle, the manufacturing company where Eugene Stoner developed the rifle for the military in the late 1950s. The military eventually adopted the selective-fire, automatic version of the rifle (capable of continuous fire) as the M-16. Colt introduced the semiautomatic version—the "AR-15 Sporter"—into the civilian market as a superb hunting rifle in the early 1960s (Dickinson, 2018).

Because of the rifle's military heritage, the overall cosmetic appearance of the AR-15 has always made the rifle virtually indistinguishable from the military M-16 rifle, and marketing hyperbole has sometimes highlighted this military connection. Further, as the Violence Policy Center has noted, individuals can customize and modify rifles of this type "to make them look even more militaristic, even more grand in the eyes of their owners" (Dickinson, 2018). Nonetheless, regardless of appearance, semiautomatic AR-15-style rifles are not capable of continuous fire, and are identical in firing function to more traditional-looking, semiautomatic hunting rifles. Nonetheless, the AR-15 has acquired such a grave reputation for lethality and gun violence that some legislators and a significant percentage of the population have generated continuous calls for its banning.

At least three factors account for the rifle's disreputable status among advocates wishing to ban the firearm. The first, as discussed above, is simply its militaristic appearance and ignorance regarding the difference between automatic and semiautomatic firing. For individuals unfamiliar with firearms, the "black rifle," as the AR-15 is sometimes called, has a chilling, deadly appearance—most often encountered in portrayals of U.S. military battle scenes and police SWAT operations using M-16s. Further, as Dickinson (2018) has noted, the rifle's marketers have often deliberately contributed to this perception with aggressive and war-themed advertising. While marketing the rifle as a military rifle does not make it one, it certainly contributes to the view among non–gun owners that the firearm is particularly lethal and dangerous.

The second factor contributing to the rifle's notoriety is its seemingly ubiquitous presence in the hands of deranged schoolhouse shooters and unbalanced spree killers. After observing that unstable individuals used AR-15-style rifles in many horrific mass shootings—from Parkland to Las Vegas to Orlando to Sandy Hook—one commentator characterized the rifle as the "mass shooters' weapon of choice" (Andavolu, 2018). Another suggested that assault weapons are "presented by the media as the gun of choice for drug dealers and criminals" and which the police want off the streets (Becket, 2014). A third noted, after listing 10 mass shootings involving assault weapons that had killed dozens all across the nation, that President Obama had wanted to reintroduce a federal ban because "weapons that were designed for soldiers in war theaters don't belong on our streets" (Gillin, 2017).

A calculated "assault rifle" media campaign organized by gun control advocates is the third factor contributing to the belief that the AR-15 and similar firearms are unsuitable for civilian ownership. In the late 1980s, Josh Sugarmann, an ardent gun control proponent and founder of the Violence Policy Center, formulated a new strategy to bolster gun control sentiment in the United States: brand the AR-15 as an "assault rifle" whose single purpose in civilian hands is simply the killing and maiming of large numbers of people. In a publication entitled *Assault Weapons and Accessories in America*, Sugarmann (1988) argued that the rifle's "menacing looks, coupled with the public's confusion over fully automatic machine guns versus semi-automatic assault weapons—anything that looks like a machine gun is assumed to be a machine gun—can only increase the chance of public support for restrictions. . . . Efforts to restrict assault weapons are more likely to succeed than those to restrict handguns." The next year, the Bureau of Alcohol, Tobacco, and Firearms prohibited the importation of over 40 models of "assault-type" semiautomatic rifles previously approved, followed by numerous state bans over the next decade (NRA-ILA, 2013).

Yet, even assuming the position of gun rights groups—that the menace and lethality of AR-15 type rifles have been deliberately overstated by gun control organizations and their legislative allies—such distortions do not negate the possibility that a ban may indeed reduce violent gun crime. Of course, evidence assessing the effectiveness of various gun control measures is always complicated, and this is particularly so in this case. Assessment involves examining three kinds of evidence: findings relevant to "normal" gun crimes; findings relevant to mass shootings; and findings relevant to the federal assault weapons ban that began in 1994 and expired in 2004.

For "normal" violent crimes (e.g., homicide, rape, robbery, and assault), the impact of an assault-style rifle ban would be minimal. A recent survey (Alper & Glaze, 2019) of state and federal prisoners determined that less than 25 percent used a firearm during the commission of their violent felony, and rifles and shotguns (of any type) were the weapon of choice in less than 2 percent of these cases. This finding is in line with a 2014 study that found that assault weapons were involved in only about 2 percent of gun crimes before the federal assault weapons ban, and that FBI data showed that rifles of any type accounted for only 322 homicides in 2012 (Beckett, 2014). In an even earlier analysis, David Kopel, Research Director of the Independence Institute and a prominent gun rights advocate, also concluded that assault weapons are used in only about 1 percent of gun crimes (Kopel, 1994). Given this already infrequent use of assault weapons in gun crimes, a ban would have little chance of providing further reduction in the actual number of gun crimes, although it might well reduce the number of injuries and fatalities on those occasions when criminals would have used assault weapons.

The evidence for assessing the effects of an assault weapons ban on mass shootings is more complicated to interpret. Described by *Rolling Stone* (a magazine with a pro–gun control editorial orientation) as the "go-to rifle of mass killers" (Dickinson, 2018), the unusual prominence of assault-type rifles in such attacks suggests that unhinged individuals have a particular attraction to the AR-15 because of its lethality. However, an alternative explanation exists. As the NRA and other commentators have observed, AR-15-style rifles represent the most popular rifle purchased in America (Dickinson, 2018), with anywhere from 8 million (Andavolu, 2018; Myre, 2018) to 16 million (Eger, 2018) in civilian hands. According to the National Shooting Sports Foundation (NSSF), manufacturers produced an estimated 2.3 million versions of "modern sporting rifles"—the industry's preferred term for AR-15-style rifles—in 2016 alone. This compares to a total of about 4.2 million rifles of all types and calibers produced that year (Egers, 2018). Indeed, the AR-15-style rifle is so popular among American gun owners that some have jested that "AR" stands for "America's Rifle" (Myre, 2018). Given such widespread popularity among gun owners generally, it is hardly surprising that this type of firearm would also prominently occupy the weapons cache of crazed spree killers. Thus, it is likely that several factors contribute to the popularity of the AR-15 among mass shooters.

None of this negates the undeniable fact that assault weapons have been used to inflict horrendous violence and harm on innocents in schools and in other public places. Just between 2012 and 2016, rampage killers using assault rifles killed 124 individuals and wounded another 150 in eight terrible mass shootings (Dickinson, 2018); and in 2017, such rifles were used in the Las Vegas massacre—America's worst mass shooting—killing 59 individuals and wounding more than 500. Nevertheless, as shocking as this carnage is, a leading criminologist researching mass shootings, Professor James Alan Fox of Northeastern University has estimated that over the past three decades, the *average* number of victims killed yearly in mass shootings is around 100 individuals (Beckett, 2014). In context, typically about 12,000–15,000 Americans are homicide victims annually.

The last type of evidence relevant to the likely effectiveness of an assault weapons ban is an assessment of the success of the 1994–2004 federal ban in reducing violent crime. This evidence is the most difficult to evaluate because the findings are complex and nuanced. For example, one major analysis of the ban's impact (Koper, Woods, & Roth, 2004) indicated that the ban had "mixed" success in reducing gun crimes. The researchers noted that any decline in gun crimes attributable to the absence of banned firearms was offset by the rising use of nonbanned firearms. They indicated that the ban resulted in no discernable reduction in the injuriousness or lethality of gun violence. However, they suggested that their assessments might be premature because the ban's effect realistically could occur only gradually (see Farley, 2013). Additionally, their report speculated that the effects of a renewed ban would be small—possibly even too small for reliable measurement.

Other investigators have reached similar negative assessments regarding the effectiveness of such bans. Research by John Lott (2003), a prominent and controversial gun rights advocate, uncovered no evidence showing that bans had any impact on violent crime; and analyses of state-level assault weapons bans indicated that they did not impact murder rates (Gius, 2014) or number of victims (Blau, Gorry, & Wade, 2016). For example, Benjamin Blau, a professor of finance at Utah State University, concluded that state and federal bans on assault weapons are unrelated to the likelihood of assault weapon use in a public shooting; and that, when assault weapons *are* used, such use is not related to greater numbers of victims or fatalities relative to other kinds of firearms (Blau, Gorry, & Wade, 2016).

In contrast, Mark Gius, a researcher in the Department of Economics at Quinnipiac University, found that both state and federal assault weapons bans had statistically significant negative effects on mass shooting fatalities; and that the federal ban also had a negative impact on mass shooting injuries. Similarly, Charles DiMaggio and his colleagues, researchers in the Department of Surgery in New York University's School of Medicine, analyzed several open-source data sets and found that assault rifles accounted for 430 of the 501 mass shooting fatalities during the period examined (1981–2017). Their regression analysis indicated that, during the federal assault weapons ban period, a statistically significant 9 fewer mass shooting–related deaths per 10,000 firearm homicides occurred (DiMaggio et al., 2019).

However, another investigator at the University of Massachusetts, examining the same data sets, has questioned these findings. He asserts that DiMaggio and colleagues (2019) misidentified the involvement of assault weapons in about half of the 44 incidents that they examined, casting doubt on the study's overall conclusions (Klarevas, 2019).

Still another set of researchers examined the difference in the number of individuals killed and wounded during active shooter incidents involving semiautomatic rifles relative to incidents involving other types of firearms (i.e., handguns, shotguns, and non-semiautomatic rifles). Using the FBI's publicly accessible database, the investigators analyzed 238 active shooter incidents covering the period 2000 through 2017. Of these 238 incidents, 61 (24.6 percent) involved a semiautomatic rifle and 187 incidents (75.4 percent) involved only handguns (n = 154), shotguns (n = 38), non-semiautomatic rifles (n = 15), or some combination of these firearms.

The researchers found that more individuals were wounded or killed in those incidents where a semiautomatic rifle was present than in incidents involving other firearms (de Jager et al., 2018).

Overall, however, the empirical findings regarding the effectiveness of assault weapons bans are contradictory. Assault rifles are rarely used in "normal" crime, and while they are prominently highlighted in mass shooting, mass shootings—despite their media notoriety—account for only a small fraction of the country's violent incidents. Further, as the earlier ban demonstrated, determined lawbreakers can circumvent the ban's restrictions either by moving to nonbanned semiautomatic guns, or even by acquiring a banned rifle that has been legally grandfathered and exempted from the ban.

FURTHER READING

Alper, Mariel, & Glaze, Lauren, 2019. "Source and Use of Firearms Involved in Crimes: Survey of Prison Inmates, 2016." Bureau of Justice Statistics, January. https://www.bjs.gov/index.cfm?ty=pbdetail&iid=6486

Andavolu, Krishna, 2018. "Banning the AR-15 Won't Solve the Mass Shooting Crisis." Vice, September 10. https://www.vice.com/en_us/article/438ydn/banning-the-ar-15-wont-solve-the-mass-shooting-crisis

Beckett, Lois, 2014. "The Assault Weapon Myth." New York Times, September 12. https://www.nytimes.com/2014/09/14/sunday-review/the-assault-weapon-myth.html

Blau, Benjamin, Gorry, Devon, & Wade, Chip, 2016. "Guns, Laws and Public Shootings in the United States." Applied Economics, 48, 4732–4746.

de Jager, Elzerie, et al., 2018. "Lethality of Civilian Active Shooter Incidents with and without Semiautomatic Rifles in the United States." Journal of the American Medical Association, 320(10), 1034–1035. https://jamanetwork.com/journals/jama/fullarticle/2702134

Dickinson, Tim, 2018. "All-American Killer: How the AR-15 Became Mass Shooters' Weapon of Choice." Rolling Stone, February 22. https://www.rollingstone.com/politics/politics-features/all-american-killer-how-the-ar-15-became-mass-shooters-weapon-of-choice-107819/

DiMaggio, Charles, et al., 2019. "Changes in US Mass Shooting Deaths Associated with the 1994–2004 Federal Assault Weapons Ban: Analysis of Open-Source Data." Journal of Trauma and Acute Care Surgery, 86(1), 11–19. https://journals.lww.com/jtrauma/Abstract/2019/01000/Changes_inUS_mass_shooting_deaths_associated_with.2.aspx

Eger, Chris, 2018. "NSSF: AR-15/AK Numbers Top 16 Million." Guns.Com, September 17. https://www.guns.com/news/2018/09/17/nssf-ar-15-ak-numbers-top-16-million

Farley, Robert, 2013. "Did the 1994 Assault Weapons Ban Work?" The Wire, FactCheck.Org, February 1. https://www.factcheck.org/2013/02/did-the-1994-assault-weapons-ban-work/

Fox, James, & DeLateur, Monica, 2014. "Mass Shootings in America: Moving beyond Newtown." *Homicide Studies*, 18(1), 125–145. jpfo.org/pdf03/Homicide%20Studies-2014-Fox-125-45.pdf

French, David, 2018. "It's Time for Real Talk about the Assault Weapons 'Ban.'" *National Review*, February 27. https://www.nationalreview.com/2018/02/assault-weapons-ban-not-answer-mass-shootings/

Gillin, Joshua, 2017. "Congress Blocked Obama's Call for New Gun Laws after Mass Shootings." PolitiFact, January 6. https://www.politifact.com/truth-o-meter/article/2017/jan/06/congress-blocked-obama-call-gun-control-mass-shoot/

Gius, Mark, 2014. "An Examination of the Effects of Concealed Weapons Laws and Assault Weapons Bans on State-Level Murder Rates." *Applied Economics Letters*, 21(4), 265–267.

Gius, Mark, 2015. "The Impact of State and Federal Assault Weapons Bans on Public Mass Shootings." *Applied Economics Letters*, 22(4), 281–284. https://www.researchgate.net/publication/271939348_The_impact_of_state_and_federal_assault_weapons_bans_on_public_mass_shootings

Klarevas, Louis, 2019. "Letter to the Editor Re: DiMaggio, C. et al. 'Changes in US Mass Shooting Deaths Associated with the 1994–2004 Federal Assault Weapons Ban: Analysis of Open-Source Data.' J. Trauma Acute Care. 2019; 86(1), 11–19." *Journal of Trauma and Acute Care Surgery*, 86(5), 926–928. https://journals.lww.com/jtrauma/Citation/2019/05000/Letter_to_the_editor_re_DiMaggio,_C_Et_al_.24.aspx

Kopel, David, 1994. "Rational Basis Analysis of 'Assault Weapon' Prohibition." *Journal of Contemporary Law*, 20, 381–417. https://constitution.org/1-Constitution/2ll/2ndschol/62rati.pdf

Koper, Christopher, Woods, Daniel, & Roth, Jeffrey, 2004. "An Updated Assessment of the Federal Assault Weapons Ban: Impacts on Gun Markets and Gun Violence, 1994–2003." *Report to the National Institute of Justice*, June. https://www.ncjrs.gov/pdffiles1/nij/grants/204431.pdf

Lott, John, 2003. *The Bias against Guns*. Washington, DC: Regnery Publishing, 207–210.

Myre, Greg, 2018. "A Brief History of the AR-15." NPR, February 28. https://www.npr.org/2018/02/28/588861820/a-brief-history-of-the-ar-15

NRA-ILA (National Rifle Association Institute for Legislative Action), 2013. "Semi-automatic Firearms and the 'Assault Weapon' Issue Overview." NRA-ILA, February 15. https://www.nraila.org/articles/20130215/assault-weapons-overview

Sugarmann, Josh, 1988. "Assault Weapons and Accessories in America." Violence Policy Center. https://www.vpc.org/studies/awacont.htm

2

Guns and Personal Safety

American humorist Mark Twain is reputed to have remarked that people get into difficulties not because of what they do not know, but because of what they know that is simply not so. This aphorism seems especially pertinent when examining the place of firearms in securing an individual's personal safety. A 2018 NBC/*Wall Street Journal* poll indicated that almost 60 percent of Americans believe that gun ownership increases an individual's safety (Murray, 2018), and an earlier Gallup poll (McCarthy, 2014) showed that more than 60 percent believe that having a gun in the house makes the home a safer place. Indeed, when asked about reasons for owning a firearm, a majority of gun owners (63 percent) cited self-defense as a primary motive (Masters, 2016).

At first glance, these findings may appear self-evident. Firearms—particularly handguns—are preeminent personal protection tools, specifically designed to keep individuals safe from attack, whether by dangerous beasts or dangerous persons. But is this belief in the efficacy of the gun to keep us safe just an example of "knowing something that simply is not so"? Gun control proponents argue exactly that. Rather than heighten personal safety, as gun rights advocates have claimed, they believe that gun ownership actually increases an individual's likelihood of injury and harm (Lopez, 2018). So, does a firearm enhance or diminish individual safety? The first question in this chapter examines this important issue.

The next two questions focus on actions that individuals might take that are thought to increase safety and lessen the possibility that gun ownership results in an accidental tragedy or some other avoidable mishap. The first examines the question of mandatory gun safety training and its likely efficacy in reducing gun accidents and gun suicides. The second question evaluates the same issues, but from the perspective of mandatory safe storage regulations. The last two questions in the chapter examine two other laws assumed to increase the safety of individual gun owners: stand your ground laws, and "red flag"/extreme risk laws. Both have generated significant controversy and hold implications not just for the individual but for society as well.

FURTHER READING

Lopez, German, 2018. "Poll: Most Americans Say Gun Ownership Increases Safety. Research: Nope." Vox, March 23. https://www.vox.com/policy-and-politics/2018/3/23/17155596/gun-ownership-polls-safety-violence

Masters, Kate, 2016. "Fear of Other People Is Now the Primary Motivation for American Gun Ownership, a Landmark Survey Finds." The Trace, September 19. https://www.thetrace.org/2016/09/harvard-gun-ownership-study-self-defense

McCarthy, Justin, 2014. "More than Six in 10 Americans Say Guns Make Homes Safer." Gallup, November 7. https://news.gallup.com/poll/179213/six-americans-say-guns-homes-safer.aspx

Murray, Mark, 2018. "Poll: 58 Percent Say Gun Ownership Increases Safety." NBC News, March 22. https://www.nbcnews.com/politics/first-read/poll-58-percent-say-gun-ownership-increases-safety-n859231

Q7. DOES GUN OWNERSHIP AND HAVING A GUN IN THE HOME INCREASE PERSONAL SAFETY?

Answer: A clear majority of Americans believe that gun ownership increases personal safety. Further, judging by a popular ironic maxim endorsed by firearms enthusiasts—"when seconds count, the police are only minutes away"—gun owners and gun rights proponents subscribe to this belief even more strongly. They point to the statistics on defensive gun uses (DGUs)—the presentation or use of a firearm to protect oneself or others from harm—as vindicating the belief that firearms enhance personal safety. However, DGU estimates vary widely, from a low of less than 70,000 annually to a high of more than 2.5 million (Hemenway, 1997). If the estimates (e.g., Kleck & Gertz, 1995; Kleck, 2015) that have placed the annual frequency of DGUs at more than 2 million are accurate, then the personal security a gun provides an individual is compellingly substantial.

Gun control proponents dispute these high estimates, arguing that the DGU figures do not tally with relevant police and hospital reports and are heavily exaggerated (e.g., DeFilippis & Hughes, 2015; Hemenway, 1997; 2004). An attempt in the mid-1990s to reconcile the wide discrepancies in DGU estimates concluded that 1.2 million DGUs annually appeared reasonable (Smith, 1997). In 2018, Florida State University criminology professor Gary Kleck, a prominent gun rights advocate, analyzed Centers for Disease Control data on DGUs that the center collected in the years 1996–1998 but did not examine. This analysis also provided an estimate of over a million DGUs annually (Doherty, 2018).

Aside from DGUs, the consequences of keeping a gun in the home is also relevant in examining the impact of gun ownership on an individual's personal safety. The Giffords Law Center to Prevent Gun Violence, a pro-gun control–oriented organization, asserts that a gun in the home is more likely to result in harm to the gun owner or family members—through accidents, domestic violence, and suicide—than it is likely to protect them from home invaders or robbers (Giffords Law Center, n.d.). Other studies have found that relative to homes without guns, having a gun available appears to increase the risk of homicide and suicide (Dahlberg, Ikeda, & Kresnow, 2004; Kellermann et al., 1993). Studies have also found increased incidents of female intimidation and homicide in homes with firearms (Hemenway, 2011).

Gun rights proponents have criticized the validity of this body of research, by citing contradictory findings (e.g., Smith, 2017) or by questioning the methodological procedures used in the studies (e.g., Schaffer, 1993). Additionally, the National Rifle Association (NRA), the most influential gun rights group in the country, has emphasized that the researchers conducting much of the research are gun control advocates. Questioning the objectivity of the investigators, the NRA dismissed their findings as "junk science . . . designed to provide ammunition for the gun control lobby" (Henderson, 2013).

In the absence of additional empirical evidence, no objective method can satisfactorily resolve these disputes over DGU prevalence or the impact of having a firearm in the home. Whether gun ownership appears to provide increased safety or increased jeopardy devolves into an individual's subjective assessment of the available research. Such orientations are generally culturally derived and shape whether an individual emphasizes the possible harms linked to gun ownership, or stresses the possible benefits of heightened security (see Kahan & Braman, 2003).

The Facts: Despite downward trends in the nation's violent crime rate, gun owners see the dangers of physical assault or worse as a remote but real possibility, and assert that a gun for self- and home protection fosters a sense of personal safety (Masters, 2016). For example, one 2014 Gallup survey found that 63 percent of Americans think that the presence of a firearm increases home security, while only 30 percent fear that a gun makes the home more dangerous (McCarthy, 2014). Similarly, a *Wall Street Journal*/NBC poll found that 58 percent of Americans believe that gun ownership increases individual safety by allowing law-abiding citizens to protect themselves from violent criminals and other lawbreakers, while only 38 percent think that gun ownership reduces safety by giving too many untrained people access to firearms, thus increasing the chances for accidents and misuse (Murray, 2018). Nonetheless, regardless of what people may believe, some researchers (e.g., Hemenway, 2004) and commentators (e.g., Lopez, 2018) argue that this faith in the efficacy of firearms for safety and security is badly misplaced, suggesting that the potentially lethal hazards associated with firearms far outweigh the safety and security advantages they are presumed to supply.

Two kinds of evidence are relevant in determining the net value of guns for enhancing a person's well-being. The first is the frequency of firearms' use in warding off assailants from doing harm. Researchers have examined this evidence under the heading of "defensive gun uses" (DGUs). The second is the likelihood and severity of gun mishaps in firearms-present homes. This evidence has been generated and examined primarily by public-health-and-safety–oriented investigators.

Wide variations exist in estimates of the prevalence of DGUs, due to differences in data collection methodologies, the number of respondents involved in a particular survey, and the analytical procedures used by the investigators. The research of prominent gun control advocates such as David Hemenway (1997; 2004) and his colleagues (DeFilippis & Hughes, 2015) indicate that DGUs are relatively rare, averaging no more than 50–60,000 annually. Prominent gun rights advocates, such as Gary Kleck and his colleagues (Kleck & Gertz, 1995; Kleck, 2015), indicate that DGUs are significantly more prevalent, averaging more than 2 million annually. Estimates from other surveys, such as the National Crime Victimization Survey and the Centers for Disease Control (Doherty, 2018) fall between these two extremes.

For example, one estimate of DGUs using FBI and National Crime Victimization Survey data for the five-year period 2007–2011 found that victims of crime used a firearm for self-defense in less than 1 percent of the total number of crime incidents. Nevertheless, this tiny percentage produced over 300,000 incidents where a firearm offered a person increased security and protection (Violence Policy Center, 2015). Similarly, Kleck derived an estimate of over a million DGUs annually from data collected (but not analyzed) by the Centers for Disease Control in 1996–1998

(Doherty, 2018). This statistic is in line with the 1.2 million figure generated in an early attempt to reconcile DGU estimates (Smith, 1997). Other estimates have ranged from 500,000 to 3 million DGUs yearly. Amy Swearer, a legal analyst with the conservative Heritage Foundation, asserts that even the lower end of this range is substantially greater than the number of times otherwise law-abiding Americans misuse firearms (Swearer, 2019).

None of these estimates—high or low—directly addresses the issue of whether guns increase personal safety. Most Americans have a very low likelihood of ever needing a firearm for self-defense. In a country of 350 million individuals, even with a million DGUs annually, possessing a firearm only enhances the safety of a small percentage of the total population and does little to enhance the objective safety of the millions of citizens who carry a gun but never need it. Of course, this assessment minimizes the sense of preparedness a firearm provides these gun-carrying individuals, and discounts their subjective feelings of enhanced security.

The second type of evidence relevant to judging the safety implications of gun ownership is the severity and frequency of gun mishaps in homes where firearms are present. Many gun control–oriented researchers assert that having a gun in the home significantly raises the risk of death for everyone living in the home—for gun owners, for spouses, and for children. The basis for these claims and recommendations comes from investigations conducted by public-health researchers having an epidemiological orientation to gun violence, one stressing the environmental factors contributing to gun damage and lethality. Arthur Kellermann pioneered this approach in the 1980s by examining all the gunshot deaths that occurred in Seattle and its environs (i.e., King County, Washington) over a six-year period. Of the 743 deaths from firearms, more than half—398—occurred in homes with guns. Suicides accounted for more than 80 percent, followed by homicides (13 percent) and accidents (3 percent). Since only 9 of the 398 deaths involved some form of self-defense, Kellermann dramatically concluded that his study found "43 suicides, criminal homicides, or accidental gunshot deaths involving a gun kept in the home for every case of homicide for self-protection" (Thompson, 1998). In follow-up investigations, Kellermann, his colleagues, and other epidemiologically oriented researchers have consistently found that the dangers of having a gun in the home far outstrip the benefits of self-protection it appears to provide (see Dahlberg, et al., 2004; Hemenway, 2011; Kellermann et al., 1993).

Gun rights advocates generally dismiss epidemiologically oriented gun research as invalid, either because of poor methodological procedures (e.g., Schaffer, 1993), contradictory evidence (e.g., Smith, 2017), or because the research overlooks the implications of the two-way relationship between gun availability and violence. Specifically, in cases where violence may have initially prompted the household to acquire a gun, matching that home to a home without a firearm (as is the case in many epidemiological studies) is not appropriate. Although the homes may appear equivalent, they clearly are different. Along these lines, Kleck has asserted that epidemiologically oriented gun investigations often confuse cause and effect, and show unprofessional bias in interpreting their results. He goes so far as to describe one well-known epidemiologically oriented study as "the most technically primitive study of gun violence . . . ever published in a professional journal" (Thompson, 1998). The NRA has echoed similar criticisms, labeling the whole body of epidemiologically oriented research as a clear effort to buttress gun control efforts (Union of Concerned Scientists, n.d.).

Does an assessment of the overall evidence justify a conclusion that firearms increase personal safety? It seems apparent that gun control and gun rights advocates will answer this question differently. For gun control advocates, the conflicting findings doubtless demonstrate that even if firearms provide *any* increase in personal security, this increase is minimal and cannot justify the much greater harm guns inflict on other individuals and on society generally. For gun rights advocates, the findings demonstrate just the opposite. Even if most gun owners never need or use a gun for self-protection, for those individuals that need protection, firearms offer vital security regardless of possible mishaps associated with their ownership.

In the absence of an empirical answer to the question, some analysts (Kahan & Braman, 2003) have proposed a psychological resolution, suggesting that a person's idiosyncratic risk perceptions determine whether guns are believed to enhance safety or foster harm. These risk perceptions are culturally derived, shaped by the individual's larger cultural worldview. Individuals having an egalitarian worldview tend to center on the hazards firearms present, while those with an individualistic worldview tend to center on benefits they provide (see Campbell, 2019).

FURTHER READING

Campbell, Donald, 2019. *America's Gun Wars: A Cultural History of Gun Control in the United States.* Santa Barbara, CA: Praeger.

Dahlberg, Linda, Ikeda, Robin, & Kresnow, Marcie-jo, 2004. "Guns in the Home and Risk of a Violent Death in the Home: Findings from a National Study." *American Journal of Epidemiology,* 160(10), 929–936. https://academic.oup.com/aje/article/160/10/929/140858#ref-30

DeFilippis, Evan, & Hughes, Devin, 2015. The Myth behind Defensive Gun Ownership." Politico, January 14. https://www.politico.com/magazine/story/2015/01/defensive-gun-ownership-myth-114262

Doherty, Brian, 2018. "A Second Look at a Controversial Study about Defensive Gun Use." *Reason*, September 4. https://reason.com/2018/09/04/what-the-cdcs-mid-90s-surveys-on-defensi/

Giffords Law Center, n.d. "Statistics on Guns in the Home & Safe Storage." https://lawcenter.giffords.org/guns-in-the-homesafe-storage-statistics/

Hemenway, David, 1997. "Survey Research and Self-Defense Gun Use: An Explanation of Extreme Overestimates." *Journal of Criminal Law and Criminology*, 87(4), 1430–1445.

Hemenway, David, 2004. *Private Guns, Public Health*. Ann Arbor: University of Michigan Press.

Hemenway, David, 2011. "Risks and Benefits of a Gun in the Home." *American Journal of Lifestyle Medicine*, 5(6). https://journals.sagepub.com/doi/10.1177/1559827610396294

Henderson, Peter, 2013. "Scientists Urge End to Limits on Gun Safety Research." Reuters, January 10. https://www.reuters.com/article/us-usa-guns-scientists-idUSBRE90915F20130110

Kahan, Dan, & Braman, Donald, 2003. "More Statistics, Less Persuasion: A Cultural Theory of Gun-Risk Perceptions." *University of Pennsylvania Law Review*, 151(4), 1291–1327. https://scholarship.law.upenn.edu/cgi/viewcontent.cgi?article=3212&context=penn_law_review

Kellermann, Arthur L., Rivara, Frederick P., Rushforth, Norman B., Banton, Joyce G., Reay, Donald T., Francisco, Jerry T., Locci, Ana B., et al., 1993. "Gun Ownership as a Risk Factor for Homicide in the Home." *New England Journal of Medicine*, 329, 1084–1091. https://www.nejm.org/doi/full/10.1056/NEJM199310073291506

Kleck, Gary, 2015. "Defensive Gun Use Is Not a Myth." Politico, February 17. https://www.politico.com/magazine/story/2015/02/defensive-gun-ownership-gary-kleck-response-115082

Kleck, Gary, & Gertz, M., 1995. "Armed Resistance to Crime: The Prevalence and Nature of Self-Defense with a Gun." *Journal of Criminal Law and Criminology*, 86(1), 150–187. https://scholarlycommons.law.northwestern.edu/cgi/viewcontent.cgi?article=6853&context=jclc

Lopez, German, 2018. "Poll: Most Americans Say Gun Ownership Increases Safety. Research: Nope." Vox, March 23. https://www.vox.com/policy-and-politics/2018/3/23/17155596/gun-ownership-polls-safety-violence

Masters, Kate, 2016. "Fear of Other People Is Now the Primary Motivation for American Gun Ownership, a Landmark Survey Finds." The Trace, September 19. https://www.thetrace.org/2016/09/harvard-gun-ownership-study-self-defense

McCarthy, Justin, 2014. "More than Six in 10 Americans Say Guns Make Homes Safer." Gallup, November 7. https://news.gallup.com/poll/179213/six-americans-say-guns-homes-safer.aspx

Murray, Mark, 2018. "Poll: 58 Percent Say Gun Ownership Increases Safety." NBC News, March 22. https://www.nbcnews.com/politics/first-read/poll-58-percent-say-gun-ownership-increases-safety-n859231

Perry, Susan, 2012. "The Health Risk of Having a Gun in the Home." Minnpost, December 17. https://www.minnpost.com/second-opinion/2012/12/health-risk-having-gun-home/

Raphelson, Samantha, 2018. "How Often Do People Use Guns in Self-Defense" NPR, April 13. https://www.npr.org/2018/04/13/602143823/how-often-do-people-use-guns-in-self-defense

Schaffer, Henry, 1993. "Serious Flaws in Kellermann, et al. (1993) NEJM." https://www.firearmsandliberty.com/ResearchContent/kellerman-schaffer.html

Smith, Guy, 2017. *Gun Facts*. www.gunfacts.info/pdf/gun-policy-info/accidental-deaths/ [and] gun-policy-info/guns-and-crime-prevention/

Smith, Tom, 1997. "A Call for a Truce in the DGU War." *Journal of Criminal Law and Criminology*, 87(4), 1462–1469.

Swearer, Amy, 2019. "Latest News of Self-Defense with Firearms Contradicts Gun Control Rhetoric." Daily Signal, April 9. https://www.dailysignal.com/2019/04/09/latest-news-of-self-defense-with-firearms-contradicts-gun-control-rhetoric/

Thompson, B., 1998. "Trigger Points." *Washington Post Magazine*, March, 29. https://www.washingtonpost.com/wp-srv/national/longterm/trigger/trigger4.htm

Union of Concerned Scientists, 2017. "How the NRA Suppressed Gun Violence Research." https://www.ucsusa.org/suppressing-research-effects-gun-violence

Violence Policy Center, 2015. "Firearm Justifiable Homicides and Non-Fatal Self-Defense Gun Use." https://vpc.org/studies/justifiable17.pdf

Q8. DOES MANDATORY GUN SAFETY TRAINING REDUCE GUN ACCIDENTS AND SUICIDES?

Answer: Both gun control and gun rights proponents agree on the importance of gun safety training. They both endorse the idea that individuals intending to own or use a gun should have proper gun safety training. As one firearms instructor notes, "proper and continued training enhances safety, physical skill and mindset, and mitigates legal risk" (Cole, 2014). Given such rare agreement between the two sides, it is a bit ironic that virtually no empirical evidence exists showing that gun safety training actually increases gun safety or reduces suicides. For example, data examining the relationship between firearms training and accidents rates across different states—some with strict training requirements, others with low training requirements, and still others with no training requirements—uncovered no apparent pattern linking firearms training (or its absence) to firearm accidents (Cole, 2014).

Additionally, a review of the effectiveness of a specialized children's gun safety education program—the National Rifle Association's (NRA) Eddie Eagle program—concluded that the primary assessment evidence consisted of anecdotal testimonials provided by adults rather than empirical data (Haelle, 2017). Similarly, possible correlations between firearms safety training and gun suicides have not been a focus of study.

In the absence of hard criteria for determining the effectiveness of gun safety training, reasonable individuals disagree regarding the appropriateness of *mandating* such training. Gun control proponents typically assert that, even without empirical evidence, logical considerations suggest that firearms safety programs make sense. At worst, such programs will have no impact on reducing accidents and suicides, but more likely, they will have a positive impact. Gun rights proponents typically argue that mandating *any* type of training to exercise a constitutional right, even training that may make logical sense, is only justified in the face of substantial evidence that such training is absolutely necessary. According to this perspective, mandating firearms safety training requires individuals to spend time and money on an enumerated constitutional right, and disenfranchises those citizens who have neither the time nor the money (Cole, 2014).

Thus, an answer to this question is complicated. Logical considerations and conventional wisdom support firearms training, but mandating safety programs is problematic. While most gun control proponents favor required training enforced with legal penalties, most gun rights advocates endorse voluntary training encouraged by educational campaigns (Campbell, 2019, 141).

The Facts: Gun safety training programs are not standardized, and training requirements, content, and approach reflect the philosophy and expertise of the individual instructors and the organizations sponsoring the training. Programs vary in length from a few hours to as many as 12 or more, and class fees vary in cost from about $35 for shorter programs to $185 for the more extensive programs. Some programs include range time and actual shooting experience, while others are limited to just classroom instruction and audiovisual presentations. Typically, good programs cover revolver and pistol nomenclature, general firearm operations, gun safety rules and safe gun handling, shooting accuracy, and legal issues and considerations.

As the content summary suggests, training programs offer much useful information ancillary to safety, and do provide content that, if taken seriously and practiced (e.g., safety rules and safe handling), should positively influence accident reduction. Consequently, despite the absence of hard empirical evidence confirming that gun safety programs reduce accidents or suicides, the idea that gun users should receive gun safety training has been championed by both gun control and gun rights advocates. The divisive issue separating the two groups is the issue of mandatory versus voluntary training. Gun control proponents assert that gun safety training is essential, contending that such instruction will at least limit egregious incidents of dangerous gun handling and avoidable gun accidents, such as injuries and fatalities suffered by small children who find and play with unsecured firearms. Additionally, it may also reduce incidents of gun suicides by increasing individual awareness of this potential gun-owning danger, and by heightening acceptance of the need for safe storage practices.

Gun rights proponents argue that the most effective training is voluntary training, since in these circumstances individuals are likely to be motivated and receptive to the presented material and instructor guidance. With mandatory training, a certain percentage of the class, inattentive or resentful of the time and money expenditures, may distract other class participants and reduce overall training effectiveness. Additionally, the financial and time commitments associated with mandated gun training means that some individuals particularly in need of a firearm for self-protection—for example, low-income citizens living in high-crime areas—will find themselves shut out of an enumerated constitutional right (Cole, 2014).

In attempting to reconcile these opposite positions, an examination of three types of gun safety training programs—handgun oriented, child oriented, and hunter oriented—is useful. Even in the absence of empirically driven data assessment, such an examination can provide a basis for judging whether a program's presumed benefits appear clear enough to justify a mandated approach.

The largest and most relevant of the three types of programs are those focused on handgun safety. The NRA's firearms safety programs are the nation's oldest and probably the best known. These programs are voluntary, and more than 125,000 NRA certified instructors and range safety officers train over 1 million participants annually. The NRA reports that since data were first collected in 1903, the per capita rate of gun accident deaths has decreased 94 percent; and that over the last 20 years, the annual number of accidental gun deaths has decreased by more than half. Based on such evidence, the association concludes that voluntary firearms training and education are already successful and that mandating firearms training is unnecessary and a constitutional infringement (NRA-ILA, 2016).

On the other hand, a 2018 University of Washington study found that only about 60 percent of U.S. firearm owners receive any formal gun training, a percentage identical to 20 years ago; and that only 14 percent of nonowners living with a firearms owner had received some type of formal gun safety training. Additionally, because instructors primarily determine the content of the programs, the impact of gun ownership on suicide attempts—that is, the substantial increase in lethality of such attempts—is often under-addressed, with only about 15 percent of gun-owning respondents reporting that their training covered suicide prevention. Considering that two-thirds of all firearm deaths in the country are suicides, this omission has potentially significant implications, and suggests that mandatory gun training with standardized content might well save lives (Rowhani-Rahbar et al., 2018).

Gun safety education for children is a second area that can indirectly address the impact of voluntary safety training on reducing gun accidents. These educational programs, such as the NRA Eddie Eagle program, generally attempt to impress upon youngsters that guns are not toys, that they should avoid even touching the gun should they come upon an unsecured firearm, and that they should leave the area and tell an adult about the firearm. The effectiveness of such programs, as with voluntary adult gun safety programs, is hotly disputed.

For example, the NRA marshals several types of evidence to demonstrate the effectiveness of its Eddie Eagle program. The association states that multiple agencies and groups, such as the National Sheriffs' Association, the U.S. Department of Justice, and the Association of American Educators, have endorsed the program, as well as 26 state governors and 23 state legislatures. Further, noting that 26,000 school teachers and law enforcement officers have taught the program to over 28 million children, the association argues that the very popularity of the program speaks to its effectiveness. The association also points to academic research (i.e., Howard, 2001) that evaluated the Eddie Eagle program and concluded that it was the best of the 80 programs examined. Finally, based on National Center for Health statistics, proponents of the program note that fatal firearms accidents decreased more than 80 percent in the Eddie Eagle age group since the program's nationwide launch in 1988 (NRA Explore, n.d.).

Critics, however, have questioned the effectiveness of a voluntary educational approach to children's gun safety, typically preferring child access prevention laws. While acknowledging that educational programs may prevent some youngsters from touching an unsecured firearm, these programs cannot predict which children will follow the guidelines and which children will not. As one commentator observed, "firearms hold an allure that is hard to resist . . . and despite kids' and parents' best intentions, most children will pick up the gun. A third or so will pull the trigger" (Haelle, 2017; see also Jackman et al., 2001). Such critics dismiss the evidence supporting the effectiveness of programs like Eddie Eagle as simply reflecting the anecdotal testimonials of adults, and note that anecdotes do not qualify as scientific data. Other commentators have been especially critical of the Eddie Eagle program, describing it as not just ineffective (e.g., Aran, 2018) but as a disguised attempt to market guns to kids and a cynical ploy to kill child safety legislation (Violence Policy Center, n.d.).

The little empirical research that has examined the effectiveness of children's gun safety educational programs has produced ambiguous results. For example, while the Howard (2001) study endorsed the effectiveness of the educational Eddie Eagle program, critics note that the endorsement was essentially conjectural, based on the researcher's assessment that the program incorporated the most elements of a successful educational program—not measurable outcome criteria (Haelle, 2017). Other research comparing the effectiveness of the Eddie Eagle educational approach with a behavioral skills training approach (using instruction, modeling, rehearsal, and feedback) found that while both programs were effective for teaching children to verbalize gun safety rules, neither program appeared effective in transferring these safety skills beyond the training situation (Himle et al., 2004). A similar research study also found that both programs were effective in getting the children to produce the appropriate verbal responses, but only behavioral training was effective in getting the children to demonstrate the safety skills in role-playing assessments (Gatheridge et al., 2004).

Hunter safety courses are also relevant to consider. Originally voluntary, such programs date back to the 1940s. The NRA, alarmed at the unfavorable attention hunting accidents were garnering in popular periodicals, introduced its first hunter safety program in 1950. By the late 1990s, every state mandated hunter safety education for some segment of its hunters (McKibbin, 2017). Proponents of such mandatory training tout statistics documenting the general decline of hunting accidents over the decades. For example, New York's hunter education course was cited for the state's declining trend in firearms-related hunting injuries (Moran, 2000); similarly, Pennsylvania's hunter safety program was credited with reducing hunting-related shooting incidents by nearly 80 percent since 1959 (Hayes, 2009). Such reductions are representative, with one commentator observing, "hunter education has made hunting safer, as firearm accidents involving hunters are at a historic low" (McKibbin, 2017). Gun control proponents have pointed to these findings as clear evidence of the effectiveness of mandatory gun safety training. But as with virtually all evidence assessing mandatory versus voluntary training, the decline in hunting firearm accidents is only suggestive, since the potential effect of voluntary programs on such accidents is unknown.

In considering all three gun safety programs, the evidence is equivocal regarding whether the benefits of mandatory training are sufficient to outweigh the constitutional and practical costs imposed by such a requirement. While logic and conventional wisdom indicate that gun safety training is valuable, its actual effectiveness in reducing accidents or in reducing suicides presumably hinges on individual characteristics, for example, a person's ability to attend such training and motivation to take training content seriously. If so, gun rights advocates would likely conclude that voluntary training is sufficient, and see mandatory training backed with legal penalties as both unnecessary and excessive. Gun control proponents would likely conclude that relying on voluntary educational campaigns is simply insufficient and irresponsible, and see mandated training as essential.

FURTHER READING

Aran, Isha, 2018. "Meet Eddie Eagle, the NRA's Ineffective Approach to Gun Safety for Children." Splinter, March 23. https://splinternews.com/meet-eddie-eagle-the-nras-ineffective-approach-to-gun-1823990269

Campbell, Donald, 2019. *America's Gun Wars: A Cultural History of Gun Control in the United States.* Santa Barbara, CA: Praeger.

Cole, David, 2014. "Mandatory Firearms Training? What if We Had Mandatory Free Speech Training." Ammoland, June 13. https://www.ammoland.com/2014/06/mandatory-firearms-training/

Gatheridge, Brian, Miltenberger, Raymond G., Huneke, Daniel F., Satterlund, Melisa J., Mattern, Amanda R., Johnson, Brigette M., & Flessner, Christopher A., 2004. "Comparison of Two Programs to Teach Firearm Injury Prevention Skills to 6- and 7-year-old Children." *Pediatrics, 114*(3), e294–e299. https://pubmed.ncbi.nlm.nih.gov/15342889/

Giffords Law Center, n.d. "Licensing." https://lawcenter.giffords.org/gun-laws/policy-areas/gun-owner-responsibilities/licensing/

Haelle, Tara, 2017. "Gun Safety Programs Won't Save Your Child, but This Question Might." *Forbes,* June 21. https://www.forbes.com/sites/tarahaelle/2017/06/21/gun-safety-programs-wont-save-your-child-but-this-question-might/#52104d5a55b8

Hayes, John, 2009. "State's Hunter-Trapper Safety Course Reduces Accidents by Nearly 80 Percent." *Pittsburgh Post-Gazette*, September 13. https://www.post-gazette.com/sports/hunting-fishing/2009/09/13/State-s-hunter-trapper-safety-course-reduces-accidents-by-nearly-80-percent/stories/200909130183

Himle, Michael B., Miltenberger, Raymond G., Gatheridge, Brian J., & Flessner, Christopher, 2004. "An Evaluation of Two Procedures for Training Skills to Prevent Gun Play in Children." *Pediatrics, 113*(1), 70–77. https://pubmed.ncbi.nlm.nih.gov/14702451/

Howard, Patricia, 2001. "An Overview of a Few Well-Known National Children's Gun Safety Programs and ENA's Newly Developed Program." *Journal of Emergency Nursing, 27,* 485–488. https://docslide.us/documents/an-overview-of-a-few-well-known-national-childrens-gun-safety-programs-and.html?h=documents.onl

Jackman, G. A., Farah, M. M., Kellermann, A. L., & Simon, H. K., 2001. "Seeing Is Believing: What Do Boys Do When They Find a Real Gun?" *Pediatrics, 107*(6), 1247–1250. https://pubmed.ncbi.nlm.nih.gov/11389238/

McKibbin, Connor, 2017. "First Light: NRA Introduces Online Hunter Education Course." *American Hunter,* December 25. https://www.americanhunter.org/articles/2017/12/25/first-light-nra-introduces-online-hunter-education-course/

Moran, Ken, 2000. "Hunter Safety Is No Accident." *New York Post,* November 17. https://nypost.com/2000/11/17/hunter-safety-is-no-accident/

NRA Explore, n.d. "Have There Been Any Evaluations of the Program's Impact in Published/Unpublished Literature? If not, How Do You Measure Its Impact?" NRA Explore Parents FAQs. https://eddieeagle.nra.org/faqs/

NRA-ILA, 2016. "Gun Safety." NRA-ILA, August 8. https://www.nraila.org/get-the-facts/gun-safety/

Rowhani-Rahbar, Ali., Lyons, Vivian H., Simonetti, Joseph A., Azrael, Deborah, & Miller, Matthew, 2018. "Formal Firearm Training among Adults in the USA: Results of a National Survey." *Injury Prevention, 24*(2), 161–165.

Violence Policy Center, 2000. "Joe Camel with Feathers." https://www.vpc.org/studies/eddieap1.htm

Q9. DO MANDATORY SAFE STORAGE LAWS REDUCE ACCIDENTAL SHOOTINGS AND SUICIDES?

Answer: Yes. Safe storage laws require gun owners to keep their firearms out of the reach of others when not in use, preferably in a locked box or safe, or rendered inoperable using a trigger lock or similar device. The regulations are aimed at keeping firearms out of the "wrong hands." Such hands belong not just to criminals and lawbreakers, but also to children, the mentally unstable, those unfamiliar with firearms, and prohibited individuals (e.g., convicted felons and domestic abusers). Proponents argue that safe storage laws "prevent tragedies due to accidental discharges, suicides, and gun theft by creating an environment helping ensure firearms are only used by their rightful owners" (Giffords Law Center, n.d.a). They assert that the laws' value in achieving these ends justifies their mandatory nature.

Critics argue, however, that the laws are generally unenforceable—the police cannot determine beforehand whether a gun owner is actually abiding by the law—and are typically invoked only *after* a tragedy has occurred. Additionally, opponents of storage laws believe that they increase reaction times under stress, and that the loss of even a few seconds in self-defense circumstances "could mean the difference between life and death" (NRA Explore, n.d.). Thus, for critics, the issue is not primarily whether safe storage regulations can avert tragedies (although some do question this; see Lott & Whitley, 2001), but whether they should be mandatory. Noting that all households are different and have different needs, they argue that individual gun owners are the best judges when it comes to firearm storage in determining the risk trade-off involved in accidents and misuse versus slowed reactions and diminished self-protection capacity.

Pragmatically, the research evidence suggests that safe storage laws do have a positive impact on reducing gun accidents and suicides. For example, a RAND Corporation analysis of child access prevention (CAP) laws—these laws go beyond safe storage regulations and impose legal penalties on adults found guilty of irresponsibly storing firearms around children—concluded that such laws appear to reduce suicides among young people aged 14–20 (Apaydin, n.d.a). The evidence also suggests that CAP laws reduce accidental self-injuries in children; and, less strongly, that they decrease accidental firearm injuries and deaths among adults as well (Apaydin, n.d.b). Nonetheless, even most gun owners who acknowledge the benefits of safe storage do not actually use gun safes or take other precautions to secure all their firearms (Yablon, 2018), presumably because they place a higher priority on having one gun easily available for emergencies. This mindset suggests that many gun owners will ignore mandated safe storage laws, making efforts to increase voluntary compliance with safe storage (perhaps through ongoing educational campaigns) essential.

The Facts: Research indicates that as of the late 2010s, more than 4.5 million children reside in homes where at least one gun is unlocked and loaded. Further, the proportion of child-rearing gun owners with unsecured firearms is increasing (Azrael et al., 2018), and unsecured guns are a leading means of youth suicides (Biette-Timmons, 2018). Other research has found that a disproportionate number of accidental firearm fatalities occur in states where owners fail to lock or secure their loaded guns, leading investigators to conclude that safer storage practices would save many lives (Miller et al., 2005). Additionally, more than 500,000 unsecured firearms are lost or stolen from private residences each year, fueling the black market in illegal weapons (see Giffords Law Center, n.d.a). Not surprisingly, then, many individuals (and particularly gun control proponents) have advocated for the passage of mandatory safe storage gun laws—requirements designed to prevent unauthorized or unqualified parties from gaining access to gun owners' not-in-use firearms.

Opponents of mandatory safe storage laws (generally gun rights advocates) question the effectiveness of such legislation. For example, they point to research by John Lott—a prominent but controversial (e.g., Moskowitz, 2018; Winkler, 2011) gun rights figure—that found no support for concluding that safe storage laws reduce juvenile accidental gun deaths or suicides. Lott asserted that their major impact, instead, is to impair people's ability to use guns defensively, encouraging increased criminal violence (Lott & Whitley, 2001). Lott's findings, however, diverge from conclusions reached by a RAND corporation analysis of CAP laws, which determined that the weight of evidence *supports* the effectiveness of safe storage practices for reducing gun accidents and suicides (Apaydin, n.d.a; n.d.b).

However, opponents' objections to safe storage laws are not limited to their potential effectiveness but also to the underlying philosophy of mandatory gun safety laws in general. As the secretary of the Buckeye Firearms Association put it, "education is really the key: we teach kids 'don't touch a hot stove'—we don't ignore the fact that hot stoves exist. So kids need to be taught: don't touch, leave the area, tell an adult about [unsecured] guns . . ." (Baus, 2014). Another journalist writing for NRA Family, an informational website for "families and beginning shooters of all ages," acknowledges that a "don't touch" policy may not work for everyone. In an analysis of the strengths and limitations of a variety of safe storage systems, he concluded that "the right safe storage solution for everyone is different. The determination of what is 'adequate protection' is a matter of judgment on the part of the individual gun owner" (Horman, 2019).

Child access prevention (CAP) laws are also relevant to this discussion. While safe storage laws require gun owners to responsibly store their firearms, CAP laws are particularly designed to reduce storing firearms negligently around children. These laws also mandate safe firearms storage, but they additionally authorize law enforcement (typically using a weaker standard of criminal liability) to bring criminal charges against adults who negligently allow children access to firearms. The laws themselves vary from state to state. For example, California has the most stringent CAP law, imposing criminal liability if a minor is *likely* to gain access to a negligently stored firearm, even in the absence of actual possession. Utah has the weakest, merely prohibiting adults from directly providing a firearm to an unsupervised minor (Giffords Law Center, n.d.b). CAP laws and safe storage laws have similar goals—reducing accidental gun injuries, suicides, and criminal shootings—and the arguments for and against such laws are also highly similar.

Safe storage laws and CAP laws, then, are both specifically designed to reduce negligent gun-related behaviors. This duplication may reflect in part the advantage a "child safety" bill has for legislative passage relative to a mundane "safe storage" bill. For example, only 11 states have safe storage laws (Giffords Law Center, n.d.a), while 27 states and the District of Columbia have enacted CAP laws (Giffords Law Center, n.d.b). In the propaganda war waged over guns, such legislative outcomes have been noted by both camps. Further, disagreements over mandated requirements versus voluntary compliance are not specific to only this legislation. Gun control advocates generally favor the mandatory implementation of "gun problem" solutions, enforced with legal penalties; while gun rights proponents favor voluntary implementations, founded on educational campaigns (see Campbell, 2019, 140–142).

The severe divisions—and suspicions—that separate gun control and gun rights advocates on virtually all issues related to firearms are captured by a prominent gun rights researcher commenting on safe storage laws. After insisting that such laws really are unnecessary, since all states have reckless endangerment and negligence laws that would fully apply to guns, and that parents know plenty of ways to keep items away from children without the need for locks, he states, "The hidden agenda behind safe-storage laws has nothing to do with safety . . . the anti-gun lobby believes that armed self-defense . . . is inherently immoral . . . in Canada, gun prohibitionists have used storage laws as a justification for imposing [more and harsher restrictions] . . . parents, not legislators know best how to keep their children safe" (Kopel, Gallant, & Eisen, 2000).

Proponents of a federal safe storage mandate, however, insist that state-level endangerment and negligence laws are insufficient. "According to a national survey conducted in 2015, about two in 10 gun-owning households with children store at least one weapon in the least safe manner—loaded and unlocked," declared a 2019 editorial by the pro-gun control Bloomberg News Editorial Board. "That means that about 7 percent of U.S. children, some 4.6 million, are living with a daily risk that is lethal, persistent and inexcusable." The Board urged passage of a robust federal law to reduce these numbers, pointing to a 2019 study from the T. H. Chan Harvard School of Public Health that found that safe storage of guns could reduce teen and childhood firearm deaths by a third (Bloomberg News Editorial Board, 2019).

Overall, what conclusions about accidents, suicides, and mandatory safe storage laws can be drawn? As with firearms-related evidence generally, research findings are complicated and mixed, but the weight of the evidence suggests that such laws can result in decreased firearm accidents and mishaps. However, the evidence also suggests that many gun owners, even aware of the benefits associated with safe storage, prefer to have a firearm at the ready for self- and family defense. These individuals are likely to ignore mandated safe storage requirements, as are individuals and parents who believe they are better equipped to make personal gun safety decisions than the government. Thus, while mandated safe storage laws may reduce accidents and suicides, their effectiveness relative to voluntary guidelines buttressed with sustained education campaigns is unknown. Such campaigns are likely necessary to influence those gun owners who ignore mandated regulations.

FURTHER READING

Apaydin, Eric, n.d.a. "Effects of Child-Access Prevention Laws on Suicide." RAND Corporation. https://www.rand.org/research/gun-policy/analysis/child-access-prevention/suicide.html

Apaydin, Eric, n.d.b. "Effects of Child-Access Prevention Laws on Unintentional Injuries and Deaths." RAND Corporation. https://www.rand.org/research/gun-policy/analysis/child-access-prevention/unintentional-injuries.html

Azrael, Deborah., Cohen, Joanna, Salhi, Carmel, & Miller, Matthew, 2018. "Firearm Storage in Gun-Owning Households with Children: Results of a 2015 National Survey." *Journal of Urban Health*, 95(3), 295–304. https://link.springer.com/article/10.1007/s11524-018-0261-7

Baus, Chad, 2014. "Common Sense: Gun Storage Laws Don't Work; Firearm Safety Education Does." Buckeye Firearms Association, March 21. https://www.buckeyefirearms.org/common-sense-gun-storage-laws-dont-work-firearm-safety-education-does

Biette-Timmons, Nora, 2018. "Roughly 4.6 Million American Kids Live in Homes with Unlocked, Loaded Guns." The Trace, May 21. https://www.thetrace.org/newsletter/study-american-children-unlocked-loaded-gun-storage/

Bloomberg News Editorial Board, 2019. "We Need Safe Storage Laws for Firearms." Bloomberg Opinion, July 17. https://www.bloomberg.com/opinion/articles/2019-07-17/u-s-needs-safe-gun-storage-laws

Campbell, Donald, 2019. *America's Gun Wars: A Cultural History of Gun Control in the United States*. Santa Barbara, CA: Praeger.

Giffords Law Center, n.d.a. "Safe Storage." https://lawcenter.giffords.org/gun-laws/policy-areas/child-consumer-safety/safe-storage/

Giffords Law Center, n.d.b. "Child Access Prevention." https://lawcenter.giffords.org/gun-laws/policy-areas/child-consumer-safety/child-access-prevention/

Horman, B. Gil, 2019. "6 Ways to Safely Store Your Firearms." NRA Explore, November 5. https://www.nrafamily.org/articles/2019/11/5/6-ways-to-safely-store-your-firearms/

Kopel, David, Gallant, Paul, & Eisen, Joanne, 2000. "Not-So-Safe Storage Laws." http://www.davekopel.com/NRO/2000/Not-so-Safe-Storage-Laws.htm

Lott, John, & Whitley, John, 2001. "Safe Storage Gun Laws: Accidental Deaths, Suicides, and Crime." *Journal of Law and Economics*, 44(2), 659–689.

Miller, Matthew, Azrael, Deborah, Hemenway, David, & Vriniotis, Mary, 2005. "Firearm Storage Practices and Rates of Unintentional Firearm Deaths in the United States." *Accident Analysis and Prevention*, 37(4), 661–667. https://pubmed.ncbi.nlm.nih.gov/15949457/

Moskowitz, Peter, 2018. "Inside the Mind of America's Favorite Gun Researcher." Pacific Standard, September 23. https://psmag.com/magazine/inside-the-mind-of-americas-favorite-gun-researcher

NRA Explore, 2018. "Delaware: Mandatory Gun Storage Legislation to Be Heard in Committee Today." NRA Explore, April 25. https://www.nraila.org/articles/20180425/delaware-mandatory-gun-storage-legislation-to-be-heard-in-committee-today

Winkler, Adam, 2011. *Gunfight: The Battle over the Right to Bear Arms in America*. New York: W. W. Norton.

Yablon, Alex, 2018. "Gun Safes Work. But Most Gun Owners Don't Use Them." *Washington Post*, June 4. https://www.washingtonpost.com/news/posteverything/wp/2018/06/04/gun-safes-work-but-most-gun-owners-dont-use-them/

Q10. DO "STAND YOUR GROUND" LAWS INCREASE AN INDIVIDUAL'S PERSONAL SAFETY?

Answer: Stand your ground (SYG) laws permit a person to use defensive force—up to and including lethal force—against perceived threats in confrontational situations, even if a safe retreat from the situation might have been possible. While SYG laws vary from state to state, they commonly assert that individuals in threatening circumstances have no obligation to retreat from any place that they have a lawful right to be; and that if those individuals reasonably believe they (or others) are in imminent danger of serious bodily harm or death, they may use any level of force necessary to protect themselves.

As an expansion of the concept of self-defense, proponents of SYG laws argue that these laws increase personal safety in at least two ways. First, they allow individuals facing danger to concentrate their attention on the perceived threat, without having to divide their focus between the aggressor and determining if a potential retreat is feasible and safe. Second, SYG laws provide emotional safety by eliminating the psychological stresses and financial hardships that defending against a criminal prosecution for simply engaging in self-defense inflicts on an individual (Stand Your Ground, n.d.).

Opponents of SYG laws argue that, far from making people safer, these laws actually encourage violence, threaten the safety of bystanders, and allow individuals to "more easily get away with murder" (Giffords Law Center, n.d.). Disparaging SYG laws as "shoot first" laws, opponents note that the "stand your ground" concept ignores centuries of legal precedent and addresses a nonexistent problem: the law has always allowed individuals to ward off serious threats with deadly force if no safe retreat was available. By removing a "duty to retreat" in such circumstances, these critics contend that SYG laws endanger public safety by legally sanctioning the sometimes needless escalation of conflicts into violence (Giffords Law Center, n.d.).

Research in this area is limited, but a 2018 RAND analysis of the available evidence concluded that SYG laws increase both total homicides and firearms homicides, and have uncertain effects on other types of violent crime (Xenakis, 2018a). Additionally, these laws increase the number of justifiable homicides, although limitations in the data make this finding provisional (Xenakis, 2018b). Overall, the research evidence remains unclear regarding the impact of SYG laws on personal safety. More violent deaths certainly suggest a *decrease* in individual safety, but that conclusion warrants further scrutiny. In Florida, for example, justifiable homicides reported to the Florida Department of Law Enforcement increased threefold since the SYG law was enacted (Giffords Law Center, n.d.). Presumably, threatened victims whose SYG actions avert danger to themselves—even if their actions result in the death of a perceived assailant—would view SYG laws as *increasing* personal safety. Similarly, the continuing passage of SYG laws by state legislatures—as of 2019 at least 36 states (including so-called "blue" states such as California, Illinois, and Virginia) have SYG laws or variants, and no state having such a law has repealed it—also implies that, regardless of their objective impact, the perceived impact of SYG laws is that they increase individual safety. Opponents of these laws contend that, regardless of the laws' *perceived* impact, their *actual* impact is nonetheless to encourage violence and decrease safety.

The Facts: "Stand your ground" or SYG laws are an extension of the "castle doctrine"—the common law doctrine that established a person's right to use reasonable force (including lethal force) with no obligation to retreat when defending against intruders in the home. *Outside* the home, in the absence of SYG laws, common law doctrine requires an individual to retreat from a threat if withdrawal can be done safely. Failure to do so invalidates a claim of self-defense, and exposes the individual to criminal prosecution for any use of deadly force in that situation.

Although the State of Utah passed an SYG law in 1994, commentators often cite Florida's 2005 SYG law as "the first of its kind in the nation" (Parsons & Vargas, 2018), or assert that Florida was the "first state" (Margolin, 2016) to enact such a law. The implication that an SYG defense is a relatively recent development in American jurisprudence is misleading, however. Both "duty to retreat" and "stand your ground" approaches have coexisted in American legal doctrine for well over a hundred years, long before SYG laws captured the nation's headlines after the exoneration of George Zimmerman in the July 2016 homicide of an unarmed Black teenager named Trayvon Martin. Zimmerman, a man variously described as white, white Hispanic, and mixed race, shot Martin on the sidewalk of a gated community in Sanford, Florida, where Martin was visiting his father. Ironically, although the Zimmerman-Martin confrontation brought Florida's SYG law to the forefront of public discourse, Zimmerman did not invoke an SYG defense, with his acquittal on multiple homicide charges apparently resulting from traditional self-defense arguments (see Ward, 2015). Nonetheless, the Zimmerman-Martin case provided opponents of SYG laws a potent opportunity to attack these statutes.

These condemnations of SYG laws incorporated three main arguments. First, SYG laws generally encourage and increase the rate of lethal violence in society. Second, such laws reflect attempts by the National Rifle

Association (NRA) to advance gun ownership, and have little to do with increased personal safety. Third, as statistical analyses of SYG acquittals demonstrate, the laws are inherently racist (see Ward, 2015). Supporting the first argument, opponents of SYG often cite a trio of research studies showing increases in homicide rates apparently due to the implementation of SYG statutes. For example, McClellan and Tekin (2012) used state-level monthly data to examine the effects of SYG laws on homicides and firearm injuries. They found that while these laws did not increase Black homicides, they significantly increased homicides among Caucasians, especially white males. Additionally, they found significant increases in firearms-related emergency room visits and hospital discharges. The researchers concluded that their findings contradict the belief that SYG laws make the public safer.

A second investigation (Cheng & Hoekstra, 2013) also reported finding a significant increase in homicides in states that have passed SYG laws. In attempting to explain the 8 percent average increase in homicides and nonnegligent manslaughters, the investigators speculated that individuals in SYG jurisdictions were more likely to engage in potentially violent situations that they previously would have avoided (Sanburn, 2016). The third investigation (Humphreys, Gasparrini, & Wiebe, 2017) used a time-series design to analyze monthly rates of both homicide and firearm homicide in Florida from 1999 to 2014. Results showed that, prior to the passage of Florida's SYG law, the mean monthly homicide rate was .49 deaths per 100,000 people; and .29 deaths per 100,000 for firearm homicides. After passage, both rates increased, to .53 per 100,000 for homicides, and to .37 per 100,000 for gun homicides. These increases represented about a 24 and 32 percent increase respectively. While noting that the study could not address the SYG law's potential for deterring crime and improving public safety, the investigators concluded that the 2005 law did appear to result in abrupt and sustained increases in homicides and gun homicides.

Despite the investigators' own cautious interpretation of their findings, many popular reports of the results (e.g., Margolin, 2016; Parsons & Vargas, 2018; Sanburn, 2016) presented the increased homicide rate as potentially indicating that SYG laws made individuals less safe rather than more. One commentary observed, "Floridians have ample information to determine whether this law has proven beneficial to the safety of all communities statewide, or whether it is a failed experiment in need of immediate repeal" (Parsons & Vargas, 2018).

Proponents of SYG statutes, however, dispute both the empirical homicide findings and the implication that SYG laws make people less safe. The

Crime Prevention Research Center (2016), a pro-gun research and advocacy center founded by prominent but controversial gun researcher John Lott, has criticized the Humphreys et al. (2017) study. The center claimed that Florida homicides were increasing even before implementation of the 2005 SYG law, and it asserted that other factors, such as declining arrest rates for murder, also likely impacted the homicide findings. The critique additionally objected to using a single state to evaluate the impact of SYG laws around the country. In *More Guns Less Crime* (1998), Lott's most influential and most heavily criticized book, the author had examined all states that had these laws and reported a nonsignificant *decrease* in murders after enactment.

Regardless of the effects of SYG laws on homicide rates, advocates have asserted that such laws accomplish what they are supposed to accomplish. Dennis Baxley, the state representative who sponsored Florida's SYG law in 2005, said that the law allows innocent people to defend themselves and stop violent acts. He also pointed out that Florida's violent crime rate dropped since SYG went into effect, and contended that the law was at least a contributing factor in that decline (Vedantam, 2013). He questioned the studies showing an uptick in homicides relative to the law, asserting that the researchers had an anti-gun agenda. In reply, one of those researchers, David Humphreys, denied having an agenda. He also described Baxley's criticisms as "an easy way to undermine findings that you don't want to believe are true" (Sanburn, 2016).

The Baxley-Humphreys clash illustrates that gun politics—as with virtually all policy questions centered on firearms in America—is an important element influencing judgments about the efficacy of SYG laws. The NRA has strongly supported the enactment of SYG laws since the passage of Florida's law. Indeed, Marion Hammer, a former president of the organization, helped shape Florida's statute (Spies, 2018). Critics of these laws are quick to emphasize the NRA's championing of SYG statutes, since the organization is well known for its promotion of gun ownership and gun rights (see Ward, 2015). In response, the organization claims that "duty to retreat" laws make it more difficult for individuals to exercise their right of self-defense because they permit post-hoc analyses—in the courtroom's quiet safety—of whether retreat was perhaps feasible. On this point, the NRA quotes former Supreme Court Justice Oliver Wendell Holmes, "Detached reflection cannot be demanded in the presence of an uplifted knife. Therefore . . . it is not a condition of immunity that one in that situation should pause to consider whether . . . it [is] possible to fly with safety . . ." (Cox, 2019). As with any complex issue, an organization might pursue a particular policy for multiple reasons, some pragmatic (e.g., increasing gun ownership) and some philosophical (e.g., protecting the Second Amendment and enhancing individual safety).

Race is also relevant to whether SYG laws boost personal safety. Opponents have attacked the *application* of SYG laws as racially biased. Evidence suggests that the race of the attacker and the race of the victim influence whether an SYG shooting is deemed justified (Roman, 2013). Cases of white shooters and Black victims are almost three times more likely to be ruled justified than cases where both the shooter and the victim are white. Further, when the shooter and the victim are both Black, the shooter is more likely to be convicted. Additionally, individuals who kill a Black victim are substantially less likely to suffer a penalty than those who kill a white victim (see Giffords Law Center, n.d.).

Of course, racial disparities in the criminal justice system are fairly pervasive (e.g., Sommers & Marotta, 2014) and not just limited to SYG laws. Interpreting the significance of such disparities—do these disparities indicate a fundamental unfairness in the law?—is complex and difficult (see Berk, 2017). As Roman (2013) notes about SYG disparities, "If the facts of white-on-black homicides differ from the facts associated with black-on-white homicides such that one routinely occurs as part of self-defense and the other as part of street crime, then there is no animus." Since the reported statistical data used in SYG analyses typically do not include the setting of incidents, determining the significance of racial disparities in this area is not possible.

As with other empirical assessments of gun-related laws, the objective evidence remains ambiguous regarding the degree of increased personal safety—if any—that SYG laws offer the individual. Such laws can lead to a greater number of homicides, but this may simply indicate that threatened individuals now feel more secure legally in using lethal force to defend themselves. As of 2019, 36 states have enacted SYG laws, and the continuing passage of these laws suggests that individuals at least *believe* SYG laws enhance their safety.

FURTHER READING

Berk, Richard, 2017. "Fairness in the Criminal Justice System." Omnia, September 28. https://omnia.sas.upenn.edu/story/fairness-criminal-justice-system

Cheng, Cheng, & Hoekstra, Mark, 2013. "Does Strengthening Self-Defense Law Deter Crime or Escalate Violence?" *Journal of Human Resources*, 48(3), 821–854. jhr.uwpress.org/content/48/3/821.short

Cox, Chris, 2019. "Working Together to Save the Second Amendment Part II: State Success Stories." NRA-ILA, May. https://www.nraila.org

/articles/20190521/working-together-to-save-the-second-amendment-part-ii-state-success-stories

Crime Prevention Research Center, 2016. "Misleading Journal of the American Medical Association Research about Florida's Stand Your Ground Law." Crime Prevention Research Center, November 28. https://crimeresearch.org/2016/11/misleading-journal-american-medical-association-research-floridas-stand-ground-law/

Gehrke, Robert, 2012. "Utah's 'Stand-Your-Ground' Law Dates to 1994." *Salt Lake Tribune*, March 27. https://archive.sltrib.com/article.php?id=53796323&itype=CMSID

Giffords Law Center, n.d. "Stand Your Ground." https://lawcenter.giffords.org/gun-laws/policy-areas/guns-in-public/stand-your-ground-laws/

Holan, Angie, 2012. "Crime Rates in Florida Have Dropped Since 'Stand Your Ground,' Says Dennis Baxley." PolitiFact Florida, March 23. https://www.politifact.com/florida/statements/2012/mar/23/dennis-baxley/crime-rates-florida-have-dropped-stand-your-ground/

Humphreys, David, Gasparrini, Antonio, & Wiebe, Douglas, 2017. "Evaluating the Impact of Florida's 'Stand Your Ground' Self-Defense Law on Homicide and Suicide by Firearm." *JAMA Internal Medicine*, 177(1), 44–50. https://jamanetwork.com/journals/jamainternalmedicine/fullarticle/2582988

Margolin, Emma, 2016. "Florida's 'Stand Your-Ground' Law Linked to Increase in Homicides, Study Finds." NBC News, November 15. https://www.nbcnews.com/news/us-news/florida-s-stand-your-ground-law-linked-increase-homicides-study-n683806

McClellan, Chandler, & Tekin, Erdal, 2012. "Stand Your Ground Laws, Homicides, and Injuries." NBER Working Paper, No. 18187, October. https://www.nber.org/papers/w18187 Revised version published in *Journal of Human Resources*, 2017, 52(3), 621–653.

Parsons, Chelsea, & Vargas, Eugenio, 2018. "The Devastating Impact of Stand Your Ground in Florida." Center for American Progress Action Fund, October 17. https://www.americanprogressaction.org/issues/guns-crime/news/2018/10/17/172031/devastating-impact-stand-ground-florida/

Roman, John, 2013. "Race, Justifiable Homicide, and Stand Your Ground Laws: Analysis of FBI Supplementary Homicide Report Data." Urban Institute, July. https://www.urban.org/sites/default/files/publication/23856/412873-Race-Justifiable-Homicide-and-Stand-Your-Ground-Laws.PDF

Sanburn, Josh, 2016. "Florida's 'Stand Your Ground' Law Linked to Homicide Increase." *Time*, November 14. https://time.com/4569145/florida-stand-your-ground-law-homicide-increase-study/

Sommers, Samuel, & Marotta, Satia, 2014. "Racial Disparities in Legal Outcomes: On Policing, Charging Decisions, and Criminal Trial

Proceedings." *Policy Insights from the Behavioral and Brain Sciences*, 1(1), 103–111. https://journals.sagepub.com/doi/full/10.1177/2372732214548431

Spies, Mike, 2018. "The N.R.A. Lobbyist behind Florida's Pro-Gun Policies." *New Yorker*, February 23. https://www.newyorker.com/magazine/2018/03/05/the-nra-lobbyist-behind-floridas-pro-gun-policies

Stand Your Ground, n.d. Pros and Cons of the Law. https://standyourgroundtoday.weebly.com/pros-and-cons.html

Vedantam, Shankar, 2013. "'Stand Your Ground' Linked to Increase in Homicides." NPR, January 2. https://www.npr.org/2013/01/02/167984117/-stand-your-ground-linked-to-increase-in-homicide

Ward, Cynthia, 2015. "'Stand Your Ground' and Self Defense." William & Mary Law School Scholarship Repository, Faculty Publications, 1800. https://scholarship.law.wm.edu/cgi/viewcontent.cgi?referer=https://www.google.com/&httpsredir=1&article=2841&context=facpubs

Xenakis, Lea, 2018a. "Effects of Stand-Your-Ground Laws on Violent Crime." RAND Corporation, March 2. https://www.rand.org/research/gun-policy/analysis/stand-your-ground/violent-crime.html

Xenakis, Lea, 2018b. "Effects of Stand-Your-Ground Laws on Defensive Gun Use." RAND Corporation. https://www.rand.org/research/gun-policy/analysis/stand-your-ground/defensive-gun-use.html

Q11. DO "RED FLAG LAWS"/EXTREME RISK ORDERS INCREASE DOMESTIC AND FAMILY SAFETY?

Answer: Red flag laws, variously known as "extreme risk protection orders (ERPO)," "risk warrants," and "gun violence restraining orders," are civil orders that allow police to temporarily confiscate the firearms of individuals deemed to present a danger to themselves or others. The process is specific to each state, but typically a petitioner (usually a family/household member, close acquaintance, medical professional, or law enforcement officer) brings concerns about the behavior and mental stability of the person in question (the respondent) before a judge. If the presented evidence convinces the judge that the person is indeed at risk for harming himself or others, these laws allow the judge to issue an emergency order—without the presence or knowledge of the respondent—authorizing the police to immediately seize the person's firearms (Dunn, 2019).

Proponents of red flag laws assert that the laws prevent emergency situations from worsening. They permit legal interventions to curb unbalanced individuals from potentially engaging in violent behaviors, such as mass shootings; potentially fatal attacks on spouses; partners, and other family members; and gun suicides. Noting that shooters frequently display warning signs before they actually resort to violence, supporters argue that ERPOs can prevent not only large-scale tragedies (e.g., school and nightclub shootings) but also small tragedies that devastate families (e.g., suicides and partner homicides). Supporters observe that nearly two-thirds of gun deaths in the country—around 22,000—are suicides, including over 1,000 children and teens (Everytown for Gun Safety, 2019).

Opponents of red flag laws do not object to the laws on the basis of their potential effectiveness for reducing suicides or mass shootings, however. Rather, they oppose these laws because they believe that they violate fundamental constitutional rights and core American values. For example, opponents argue that ERPOs assume a respondent is dangerous (i.e., "guilty") until the individual proves otherwise, at a hearing often not convened until two or three weeks later. The respondent usually receives no notice of the ERPO until the arrival of law enforcement at the person's residence, and has no due process rights—the identity of the petitioner (the "accuser") is often kept secret as is the evidence supporting the ERPO prior to the presumed temporary confiscation of the firearms. Because of this, adversaries see red flag laws as both legally questionable (undermining the Second, Fourth, Fifth, and Sixth Amendments of the Constitution) and rife with potential for personal vindictiveness and governmental abuse (Ammoland, 2019; Dunn, 2019).

Do such laws increase family safety? As the *New York Times* noted, it is hard to gauge the effectiveness of red flag laws because it is impossible to know how many mass shootings or family tragedies ERPOs have prevented (Johnson, 2018). Nonetheless, with one exception (Lott & Moody, 2018), the available research evidence generally indicates that red flag laws reduce suicides (Dunn, 2019; Everytown for Gun Safety, 2019). Thus, while critics contend that ERPOs pose threats to Second Amendment and due process rights, gun control advocates claim that they can enhance the well-being of at-risk individuals and their families.

The Facts: Connecticut and Indiana enacted the country's first "red flag" laws, in 1999 and 2005 respectively. Connecticut's law was in response to a rampage shooting at a state lottery office (Silber, 2018), while Indiana's statute was motivated by a shooting spree carried out by a deranged individual previously hospitalized. The police had earlier seized his cache of firearms, but without a legal basis for holding the guns, they had to return everything—five months before the shooting (Hussein & Martin, 2018). Thus, the initial purpose of these laws was to avert similar tragedies, by authorizing the police to temporarily confiscate firearms from unbalanced individuals signaling or threatening harm. While ERPOs surely have the potential to prevent spree shootings (see Crimesider Staff, 2018), suicide is actually the gun tragedy most likely to impact Americans (Associated Press, 2018), and ERPOs are much more commonly used to intervene in potential suicide situations. For example, in every state reviewed by the *Denver Post* in a 2019 report, suicide was the number one reason for gun removal (Staver, 2019).

The research evidence regarding the impact of ERPOs on suicide is mixed, but suggests that these orders can save lives. In an analysis of Connecticut's and Indiana's red flag laws, investigators uncovered a 7.5 percent reduction in firearm suicides in the 10 years following Indiana's enactment of ERPOs; and in Connecticut, an almost 14 percent reduction two years after enactment. However, Connecticut's reduction in firearm suicides was offset by an increase in non-firearm suicides, a "replacement effect" not evident in the Indiana findings (Kivisto & Phalen, 2018). A second study also examined the influence of Connecticut's law on suicide and, using a process of extrapolation from fatality rates associated with different methods of suicide, estimated that 10 to 20 gun seizures produced one averted suicide (Swanson, et al., 2017). A similar analysis of Indiana's risk-based gun seizure law produced comparable findings: the extrapolation estimated that every 10 gun-seizure actions averted one suicide (Swanson, et al., 2019).

However, not all investigations have concluded that red flag laws increase safety or limit suicides. Using data covering the 13 states having ERPO statutes in 2018, John Lott, a prominent but controversial (e.g., Winkler, 2011) gun rights advocate and president of the Crime Prevention Research Center, examined the impact of red flag laws on murder, suicide, and deaths due to multiple-victim public shootings. Lott claimed that red flag laws had no significant impact on murder, suicide, or the number of individuals killed in mass public shootings (Lott & Moody, 2018).

In the court of public opinion, Americans have historically accepted that red flag laws increase safety and prevent suicide, with some polls showing almost 90 percent support for such laws (Everytown for Gun Safety, 2019). Opposition to these laws is not centered on their potential lifesaving possibilities but on their potential for misuse or abuse, and on their threat to due process. For example, while even the Republican Senator from South Carolina, Lindsey Graham, endorsed ERPOs at a Judiciary Committee meeting examining such laws—he noted, "If you stop just one [shooting or suicide], that's enormous"—he also noted that "there has to be due process, we all get that" (McLeod, 2019).

David Kopel, a gun rights proponent, research director of the Independence Institute and an adjunct professor of constitutional law at the

University of Denver's Sturm College of Law, notes that red flag laws make sense "in concept," but because of how they are typically written, not in practice. "There are huge problems of due process—you're having your constitutional rights taken away with no opportunity to present your side of the case. . . . The cops show up at your door to take your guns, in many cases with 'no knock warrants,' which are inherently violent and increase the risk of both the public and the officers' safety" (Vlahos, 2018).

Other critics assert that the ERPOs of many states contain no penalties to dissuade malicious individuals—a disgruntled ex-spouse or a feuding neighbor—from attempting to use the law to punish a disliked gun owner (Knighton, 2019). For example, critics of Colorado's red flag law note that there is no accountability for false accusers, and even no filing fee for requesting an ERPO, even though the filing fee for a temporary restraining order is $97.00 (Ammoland, 2019). More broadly, the American Civil Liberties Union of Rhode Island (ACLU-RI) took issue with that state's red flag law, expressing concern about "the precedent it sets for the use of coercive measures against individuals not because they . . . have committed any crime, but because somebody believes they might, someday, commit one."

The ACLU-RI observed that the state's ERPO gave police the authority to search the gun owner's property, perhaps allowing officers to "stumble across" evidence of unrelated illegal activity. Additionally, the police could conceivably use the ERPO against people engaging in exaggerated political rhetoric, or as a shortcut for seizing lawfully owned firearms from alleged gang members. Noting that the ERPO process entails speculation by petitioners and judges about a person's likelihood of violence, the organization argues that "psychiatry and the medical sciences have not succeeded in this realm, and there is no basis for believing courts will do any better. The result will likely be a significant impact on the rights of many innocent individuals in the hope of preventing a tragedy" (ACLU-RI, 2018).

The legislative counsel for Gun Owners of America, Michael Hammond, has emphasized the "ex-parte" nature of many ERPOs, where the opposing party receives no notice and is not present for the legal proceeding. According to Hammond, "when you are the only guys in the room, you can get the judge to sign a ham sandwich" (Vlahos, 2018). Other opponents list additional legal and constitutional issues raised by ERPOs. For example, the Fifth and Fourteenth Amendments to the Constitution limit the government's ability to deprive individuals of their property. Before doing so, the government typically must provide the owner the opportunity to have legal representation, cross-examine witnesses, and refute the alleged charges. Although guns are property, many red flag orders ignore these legal safeguards (Natelson, 2019).

Similarly, the Sixth Amendment insures that a criminal defendant can confront the witnesses against him. While ERPOs are not criminal prosecutions, given their serious consequences, opponents argue that ERPOs should be held to Sixth Amendment standards. However, some red flag statutes allow the court to issue emergency ERPOs using a "reasonable cause" standard of evidence—the lowest standard (Vlahos, 2018); and others allow the court to conduct hearings by telephone, or accept evidence by affidavit, with no possibility for questions (Natelson, 2019). The constitutional issues associated with some red flag laws have added fuel to the "Second Amendment Sanctuary" movement (see Durden, 2019), and are substantial enough that numerous county sheriffs have stated publicly that they will not serve such orders (see Raleigh, 2019).

Unlike other gun control issues, the assessment of red flag laws does not easily reduce to whether such laws increase safety or whether they are effective. As some investigators (Swanson et al., 2017) have observed, does averting one suicide justify 10 to 20 gun seizures? Given the law's due process and other pitfalls, is this a fair trade-off? Reasonable people may surely answer these questions differently.

FURTHER READING

ACLU-RI, 2018. "An Analysis of 18-H 7688 and 18-S 2492, Relating to Extreme Risk Protective Orders," March 2018. riaclu.org/images/uploads/180302_analysis_RedFlagsLegislation.pdf

Ammoland, 2019. "Why Colorado's Red Flag ERPO Bill Is the Most Dangerous in the Nation." Ammoland Shooting Sports News, March 27. https://www.ammoland.com/2019/03/colorados-red-flag-erpo-bill-most-dangerous-nation/

Associated Press, 2018. "Red Flag Laws May Prevent More Suicides than Mass Shootings." WUSF News, April 13. https://wusfnews.wusf.usf.edu/post/red-flag-laws-may-prevent-more-suicides-mass-shootings

Crimesider Staff, 2018. "New Vermont Law Used to Keep School Shooting Plot Suspect from Getting Gun." CBS News, April 16. https://www.cbsnews.com/news/new-vermont-law-used-to-keep-school-shooting-plot-suspect-from-getting-gun/

Dunn, Travis, 2019. "Red Flag Laws and the Consequences of Good Intentions." Who.What.Why., March 18. https://whowhatwhy.org/2019/03/18/laws-and-the-consequences-of-good-intentions/

Durden, Tyler, 2019. "'Second Amendment Sanctuary' Cities, Counties, & States Spring Up across the Country." ZeroHedge, March 21. https://www.zerohedge.com/news/2019-03-20/second-amendment-sanctuary-cities-counties-states-spring-across-country

Everytown for Gun Safety, 2019. "Extreme Risk Laws." Everytown for Gun Safety, March 25. https://everytownresearch.org/extreme-risk-laws/

Hussein, Fatima, & Martin, Ryan, 2018. "Indiana's 'Red Flag' Gun Law Is Getting National Attention. But Does It Work?" *IndyStar*, February 24. https://www.indystar.com/story/news/2018/02/22/indianas-red-flag-gun-law-getting-national-attention-but-does-work/355132002/

Johnson, Kirk, 2018. "States Mull 'Red Flag' Gun Seizures from People Deemed Dangerous." *New York Times*, February 23. https://www.nytimes.com/2018/02/23/us/red-flag-laws-guns.html

Kivisto, Aaron, & Phalen, Peter, 2018. "Effects of Risk-Based Firearm Seizure Laws in Connecticut and Indiana on Suicide Rates, 1981–2015." *Psychiatric Services*, 69(8), 855–862. https://ps.psychiatryonline.org/doi/10.1176/appi.ps.201700250

Knighton, Tom, 2019. "Maine Reaches Compromise on 'Red Flag' Bill." Bearing Arms, May 29. https://bearingarms.com/tom-k/2019/05/29/maine-reaches-compromise-red-flag-bill/

Lott, John, & Moody, Carlisle, 2019. "Do Red Flag Laws Save Lives or Reduce Crime?" January 27. https://papers.ssrn.com/sol3/papers.cfm?abstract_id=3316573

McLeod, Paul, 2019. "Lindsey Graham Is Writing a Bill to Take Guns Away from People Deemed Dangerous." BuzzFeed News, April 4. https://www.buzzfeednews.com/article/paulmcleod/lindsey-graham-guns-red-fla-laws

Natelson, Rob, 2019. "Natelson: Rights Violating 'Red Flag' Laws May Kill More than They Save." Complete Colorado Page Two, April 7. https://pagetwo.completecolorado.com/2019/04/07/natelson-rights-violating-red-flag-laws-may-kill-more-people-than-they-save/

Raleigh, Helen, 2019. "Colorado Counties Declare Themselves Second Amendment Sanctuaries in Face of Gun-Grabbing Bill." Federalist, March 29. https://thefederalist.com/2019/03/29/colorado-counties-declare-second-amendment-sanctuaries-face-gun-grabbing-bill/

Silber, Clarice, 2018. "White House Encouraging States to Consider Red-Flag Law CT Pioneered." CT Mirror, March 26. https://ctmirror.org/2018/03/26/white-house-encouraging-states-consider-red-flag-laws-ct-pioneered/

Staver, Anna, 2019. "What Colorado Can Learn from 'Red Flag' Gun Laws in Other States as Lawmakers Debate Passing Their Own Version."

 Denver Post, February 25. https://www.denverpost.com/2019/02/25/gun-laws-red-flag-colorado/

Swanson, Jeffrey., Easter, Michele, Alanis-Hirsch, Kelly, Belden, Charles, Norko, Michael, Robertson, Allison, Frisman, Linda, et al., 2019. "Criminal Justice and Suicide Outcomes with Indiana's Risk-Based Gun Seizure Law." *Journal of the American Academy of Psychiatry and Law*, 47(2), 1–10. jaapl.org/content/jaapl/early/2019/04/15/JAAPL.003835-19.full.pdf

Swanson, Jeffrey, Norko, Michael, Lin, Hsiu-Ju, Alanis-Hirsch, Kelly, Frisman, Linda, Baranoski, Madelon, Easter, Michele, et al., 2017. "Implementation and Effectiveness of Connecticut's Risk-Based Gun Removal Law: Does It Prevent Suicides?" *Law and Contemporary Problems*, 80(2), 179–208. https://scholarship.law.duke.edu/cgi/viewcontent.cgi?refer=&httpsredir=1&article=4830&context=lcp

Vlahos, Kelley, 2018. "Emergency Confiscation Is Easy Target in New Gun Control Congress." *American Conservative*, December 11. https://www.theamericanconservative.com/articles/emergency-gun-confiscation-may-be-easy-target-in-new-congress/

Winkler, Adam, 2011. *Gunfight*. New York: W. W. Norton, pp. 76–77.

3

Guns and Societal Safety

Is American society made better and more secure by firearms, as gun rights activists argue, or do firearms make America a more violent and dangerous country, as gun control proponents assert? The answer to this question is crucial if the country is ever to develop effective national policies on firearms, but no single set of metrics offers a satisfactory response. As a 2017 Pew Research Center report suggests, Americans have a complex relationship with guns, and little agreement exists among gun owners and nonowners on even fundamental gun concerns. To the contrary, the two sides are polarized on almost every issue related to gun policy, gun violence, and the role of firearms in American society. For example, while the aforementioned 2017 Pew poll found that a substantial majority (59 percent) of non-gun owners see gun violence as a major problem in the United States, only a third (33 percent) of gun owners agree. A similar divide exists among owners and nonowners on whether gun violence is a major problem in their local community, with non-gun owners twice as likely as gun owners (22 versus 11 percent) to claim that it is. Comparable divisions exist among owners and nonowners on specific policies, such as on the usefulness of banning high-capacity magazines or the value of creating comprehensive federal gun registration databases (Parker et al., 2017).

Much of the difference in these attitudes about the societal impact of firearms stems from the antagonistic cultural orientations of owners and nonowners (Campbell, 2019). Since these attitudes and beliefs do not always capture the actual effect of guns on societal life, this chapter examines seven questions that sample a range of gun issues that offer a more empirical evaluation of firearms' influence on general societal safety. The opening question examines the extent and nature of gun violence in America, and whether such violence is trending up or down. The second question explores the role of the armed citizen in American life and whether law enforcement officers see armed citizens as adding to or subtracting from general safety. The next two questions weigh the likely impact of two gun-focused interventions on societal well-being: the implementation of "smart gun" technology, and the banning of "bump" stocks and large capacity magazines (LCMs). Then the chapter considers two administratively focused questions: could centralized databases (e.g., tracking gun violence and gun sales) improve general safety; and would mandatory gun liability insurance enhance societal well-being? The chapter's final question examines whether gun control regulations have a detrimental safety impact on minority communities relative to the larger society.

FURTHER READING

Campbell, Donald, 2019. *America's Gun Wars: A Cultural History of Gun Control in the United States.* Santa Barbara, CA: Praeger.

Parker, K., Horowitz, J., Igielnik, R., Oliphant, J. Baxter, & Brown, A., 2017. "America's Complex Relationship with Guns." Pew Research Center, June 22. https://www.pewsocialtrends.org/2017/06/22/americas-complex-relationship-with-guns/

Q12. IS GUN VIOLENCE INCREASING IN AMERICA?

Answer: The portrayal of gun violence in a society can encompass various metrics, and these different metrics often conjure up quite dissimilar impressions of the level of overall gun violence. For example, one analysis of American gun violence from a leading gun control advocacy organization notes that guns kill 100 individuals every day, and injure hundreds more. It further notes that the U.S. gun homicide rate is 25 times higher (and the U.S. gun suicide rate is 10 times higher) than other "high-income" countries (Everytown for Gun Safety, 2019). Another analysis notes that homicide is the 16th leading cause of death in the United States, with guns responsible for 74 percent of those deaths. This report, citing statistics from the Centers for Disease Control and Prevention (CDC), observes that "Homicides and suicides involving guns have been increasing . . . after years of declines in gun deaths" (Christensen, 2018). These statistics, often highlighted in popular media after a particularly gruesome shooting tragedy, give the impression that gun violence in America is spiraling out of control and getting progressively worse (Cooke, 2015). The reality is more complex, however.

For instance, gun deaths (homicides plus suicides plus accidents) increased in the United States from about 36,000 in 1990 to about 37,000 in 2016. But because of population growth over this period, the *rate* of gun deaths actually *decreased* from about 14 gun deaths per 100,000 in 1990 to about 11 per 100,000 in 2016 (see Naghavi, 2018). In another similar analysis by the CDC, covering the years 1999 through 2017, the rate of gun deaths (now also including legal interventions) averaged about 11 per 100,000 varying from a low of 10.2 in 2000 to a high of 12.2 in 2017. While these figures indicate an upward trend beginning in 2015 (11.3 per 100,000 to 12.2 in 2016), a closer examination of the data shows that this increase is primarily related to increases in suicides. The suicide rate—which had hovered around 5.8 per 100,000 for a decade—began a steady climb in 2008 from 6.0 suicides per 100,000 to 7.3 in 2017. In contrast, the homicide rate, which had hovered around 4.0 homicides per 100,000, began a *decrease* in 2008 through 2014, returning to 4.0 in 2015, and increasing to 4.5 per 100,000 in 2016 and 2017 (see CDC, 2018).

More broadly, other metrics of violence reveal a similar pattern. For instance, an analysis of Federal Bureau of Investigation (FBI) statistics covering the period 1990 to 2017 showed that violent crime (i.e., murder, nonnegligent manslaughter, forcible rape, robbery, and aggravated assault) peaked at about 1.93 million crimes in 1992, and steadily declined to a low of about 1.15 million crimes in 2014. Then in 2016 and 2017, this figure rose to about 1.25 million crimes in each of these years, declining to about 1.21 million in 2018 (Statista Research, 2020).

What generalization about gun violence in America do these data permit? As some commentators have noted, it seems fair to claim that such violence "is down and has been on the decline for decades" (Malcolm & Swearer, 2018); and that "America is safer today than it has been for a long, long time" (Cooke, 2015). Nonetheless, the recent uptick in gun violence and violent crime generally raises concerns about a potential shift in this pattern. One CDC investigator, in discussing a similar rise in the firearm homicide and suicide rates of large metropolitan areas, noted that the significance of these increases is unknown. It is simply too soon to determine whether the observed changes represent a short-term fluctuation in rates or the beginning of a longer-term trend (Kegler, Dahlberg, & Mercy, 2018). While this cautious optimism is also appropriate for viewing the question of gun violence generally, the current data suggest that overall, gun violence in America has declined markedly over the last several decades, despite public perceptions to the contrary.

The Facts: As suggested above, gauging the objective level of gun violence in society is in itself a complex undertaking, and subjective impressions of changes in this level are readily distorted by arbitrary considerations. Determining the type of incidents to include in "gun violence," the way information is summarized and packaged, the choice of the time periods examined, the cognitive impact of dramatic but unrepresentative incidents, and so on, all influence general perceptions of the prevalence of gun violence.

As an example, consider the likely impact of mass shootings on subjective assessments of gun violence. Depending on the definition of "mass shooting," the United States experienced anywhere between 7 mass shootings in 2015 (according to *Mother Jones*) and 371 (according to Mass Shooting Tracker). Other sources range from 65 to 332 (see Smart, 2018). Popular commentaries and news stories using high-end estimates based on the different definitions of a "mass shooting" may alarm the average individual. Further, the term "mass shooting" itself appears much more frequently in current media reports than it has in the past—also fostering the perception that gun violence is on the rise (Smart, 2018).

Sobering contrasts with levels of gun violence in other nations may also evoke a perception that America's degree of gun violence is escalating. For instance, CBS News, using research that compared gun deaths in the United States with gun deaths in 22 other "high income" nations, showed that not one of the other 22 countries had a firearms homicide rate greater than 0.5 per 100,000 individuals. The U.S. rate was 3.6 per 100,000. Quoting the original researchers, the report notes, "Overall, our results show that the U.S. . . . suffers disproportionately from firearms compared with other high-income countries" (Preidt, 2016).

The impression created by these comparisons is somewhat misleading, however. For instance, in the report discussed above, while the American firearms homicide rate is disproportionately large relative to *high-income* countries, it is actually in line with the *global* average gun death rate of 4 per 100,000 individuals. Further, it is only about a tenth of the highest rates (e.g., 40 per 100,000) reached in parts of Central and South America (CBS News, 2018). Gun rights organizations and advocates claim that the comparison group is unfairly biased and misleading when it is limited to Organization for Economic Cooperation and Development (OECD) countries. Supporters of gun control, however, argue that using poorer and politically unstable developing nations as a yardstick for measuring gun violence in the United States is problematic.

Additionally, a country's gun control policies may also skew perceptions of gun violence. Just as a society with more cars will have more car accidents, the United States, with "permissive" gun regulations and more freely available firearms, will have more gun incidents than comparable countries with "restrictive" regulations and fewer firearms—the case with all 22 countries in the research discussed above. Thus, although America's more permissive gun regulations produce a gun homicide rate greater than more restrictive countries, it is not because America society is necessarily more violent, but because Americans simply have more firearms. Of course, proponents of greater gun regulation would argue that this is precisely their point: regardless of whether gun violence is increasing or decreasing, the number and easy availability of firearms in American society make individuals less safe overall (see Hemenway, 2015).

An examination of crime rates associated with different types of crime can also provide useful information about the prevalence of violent crime. While these comparisons are static and do not directly address changes over time, they can illuminate the general extent of violent crime relative to other kinds of crime. For instance, in 2017, the FBI recorded a total of about 9 million crimes in the United States. Of this total, property crime accounted for about 7.7 million cases, with larceny-theft making up the great majority of these crimes, followed by burglary.

In contrast, the total number of violent crimes in 2017 was about 1.3 million cases, with aggravated assault making up the majority, followed by robbery. Murder and nonnegligent manslaughter accounted for less than 18,000 cases (Statista Research, 2019). The violent crime numbers include *all* violent incidents, not just incidents involving firearms. To the extent that these findings generalize, the numbers suggest that those Americans unfortunate enough to experience crime personally are substantially more likely to encounter theft and burglary (property crimes) rather than murder or assault (violent crimes).

Yet another reason perceptions of American gun violence may exceed objective reality is the intensity and visibility of the propaganda war waged by pro-gun and anti-gun proponents. Ironically, despite having deep-seated opposing values, both sides have a vested interest in emphasizing—and perhaps exaggerating—gun violence in America. For gun control advocates, every incident of gun violence presents an opportunity to highlight the potentially lethal dangers that firearms introduce into civilized societies. By widely broadcasting and amplifying such incidents—and by stressing the word "gun" in gun violence—proponents of gun control can better support their pleas for additional and more stringent gun regulations. For gun rights advocates, meanwhile, every incident of gun violence is an object lesson in the unpredictable and random perils of modern society—and the need for Americans to be able to defend themselves from those potential perils. By stressing and inflating the "violence" in gun violence, proponents of gun rights can underscore the value of firearms for proactive self-protection, and the importance of the Second Amendment for securing the instruments of such protection—gun ownership.

So is gun violence increasing or not? Despite subjective perceptions that such violence is spiraling upward—perhaps driven by the heavy media coverage of mass shooting events of the past decade or so—the objective data show that overall, violent crime in the United States (including gun crime) has been steadily decreasing for almost three decades. While the statistics for 2016–2017 reveal a small reversal in this pattern, gun violence levels still remain well below the peak levels of the early 1990s.

FURTHER READING

CBS News, 2018. "Gun Deaths Top 250,000 per Year Worldwide, Study Finds." CBS News, August 28. https://www.cbsnews.com/news/gun-deaths-top-250000-per-year-worldwide-study-finds/

CDC (Centers for Disease Control), 2018. Firearms Deaths by Intent, 1999–2017. CDC Wonder Online Database, December. https://wonder.cdc.gov/controller/datarequest/D76;jsessionid=7B6F7CCF9E05D6279DC0FEF55CC9597D

Christensen, Jen, 2018. "Gun Deaths Increasing after Years of Decline, Study Finds." CNN, November 8. https://www.cnn.com/2018/11/08/health/firearm-homicide-suicides-increasing-study/index.html

Cooke, Charles, 2015. "Careful with the Panic: Violent Crime and Gun Crime Are Both Dropping." *National Review*, November 30. https://www.nationalreview.com/corner/careful-panic-violent-crime-and-gun-crime-are-both-dropping-charles-c-w-cooke/

Everytown for Gun Safety, 2019. "Gun Violence in America." Everytown for Gun Safety, April 4. https://everytownresearch.org/gun-violence-america/

GunPolicy.org, n.d. "Compare the United Nations: Firearms Regulation—Guiding Policy." https://www.gunpolicy.org/firearms/compare/193/firearm_regulation_-_guiding_policy/

Hemenway, David, 2015. "There's Scientific Consensus on Guns—and the NRA Won't Like It." *Los Angeles Times*, April 22. https://www.latimes.com/nation/la-oe-hemenway-guns-20150423-story.html

Kegler, Scott, Dahlberg, Linda, & Mercy, James, 2018. "Firearm Homicides and Suicides in Major Metropolitan Areas—United States, 2012–2013 and 2015–2016." *Morbidity and Mortality Weekly Report, 67*, 1233–1237. https://www.cdc.gov/mmwr/volumes/67/wr/mm6744a3.htm#contribAff

Malcolm, John, & Swearer, Amy, 2018. "Here Are 8 Stubborn Facts on Gun Violence in America." Heritage Foundation, March 14. https://www.heritage.org/crime-and-justice/commentary/here-are-8-stubborn-facts-gun-violence-america

Naghavi, Mohsen, 2018. "Global Mortality from Firearms, 1990–2016." *Journal of the American Medical Association, 320*(8), 792–814. https://jamanetwork.com/journals/jama/fullarticle/2698492

Preidt, Robert, 2016. "How U.S. Gun Deaths Compare to Other Countries." CBS News, February 3. https://www.cbsnews.com/news/how-u-s-gun-deaths-compare-to-other-countries/

Smart, Rosanna, 2018. "Mass Shootings: Definitions and Trends." RAND Corporation, March 2. https://www.rand.org/research/gun-policy/analysis/essays/mass-shootings.html

Statista Research, 2019. "Number of Committed Crimes in the United States in 2017, by Type of Crime." https://www.statista.com/statistics/202714/number-of-committed-crimes-in-the-us-by-type-of-crime/

Statista Research, 2020. "Total Violent Crime Reported in the United States from 1990 to 2018." https://www.statista.com/statistics/191129/reported-violent-crime-in-the-us-since-1990/

Q13. ARE THE POLICE IN FAVOR OF ARMED CITIZENS?

Answer: As Americans increasingly purchase firearms, the number of individuals holding a concealed handgun permit—legally allowing the holder to carry a weapon (typically a handgun) in public concealed on his person—has also ballooned. In 2018, about 17 million Americans had such permits, representing about 7 percent of the adult population (Crime Prevention Research Center, 2018).

Gun rights advocates assert that this development increases societal safety. With more armed citizens, the argument goes, criminals are discouraged from accosting individuals who may be carrying a firearm for protection and violent crime declines (see Lott, 2010; Lott & Mustard, 1996). In contrast, gun control proponents argue the opposite, that armed citizens actually contribute to violence and decrease general safety. For example, after his research indicated that states with right-to-carry concealed handgun laws appear to have about a 14 percent increase in crime, one investigator declared that the net effect of elevated gun carrying is elevated violent crime (Martinovich, 2017). The Violence Policy Center, a noted pro-gun control organization, also asserted in 2018 that "innocent victims continue to die at the hands of private citizens with permits to carry concealed handguns. . . . Concealed carry killers continue to take the lives of innocent people at a shocking pace. . . . The evidence is clear that allowing random people to carry guns in public endangers public safety" (Violence Policy Center, 2018).

Such contradictory and mutually exclusive assertions about the influence of armed citizens on public safety reflect the complexity of assessing objectively the impact of *any* firearms-related policy in gun-divided America. However, gun rights proponents assert that another perspective worth considering is the experienced-based perspective of law enforcement officers—individuals for whom gun violence is an ongoing occupational reality and who have a considerable stake in minimizing dangerous encounters.

In 2013, PoliceOne.com—an online information and resource exchange website dedicated to law enforcement professionals—invited its 400,000 members to complete a 28-item survey focused on gun policy and law enforcement. Over 15,000 verified police professionals covering all ranks and department sizes responded. More than 91 percent supported concealed carry by civilians not convicted of a felony or deemed psychologically or medically incapable (Avery, 2013). Further, the 2018 yearly survey conducted by the National Association of Chiefs of Police covering a cross section of police chiefs and sheriffs in the United States produced indirectly related results. Although not specifically focused on concealed carry, 79 percent of the respondents believed that qualified, law-abiding armed citizens help law enforcement reduce violent criminal activity. Further, this endorsement of an armed citizenry never dipped below 69 percent in the 10 years the survey posed the question (see National Association of Chiefs of Police, n.d.).

Thus, while police officers may object to certain aspects of an armed citizenry—carrying concealed handguns without a permit, or without training, or without a background check (Robertson & Williams, 2016)—the evidence indicates that they strongly favor legally armed citizens, viewing them as an asset in reducing violent crime and increasing public safety.

The Facts: An examination of annual NICS federal firearm background requests—typically used as a rough stand-in for the number of guns purchased—show that over a 21-year period, background checks have grown steadily from about 9 million in 1999 to over 28 million in 2019 (NICS Documents, 2020). In an irony of American gun politics, checks (and actual sales of firearms) usually mushroom during the terms of presidents who are perceived as being in favor of stronger gun control laws. For example, during the eight years (2001–2008) of George W. Bush's gun-friendly Republican presidency, background checks totaled about 77.6 million. During the next eight years (2009–2016) of Barack Obama's presidency—perceived by gun rights advocates as strongly anti-gun—they swelled by 75 percent, to about 136.0 million (Smith, 2016). Simultaneously, the number of Americans having concealed carry permits also consistently increased, from 4.6 million in 2007, to 14.5 million in 2016, to 17.25 million in 2018 (Crime Prevention Research Center, 2018).

Many gun control proponents see this escalation in the number of civilians carrying concealed firearms in public as a classic recipe for lethal tragedies. During the mid-2010s, the *New York Times* Editorial Board categorized the growing concealed carry trend as a homicide and suicide "body count" producer (2015a), as a reckless "fantasy" that encourages a dangerous vigilantism (2015b), as a threat to public safety (2016), and as a "delusional" vision of civilian "good shooters gunning down bad shooters" (2017).

Similarly, Mark Kelly, husband of gunshot victim Gabrielle Giffords and a prominent gun control advocate, expressed deep reservations about the safety implications of concealed carry. Recalling the horrendous incident in which his wife was shot in the head and six other people killed, he recounts how one concealed carry holder, hearing the shots and wanting to help, rushed to the scene, saw a man holding a handgun, and almost shot him. But that man was one of the individuals who had wrestled the real shooter to the ground. As Kelly puts it, "that man with a gun was a good guy, too. . . . And he was moments away from being shot for the wrong reason" (Kelly, 2017).

Further, citing research examining concealed carry shooting incidents, the Violence Policy Center has consistently asserted that permitting private citizens to carry concealed handguns simply exposes the public to heightened dangers. Kristen Rand, VPC's legislative director, maintains that, "Far more often than they use their guns to kill in self-defense, concealed handgun permit holders kill themselves or others. [These] tragic incidents . . . should put an end to the gun industry myth that concealed carry permit holders increase public safety" (Violence Policy Center, 2015).

Gun rights proponents rigorously dispute the claim that concealed carry decreases public safety. They assert that, far from making the public less safe, concealed carry holders deter violent crime and heighten community well-being. Police attitudes toward armed civilians offer a valuable alternative perspective on the public safety implications of concealed carry. More than most individuals, law enforcement officers have a vested interest in minimizing the dangers associated with gun violence. If legally armed civilians pose a public safety problem, the experiences of streetwise police officers should detect such a safety issue. If so, they certainly would be foremost among the groups condemning concealed carry. But as a number of research surveys indicate, they are not.

As noted earlier, a major online survey of over 15,000 police officers—9,000 of whom were at the rank of lieutenant or below—indicated that these officers not only overwhelmingly endorsed the idea of legally armed civilians (91.3 percent) but that they also believed legally armed civilians are important (21.7 percent) or very important (54.7 percent) for reducing overall crime rates. Indeed, about 86 percent of the respondents indicated that legally armed citizens likely would reduce casualties at mass shootings (PoliceOne.com, 2013). The annual surveys of police chiefs and sheriffs conducted by the National Association of Chiefs of Police have also produced results supporting (80.6 percent in 2017) the perceived value of armed citizens in reducing violent crime—as it has for all 10 years the survey has asked the question.

Police support for armed civilians is not unconditional, however. As noted, the "legally armed" stipulation immediately excludes from concealed carry individuals convicted of a felony, and those individuals deemed psychologically or medically incapable. Additionally, more than half of the respondents to an online poll of police officers (about 57 percent) indicated that civilians should undergo mandatory safety training before buying *any* gun (42.3 percent) or at least for certain firearms (14.4 percent) (PoliceOne.com, 2013). More broadly, these results imply much weaker police support for an armed citizenry under two other forms of firearms carry—"open carry" and "constitutional carry."

Open carry—the practice of visibly and openly carrying a firearm on one's person in public legally—complicates police interactions with armed citizens, and can sometimes impede public safety. For example, as Steve Loomis, leader of Cleveland's police union noted, if an armed civilian is openly carrying an AR-15 in downtown Cleveland—legally or not—"there's going to be multiple police officers watching that person with that AR-15, when they should be over here watching for the guy that's not on his meds that has a couple of handguns" (Kaste, 2016). Gun control advocates have also elaborated on this theme, arguing that open carry makes it difficult for the police to distinguish between credible threats and citizens with legal open carry permits. Officers responding to 911 calls about individuals carrying firearms encounter situations potentially dangerous for both the police officer and the gun carrier. Further, in the event of an actual shooting, distinguishing between the shooters and individuals legally carrying guns openly is problematic (Giffords Law Center, n.d.).

Constitutional carry is the practice of legally carrying on one's person a handgun in public, openly or concealed, without the need for a state permit or license. Currently, at least 16 states have some version of constitutional carry (Shaw, 2019). This approach to firearms carry is frequently endorsed by staunch gun rights advocates who assert that every law-abiding citizen has (or should have) the right to carry a firearm without government permission (see Brown, 2019). Not surprisingly, gun control advocates rigorously oppose constitutional carry—sometimes called "permit-less carry" or "Vermont carry"—claiming that in some cases this approach to firearms carry "would let violent criminals, teenagers, and people with no safety training legally carry in crowded town centers and on city streets" (Everytown for Gun Safety, 2019). Although the police are generally more supportive of gun rights than the public (Morin et al., 2017), the absence of a training requirement with constitutional carry would likely raise concerns with police officers—as it does even with some ardent Second Amendment supporters (see Vandenberge, 2019).

Despite all the practical problems that concealed, open, and constitutional carry create for the police, the weight of the evidence is that a significant majority of police officers believe a legally armed citizenry is an important resource in fighting violent crime, and see legally armed and trained civilians not as threats but as assets.

FURTHER READING

Avery, Ron, 2013. "Police Gun Control Survey: Are Legally-Armed Citizens the Best Solution to Gun Violence?" PoliceOne.com. https://www.police1.com/gun-legislation-law-enforcement/articles/police-gun-control-survey-are-legally-armed-citizens-the-best-solution-to-gun-violence-7uwWgZ75iwWz9vI9/

Brown, Dudley, 2019. "Your Right to Constitutional Carry." National Association for Gun Rights, April 15. https://nationalgunrights.org/from-the-desk-of-dudley-brown/your-right-to-constitutional-carry/

Crime Prevention Research Center, 2018. "New Study: 17.25 Million Concealed Handgun Permits, Biggest Increases for Women and Minorities."

Crime Prevention Research Center, August 17. https://crimeresearch.org/2018/08/new-study-17-25-million-concealed-handgun-permits-biggest-increases-for-women-and-minorities/

Everytown for Gun Safety, 2019. "Permitless Carry: Concealed Carry in Public with No Permit and No Training." Everytown for Gun Safety, February 7. https://everytownresearch.org/permitless-carry/

Giffords Law Center, n.d. "Open Carry." https://lawcenter.giffords.org/gun-laws/policy-areas/guns-in-publiv/open-carry/

Kaste, Martin, 2016. "Gun Carry Laws Can Complicate Police Interactions." NPR, July 19. https://www.npr.org/2016/07/19/486453816/open-carry-concealed-carry-gun-permits-add-to-police-nervousness

Kelly, Mark, 2017. "'Good Guys with Guns' Can Be Dangerous, too. Don't Gut Concealed Carry Laws." *Washington Post*, December 6. https://www.washingtonpost.com/news/posteverything/wp/2017/12/06/good-guys-with-guns-can-be-dangerous-too-dont-gut-concealed-carry-laws/

Lott, John, 2010. *More Guns, Less Crime.* Chicago: University of Chicago Press.

Lott, John, & Mustard, David, 1996. "Crime, Deterrence, and Right-to-Carry Concealed Handguns." *University of Chicago Law School Working Paper*, No. 41. https://chicagounbound.uchicago.edu/cgi/viewcontent.cgi?article=1150&context=law_and_economics

Martinovich, Milenko, 2017. "States with Right-to-Carry Concealed Handgun Laws Experience Increases in Violent Crime, According to Stanford Scholar." *Stanford News*, June 21. https://news.stanford.edu/2017/06/21/violent-crime-increases-right-carry-states/

Morin, Rich, Parker, Kim, Stepler, Renee, & Mercer, Andrew, 2017. "6. Police Views, Public Views." Pew Research Center, January 11. https://www.pewresearch.org/social-trends/2017/01/11/police-views-public-views/

National Association of Chiefs of Police, n.d. Survey Results. https://www.nacoponline.org/programs

New York Times Editorial Board, 2015a. "Concealed-Carry's Body Count." *New York Times*, February 11. https://www.nytimes.com/2015/02/11/opinion/concealed-carrys-body-count.html?emc=edit_ty_20150211&nl=opinion&nlid70310150&_r=4

New York Times Editorial Board, 2015b. "The Concealed-Carry Fantasy." *New York Times*, October 26. https://www.nytimes.com/2015/10/26/opinion/the-concealed-carry-fantasy.html?_r1&refere=

New York Times Editorial Board, 2016. "The Threat to Public Safety if 'Concealed Carry' Goes National." *New York Times*, December 1. https://

www.nytimes.com/2016/12/01/opinion/the-threat-to-public-safety-if-concealed-carry-goes-national.html?_r=2&mtrref=crimeresearch.org

New York Times Editorial Board, 2017. "The Shootout Myth at the Airport." *New York Times*, January 12. https://www.nytimes.com/2017/01/12/opinion/the-shootout-myth-at-the-airport.html?ref=opinion

NICS Documents, 2020. "NICS Firearm Checks: Month/Year." https://www.fbi.gov/file-repository/nics_firearm_checks_-_month_year.pdf/view

PoliceOne.com, 2013. "PoliceOne's 2013 Gun Policy & Law Enforcement Survey Results: Executive Summary." April 8. https://www.policeone.com/police-products/firearms/articles/6188462-PoliceOnes-2013-Gun-Policy-Law-Enforcement-Survey-Results-Executive-Summary/

Robertson, Campbell, & Williams, Timothy, 2016. "As States Expand Gun Rights, the Police Object." *New York Times*, May 3. https://www.nytimes.com/2016/05/04/us/as-states-expand-gun-rights-police-join-opposition.html

Shaw, C. Mitchell, 2019. "Constitutional Carry Gaining Ground: Kentucky 16th State to Allow Permitless Concealed Carry." *New American*, March 13. https://www.thenewamerican.com/usnews/constitution/item/31734-constitutional-carry-gaining-ground-kentuchy-16th-state-to-allow-permitless-concealed-carry

Smith, Aaron, 2016. "Guns, Guns, Guns: 2015 Was a Record Year for FBI Background Checks." *CNN Money*, January 4. https://money.cnn.com/2016/01/04/news/guns-fbi-background-checks/

Vandenberge, Jordan, 2019. "Proposed 'Constitutional Carry' Measure Would Eliminate Need for Gun Safety Training." *ABC News 5 Cleveland*, March 29. https://www.news5cleveland.com/news/local-news/cleveland-metro/proposed-constitutional-carry-measure-would-eliminate-need-for-gun-safety-training

Violence Policy Center, 2015. "Concealed Carry Permit Holders Threaten Public Safety, VPC Research Shows." Violence Policy Center, October 14. https://vpc.org/press/concealed-carry-permit-holders-threaten-public-safety-vpc-research-shows/

Violence Policy Center, 2018. "More than 1,250 Non-Self Defense Deaths Involving Concealed Carry Killers since 2007, Latest Violence Policy Center Research Shows." Violence Policy Center, August 2. https://vpc.org/press/more-than-1250-non-self-defense-deaths-involving-concealed-carry-killers-since-2007-latest-violence-policy-center-research-shows/

Q14. CAN IMPLEMENTING "SMART GUN" TECHNOLOGY MAKE SOCIETY SAFER?

Answer: "Smart gun" or "personalized gun" technology refers to the attempt to design a firearm that recognizes an authorized user, and allows only an authorized user to operate and fire the gun (Keane, 2019). Various technologies are involved in this quest, such as grip recognition algorithms, fingerprint readers, and radio frequency identification (RFID) chips (Mearian, 2012b). Regardless, they all have the common goal of preventing the fatal misuse of firearms by children and other unauthorized people, and of rendering stolen or lost guns useless (Violence Policy Center, 2016).

Two factors appear paramount in determining whether smart gun technology can make society safer. First, if smart guns were available, would the gun-buying public actually purchase this type of firearm? Second, if such guns were purchased, would their presence have a noticeable impact on reducing common gun safety problems, such as criminal or child use, or impulse suicides, or school and mass shootings? The research conducted on these questions has not been encouraging to date.

Surveys have generally indicated that firearm owners question both the reliability of the technology and the cost premium such technology adds to the firearm's purchase price. For example, only 5 percent of gun-owner respondents in a 2019 survey indicated that they were "very likely" to buy such a gun, with another 13 percent indicating they were "somewhat likely." About 70 percent of the total respondents (which included both gun owners and non-gun owners) expressed concerns about whether the firearm would always work when needed, and 56 percent had concerns about price (Crifasi et al., 2019). These results parallel findings of an earlier National Shooting Sports Foundation (NSSF) poll where only 14 percent of respondents indicated that they were "very" or "somewhat" likely to purchase a smart gun. The same survey indicated that the majority of both gun owners (84 percent) and non-gun owners (60 percent) believe that a smart gun would not be reliable (NSSF, 2013).

Other investigations have indicated that Americans accept smart gun technology at much higher rates than the above polls suggest, but gun rights advocates assert that these surveys have notable limitations. One web-based study conducted by the Johns Hopkins Bloomberg School of Public Health examined the public's interest in smart guns, and found that 59 percent of all respondents (and 43 percent of gun owners) indicated that they were willing to buy a "childproof" gun (Wolfson et al., 2016). However, critics in the gun rights community stated the research did not examine whether the respondents would choose such a firearm (with its potential reliability issues) over a traditional gun, or whether the respondents' willingness to purchase was predicated on some imagined "childproof" firearm without such issues. A second study also found a high acceptance rate of smart gun technology—52 percent favored a smart gun over a traditional gun—but the research used a relatively small and not nationally representative sample of the general public (both gun owners and non-gun owners) (Wallace, 2016).

Even if gun buyers are willing to purchase smart guns, the Violence Policy Center (2016)—an organization with a strong gun control orientation—has questioned the impact these guns could reasonably have on gun violence. The center notes that over 300 million firearms are already in circulation in the United States, with the typical gun owner possessing more than one firearm. Thus, many purchasers of smart guns would still have nonpersonalized guns in the household, preventing smart guns from having more than just minimal preventive effects on suicides and homicides.

Further, even in those cases where a smart gun is the only firearm in the home, despondent owners (as authorized users) can still harm themselves with the firearm. Similarly, in many gun-owning households, teenagers frequently have parentally approved access to family firearms. In these circumstances, some teens would be "authorized" to use the family's smart guns. Additionally, many homicides occur among people who know each other—spouses, intimate partners, other family members. Assailants in these incidents typically use their own guns, and they would be authorized users even if the weapon was personalized. Thus, a smart gun would not prevent such violence.

While smart gun proponents particularly emphasize the gun's potential for limiting tragedies involving young children, the VPC and other opponents of the technology assert that such horrific events occur relatively infrequently—less than 75 juvenile gun accident fatalities annually (Penzenstadler, 2019). They suggest the use of existing technology (such as a trigger lock) could have prevented many of these incidents. Opponents also argue that smart guns are unlikely to seriously hamper the criminal market for illegal guns. Criminals acquire a large percentage of their firearms through "straw purchases," where an individual who can legally purchase firearms buys a gun and then illegally transfers the firearm to the prohibited person. In the case of smart guns, the straw purchaser would merely pass along the authorization procedure with the gun. Nor would smart gun technology have much impact on firearm theft: it is highly unlikely that criminals and thieves would pass up stealing guns simply because some may be personalized and inoperable (Violence Policy Center, 2016).

Overall, then, little likelihood exists that implementing current smart gun technology will noticeably increase societal safety. Issues with the gun's reliability and cost still abound after decades of development, and few such guns are presently available in the United States. Of course, as innovators refine smart gun technology, current questions about the functionality and market competitiveness of such firearms may fade, and some of the hoped-for societal benefits of the technology might eventually appear.

The Facts: Interest in smart gun technology dates back at least to the 1970s, when Magna-Trigger marketed a magnetic device that prevented a revolver from firing unless the user was wearing a compatible magnetic ring (Wallace, 2016). Congress then became interested in smart gun technology in the 1990s, seeing it as a potential method for reducing the number of police killed with their own firearms during struggles with assailants (Mearian, 2012a). Despite ongoing developmental efforts—innovators had filed more than 100 smart gun-related patents by 2000 alone—questions concerning the speed and reliability of the technology have continued to plague its practical application.

For example, Sandia National Laboratories tested several systems in the 1990s. It found that the speed of RFID systems appeared satisfactory, but the speed of some biometric-based systems (e.g., fingerprint recognition) was not (Wallace, 2016). Since any delay in identifying an authorized user could put that individual in lethal danger, the possibility of delay—or not being recognized for some other reason—represents a significant concern for potential gun owners, and a significant drawback for the technology. While steadily improving technology may reduce these concerns, improvements cannot eliminate them. Even the best technology sometimes malfunctions, and sometimes even low-tech batteries expire at a crucial moment (see Keane, 2019). Surveys have found that these kinds of reliability worries remain high among gun-oriented individuals evaluating smart gun technology (Crifasi et al., 2019; NSSF, 2013).

Similarly, since smart gun technology would affect only newly manufactured firearms, even some gun control proponents remain skeptical about the societal benefits smart guns are likely to provide. As noted above, with more than 300 million traditional firearms already circulating in America, the societal safety increment smart guns could likely add would necessarily remain limited. In fact, some analysts have speculated that widespread smart gun availability might *decrease* societal safety by enticing Americans who currently do not own firearms to acquire personalized guns, thus bringing dangerous weapons into previously safe homes (Violence Policy Center, 2016). Other analysts, such as NSSF—the firearm manufacturers' trade association—worry that smart guns might entice owners—relying on the gun's technology—to relax safe storage practices and leave loaded guns where children could access them. Noting that technology can fail, they fear a possible spike in gun accidents (NSSF, 2016).

Additional questions about the efficacy of smart guns arise when considering their likely usefulness in limiting school and mass shootings. As one commentator noted in 2018, since 1982, unbalanced mass murderers have used about 143 guns in carrying out their horrendous rampages. In 75 percent of cases, they obtained their guns legally. In such cases, smart guns could not have foiled these tragedies (Nguyen, 2018). And, as indicated above, with more than 300 million conventional firearms in circulation, professional criminals and others intent on doing harm will merely use a nonpersonalized gun during their illegal forays.

Concerns about the cost of smart gun technology and its effect on the market competitiveness of such firearms also remain an issue. While some researchers have suggested in their survey questions that smart gun technology would entail only a small additional price increase (Crifasi et al., 2019), the actual premiums often are substantial. For example, the German arms maker Armatix attempted to introduce two smart guns into the U.S. market in the 2010s: the iP1 .22 caliber pistol (using RFID technology) in 2014, and the iP9 9 mm pistol (using fingerprint recognition technology) in 2016. Armatix priced the iP1 at $1,798—$1,399 for the pistol and $399 for the enabling watch. This price was about five times the $300 to $400 selling price of many traditional quality .22 caliber pistols at the time (Turner & Winn, 2015). Marketed at about the same retail price as the iP1, the price of the iP9 was still more than twice the cost of many traditional 9 mm pistols (Mearian, 2016a).

Another smart gun system—the Intelligun by Kodiak Industries—also uses fingerprint recognition technology and is less expensive than the Armatix pistols, but it has other limitations. For instance, the system works only with a certain type of pistol (a Model 1911) and requires special installation (Nguyen, 2018). More generally, the purchasing options for individuals wanting a smart gun are severely limited, and despite decades of interest and effort, most smart gun systems remain in a developmental or prototype stage (see Mearian, 2014; Mearian, 2016b; Peak, 2016). While this is primarily related to the inability of smart gun innovators to overcome reliability and cost issues (e.g., Winn, 2014), it is also due to politics.

While gun rights groups such as the National Rifle Association (NRA) and the National Shooting Sports Foundation have asserted that they are not opposed to the development or marketing of smart guns (e.g., Turner & Winn, 2015; NSSF, 2013), they *are* staunchly opposed to government mandates *requiring* the use of such technology. The State of New Jersey had such a mandate for 17 years, and it apparently deterred the major gun manufacturers from pursuing smart gun technology. The New Jersey Childproof Handgun Law, passed in 2002, mandated that once smart guns were certified as viable *anywhere* in the country, New Jersey gun stores could stock only handguns using this technology. At that point, the law would have essentially banned the retail sale of conventional handguns in the state. Gun rights supporters across the country vehemently assailed the law, making smart guns controversial for both manufacturers and retailers (Nguyen, 2018).

For example, when the owner of a Maryland gun shop indicated in 2014 that he planned to carry the Armatix iP1 pistol, he received so many threatening calls and emails—presumably from individuals fearing his action would trigger the New Jersey law and lead to similar governmental mandates in other states—he backed down and reversed his decision. Similarly, gun manufacturers such as Smith & Wesson and Colt saw perils in the New Jersey law. If such mandates spread, they obviously would severely damage the market for the companies' traditional handguns. Thus, losses sustained in the conventional gun market would offset any benefits gained by perfecting smart gun technology—to say nothing of the massive backlash manufacturers would likely encounter from a sizable segment of gun owners and firearm enthusiasts (Nguyen, 2018).

In 2019, New Jersey passed a new smart gun mandate that modified the 2002 law. The law now allows New Jersey gun shops to continue selling conventional handguns even after smart guns are commercially viable, but it obliges them to stock at least one smart gun model for sale. The potential impact of this change on smart gun development is uncertain. Gun manufacturers Smith & Wesson and Ruger recently rejected activist shareholder attempts to force the companies to engage in smart gun research and development, citing reliability problems with the technology and the lack of significant consumer demand (NRA, 2019); and the Violence Policy Center notes that the firearms industry is a low-tech industry that may not have the manufacturing expertise to implement smart gun technology (Violence Policy Center, 2016). Overall, then, given the multiple practical and political issues that smart gun technology currently confronts, it is unlikely that this technology will noticeably increase societal safety in the foreseeable future.

FURTHER READING

Crifasi, Cassandra, O'Dwyer, Jayne, McGinty, Emma, Webster, Daniel, & Barry, Colleen, 2019. "Desirability of Personalized Guns among Current Gun Owners." *American Journal of Preventive Medicine*, 57(2), 191–196. https://pubmed.ncbi.nlm.nih.gov/31196718/

Keane, Larry, 2019. "'Smart Gun' Legislation Misses the Mark." NSSF, June 25. https://www.nssf.org/smart-gun-legislation-misses-the-mark/

Mearian, Lucas, 2012a. "Missing from the NRA Plan: Smart Gun Technology." *Computerworld*, December 21. https://www.networkworld.com/article/2162363/missing-from-nra-plan--smart-gun-technology.html

Mearian, Lucas, 2012b. "Could Smart Gun Technology Make Us Safer?" *Computerworld*, December 20. https://www.computerworld.com/article/2494099/could-smart-gun-technology-make-us-safer-.html

Mearian, Lucas, 2014. "Armatix Smart-Gun Tech Reignites Gun Fight, with Retailers in the Middle." *Computerworld*, May 20. https://www.computerworld.com/article/2489588/emerging-technology-armatix-smart-gun-tech-reignites-gun-fight-with-retailers-in-the-middle.html

Mearian, Lucas, 2016a. "German Arms Maker Armatix to Release Second Smart Gun in U.S." *Computerworld*, October 19. https://www.computerworld.com/article/3132572/german-arms-maker-to-release-second-smart-gun-in-u-s.html

Mearian, Lucas, 2016b. "Efforts to Restart Smart-Gun Innovation Could Misfire Again." *Computerworld*, October 14. https://www.computerworld.com/article/3131068/efforts-to-restart-smart-gun-innovation-could-misfire-again.html

Nguyen, Nicole, 2018. "Here's What's Up with 'Smart Guns'—and Why You Can't Buy One in the US." Buzzfeed News, March 13. https://www.buzzfeednews.com/article/nicolenguyen/what-is-smart-gun-technology/

NRA (National Rifle Association), 2019. "The Truth about 'Smart Guns.'" *America's 1st Freedom*, 20(8), August, p. 56.

NSSF (National Shooting Sports Federation), 2013. "Americans Skeptical of 'Smart Guns'; Oppose Their Legislative Mandate, National Poll Finds." NSSF, November 13. https://www.nssf.org/americans-skeptical-of-smart-guns-oppose-their-legislative-mandate-national-poll-finds/?hilite=%27smart%27%2c%27gun%27

NSSF (National Shooting Sports Federation), 2016. "Smart Guns, Dumb Survey." NSSF, February 1. https://www.nssf.org/smart-guns-dumb-survey/

Peak, Chris, 2016. "These 5 Smart Gun Technologies Could Be the Future of Firearms in America." Nation Swell, June 2. nationswell.com/these-5-smart-gun-technologies-could-be-the-future-of-firearms-in-america/

Penzenstadler, Nick, 2019. "A Toddler Found a Handgun and Fatally Shot Himself. His Case Is One of at Least 73 Accidental Child Deaths Involving a Gun in 2018." *USA Today*, March 19. https://www.usatoday.com/story/news/investigations/2019/03/19/gun-deaths-shooting-accidents-killed-73-kids-last-year/3032060002/

Turner, Clay, & Winn, Frank, 2015. "We Test the Armatix iP1, the Not-So-Smart Gun." https://www.americas1stfreedom.org/articles/2015/11/12/exclusive-we-test-the-armatix-ip1-the-not-so-smart-gun/

Violence Policy Center, 2016. "Smart Guns." https://vpc.org/regulating-the-gun-industry/smart-guns/

Wallace, Lacey, 2016. "American Preferences for 'Smart' Guns versus Traditional Weapons: Results from a Nationwide Survey." *Preventive Medicine Reports*, 4, 11–16. https://www.sciencedirect.com/science/article/pii/S2211335516300353#bb0105

Winn, Frank, 2014. "What's So Smart about This Gun?" America's1st Freedom, August 8. https://www.americas1stfreedom.org/articles/2014/8/8/whats-so-smart-about-this-gun/

Wolfson, Julia, Teret, Stephen, Frattaroli, Shannon, Miller, Matthew, & Azrael, Deborah, 2016. "The US Public's Preference for Safer Guns." *American Journal of Public Health*, 106(3), 411–413. https://www.ncbi.nlm.nih.gov/pmc/articles/PMC4815965/

Q15. WOULD BANNING "BUMP" STOCKS AND LARGE-CAPACITY MAGAZINES (LCMS) REDUCE SHOOTING CASUALTIES?

Answer: "Bump" stocks are rifle stocks that modify a semi-automatic firearm in a way that accelerates the gun's rate of fire, mimicking the rate of a fully automatic weapon. By using the firearm's recoil to push the trigger against the shooter's finger (rather than having the shooter pull the trigger), bump stocks essentially transform the rifle into a machine gun, capable of firing over 400 rounds per minute (Diamond, 2018). Large-capacity magazines are ammunition feeding devices that can hold more than a specified number of rounds. The actual number varies by state, but typically magazines of more than 10 or 15 rounds are considered LCMs.

Gun control/gun safety proponents argue that both types of devices increase the lethality of commonly owned firearms and pose a substantial threat to public safety. For example, they note that Stephen Paddock, the Las Vegas gunman who killed 58 people and wounded hundreds more in 2017, used bump stocks and multiple LCMs to shoot into the crowd of 22,000 concertgoers attending a music festival across from his hotel (Giffords, 2019). The death toll and devastation were so terrible, these proponents assert, because bump stocks and LCMs (some containing 100 rounds) allowed Paddock to fire over 1,100 rounds of ammunition in about 11 minutes. Without bump stocks and with having to reload more frequently, the attack would have produced many fewer casualties (Everytown for Gun Safety, 2019). They argue that a federal government ban on such devices would reduce the lethality of future mass shootings, significantly increasing everyone's safety.

Gun rights proponents question these arguments and are skeptical of the safety benefits bans might provide. These individuals note that most shooting enthusiasts consider bump stocks a novelty accessory. While they increase a rifle's rate of fire, they do so at the cost of severely degraded accuracy. Shooters use them once or twice, note how they function, and then never use them again. Even in the military, automatic fire—the type of fire mimicked by bump stocks—is typically discouraged because it results in poor accuracy and wasted ammunition (Diamond, 2018). They acknowledge that a ban on bump stocks might have reduced casualties at the tragic Las Vegas massacre, but they also emphasize that such attacks are not the source of most shooting casualties. In actuality, handguns (which do not use bump stocks) are the source of most shooting casualties (Malcolm & Swearer, 2018). In their view, public mass shootings simply receive disproportionate attention in the media, both generally and in terms of the number of casualties they produce (see Swearer, 2019).

Similarly, while LCMs reduce a shooter's reloading frequency, the average shooter can exchange one magazine for another in two to three seconds, and no evidence suggests that such a short delay would lessen the lethality of murderous attacks (Malcolm & Swearer, 2018). If LCMs are banned, some analysts argue that mass shooters will simply carry more magazines (Petulla, 2017). For example, the Virginia Tech killer murdered 32 and injured 17 using two handguns with standard-capacity magazines of 10 and 15 rounds. He merely carried 19 extra magazines (Malcolm & Swearer, 2018).

Empirical evidence examining the likely effectiveness of an LCM ban is limited. In an unpublished study conducted for CNN, Michael Siegel, a community health science professor at Boston University, found that states with an LCM ban had a substantially lower rate of mass shootings relative to states without such a ban, but the ban's actual effectiveness on shooting casualties was not known (Petulla, 2017). Other researchers (Koper, Woods, & Roth, 2004) have also suggested that an LCM ban could reduce shooting casualties, but the exemption of *previously owned* LCMs during the federal assault weapons ban (1994–2004) prevented definitive testing of this possibility. Anecdotal evidence exists suggesting that, at least sometimes, the need to reload can reduce shooting casualties. For instance, when the Tucson, Arizona, spree killer who murdered 6 people and wounded 13 others (including U.S. representative Gabrielle Giffords) stopped to reload his pistol, a bystander in the crowd tackled and brought him down, ending the spree.

Perceptually, the public appears to believe that banning LCMs would reduce shooting casualties. One 2017 Ipsos poll found that 78 percent of the citizenry favor a ban (with 82 percent also favoring a ban on bump stocks). On the other hand, an online survey of law enforcement officers found overwhelming agreement (96 percent) that a federal ban on LCMs would have no effect on violent crime (PoliceOne.com, 2013).

In the case of bump stocks, violent criminals typically use handguns in their predations, and rarely use rifles—much less rifles with bump stocks. This suggests that a bump stock ban would be of limited utility at best in reducing gun violence. (The terrible Las Vegas mass shooting of October 2017 that killed 58 people and wounded 469 others is the single such mass shooting incident involving bump stocks as of mid-2020.) Additionally, since a shooter can achieve bump firing by other means—even a simple rubber band, for instance—a deranged killer can still bump-fire even in the face of a ban (see Green, 2018). In the case of LCMs, a ban's impact on casualties assumes that a reloading delay of two or three seconds—1.5 seconds according to some gun experts (Howerton, 2013)—allows some victims to escape and gives law enforcement extra time to intervene. Further, as gun control proponents note, while banning bump stocks and LCMs alone may be insufficient to stop mass shootings or significantly reduce gun casualties, their effectiveness as part of a *comprehensive* package of gun control measures remains untested and unknown.

The Facts: William B. Ruger—a founder of Sturm, Ruger & Co., a major American firearms manufacturing company—believed that civilians did not require LCMs ("No honest man needs more than 10 rounds in any gun"), but this attitude was (and is) atypical in the firearms community. Most firearms enthusiasts endorse the position of a later Sturm, Ruger & Co. CEO, Michael Fifer, who strenuously argued against a proposed Connecticut ban on large-capacity magazines (which gun enthusiasts refer to as "standard-capacity" magazines). Fifer contended that regulating magazine capacity would do nothing to deter crime, and would unnecessarily "put law-abiding citizens at risk of harm" (Harkinson, 2016).

Gun control advocates have traditionally sided with Ruger, viewing Fifer's contention skeptically. They point to the 2019 mass shooting in Dayton, Ohio, where the killer used a 100-round LCM to murder 10 individuals and wound 17 others in 32 seconds, and they ask rhetorically, "Who needs 100 rounds to defend themselves against harm?" In response to this argument, U.S. representative Thomas Massie of

Kentucky noted, "If 6 brave, trained, and alert police officers with professionally maintained weapons fired 58 rounds to subdue the Dayton shooter, I'd say my wife deserves at least that many chances to protect herself and my kids when I'm not home" (Knighton, 2019a). From this perspective, gun rights proponents argue that any reduction in the number of spree shooting victims brought about by an LCM ban is likely to be offset by increased victim casualties in home invasions where individuals defending themselves with reduced-capacity magazines run out of ammunition.

Enforcement is another obstacle limiting the ability of an LCM ban to reduce shooting casualties. From 1994 to 2004, the Violent Crime Control and Law Enforcement Act (commonly referred to as the "Assault Weapons Ban" Act) prohibited the manufacture and possession of LCMs. But the law "grandfathered" in (exempted) the sale and possession of LCMs made before the law's enactment. Since magazines typically do not carry manufacturing dates, it was not possible to distinguish banned LCMs from grandfathered LCMs, and thus the ban had little impact on the practical availability of LCMs during the decade-long prohibition (Giffords Law Center, n.d.). Since the expiration of the federal ban, nine states (and the District of Columbia) have enacted state laws restricting LCMs, many without grandfathering provisions, but enforcement remains an issue.

For example, in 2018, the State of New Jersey passed legislation that prohibited magazines of more than 10 rounds. The law required owners to surrender these magazines to police, render them inoperable, modify them to hold 10 rounds or less, or sell them out of state. Informal investigations of compliance with the law suggested that, of New Jersey's 1 million gun owners, *none* had surrendered the now-banned magazines to any of the local and state police agencies that were queried. While some owners may have complied with the law using an alternative approved method, there is no evidence to suggest this (Sullum, 2018). Further, the state apparently has no strategy for enforcing the law (Knighton, 2018). Thus, if New Jersey's experience is any indication, massive noncompliance is likely to plague any federal LCM ban, significantly curtailing whatever benefits the ban might provide.

Similarly, a ban on bump stocks is also unlikely to noticeably reduce shooting casualties, for two reasons. First, because bump stocks degrade a shooter's accuracy, they have the greatest possibility of inflicting a high casualty count when the killer is firing into a crowd, such as during a mass shooting. Yet, despite the fact that multiple mass shooting tragedies rocked the United States over the course of the 2010s decade, such shooting sprees (like air disasters) are exceptional, with psychologically shocking but relatively small casualty numbers overall. For instance, in August

2019, the *Washington Post* identified every mass shooting victim since 1966. The list contained 1,196 names. During the same period, 2,236 individuals died from lightning strikes: a person was almost twice as likely to be a lightning strike casualty as a victim in a mass shooting (Knighton, 2019b).

Second, while bump stocks offer a shooter a more convenient and more accurate method (Peters, 2013) for mimicking automatic fire, they are not essential for achieving this effect. As noted earlier, shooters can use rubber bands, belt buckles and belt loops, and other means to bump fire semi-automatic rifles. Thus, a ban on bump stocks cannot prevent a determined shooter from simulating machine-gun fire if the individual is so inclined.

In 2018, the Trump administration proposed changes to the regulatory status of bump stocks. It reclassified the devices as machine guns, thus making them illegal under current federal gun laws. The federal ban went into effect in March 2019, complementing about a dozen state-level bans enacted earlier. Assuming these bans pass judicial muster—several suits have challenged the federal ban—the bans' effectiveness in reducing shooting casualties may become clearer over time. Until then, historical crime data available to 2020 indicate that banning bump stocks (and LCMs) would have little overall effect on shooting casualties.

FURTHER READING

Baumann, Beth, 2018. "Whoa: Gun Grabber Dianne Feinstein Admits There's Issues with the Bump Stock Ban." Townhall, December 29. https://townhall.com/tipsheet/bethbaumann/2018/12/29/whoa-gun-grabber-dianne-feinstein-admits-theres-issues-with-the-bump-stock-ban-n2538231

Diamond, Michael, 2018. "Opinion: Federal Bump Stock Ban the Right Move for Gun Safety." Daily Caller, December 7. https://dailycaller.com/2018/12/07/bump-stocks-safety/

Everytown for Gun Safety, 2019. "Assault Weapons and High-Capacity Magazines." Everytown for Gun Safety, March 22. https://everytownresearch.org/assault-weapons-high-capacity-magazines/

Giffords, 2019. "Giffords Law Center Reacts to Judicial Decision Upholding a Federal Ban on Bump Stocks." Giffords Press Release, April 1. https://giffords.org/press-release/2019/04/dc-appeals-bump-stock-rule/

Giffords Law Center, n.d. "Large Capacity Magazines." https://giffords.org/lawcenter/gun-laws/policy-areas/hardware-ammunition/large-capacity-magazines/

Green, Gary, 2018. "When Rubber Bands Become 'MACHINE GUNS': Why the Proposed Ban on Bump-Fire Devices Won't Stop Criminals."

Daily Caller, April 3. dailycaller.com/2018/04/03/when-rubber-bands-become-machine-guns-because-of-bump-stock-ban/

Harkinson, Josh, 2016. "Fully Loaded: Inside the Shadowy World of America's 10 Biggest Gunmakers." *Mother Jones*, June 14. https://www.motherjones.com/politics/2016/06/fully-loaded-ten-biggest-gun-manufacturers-america/

Howerton, Jason, 2013. "Gun Experts: Limits on Magazine Size Will Only Slow Determined Killer Down by a Few Seconds." Blaze, January 17. Accessed August 2019. theblaze.com/news/2013/01/17/gun-experts-limits-on-magzine-size-will-only-slow-determined-killer-down-by-a-few-sseconds (URL no longer active).

Ipsos, 2017. "Majority of Americans Hold Incorrect Assumptions about Guns." Ipsos, October 13. https://www.ipsos.com/en-us/news-polls/npr-gun-control-2017-10

Knighton, Tom, 2018. "Still No Word on How NJ Will Enforce Magazine Ban." Bearing Arms, December 13. https://bearingarms.com/tom-k/2018/12/13/still-no-word-nj-will-enforce-magazine-ban/

Knighton, Tom, 2019a. "Rep. Thomas Massie Rips Apart 'Who Needs 100 Rounds' Argument with Single Tweet." Bearing Arms, August 8. https://bearingarms.com/tom-k/2019/08/08/rep-thomas-massie-rips-apart-needs-100-rounds-argument/

Knighton, Tom, 2019b. "You're More Likely to Die from Lightning Strike than in Mass Shooting." Bearing Arms, August 13. https://bearingarms.com/tom-k/2019/08/13/youre-likely-die-lightning-strike-mass-shooting/

Koper, Christopher, Woods, Daniel, & Roth, Jeffrey, 2004. "An Updated Assessment of the Federal Assault Weapons Ban: Impact on Gun Markets and Gun Violence, 1994–2003." Report to the National Institute of Justice, June. ncjrs.gov/pdffiles1/nij/grants/204431.pdf

Malcolm, John, & Swearer, Amy, 2018. "6 Reasons Gun Control Will Not Solve Mass Killings." Heritage Foundation, March 16. https://www.heritage.org/firearms/commentary/6-reasons-gun-control-will-not-solve-mass-killings

Peters, Justin, 2013. "This Simple, Legal Add-On Lets an AR-15 Rifle Fire 900 Rounds per Minute." *Slate*, January 7. slate.com/news-and-politics/2013/01/slide-fire-this-simple-legal-add-on-lets-an-ar-15-fire-900-rounds-per-minute.html

Petulla, Sam, 2017. "Here Is 1 Correlation between State Gun Laws and Mass Shootings." *CNN Politics*, October 5. https://www.cnn.com/2017/10/05/politics/gun-laws-magazines-las-vegas/index.html

PoliceOne.com, 2013. "PoliceOne's 2013 Gun Policy & Law Enforcement Survey Results: Executive Summary." April 8. https://www.policeone

.com/police-products/firearms/articles/6188462-PoliceOnes-2013-Gun-Policy-Law-Enforcement-Survey-Results-Executive-Summary/

Sullum, Jacob, 2018. "Gun Owners Don't Seem Eager to Comply with New Jersey's New Magazine Ban." *Reason*, December 20. https://reason.com/2018/12/20/new-jerseys-gun-owners-do-not-seem-eager/

Swearer, Amy, 2019. Quoted in Richardson, Valerie, 2019. "'Myth': Narrative of Rampant White Nationalist Mass Shootings Overblown." *Washington Times*, August 5. https://www.washingtontimes.com/news/2019/aug/5/white-nationalist-mass-shootings-not-rising-resear/

Q16. CAN A COMPREHENSIVE DATABASE ON GUN SALES REDUCE GUN VIOLENCE?

Answer: At the federal level, a comprehensive gun sales database—a national registry linking the serial numbers of sold firearms to the names and addresses of specific owners—does not exist. In fact, federal law explicitly prohibits the federal government from creating such a database. Consequently, judgments about the effectiveness of this type of database for reducing gun violence involve drawing inferences from logical considerations and from examinations of the impact of more limited, state- and city-level gun registries.

The logical arguments for anticipating that a comprehensive gun registry would deter gun violence are three: 1) a registry would increase gun owner accountability, and likely decrease illegal or questionable gun sales; 2) it would help law enforcement solve felonies by identifying guns recovered at crime scenes; and 3) it would aid in the timely retrieval of firearms from dangerous (e.g., domestic abusers) or at-risk (e.g., severely depressed) individuals prohibited from possessing firearms (Giffords Law Center, n.d.a; Holter, 2018). Further, some empirical evidence also suggests that gun registries might reduce gun violence.

For example, a 2001 study of 25 U.S. cities (Webster, Vernick, & Hepburn, 2001) found that states with some combination of gun registration and licensing had fewer in-state-sold firearms recovered at crime scenes than states without registration and licensing. Similarly, Massachusetts, which has one of the most comprehensive gun control regimes in the country, requires both gun registration and licensing, and it consistently reports the lowest gun death rates in the country (Lopez, 2018). Proponents for a national gun registry point to such findings and assert that a national registration and licensing system would reduce gun violence simply by virtue of one of its several features: blocking prohibited individuals (e.g., criminals and juveniles) from obtaining guns.

Gun rights proponents reject these assertions. They argue that a national gun registry is unlikely to reduce gun violence noticeably, but that it would pose a significant threat to gun ownership and Second Amendment safeguards. For example, the National Rifle Association (2016) notes that while neither the federal government nor the vast majority of states require gun registration or licensing, violent crime in the country fell to a 44-year low in 2014, and murder to an all-time low. Gun homicides and overall rates of violent crime rose in 2015–2017, but violent crime in 2018 began to fall again and still remains at substantially lower levels than in previous decades (Statista, 2020). Gun rights advocates also state that a 2003 review of gun registration and licensing studies by the Centers for Disease Control and Prevention (CDC) concluded that the effects of registration and licensing on violent outcomes were "insufficient" and "inconsistent" (Hahn, et al., 2003). Similarly, an analysis by Gun Facts—a pro-gun website providing indexed research information on multiple gun control issues—of California's handgun registration law and its impact on violent crime suggested that registration had no noticeable impact (Smith, 2019).

Gun rights activists also assert that a national gun registry poses a potentially serious threat to Second Amendment protections, specifically in the form of gun confiscations. As John Whitehead, president of the conservative Rutherford Institute notes, "If there is a centralized system with information relating to firearm possession, it becomes much easier for governments at all levels to seize firearms when it suits them. A centralized registry allows not only federal law enforcement, but state and local as well, to quickly and efficiently deprive lawful owners of their guns if they feel there is some emergency justifying it" (Dunn, 2019). These critics claim that if a national registry could be used by law enforcement to disarm criminals and domestic abusers, it could also be utilized to disarm *anyone* (Holter, 2018). They point out that authorities in both California and New York City have used gun registries to compel registered gun owners to either surrender or remove firearms that had previously been legal to own and possess (Campbell, 2019; Smith, 2019).

Overall, limited and inconsistent research evidence makes judging the effects of a comprehensive gun sales database on gun violence complicated, but public opinion polls do indicate consistent majority support for a national gun registry (Frankovic, 2019). However, this sentiment is not shared by police professionals—70 percent of respondents to one online poll of law enforcement professionals expressed opposition to such a database (PoliceOne.com, 2013).

The Facts: In 1986, Congress enacted the Firearm Owners' Protection Act (FOPA). As a concession to gun advocates perpetually worried that gun registration inevitably leads to gun confiscation (Campbell, 2019; Dunn, 2019), FOPA included a provision that specifically prohibits the federal and state governments from creating any sort of permanent database that directly links firearms to owners. FOPA, however, did make some exceptions. It permitted the continuation of any state or local gun registries that existed before the passage of FOPA. It also allowed for registries of guns recovered at crime scenes; stolen from licensed dealers and interstate carriers; and firearms expressly covered by the National Firearms Act (Paulsen, 2015).

The National Instant Criminal Background Check System (NICS)—used by licensed gun dealers to determine an individual's eligibility to purchase a firearm—is likely the country's closest approximation to a national gun registry, and NICS only determines purchase eligibility. It does not take note of the firearms involved, and requires the FBI to destroy records of approved NICS checks within 24 hours. Gun control advocates, meanwhile, have periodically pushed for some form of national firearms registration ever since the Gun Control Act of 1934, which contained no such provision for handgun registration. That 1934 law only required the registration of automatic weapons (i.e., machine guns), "silencers" (i.e., sound suppressors on guns), and shotguns and rifles with barrels less than 18 inches in length. For example, in 1968, when the Gun Control Act was enacted, President Lyndon Johnson lamented that the act did not include gun registration; and in the 1970s and 1980s, the Brady Campaign to Prevent Gun Violence regularly called for the implementation of a national firearms registry. In the run-up to the 2020 presidential election, a number of Democratic candidates—most notably Beto O'Rourke and Cory Booker (e.g., Brooks, 2019)—included the establishment of a national gun registry as part of their campaign platform.

The arguments justifying a national registry typically center on the registry's assumed utility in reducing gun violence. Supporters point to a national registry's usefulness in helping police trace crime guns, presumably by allowing the National Trace Center to modernize its deliberately archaic record-keeping systems. Because of FOPA's gun database prohibition, the center's current systems are intentionally designed to make a search of the center's 285 million gun records difficult. For example, the systems do not allow (as would a real database) searches by particular fields. Keyword searches, date sorting, serial number sorting, and so forth are simply not possible. Consolidating the center's records into a comprehensive database, using modern computer technology, would allow the police to receive the results of a crime gun trace almost immediately, instead of the average four to seven business days it currently takes (Friedman, 2016).

A second potential benefit of a comprehensive database, according to gun control advocates, is its possible impact on questionable firearms transactions. They claim that a registration system, by creating a permanent record of gun sales and purchases, may create a sense of heightened accountability in legal gun owners, and thereby discourage dubious private sales (Giffords Law Center, n.d.a). Similarly, a permanent database of background checks might help uncover the fraudulent transactions of corrupt dealers who provide false purchaser names or other information. The database might also deter gun trafficking. While federal law mandates dealers to report the sale of three or more firearms in a five-day period, traffickers currently evade this obstacle by purchasing from multiple dealers. A comprehensive database would prevent this evasion (Giffords Law Center, n.d.b).

Finally, a comprehensive gun sales database might reduce gun violence by helping the police identify and retrieve firearms from gun owners newly disbarred from possession due to a recent criminal conviction, domestic abuse charges, or some other disqualifying prohibition. If the registration requirement also mandated periodic renewal, the process could insure that the registered gun owner still possessed the listed firearms and remained eligible to possess firearms. Additionally, registration could give police responding to a home disturbance advance warning that the address contains firearms, allowing officers to proceed accordingly (Giffords Law Center, n.d.a).

Opponents of a national gun registry argue that most criminals obtain guns illegally—only about 10 percent acquire their firearms through a retail purchase (McKay, 2020)—so they claim that even a comprehensive sales database will not significantly improve the outcome of gun traces. They assert that because a successful trace merely links the gun to the first retail buyer, and since the vast majority of crime guns are not acquired through retail purchase, the trace typically leads to a legal gun owner reporting that the firearm was lost, stolen, traded, or sold in a private transaction to a stranger or an unfamiliar acquaintance (Holter, 2018).

Opponents also assert that a national registry of retail gun sales alone is unlikely to discourage questionable gun transactions among private individuals. Because private transactions do not require a background check, and occur after the retail sale, unscrupulous buyers and sellers could still engage in suspect transactions. Even the institution of a "universal" background check system (i.e., mandating a background check on all gun transactions, including private transfers) would not necessarily discourage questionable transactions unless the background check linked buyers to firearms, with this information becoming a permanent part of a gun sales registry. But at that point, the comprehensive registry of just initial gun dealer sales has become a comprehensive registry of guns and owners—a development that would certainly trigger gun activists' fears of eventual confiscation and major political opposition (Dunn, 2019; NRA-ILA, 2016).

As for a registration scheme aiding the police in confiscating firearms from disbarred gun owners, gun rights proponents assert that current gun laws make the possession of firearms by prohibited individuals a serious crime, yet only a few states have explicit processes for removing guns from prohibited individuals (e.g., those guilty of domestic violence). Many police and sheriff's departments find gun confiscations too labor-intensive and dangerous to undertake (Oppel, 2019), and authorities frequently employ court-decreed "surrender of weapons" orders instead. These orders rely on the prohibited individual's voluntary compliance with the order to obtain the firearms (e.g., Dexheimer, 2019; Kaste, 2018). Given this approach to firearms confiscation, gun rights proponents question whether police access to gun registration information would substantially increase officer safety or have much utility for decreasing gun violence.

Further, the empirical evidence examining the effectiveness of a comprehensive gun database is limited and ambiguous. As noted earlier, a CDC analysis of registration and licensing schemes, as well as other registration-focused research, was unable to document a connection between these less comprehensive registration approaches and reductions in gun violence, although the analysis did show some limited success with additional gun control measures in certain states. Even those approaches considered successful in reducing such violence (e.g., Lopez, 2018), however, are less likely to have a significant impact unless introduced as part of a package of more comprehensive, federal gun control measures, and the staunch opposition of gun rights proponents to such proposals, both in Washington and in the nation at large, have thus far prevented such packages from gaining much political traction.

Overall, the logical and empirical evidence suggests that a comprehensive database may reduce gun violence to a limited degree. However, given gun proponents' vociferous opposition to a national registry, the creation of such a comprehensive gun database would entail a fierce political fight (Holter, 2018). Whether an individual sees that fight as justifiable is likely determined by whether the individual sees granting the government the authority to track gun owners and their firearms as a potentially effective tool in reducing gun violence; and as constitutionally defensible in light of Second Amendment legal protections.

FURTHER READING

Bradner, Eric, 2019. "O'Rourke Calls for Licensing in Plan to Curb Gun Violence and White Nationalism." *CNN Politics*, August 16. https://

www.cnn.com/2019/08/16/politics/beto-orourke-plan-gun-violence-white-nationalism/index.html

Brooks, Emily, 2019. "Cory Booker Plans National Gun Registry." *Washington Examiner*, May 6. https://www.washingtonexaminer.com/news/cory-booker-plans-national-gun-registry

Campbell, Donald, 2019. *America's Gun Wars: A Cultural History of Gun Control in the United States*. Santa Barbara, CA: Praeger, pp. 11, 89.

Dexheimer, Eric, 2019. "Come and Take It: Confiscating Guns in Texas Isn't Easy." *Houston Chronicle*, January 16. https://www.houstonchronicle.com/politics/texas/article/Come-and-Take-It-Confiscating-guns-in-Texas-13541748.php

Dunn, Travis, 2019. "Would Universal Background Checks Create National Gun Registry?" Who.What.Why., April 8. https://whowhatwhy.org/2019/04/08/would-universal-background-checks-create-national-gun-registry/

Frankovic, Kathy, 2019. "Is Gun Control Legislation Even Possible in America?" YouGov, August 14. today.yougov.com/topics/politics/articles-reports/2019/08/14/gun-control-legislation-even-possible-america

Friedman, Dan, 2016. "The ATF's Nonsensical Non-Searchable Gun Databases, Explained." The Trace, August 24. https://www.thetrace.org/2016/08/atf-non-searchable-databases/

Giffords Law Center, n.d.a. "Registration." lawcenter.giffords.org/gun-laws/policy-areas/gun-owner-responsibilities/registration/

Giffords Law Center, n.d.b. "Maintaining Records of Gun Sales." https://giffords.org/lawcenter/gun-laws/policy-areas/gun-sales/maintaining-records/

Hahn, Robert, Bilukha, Oleg, Crosby, Alex, Fullilove, Mindy, Liberman, Akiva, Moscicki, Eve, & Snyder, Susan, et al., 2003. "First Reports Evaluating the Effectiveness of Strategies for Preventing Violence: Firearm Laws." CDC Task Force on Community Preventive Services Report, October 3. https://www.cdc.gov/mmwr/preview/mmwrhtml/rr5214a2.htm

Holter, Lauren, 2018. "These National Gun Registry Pros & Cons Show Why the Debate Is So Thorny." Bustle, June 1. https://www.bustle.com/p/5-national-gun-registry-pros-cons-show-why-the-debate-is-so-thorny-9242571

Kaste, Martin, 2018. "What It Takes to Get Guns Out of the Wrong Hands." NPR, January 26. https://www.npr.org/2018/01/26/580143957/what-it-takes-to-get-guns-out-of-the-wrong-hands

Lopez, German, 2018. "I Looked for a State That's Taking Gun Violence Seriously. I Found Massachusetts." *Vox*, November 13. https://www.vox.com/2018/11/13/17658028/massachusetts-gun-control-laws-licenses

McKay, Hollie, 2020. "Where Do Criminals Really Get Their Guns?" Fox News, February 19. https://www.foxnews.com/us/where-do-criminals-get-guns

NRA-ILA, 2016. "Gun Registration | Gun Licensing." NRA-ILA, August 8. https://www.nraila.org/get-the-facts/registration-licensing/

Oppel, Richard, 2019. "How So Many Violent Felons Are Allowed to Keep Their Illegal Guns." *New York Times*, February 20. https://www.nytimes.com/2019/02/20/us/gun-seizures-felons-abusers.html

Paulsen, Jacob, 2015. "Are Guns Registered in a National Firearms Registry." ConcealedCarry.com, June 18. https://www.concealedcarry.com/law/are-guns-registered/

Picket, Kerry, 2019. "Democrats Express Openness to Federal Gun Registry." Daily Caller, February 13. https://dailycaller.com/2019/02/13/dems-open-allow-doj-firearms-registry/

PoliceOne.com, 2013. PoliceOne's 2013 Gun Policy & Law Enforcement Survey Results: Executive Summary. https://www.policeone.com/police-products/firearms/articles/6188462-PoliceOnes-2013-Gun-Policy-Law-Enforcement-Survey-Results-Executive-Summary/

Smith, Guy, 2019. "Licensing and Registration." Gun Facts. https://www.gunfacts.info/gun-policy-info/licensing-and-registration/

Sobieck, Benjamin, 2016. "Can a Government Database Match a Gun to a Person?" The *Writer's Guide to Weapons*, May 12. https://crimefictionbook.com/2016/05/12/can-a-government-database-match-a-gun-to-a-person/

Statista Research, 2020. "Total Violent Crime Reported in the United States from 1990 to 2019." https://www.statista.com/statistics/191129/reported-violent-crime-in-the-us-since-1990/

Webster, Daniel, Vernick, J. S., & Hepburn, L. M., 2001. "Relationship between Licensing, Registration, and Other Gun Sales Laws and the Source State of Crime Guns." *Injury Prevention*, 7(3), 184–189.

Q17. WOULD MANDATORY GUN LIABILITY INSURANCE DECREASE GUN VIOLENCE?

Answer: The idea that mandatory gun liability insurance could decrease gun violence assumes that insurance charges can accomplish one or more objectives. First, insurance costs might discourage an unknown but presumably sizable number of non-gun-owning individuals from ever purchasing firearms, thus decreasing the number of guns that might be stolen, used for suicide or criminal activities, or result in accidental discharges and injuries. Second, mandatory insurance might discourage actual gun owners from acquiring additional firearms if insurance fees increased with each gun owned. Third, to obtain discounted rates, gun owners might be more likely to store their firearms more securely (Insurance Information Institute, 2018).

Other observers question these presumed benefits of gun liability insurance and call it "murder insurance." They argue that such insurance may give individuals an increased sense of security in using firearms for self-defense. If so, these critics suggest that gun liability insurance policies might actually encourage gun owners to employ lethal force in situations they otherwise might not (Yablon & Spies, 2017). As Igor Volsky, the director of Guns Down (a gun control organization), put it, "I call it murder insurance . . . because if you look at the way this is marketed, it's really sold in the context of 'There's a threat around every corner. . . . So when you inevitably have to use your gun to defend yourself . . . you have insurance to protect you'" (CBS News, 2017).

For their part, gun rights organizations typically support the purchase of gun liability insurance, but on a *voluntary* basis. In fact, gun rights organizations—the NRA, the U.S. Concealed Carry Association, the Armed Citizens' Legal Defense Network, U.S. Law Shield, and others—first pioneered this type of insurance. The policies they offer cover attorney fees, associated legal costs, and other miscellaneous expenses arising from the frequent civilian (and sometimes criminal) lawsuits following a self-defense shooting. As spokesperson Dana Loesch contended in her pitch for NRA's Carry Guard insurance, "The truth is, right behind your firearm, your second most important self-defense protection is a rock-solid carry policy" (Barnes, 2017).

The insurance industry overall has been less enthusiastic about mandatory gun liability insurance, noting both regulatory and practical obstacles in providing such coverage. Legally, many states prohibit insurance companies from insuring intentional acts expected to cause harm. Even in those states permitting self-defense insurance coverage, it is rarely offered by insurers; and when it is offered, it typically only protects against accidental shootings and limited acts of self-defense. The standard homeowners' insurance policy (known as HO-3 in the industry) usually covers only the theft of firearms, and explicitly excludes "expected or intended injury" (Insurance Information Institute, 2018).

Practical obstacles also abound. Because research is limited and estimates of gun violence costs vary widely across studies (due to differences in how "cost" is defined and calculated), actuarial quantification of firearm risk is complex and difficult (Moore & Reynolds, 2018). Further, while gun owners may favor purchasing gun liability insurance voluntarily, many object to answering mandatory insurance questions about gun ownership. As one member of the U.S. Concealed Carry Association stated, "I just don't think [probing about guns in the home] should be asked. I don't have a record. If I have my legal permits, I don't think I should be asked that question" (Hembree, 2017).

A number of state legislatures—California, Connecticut, Hawaii, Maryland, Massachusetts, and New York—have considered bills mandating the purchase of gun liability insurance, but none have been enacted as of mid-2020. On the federal level, bills requiring liability insurance for firearms purchases have also been introduced, but have never been ratified (Insurance Information Institute, 2018). Complicating this issue further, some of the same states (i.e., California and New York) that have contemplated mandatory liability insurance have also brought suit against the NRA's Carry Guard program, maintaining that it violates state laws against insuring intentional harm (Yablon, 2018). Subsequently, the NRA terminated the Carry Guard program (Kohrman & Yablon, 2019), a fate that may befall the insurance programs of other gun rights associations as underwriters (wishing to avoid bad publicity and regulatory complications) decline to offer this type of coverage.

Thus, the effectiveness of gun liability insurance for diminishing gun violence remains an open question. Without actual empirical evidence—impossible to obtain in the absence of governmental mandates—it is not possible to effectively gauge the impact of gun liability insurance on firearm violence.

The Facts: Gun liability insurance and "stand your ground" laws are closely intertwined for pro-gun advocates. Because stand your ground laws allow legal gun owners to use lethal force in protecting themselves from violent criminal attacks—without any duty to retreat—these individuals frequently regard liability insurance as an essential financial protection against the vagaries of an often unfriendly and arbitrary legal system likely to question their self-defense judgments. And as suggested above, providers have specifically targeted such fears in marketing the insurance.

For some gun control advocates, the ability of gun liability insurance to help shield gun owners from the financial consequences of their self-defense judgments is precisely why they oppose such insurance. As one commentator noted, "Offering this type of insurance policy will not only make it easier for 'stand your ground' shooters to settle and even win the lawsuits they may face but it could reasonably stand to embolden gun holders to shoot first and think later. . . . Trayvon Martin was just one of the many black men and women who've been murdered in the last few years by people claiming self-defense" (Barnes, 2017).

Although neither the insurance underwriter of NRA's Carry Guard Program (Chubb) nor the program's administrator (Lockton Affinity) have offered information on the number of policies sold or the number of claims filed (CBS News, 2017), outside insurance professionals have informally assessed the program as likely quite lucrative. Peter Kochenburger, deputy director of the Insurance Law Center at the University of Connecticut, observed, "If you can insure for an event that is very unlikely, but [gun owners] think is common, you'll get a ton of money and pay out very little" (Yablon & Spies, 2017). If the policies' profitability is as high—and stand your ground shootings as infrequent—as Kochernburger believes, then fears regarding increased gun violence due to gun liability insurance may be unfounded. Without better empirical information, however, this inference is highly speculative.

Arguments buttressing the assumption that mandatory gun liability insurance may *reduce* gun violence, while similarly nonempirical, nonetheless have basic economic theory working in their favor. For example, Justin Wolfers, professor of economics and public policy at the University of Michigan, argues that individuals typically only consider the personal benefits of gun ownership when purchasing a firearm, and do not consider the potential social costs of their decision (e.g., the harm and damage inflicted on innocent others if the gun is misused). He concludes that a steep gun ownership license fee would make individuals face the real social costs of their gun-buying decisions, and would probably discourage many individuals from making the purchase.

Additionally, he argues that gun owners currently are not held responsible for covering the larger social costs associated with firearms possession. If gun owners were liable for any damage their guns do, this legal liability would not only discourage some people from buying guns, it would also motivate those who do own guns to secure them carefully. For this approach to work, Wolfers concludes that gun owners would have to carry mandatory gun liability insurance, just as car owners must carry mandatory car insurance to cover any potential damage their cars may cause. Other economists such as Robert Frank, professor of economics at Cornell University, have echoed Wolfers' analysis (Kenney, 2013).

While these economic arguments suggest that mandatory gun liability insurance *should* reduce gun violence, in the absence of empirical evidence, actual effects are unknown. Further, regardless of its potential impact on gun violence, enactment of *mandatory* gun insurance faces a host of political, legal, and practical hurdles. Politically, gun rights proponents bristle at any government mandate involving firearms, and an insurance mandate would surely generate fierce opposition. Many gun rights proponents are highly skeptical of mandatory liability insurance, believing its real purpose is not to reduce gun violence but simply to make guns more expensive for law-abiding citizens and diminish private gun ownership (Olson, 2018).

Legally, mandatory gun liability insurance would face court challenges from organizations and individuals arguing that such a mandate would be unconstitutional. The Second Amendment protects an individual's right to keep and bear arms, and the courts would strike down any serious infringement on that right. Whether courts would view mandatory gun insurance premiums as a Second Amendment infringement could depend at least in part on the cost of the premiums, but gun rights advocates and other critics of mandatory firearm insurance contend that even relatively low premiums are likely to disenfranchise those individuals needing firearms the most—low-income residents (such as the elderly and the handicapped) living in high-crime areas. Thus, statutes requiring gun owners to carry liability insurance encounter potentially difficult constitutional pitfalls (Gilles & Lund, 2013).

Practically, even if state legislatures mandated gun liability insurance, the insurance industry might only offer policies that essentially replicate the kind of coverage already generally available for non-gun hazards—accidents and negligence—and perhaps coverage of plausible self-defense shootings (similar to Carry Guard–type coverage). The mandatory insurance envisioned by gun control advocates—covering harm done to innocent individuals through another person's criminal misuse of an owner's stolen firearms—present a risk-assessment nightmare for underwriters (Moore & Reynolds, 2018). If such insurance were offered at all, the premiums would certainly be significant, thus potentially triggering the Second Amendment issues discussed above (Gilles & Lund, 2013).

Overall, then, assessing the potential role of mandatory gun liability insurance in regulating gun violence is especially difficult. In the absence of empirical evidence, only logical conclusions are available to guide judgment, and in this case, the priorities and perspectives of pro-gun rights and pro-gun control camps lead them to offer starkly contrasting conclusions.

FURTHER READING

Barnes, Steph, 2017. "Why the NRA's New 'Murder Insurance' Is So Alarming to Gun Control Activists." Hello Giggles, October 26. https://

hellogiggles.com/news/nras-new-murder-insurance-alarming-gun-control-activists/

CBS News, 2017. "NRA's Carry Guard Comes Under Fire as 'Murder Insurance.'" CBS News, October 19. https://www.cbsnews.com/news/nras-carry-guard-comes-under-fire-as-murder-insurance/

Gilles, Stephen, & Lund, Nelson, 2013. "Mandatory Liability Insurance for Firearm Owners: Design Choices and Second Amendment Limits." Federalist Society, June 28. https://fedsoc.org/commentary/publications/mandatory-liability-insurance-for-firearm-owners-design-choices-and-second-amendment-limits

Hembree, Diana, 2017. "Insurance Companies 'Should Not Get a Pass' on Gun Violence." *Forbes*, October 4. https://www.forbes.com/sites/dianahembree/2017/10/04/insurance-companies-should-not-get-a-pass-on-gun-violence/#32ed598a5277

Insurance Information Institute, 2018. "Background On: Gun Liability." Insurance Information Institute, May 16. https://www.iii.org/article/background-on-gun-liability

Kenney, Caitlin, 2013. "Should Gun Owners Have to Buy Liability Insurance?" NPR, January 31. https://www.npr.org/sections/money/2013/01/31/170700177/should-gun-owners-have-to-buy-liability-insurance

Kohrman, Miles, & Yablon, Alex, 2019. "The NRA Ends Its Carry Guard Insurance Program." The Trace, July 19. https://www.thetrace.org/rounds/the-nra-ends-its-carry-guard-insurance-program/

Moore, Kristen, & Reynolds, Craig, 2018. "Firearm Risk: An Insurance Perspective." The Actuary, June/July. https://theactuarymagazine.org/firearm-risk/

Olson, Walter, 2018. "New York: Damned if You Do Insure Guns, Damned if You Don't." Cato At Liberty, December 7. https://www. cato.org/blog/new-york-damned-you-do-insure-guns-damned-you-dont

Yablon, Alex, 2018. "The NRA and Its Partners in 'Murder Insurance' Face Widening State Probes." The Trace, August 22. https://www.thetrace.org/rounds/nra-carry-guard-insurance-state-investigations-new-jersey/

Yablon, Alex, & Spies, Mike, 2017. "The NRA Is Selling Insurance to Gun Owners Willing to Shoot in Self Defense." The Trace, April 26. https://www.thetrace.org/2017/04/nra-insurance-carry-guard-self-defense/

Zonderman, Jon, 2015. "Forum: Insurance Companies Shouldn't Get a Free Pass on Gun Violence." *New Haven Register*, December 29. https://www. https://www. https://www.nhregister.com/columns/article/Forum-Insurance-companies-shouldn-t-get-a-free-11341425.php

Q18. DO GUN CONTROL REGULATIONS INCREASE THE SAFETY OF MINORITY GROUP COMMUNITIES?

Answer: Blacks and Latinos have historically endorsed traditional gun control propositions at significantly higher rates than their white counterparts. For example, in a 2017 study conducted by researchers at the University of Illinois at Chicago, both Blacks and Latinos supported 7 of 8 gun control proposals at levels substantially higher than Caucasians: requiring trigger locks (83 and 79 percent respectively, versus 67 percent), creating a federal database of all gun sales (86 and 78 percent versus 62 percent), requiring gun liability insurance (77 and 74 percent versus 56 percent), imposing a higher sales tax on guns (67 and 64 percent versus 43 percent), banning high-capacity ammunition (73 and 67 percent versus 58 percent), banning assault-style weapons (74 and 61 percent versus 55 percent), and banning all handguns (41 and 41 percent versus 19 percent). The only proposition where no differences existed between the three groups was a five-day waiting period to purchase a firearm. Support was statistically uniform across the three clusters: 84 and 77 percent versus 79 percent (Filindra & Kaplan, 2017). Thus, minorities appear to believe that gun control regulations can make communities safer, even more so than the white majority.

In some ways, however, this finding is counterintuitive. Research has also shown that experience with crime and victimization tends to decrease support for gun control, even in communities of color (Filindra & Kaplan, 2017). Moreover, minority communities, especially those situated in urban settings, typically confront gun violence that is substantially more severe than the gun violence experienced in white communities. For example, Hispanics (29 percent) and Blacks (49 percent) indicate that gun violence is a major concern in their local communities at rates almost three and five times higher than whites (11 percent) (Parker et al., 2017). Further, the average homicide death rate for Black Americans in the country is anywhere from 8 (Mitchell & Bromfield, 2019) to 14 (Howard, 2018) times higher than for white Americans. Additionally, gun violence is intensely localized in the United States, with about 1,200 neighborhoods (housing just 1.5 percent of the U.S. population) accounting for more than a quarter of the country's gun homicides in 2015 (Lopez, 2019).

Studies have found that victimization tends to lower support for gun control (Filindra & Kaplan, 2017), and gun regulations limiting or outlawing gun ownership among ex-felons are particularly impactful on minority communities due to higher minority incarceration rates (e.g., Bazelon,

2019). But while anecdotal evidence from gun store owners indicates that minorities have been buying firearms in growing numbers, and other gun rights proponents assert that concealed carry permits have risen 75 percent faster among minorities relative to whites (Lott, 2017), the empirical research evidence nonetheless indicates that both Blacks and Latinos perceive gun control as a pathway to lessen gun violence and to make their communities safer.

The Facts: Some analysts have suggested that the problem of "gun violence" in the United States is more usefully conceptualized as at least four separate problems: suicides, urban gun violence, domestic violence, and mass shootings. In 2017, suicides (about 26,000 fatalities) accounted for almost two-thirds of total gun deaths in the country (about 40,000 individuals). Urban violence was the next largest category, accounting for the majority of the roughly 14,000 deaths due to gun homicides (Lopez, 2019). These distinctions help explain why minority communities may have a dramatically different view and understanding of gun violence relative to white communities. Public gun violence that impacts primarily white communities more typically takes the form of mass shootings at schools—such as at Columbine, Sandy Hook, Santa Fe, and Parkland—or other public gathering places (Mitchell & Bromfield, 2019). For minority communities, ongoing urban gun violence is the gun violence scourge. While both types of violence are surely horrible, fewer than 600 people have died in mass shootings since 2001, while urban violence has claimed at least 100,000 lives over that same period (Lopez, 2019). Although American news media does not provide the same level of coverage for urban gun violence as it does for mass shootings, for racial and ethnic minorities such violence is a social problem of extraordinary proportions.

For example, a Brookings examination of differences in suicide/homicide ratios starkly illustrates this issue. Suicide accounts for the largest number of white gun deaths (77 percent), with homicides adding another 19 percent. But for Blacks, homicide is the cause of the vast majority of gun deaths (82 percent), with suicides contributing another 14 percent (Reeves & Holmes, 2015). A McGill University study in 2018 uncovered a substantially similar pattern (Riddell et al., 2018). Thus, for minority communities situated in the country's major urban areas, the impact of gun violence is substantial, with almost everyone knowing (or knowing of) a gun murder victim. Such experiences with violence often motivate minority individuals to acquire firearms for self-protection—Otis McDonald, of the landmark Supreme Court gun rights case that overturned Chicago's handgun ban, is an example—and likely reduces confidence in the efficacy of gun control (Filindra & Kaplan, 2017).

Historically, early gun control laws often were racist and elitist in intent and in practice. Enacted to disarm specific classes of people—Southern Blacks and Eastern and Southern European immigrants in particular—the laws have periodically motivated militant Black leaders to become radical gun activists. Such figures include Robert F. Williams and the Black Armed Guard in the 1950s, Eldridge Cleaver and the Black Panthers in the 1960s, and General Laney and the National Black Sportsman's Association in the 1970s (Tonso, 1985). Expressions of pro-gun militancy by the Black Panthers, in fact, led both the National Rifle Association and Republican governor Ronald Reagan of California to support the Mulford Act, a state ban on the "open carry" of loaded firearms that was passed in 1967 (and was still on the books as of 2020) (Emery, n.d.). More recently, the National African American Gun Association (NAAGA)—founded by Philip Smith—has become the country's largest Black firearms organization, growing rapidly since its founding in 2015, with 75 chapters and about 30,000 members nationwide (Booker, 2019).

Further, given the widespread distrust and hostility toward police in minority communities, some minorities have argued that firearms can provide a potent method of self-defense in the absence of police protection. In fact, self-protection and self-defensive motivations have been cited as the primary fuels behind the rapid growth of NAAGA, particularly among minority women. Nezida Davis, a Black female member of NAAGA, asserted that she joined the association to learn how to protect herself from crime in her community and from rising white extremism in the country: "And, yes I wanna be armed . . . by being able to protect ourselves, by training properly and getting our practice in, and learning how to defend ourselves, at least we will be able to fight back. . . ." (CBS This Morning, 2019). Davis's focus on taking personal responsibility for self-protection is borne out by policing statistics, which suggest that law enforcement is not effective in addressing urban violence. In 2017, almost 40 percent of murder cases nationwide went unresolved, with homicide solve rates falling into single digits in some Black and Latino communities (Lopez, 2019).

Despite these informal and anecdotal reasons for minorities to acquire firearms for personal and community protection, one 2017 academic study found that Blacks and Latinos endorsed seven of eight traditional gun control regulations substantially more strongly than their white counterparts (Filindra & Kaplan, 2017). These results are consistent with earlier research. A survey from 2014 conducted by the Pew Research Center, for example, found that 71 percent of Hispanics and 60 percent of Blacks indicated it was more important to control gun ownership than it was to protect the right to own guns. These percentages were reversed for whites, with 61 percent asserting that it was more important to protect the right to own guns than to control gun ownership (37 percent) (Pew Research Center, 2014).

Of course, informal and anecdotal reasons also abound for minorities to support gun control, such as drive-by shootings into houses and schoolyards that kill youngsters, and so on. As an Urban Institute report noted, "exposure to gun violence has been linked to a variety of psychological challenges [in young people] like anger and dissociation, anxiety and depression, and posttraumatic stress disorder (PTSD). It can also affect youth in the classroom, making it difficult for them to concentrate in class and damaging their academic performance and educational or career aspirations" (Bieler, 2014).

Additionally, Philip Smith, the president and founder of NAAGA, makes the point that, for minorities, even legally carrying a gun can have fatal consequences if they encounter poorly trained, racist, or nervous law enforcement officers. Sensitized by media reports of questionable police shootings of legally armed Black citizens (examples of the latter include Philando Castile in 2016 and E. J. Bradford in 2018), many minority members may not see gun ownership as a viable self-defense strategy, leaving gun control as their only option. In these circumstances, strong gun regulation is likely seen as offering some hope for positive change.

Despite the research strongly demonstrating that minorities see tougher gun regulations as a means to increased community safety (Filindra & Kaplan, 2017; Pew Research Center, 2014), some indications suggest that attitudes toward guns and gun regulations are changing in minority communities. For example, in 1993, African American support for gun control stood at 74 percent according to one poll (Mzezewa & DiNapoli, 2015). By 2012, about 53 percent of Blacks surveyed in a poll by the Pew Research Center felt that gun ownership did more to put people's safety at risk than it did to protect people from becoming crime victims (29 percent). Two years later, only 41 percent felt that gun ownership endangered people, while 54 percent believed gun ownership protected people from crime (Pew Research Center, 2014). Additionally, minorities apparently are purchasing firearms, obtaining concealed carry permits (Lott, 2017), and joining minority-oriented gun associations in increasing numbers (Booker, 2019). These trends have led some observers to wonder if traditionally high levels of Black and Latino support for strong gun regulation are undergoing at least some modest level of erosion.

FURTHER READING

Bazelon, Emily, 2019. "Charged." *Slate*, April 17. https://slate.com/news-and-politics/2019/04/slate-presents-charged-podcast-emily-bazelon-new-york-gun-court.html

Bieler, Sam, 2014. "Raising the Voices of Gun Violence." Urban Institute. https://apps.urban.org/features/RaisingtheVoicesofGunViolence/

Booker, Brakkton, 2019. "With a Growing Membership since Trump, Black Gun Group Considers Getting Political." NPR, July 10. https://www.npr.org/2019/07/10/738493491/with-a-growing-membership-since-trump-black-gun-group-considers-getting-politica

CBS *This Morning*, 2019. "As NRA Membership Wanes, America's Largest Black Gun Group Is Thriving." CBS *This Morning*, September 11. https://www.cbsnews.com/news/gun-control-national-african-american-gun-association-im-not-goin-down-without-a-fight/

Emery, David, n.d. "Did the NRA Support a 1967 'Open Carry' Ban in California?" Snopes.com. https://www.snopes.com/fact-check/nra-california-open-carry-ban/

Filindra, Alexandra, & Kaplan, Noah, 2017. "Testing Theories of Gun Policy Preferences among Blacks, Latinos, and Whites in America." *Social Science Quarterly*, 98(2), 413–428. https://onlinelibrary.wiley.com/doi/full/10.1111/ssqu.12418

Howard, Jacqueline, 2018. "The Disparities in How Black and White Men Die in Gun Violence, State by State." *CNN Health*, April 24. https://www.cnn.com/2018/04/23/health/gun-deaths-in-men-by-state-study/index.html

Lopez, German, 2019. "How to Dramatically Reduce Gun Violence in American Cities." Vox, July 12. https://www.vox.com/policy-and-politics/2019/7/12/20679091/thomas-abt-bleeding-out-urban-gun-violence-book-review

Lott, John, 2017. "In 2017, Women and Minorities Are Buying Guns. Here's Why." Fox News, March 13. https://www.foxnews.com/opinion/in-2017-women-and-minorities-are-buying-guns-heres-why

Mitchell, Yolanda, & Bromfield, Tiffany, 2019. "Gun Violence and the Minority Experience." National Council on Family Relations, January 10. Accessed September 2019. ncfr.org/ncrf-report/winter-2018/gun-violence-and-minority-expereience (URL no longer active).

Mzezewa, Tariro, & DiNapoli, Jessica, 2015. "African-Americans Still Favor Gun Control, but Views Are Shifting." Reuters, July 15. https://www.reuters.com/article/us-africanamerican-guns/African-americans-still-favor-gun-control-but-views-are-shifting-idUSKCN0PP2N320150715

Parker, Kim, Horowitz, Juliana, Igielnik, Ruth, Oliphant, J. Baxter, & Brown, Anna, 2017. "4. Views of Guns and Gun Violence." Pew Research Center, June 22. https://www.pewsocialtrends.org/2017/06/22/views-of-guns-and-gun-violence/

Pew Research Center, 2014. "Growing Public Support for Gun Rights." Pew Research Center, December 10. https://www.https://www.people-press.org/2014/12/10/growing-public-support-for-gun-rights/#survey-report

Reeves, Richard, & Holmes, Sarah, 2015. "Guns and Race: The Different Worlds of Black and White Americans." Brookings, December 15. https://www.brookings.edu/blog/social-mobility-memos/2015/12/15/guns-and-race-the-different-worlds-of-black-and-white-americans/

Riddell, Corinne, Harper, Sam, Cerdá, Magdalena, & Kaufman, Jay, 2018. "Comparison of Rates of Firearm and Non-Firearm Homicide and Suicide in Black and White Non-Hispanic Men, by U.S. State." *Annals of Internal Medicine*, 168(10), 712–720. https://www.annals.org/aim/fullarticle/2679556/comparison-rates-firearm-nonfirearm-homicide-suicide-black-white-non-hispanic

Tonso, William, 1985. "Gun Control: White Men's Law." *Reason*, December. https://reason.com/1985/12/01/gun-control/

4

Guns and School Safety

About 42 percent of Americans live in households with firearms, according to one 2017 analysis. Protection of self and family is cited as the primary motivation for gun ownership among gun owners (Parker et al., 2017). Yet, for much of the day, the family's most vulnerable members—children and young adults—are in school, away from home and beyond the protective shield potentially provided by the family's firearms. While in previous decades parents may have viewed schools as "safe havens" where little harm aside from some playground scrapes and bruises might befall their youngsters, such untroubled attitudes are no longer the case. Depending on how we define "school shooting," the time periods we examine, the data sources we use, and other pertinent factors, the country has experienced either 68 school shootings since the 1999 Columbine High School massacre (Melgar, 2019); or at least 111 since 1970 (Cai & Patel, 2019); or 179 between April 1999 and May 2018 (Livingston, Rossheim, & Hall, 2019); or perhaps even 657 between 1999 and 2018 (Rowhani-Rahbar & Moe, 2019). Whatever the number, many parents no longer regard schools as safe sanctuaries for their kids.

As with other areas in the larger gun control debate, however, evaluating the effects of America's gun culture on schools and school safety is contentious and complicated to assess. Consequently, this chapter centers on six questions that attempt to clarify core issues related to guns and schools. The first question examines the most basic issue in this area: are schools becoming more dangerous and shootings becoming more common? The next two questions explore factors that may inadvertently foster such shootings. Thus, the second question investigates whether intense media coverage inspires copycat shootings; while the third question examines the safety impact of allowing college students to carry and possess firearms on campus.

The final three questions change the focus from possible "prompts" of school shootings to commonly touted safety implementation strategies designed to reduce or prevent such shootings. Accordingly, the fourth question examines the effectiveness of strict gun regulations in preventing school shootings. The next considers the effectiveness of a particular gun control strategy—the designation of school areas as "gun free" zones—in reducing school shootings. The final question probes the effectiveness of a strategy suggested by gun rights supporters for increasing school safety: the arming of willing teachers and school staff.

FURTHER READING

Cai, Weiyi, & Patel, Jugal, 2019. "A Half-Century of School Shootings Like Columbine, Sandy Hook and Parkland." *New York Times*, May 11. https://www.nytimes.com/interactive/2019/05/11/us/school-shootings-united-states.html

Livingston, Melvin, Rossheim, Matthew, & Hall, Kelli, 2019. "A Descriptive Analysis of School and School Shooter Characteristics and the Severity of School Shootings in the United States, 1999–2018." *Journal of Adolescent Health*, 64(6), 797–799. https://www.jahonline.org/article/S1054-139X(18)30832-2/fulltext#intraref0005d

Melgar, Luis, 2019. "Are School Shootings Becoming More Frequent? We Ran the Numbers." KCUR 89.3, May 21. https://www.kcur.org/post/are-school-shootings-becoming-more-frequent-we-ran-numbers#stream/0

Parker, Kim, Horowitz, Juliana, Igielnik, Ruth, Oliphant, Baxter, & Brown, Anna, 2017. "America's Complex Relationship with Guns." Pew Research Center, June. https://www.pewsocialtrends.org/2017/06/22/americas-complex-relationship-with-guns/

Rowhani-Rahbar, Ali, & Moe, Caitlin, 2019. "School Shootings in the U.S.: What Is the State of the Evidence?" *Journal of Adolescent Health*, 64(6), 683–684. https://www.jahonline.org/article/S1054-139X(19)30175-2/fulltext

Q19. ARE SCHOOL SHOOTINGS INCREASING IN AMERICA?

Answer: Although this seemingly straightforward question appears to have an easily obtainable answer, the reality is quite different. Despite the public nature of both schools and shootings, and the virtually comprehensive reporting of such incidents in modern American society, attempting to tally the number of shooting incidents across specified time intervals requires investigators to engage in a series of arguable decisions prior to the actual count, with each choice substantially impacting the final conclusion. For example, no widespread agreement exists on the types of incidents that qualify as a "school shooting" (e.g., do accidental discharges of firearms or those that don't result in injury or death count?), or on the appropriate metric to use for the count (e.g., the actual number of school shootings versus the number of days between school shootings versus the severity of casualties). Further, researchers have more than 20 different databases available from which to draw information, and each has its own specifications for including or excluding a shooting occurrence (Rowhani-Rahbar & Moe, 2019).

With all these differing factors in play and pro-gun rights and pro-gun control sides both eager to advance statistics that bolster their arguments, little consensus exists among analysts regarding whether school shootings are becoming more or less frequent. Nonetheless, despite the popular impression that school shootings have alarmingly mushroomed in recent years, the objective evidence is clear that these incidents "are not commonplace" (Everytown for Gun Safety, 2019) and "are still very rare" (Melgar, 2019). James Alan Fox, the Lipman Family Professor of Criminology, Law and Public Policy at Northeastern University and considered a foremost expert in school shootings, contends that while multiple-victim shootings *in general* are increasing, *school shootings* are not: "There were more back in the 90s than in recent years. The difference is the impression, the perception that people have. Today we have cell phone recordings of gunfire that play over and over and over again. So it's that the impression is very different. That's why people think things are a lot worse now, but the statistics say otherwise" (Kaste, 2018). Fox's research suggests that mass shootings occur on average 20 to 30 times per year but that only one of those incidents happens at a school (Nicodemo & Petronio, 2018). Indeed, since the beginning of the twenty-first century, lightning strikes have killed more American children than mass shootings in school (Pecanha, 2019).

The Facts: As noted, no widespread agreement exists on the types of incidents that qualify as a school shooting. For example, are shootings at after-hours events included? Are noninjurious accidental discharges by security personnel counted? Are gun suicides occurring on school grounds but posing no threat to other children included? Everytown for Gun Safety (2019) defines shooting incidents broadly—"any time a gun discharges a live round inside (or into) a school campus or grounds"—and would count all these incidents, but many other analysts would not. Because different analysts make different choices in classifying a particular occurrence as a school shooting, reports in the popular media are often contradictory, with one respected source asserting shootings are increasing (e.g., Melgar, 2019) and another declaring they are not (e.g., Kaste, 2018).

Compounding this difficulty are the different ways commentators can interpret the meaning of "frequency." While typically the term would refer to the numerical count of actual shooting incidents—however defined—frequency may also loosely incorporate other relevant metrics, such as increases or decreases in the average number of days between school shootings. For instance, between 1999 and 2014, one analysis indicated that school shootings happened on average every 124 days in America, while from 2015 to 2018 the average number of days between shootings decreased to 77 days (Melgar, 2019). Because such comparisons are highly sensitive to the time periods selected for examination, outcomes for alternative time periods produce different results—a problem in objectively measuring frequency regardless of the metric used.

The severity of a shooting incident can also influence perceptions of shooting frequency. For example, another analysis noted that 16 multiple-victim shootings involving at least 2 deaths and 4 or more victims occurred in schools since 1996 (Nicodemo & Petronio, 2018). Of these, 8 incidents involved 4 or more deaths (not including the assailant). Four of these shootings occurred before 2005, and 4 occurred after 2005, but the post-2005 incidents contained 2 shootings having markedly more fatalities than earlier occurrences. Such differences in the number of fatalities across incidents also contribute to the belief that shooting incidents are increasing or becoming more deadly.

Aside from the above ambiguities inherent in determining the frequency of school shooting incidents, another factor contributing to potential misperceptions is the likely public conflation of "school" shootings with "mass" shootings. While most mass shootings are *not* school shootings, high-profile school shootings typically *are* mass shootings, and popular media reports (e.g., Densley & Peterson, 2019; Kaste, 2018; Schulman, 2017) regularly assert that mass shootings are indeed increasing and getting deadlier. While other analysts have questioned such claims (e.g., Ferguson, 2019; Reynolds, 2018), these accounts have also undoubtedly fueled the belief that *school* shootings are on the rise.

Despite this widespread perception of mushrooming school violence, the objective evidence is much more nuanced. Fox asserts that school shootings have declined both in terms of frequency and in terms of injuries over the past two decades, with youngsters much more likely to die off school grounds (in a fall, a drowning, an accident, and so forth) than they are in a school attack (Toppo, 2018). Fox's data show that in 1992–93, about 0.55 students per million were shot and killed; while in 2014–15, the rate decreased to about 0.15 per million (Kaste, 2018).

Additionally, because school shootings are uncommon occurrences regardless of whether they are increasing or decreasing (Melgar, 2019), some commentators have argued that a more directly relevant concern is the impact societal *reactions* to such incidents have on children. These critics contend that "live shooter drills" and other security measures at schools can take a heavier emotional toll on children than news stories about actual mass shootings. In attempting to insulate schools from gun violence, school districts have gone to extraordinary efforts to made schools safe, and in the process have created a burgeoning school security market worth almost $3 billion in 2017 (Bandlamudi, 2019). The industry offers an array of high-tech products—bullet-resistant classroom doors and panels; infrared and long-range night vision cameras; locks and barricade sticks that can withstand a sledgehammer's battering—as well as a range of relatively low-tech products, such as badge-operated doors, metal detectors, lockdown toilets, and barbed wire fencing. The technology is typically coupled with active shooter training drills and lockdown exercises. While these technological additions and training efforts are well intentioned, the fear is that they may be more harmful than helpful, creating unnecessary and unproductive anxiety, worry, and apprehension in children.

For instance, a training exercise in an Indiana school had students listening to an actual segment of a Columbine High School teacher's panicky 911 call to the police during the shooting massacre. In an Ohio school, police officers carried firearms and fired blank shots during the school's active-shooter exercise. In a South Carolina school, an unannounced drill incorporated a black-clad "intruder" prowling menacingly through the corridors. In yet another school, the lockdown training included adapting a lullaby to prepare even the kindergartners for a possible incident (Pecanha, 2019). While such drills and training instill basic safety procedures in students, they can also have a significant downside.

As Jaclyn Schildkraut, an expert on school shootings and associate professor of criminal justice at the State University of New York, has observed, little research has been undertaken to examine the effectiveness of these exercises—or their potential for traumatizing children. She argues that there is no point in dramatizing lockdown drills: "All that causes is fear" (Pecanha, 2019).

James Fox, another expert on school shootings, agrees. He suggests that increased security measures are likely counterproductive. "I'm not a big fan of making schools look like fortresses because they send a message to kids that the bad guy is coming for you—if we're surrounding you with security, you must have a bull's-eye on your back. That can actually instill fear, not relieve it" (Nicodemo & Petronio, 2018).

Investigations into identifying incident characteristics with an eye toward averting future school tragedies have also become a major emphasis. For example, research has shown that while most school shootings from 1999 to 2018 involved handguns (81 percent), substantially more fatalities occur when assailants use rifles or shotguns. Similarly, incidents involving older shooters (aged 20 and above) are particularly lethal, typically resulting in more fatalities and a greater number of casualties. Further, the presence of school resource officers does not appear to reduce shooting severity (Livingston et al., 2019). Research of this type can provide both the basis for creating action plans aimed at safeguarding children and schools, as well as offer criteria for evaluating the likely effectiveness of security plans currently tendered (e.g., Everytown for Gun Safety, 2019).

FURTHER READING

Bandlamudi, Adhiti, 2019. "The Big Business of School Security." KCUR 89.3, May 9. https://www.kcur.org/community/2019-05-09/the-big-business-of-school-security

Cai, Weiyi, & Patel, Jugal, 2019. "A Half-Century of School Shootings Like Columbine, Sandy Hook and Parkland." *New York Times*, May 11. nytimes.com/interactive/2019/05/11/us/school-shootings-united-states.html

Densley, James, & Peterson, Jillian, 2019. "Opinion: We Analyzed 53 Years of Mass Shooting Data. Attacks Aren't Just Increasing, They're Getting Deadlier." *Los Angeles Times*, September 1. https://www.latimes.com/opinion/story/2019-09-01/mass-shooting-data-odessa-midland-increase

Everytown for Gun Safety, 2019. "Keeping Our Schools Safe: A Plan for Preventing Mass Shootings and Ending All Gun Violence in American

Schools." Everytown for Gun Safety, February. everytownresearch.org/wp-content/uploads/2019/02/School-Safety-Report-FINAL.pdf

Ferguson, Christopher, 2019. "Mass Shootings Aren't Becoming More Common." Salon, August 11. https://www.salon.com/2019/08/10/mass-shootings-arent-more-common_partner/

Kaste, Martin, 2018. "Despite Heightened Fear of School Shootings, It's Not a Growing Epidemic." NPR, March 15. https://www.npr.org/2018/03/15/593831564/the-disconnect-between-perceived-danger-in-u-s-schools-and-reality

Livingston, Melvin, Rossheim, Matthew, & Hall, Kelli, 2019. "A Descriptive Analysis of School and School Shooter Characteristics and the Severity of School Shootings in the United States, 1999–2018." *Journal of Adolescent Health,* 64(6), 797–799. https://www.jahonline.org/article/S1054-139X(18)30832-2/fulltext#intraref0005d

Melgar, Luis, 2019. "Are School Shootings Becoming More Frequent? We Ran the Numbers." KCUR 89.3, May 21. https://www.kcur.org/post/are-school-shootings-becoming-more-frequent-we-ran-numbers#stream/0

Nicodemo, Allie, & Petronio, Lia, 2018. "Schools Are Safer than They Were in the 90s, and School Shootings Are Not More Common than They Used to Be, Researchers Say." News@Northeastern, February 26. news.northeastern.edu/2018/02/26/schools-are-still-one-of-the-safest-places-for-children-researcher-says/

Parker, Kim, Horowitz, Juliana, Igielnik, Ruth, Oliphant, J. Baxter, & Brown, Anna, 2017. "America's Complex Relationship with Guns." Pew Research Center, June. https://www.pewsocialtrends.org/2017/06/22/views-of-guns-and-gun-violence/

Pecanha, Sergio, 2019. "Lockdown Drills: An American Quirk, Out of Control." *Washington Post,* October 11. https://www.washingtonpost.com/opinions/2019/10/11/lockdown-drills-are-an-american-quirk-out-of-control/

Reynolds, Alan, 2018. "Are Mass Shootings Becoming More Frequent?" Cato at Liberty, February 15. https://www.cato.org/blog/are-mass-shootings-becoming-more-frequent

Rowhani-Rahbar, Ali, & Moe, Caitlin, 2019. "School Shootings in the U.S.: What Is the State of the Evidence?" *Journal of Adolescent Health,* 64(6), 683–684. https://www.jahonline.org/article/S1054-139X(19)30175-2/fulltext

Schulman, Ari, 2017. "How Not to Cover Mass Shootings." *Wall Street Journal,* November 17. https://www.wsj.com/articles/how-not-to-cover-mass-shootings-1510939088

Toppo, Greg, 2018. "20 Years In, Shootings Have Changed Schools in Unexpected Ways." *USAToday*, January 24. https://www.usatoday.com/story/news/2018/01/24/20-years-school-shootings-loom-large-public-imagination/1063337001/

Q20. DOES INTENSIVE MEDIA COVERAGE INSPIRE SCHOOL SHOOTINGS?

Answer: School shootings have always garnered a great deal of attention in public print and broadcast outlets, and even on popular social media such as Twitter and Facebook. These reports invariably devote substantial coverage to the shooters, their personal backgrounds and motives, the weapons they use, and the carnage and death toll they inflict on innocent children, teachers, and staff. While such reporting is understandable—as a *Washington Post* editor argued, "comprehensive information about those responsible for mass shootings . . . informs the public debate" (Zalatoris, 2016)—some commentators (e.g., Jilani, 2019; Kohrman & Reed, 2019; Schulman, 2017) fear that such intensive media coverage is central to why these shootings keep happening. Further, empirical data suggest that these fears are well founded.

For example, researchers at Arizona State University used "contagion" modeling—a mathematical tool epidemiologists often employ to investigate the spread of diseases—to determine whether school shootings and other mass killings display similar characteristics and spread patterns. The investigators examined recent data sets of such occurrences to see whether a school shooting or a mass murder event impacted the probability of a similar event occurring in the immediate future. They found significant evidence for the hypothesized effect: each shooting incident temporarily raised the probability of another shooting incident for about 13 days afterward; and on average spurred at least 0.30 new mass shooting incidents, or 0.22 new school shooting incidents (Towers et al., 2015).

Similarly, a second study conducted by researchers at the University of Western Australia and Old Dominion University focused on day-to-day prime-time television news, and examined the connections between *ABC World News Tonight*'s coverage of mass shootings and subsequent shootings, during the period of January 1, 2013, to June 23, 2016. Results paralleled the study above, and showed that coverage had a statistically significant impact on the number of subsequent shootings. This impact lasted for about 4 to 10 days, with news coverage apparently causing about three mass shootings in the following week—a finding that accounted for

55 percent of all mass shootings in the data sample examined. Further, the research results remained significant using a more extensive data source (covering a 10-year span from 2006 to 2016) and under alternative definitions of "mass shooting" (Jetter & Walker, 2018).

Jillian Peterson, a criminologist at Hamline University in Minnesota and cofounder of The Violence Project, has found similar contagion patterns in her research. She asserts that high-profile mass shootings spark other mass shootings the way high-profile suicides spark additional suicides: "So one happens and you see another few happen right after that." Peterson speculates that at least some mass shootings are, in fact, a form of suicide: "So a mass shooting happens and then vulnerable individuals who are actively suicidal and in crisis hear about the shooting and see this as a kind of script that they could also follow" (Chatterjee, 2019).

Nonetheless, despite these findings that intensive media coverage likely incites additional shootings, some commentators remain skeptical. They assert that too many confounding variables make it impossible to say with certainty that media coverage directly causes copycat attacks. Further, these defenders of news coverage of school shootings and other mass shooting events argue that full media coverage has journalistic and practical benefits. Journalistically, such coverage upholds the press's fundamental responsibility for reporting significant events as completely as possible. As a practical matter, comprehensive reporting also can help uncover and identify warning signs and troubling patterns of behavior (Zalatoris, 2016). From this perspective, even if media coverage inspires additional school shootings, as the above research suggests, a solution that can balance the public's need-to-know with society's need to safeguard its most vulnerable members will likely be difficult to craft.

The Facts: The idea that "contagion effects" may influence school shootings has early historical roots. For instance, in the 1890s, Gabriel Tarde, an eminent French sociologist and criminologist, argued that many copy-cat murders that echoed the killing spree of Jack the Ripper, a serial killer who terrorized London in the late nineteenth century, were the result of "suggestive-imitative assaults," and he proposed that some crimes were self-spreading, like some diseases. In the early 2000s, the prominent forensic psychiatrist Paul Mullen concluded in his examination of specific mass killers that "these massacres are acts of mimesis, and their perpetrators are imitators" (Schulman, 2017). Similarly, in the 1970s and 1980s, David Phillips, a well-known sociologist and researcher, studied the effects of mass media influence on suicide and murder and reached comparable conclusions about the contagious power of imitation and suggestion (Johnston & Joy, 2016).

Although these early sociological and psychological examinations implied a connection between media coverage of suicides and homicides and a subsequent uptick in such events, research studies conducted during the 2010s provide fairly convincing evidence that the hypothesized link is real (Towers et al., 2015; Jetter & Walker, 2018). As researchers Michael Jetter and Jay Walker stated about their findings, "we believe this is the first approach . . . that allows for causal conclusions. Our findings consistently suggest that media coverage systematically *causes* future mass shootings" (Jetter & Walker, 2018).

Provided that this is the case—that the contagion effect is real and media coverage inspires additional shootings—some researchers have raised an important related issue. While "contagion" is a useful explanation for how viruses and bacteria spread from one individual to another, it is just a metaphor when applied to individual behaviors, such as a school shooting. Behaviors are not diseases that spread on contact. So, what are the behavioral mechanisms that may account for the spread of a shooter's murderous actions? Drawing on research examining social learning (e.g., Bandura, 1973; 1977) and imitation (e.g., Flanders, 1968), researchers have suggested that the fundamental behavioral mechanism of contagion is modeling, whereby one individual observes another individual performing a behavior new to the observer, notes the actions and steps involved in the new behavior, and later uses that information as a guide to reproduce the behavior (Meindl & Ivy, 2017).

Of course, effective modeling requires the observer to pay attention to the model, remember the actions the model performed, have the physical ability to reproduce those actions, and also have the motivation to do so (Bandura, 1977). A number of factors influence this process. For instance, an observer is more likely to imitate higher-status, competent models who get rewarded for their actions, but who remain similar to the observer in age and gender (Flanders, 1968; Meindl & Ivy, 2017). For disturbed and troubled individuals, the typically detailed and incessant media coverage given a school shooting invariably offers all the necessary information essential for modeling.

For example, examination of the statements and self-created archival documents left behind by the perpetrators of the Columbine High School, Virginia Tech University, and Sandy Hook Elementary School shootings (as well as other mass killings) show that the murderers relied on media accounts of prior massacres in planning and executing their attacks, related to and admired the earlier predators, and saw the carnage those mass shooters wrought as a yardstick by which to measure their own murderous efforts. As one researcher observed, "the entertainment form and logic of mass mediated news provides the inspiration and fuel for later killings" (Murray, 2017).

While the work of psychologists and researchers on social learning and modeling provides a solid theoretical foundation for understanding contagion effects, other observers and commentators—attempting to find ways to lessen the demoralizing frequency of school massacres—had already noted the possible connection between media coverage and additional shooting incidents. For instance, in 2015, a journalist from *Mother Jones*, Mark Follman, showed that mass killers looked to past incidents for inspiration and operational details to structure their attacks. His investigation of the "Columbine effect" uncovered at least 74 plots across 30 states where the perpetrators cited that shooting as a model influencing their own deadly plans. Twenty-one actual incidents resulted from the 74 plots, leaving 89 victims dead and 126 injured (Follman, 2015a). However, a major focus of Follman's reporting centered on ways the media might change their coverage of school shootings, to limit modeling effects and minimize future copycat incidents.

These suggested changes for reducing copycat shootings include not using the perpetrator's name in reports and headlines; not publishing images and "pseudo-commando" poses of the murderers; not broadcasting the killer's manifestos and essays; not fixating on body counts and sensationalizing the death toll (e.g., "the worst tragedy since . . ."). Such reporting modifications minimize the notoriety and perceived "glamour" that a disturbed individual expects to achieve with a copycat shooting, thus severely diminishing the motivation to imitate. Further, they are consistent with similar efforts to de-glamorize mass shootings. Such efforts include the "No Notoriety" campaign launched after the 2012 Aurora, Colorado, massacre, which urged the media to never use the names of mass shooters; and the "Don't Name Them" campaign, which has been endorsed by several law enforcement agencies (Follman, 2015a).

Despite precedents for this kind of limited, self-imposed journalistic censorship—reports of suicides, sexual assaults, and juvenile crime frequently receive similar press and broadcast treatment—critics have mounted strong arguments against such restrictions, framing them as in conflict with the news media's responsibility to fully report shooting events. These skeptics maintain that a full public understanding of the massacres requires disclosing such details, and that full journalistic disclosure is often necessary to correct the misinformation that often surrounds the initial accounts of a school shooting or other mass shooting event. Further, despite the anger and anguish that victims' family and friends experience when exposed to images and photographs from the scene of such attacks, some news organizations assert that they have a civic duty to publish such images. For instance, the *New York Daily News* justified such a decision because "it is so easy for the public to become inured to such senseless violence" (Follman, 2015a). Such decisions, though, open news organizations up to charges that they are engaging in prurient sensationalism for the purposes of selling their product.

Nonetheless, widespread agreement exists (e.g., Jilani, 2019; Keller, 2016; Pew et al., 2019; Tufekci, 2012) that news organizations have an ethical obligation to develop guidelines for covering these events responsibly (Follman, 2015a, 2015b; Kohrman & Reed, 2019; Meindl & Ivy, 2016; Schulman, 2017). While efforts to craft a set of industry best practices that minimize contagion effects certainly are useful, their ultimate effectiveness is uncertain. Substantial value conflicts will likely make it difficult to find solutions that correctly balance the public's right-to-know with journalists' ethical responsibilities to avoid inadvertently encouraging future shootings. Further, should *mainstream* media successfully develop and adhere to a set of appropriate practices, *social* media's freewheeling chronicling may nullify any benefits achieved.

FURTHER READING

Bandura, Albert, 1973. *Aggression: A Social Learning Analysis.* Englewood Cliffs, NJ: Prentice-Hall.

Bandura, Albert, 1977. *Social Learning Theory.* New York: General Learning Press.

Chatterjee, Rhitu, 2019. "Mass Shootings Can Be Contagious, Research Shows." NPR, August 6. https://www.npr.org/sections/health-shots/2019/08/06/748767807/mass-shootings-can-be-contagious-research-shows

Flanders, James, 1968. "A Review of Research on Imitative Behavior." *Psychological Bulletin,* 69(5), 316–337. books.google.com/books?id=FZEi7nvEseMC&printsec=frontcover&source=gbs_ge_summary_r&cad=0#v=onepage&q&f=false

Follman, Mark, 2015a. "How the Media Inspires Mass Shooters." *Mother Jones,* October 6. https://www.motherjones.com/politics/2015/10/media-inspires-mass-shooters-copycats/

Follman, Mark, 2015b. "Taking a Different Ethical Approach in the Media Coverage of Mass Shooters." *New York Times,* October 9. https://www.nytimes.com/roomfordebate/2015/10/09/how-should-the-news-media-cover-mass-shooters/taking-a-different-ethical-approach-in-the-media-coverage-of-mass-shooters

Jetter, Michael, & Walker, Jay, 2018. "The Effects of Media Coverage on Mass Shootings." I Z A Institute of Labor Economics, Discussion Papers, October. http://ftp.iza.org/dp11900.pdf

Jilani, Zaid, 2019. "How the Media Can Prevent Mass Shootings." Greater Good Magazine, January 22. https://greatergood.berkeley.edu/article/item/how_the_media_can_help_prevent_mass_shootings

Johnston, Jennifer, & Joy, Andrew, 2016. "Mass Shootings and the Media Contagion Effect." American Psychological Association. https://www.apa.org/news/press/releases/2016/08/media-contagion-effect.pdf

Keller, Jared, 2016. "Does the Media Cause Mass Shootings?" Pacific Standard, October 3. https://psmag.com/news/does-the-media-cause-mass-shootings

Kohrman, Miles, & Reed, Katherine, 2019. "Coverage of Mass Shootings Threatens Public Safety. Let's Fix It." The Trace, August 14. https://www.thetrace.org/2019/08/mass-shooting-contagion-effect-media-coverage-guidelines/

Meindl, James, & Ivy, Jonathan, 2017. "Mass Shootings: The Role of the Media in Promoting Generalized Imitation." *American Journal of Public Health*, 107(3), 368–370. https://www.ncbi.nim.nih.gov/pmc/articles/PMC5296697/

Murray, Jennifer, 2017. "Mass Media Reporting and Enabling of Mass Shootings." *Cultural Studies—Critical Methodologies*, 17(2), 114–124. https://journals.sagepub.com/doi/abs/10.1177/1532708616679144?journalCode=csca

Pew, Alex, Goldbeck, Lauren, Halstead, Caroline, & Zuckerman, Diana, 2019. "Does Media Coverage Inspire Copy Cat Mass Shootings?" National Center for Health Research, 2019. www.center4research.org/copy-cats-kill/

Schulman, Ari, 2017. "How Not to Cover Mass Shootings." *Wall Street Journal*, November 17. https://www.wsj.com/articles/how-not-to-cover-mass-shootings-1510939088

Towers, Sherry, Gomez-Lievano, Andres, Khan, Maryam, Mubayi, Anuj, & Castillo-Chavez, Carlos, 2015. "Contagion in Mass Killings and School Shootings." *PLoS One*, July 2. https://www.researchgate.net/publication/280030460_Contagion_in_Mass_Killings_and_School_Shootings

Tufekci, Zeynep, 2012. "The Media Needs to Stop Inspiring Copy Cat Murders. Here's How." *Atlantic*, December 19. https://www.theatlantic.com/national/archive/2012/12/the-media-needs-to-stop-inspiring-copycat-murders-heres-hoe/266439/

Zalatoris, Joanne, 2016. "Why the Media Must Report on Shooters and Terrorists." New America, August 25. https://www.newamerica.org/weekly/edition-132/why-media-must-report-shooters-and-terrorists/

Q21. DOES ALLOWING GUNS ON COLLEGE CAMPUSES INCREASE CAMPUS GUN VIOLENCE?

Answer: "Campus carry" refers to often controversial state laws that allow legally permitted students, staff, faculty, and visitors to carry firearms on the grounds and dormitories of public colleges and universities. These laws have generated passionate opposition and condemnation among gun control proponents, who argue that allowing firearms on campus will inevitably lead to increased gun violence, and make universities and colleges less safe (Everytown for Gun Safety, 2020; Giffords Law Center, 2018).

Equally passionately, gun rights advocates fiercely support campus carry laws, and assert that self-defense is a natural right that does not disappear at a campus boundary (Hsiao, 2019). In defending such laws, proponents argue that they are absolutely necessary to prevent college and university administrators from arbitrarily depriving students and faculty of their best self-defense option. For example, Catherine Mortenson, an NRA representative, notes that "Threats to personal safety don't disappear . . . on campus. Denying law-abiding gun owners their God-given right to self-protection on campus leaves them vulnerable to attack" (Price, 2017).

In contrast, the *New York Times* Editorial Board condemned allowing guns on campus, declaring the idea was based on a "bizarre premise that students will be more secure from the nation's epidemic of gun violence if there are more guns" (*New York Times* Editorial Board, 2017). The Giffords Law Center, one of the country's leading gun control advocacy organizations, agreed: "Calls to . . . allow college students to carry guns will only lead to more gun deaths and injuries, not fewer. Allowing guns on campus poses a grave threat . . . making the workplace more dangerous for university staff and faculty" (Giffords Law Center, 2018).

The empirical evidence examining the issue is limited, but suggests that fears of increased gun violence on campus have not been borne out as of mid-2020. For example, an analysis of Colorado State University's experience with campus carry showed that for the 12-year period examined, that campus experienced no firearms issues with any of their licensed CSU student carriers (Kopel, 2015). Similarly, in the two years after Texas allowed concealed permit holders to carry firearms inside buildings (and not just on campus open spaces, as was previously the case), Texas colleges suffered no uptick in gun violence. Lawrence Schovanec, president of Texas Tech University in Lubbock, characterized campus carry as a "non-event" at his university. Chris Meyer, associate vice president for Safety and Security at Texas A&M, echoed this sentiment, indicating that campus carry had "virtually no impact at all" (Warta, 2018).

While these indications suggest that campus carry has not *increased* gun violence, there exists little support for the opposite argument that campus carry makes colleges *safer*. For example, the campus carry law did not deter a 19-year-old student—ineligible for a concealed carry permit due to his age—from illegally carrying a firearm on the Texas Tech campus and shooting and killing a campus police officer in 2017 (Warta, 2018). Further, despite the possibility that armed, law-abiding individuals may intervene to end an active-shooter situation (an argument often advanced by proponents of campus carry legislation), it is just as likely that armed citizens will not. For example, several concealed carry holders at Umpqua Community College (where campus carry is permitted) did not use their firearms to intervene in a 2015 campus shooting. Faced with a lethal threat *and* an escape avenue, they chose the option that most rational individuals would: to flee rather than fight (Gilbert, 2017).

Opponents of campus carry have cited arguments other than increased gun violence for rejecting such legislation as well. They assert that campus carry imposes substantial additional insurance premiums on the institution; negatively impacts faculty recruitment and retention; heightens the likelihood of misplaced or stolen firearms; increases the probability of accidental discharges and injuries; has a chilling effect on free speech and contributes to a diminished sense of safety on campus; and makes suicide lethality more probable (Everytown for Gun Safety, 2019). However, overall, the available evidence does not demonstrate that campus carry results in an escalation of gun violence.

The Facts: Campus carry comes in various forms. Some states mandate that public colleges and universities allow firearms on campus (typically with certain locations specifically exempted, such as dormitories, classrooms, or stadiums). Other states allow the college or university broad discretion in determining whether and where guns are permitted. The remaining states all prohibit firearms and concealed carry on campus. As of 2017, 11 states permitted some form of concealed carry; another 23 states have left the decision to each college or university; and 16 states have banned firearms on campus (Hutchens & Melear, 2017).

While both Colorado in 2003 and Utah in 2004 had early versions of campus carry, the real driving force behind the movement was the massacre of 32 students and instructors by a lone gunman at Virginia Tech University in 2007. That same year, a group of students formed Students for Concealed Carry on Campus, later shortened to Students for Concealed Carry. The organization encourages legislation permitting licensed handgun holders to legally carry firearms on college grounds, both for their own self-defense and for the possible protection of others under lethal attack (Valentine, 2019). In championing campus carry legislation, supporters often emphasize scenarios in which armed individuals intervene and stop mass shootings (e.g., Brantley, 2017), but as suggested above, such interventions appear unlikely. Stephen Boss, a researcher at the University of Arkansas, examined lethal campus shootings between 2001 and 2016 and found no evidence that the legislation effectively prevents or deters such shootings: "Campus carriers have not intervened in any incident anywhere in the country on a campus" (Valentine, 2019).

In addition to its apparently limited effectiveness in stopping mass shootings, opponents have raised other concerns regarding campus carry. Citing research that half of college students are binge drinkers or abuse illegal drugs, these critics assert that firearms and colleges simply do not mix. They argue that alcohol and drugs impair judgment, and inevitably some students' self-defense decisions—about drawing a firearm, and determining to shoot or not—will prove faulty. Or, if these determinations are appropriate, a student's aim while firing is likely to be inaccurate (Everytown for Gun Safety, 2020).

Other detractors have suggested that student disputes and arguments could conceivably escalate into shooting incidents; and intense classroom discussions of controversial issues end in gunplay (Kopel, 2015). Additionally, opponents claim that instructors also are endangered by permitting guns on campus and in classrooms: an angry student given a bad grade or feeling disrespected may attempt to shoot the professor. Theatrically illustrating these fears, a Texas community college lecturer began the academic semester sporting a Kevlar helmet and bulletproof vest in class to protest the enactment of campus carry at the college (Hutchens & Melear, 2017). Still other objections center on the risk of firearms being pilfered from dormitory rooms (Everytown for Gun Safety, 2020); pistols being inadvertently left behind in bathroom stalls; and on shooting accidents that are statistically inevitable as students relatively unfamiliar with firearms acquire them (Valentine, 2019).

Proponents of campus carry argue that these are exaggerated concerns. They point to Colorado's experience with guns on campus. When Colorado's Concealed Carry Act was enacted in 2003, Colorado State University allowed their handgun-licensed students to carry their firearms if they so desired. As mentioned, that university experienced no firearms issues with campus carry during the 12 years examined (Kopel, 2015). Further, during this period, the campus experienced a 60 percent drop in reported crime. In contrast, gun rights proponents point out that the University of Colorado—which had claimed exemption from the law and did not allow campus carry until the Colorado Supreme Court ruled the prohibition unconstitutional in 2012—experienced a 35 percent increase in reported crimes. Noting that concealed carry holders are among the least likely to use firearms illegally (Kopel, 2015; Warta, 2018), and that the Centers for Disease Control and Prevention found that individuals use guns defensively much more frequently than criminally (Lee, 2018), an analyst of the conservative Heritage Foundation interpreted the findings this way: "the University of Colorado created a more threatening and intimidating educational environment by banning firearms than Colorado State University did by allowing students to effectively defend themselves" (Swearer, 2018). Of course, many factors in addition to campus gun policies are likely to contribute to campus crime trends, so these correlational findings must be viewed cautiously.

Additionally, campus carry advocates say that the experience of Texas with campus carry also indicates that these laws do not increase gun violence or put students at risk. One factor contributing to this lack of violence is that the law is relevant only to students aged 21 or older. This is the minimum age for obtaining a concealed handgun license in Texas, and in the majority of states. Thus, for most students—those under 21—campus carry legislation generally does not apply, and carrying a firearm remains illegal.

Further, despite faculty opposition to campus carry policies or proposals in many parts of the country, campus police departments that have firsthand familiarity with its impact have given generally favorable reviews. For example, Lt. Amy Ivey, of Texas Tech's police department, has asserted that campus carry has made the school safer, and likely deters prospective shooters fearful of encountering armed students and staff (Warta, 2018).

On the other hand, aside from deterring shooters simply *weighing* an attack, campus carry is unlikely to stop assailants resolutely *determined* to carry out a mass shooting. As noted earlier, campus carriers have not yet intervened in campus shootings anywhere in the country; and given a choice between fleeing or fighting, armed citizens are likely to simply flee (Gilbert, 2017; Torreano & Merkle, 2019). Even the argument that campus carry may reduce sexual assault crimes—a contention that supporters of campus carry frequently make—is uncertain. An investigation of sexual assault crimes on 54 college and university campuses, in three states and across 13 years, revealed that campus carry failed to reduce such assaults. Indeed, inexplicably, the trends indicated assaults *increased* after the introduction of campus carry (Biastro, Larwin, & Carano, 2017). Again, as cautioned earlier, findings like these are essentially correlational in nature, and meaningful inferences must be drawn carefully. Many factors likely influence whether campus carry decreases (or increases) campus assaults and crime.

Additionally, because gun violence on college campuses is generally quite rare (Pelosi & Johnson, 2014), some researchers and commentators have argued that campus carry addresses a relatively minor danger by creating a more substantial one. Citing data that indicate about 10 percent of college students seriously consider suicide each year, these critics further note that 85 percent of gun suicide attempts are fatal—a rate much higher than attempts by other means. Thus, by increasing students' access to firearms, campus carry may unintentionally amplify suicide lethality (Giffords Law Center, 2018; Torreano & Merkle, 2019; Valentine, 2019).

Nonetheless, despite opponents' many misgivings about campus carry, the available evidence suggests that concerns regarding increased gun violence, at least, are unfounded (e.g., Polumbo, 2019). While campus carry is unlikely to achieve the expectations of its supporters and stop mass shootings, it also is unlikely to realize the fears of its detractors and turn campuses into chaotic shooting arenas.

FURTHER READING

Biastro, Leslie, Larwin, Karen, & Carano, Marla, 2017. "Arming the Academy: How Carry-on-Campus Impact Incidence of Reported Sexual Assault Crimes." *Research in Higher Education Journal*, 32, 1–12. https://files.eric.ed.gov/fulltext/EJ1148907.pdf

Brantley, Max, 2017. "House Completes Passage of Expanded Campus Gun Bill." *Arkansas Times*, March 15. https://arktimes.com/arkansas-blog/2017/03/15/house-completes-passage-of-expanded-campus-gun-bill

Everytown for Gun Safety, 2020. "The Danger of Guns on Campus." December 22. https://everytownresearch.org/report/guns-on-campus/

Ewing, Maura, 2017. "Campus Carry: The Movement to Allow Guns on College Grounds, Explained." The Trace, April 5. https://www.thetrace.org/2017/04/campus-carry-movement/

Giffords Law Center, 2018. "Guns in Schools." https://lawcenter.giffords.org/gun-laws/policy-areas/guns-in-public/guns-in-schools/

Gilbert, Erik, 2017. "Campus Carry Is Not about Preventing Mass Shootings." Inside Higher Ed, June 12. https://www.insidehighered.com/views/2017/06/12/campus-carry-about-right-individual-self-defense-not-preventing-mass-shootings

Hsiao, Timothy, 2019. "I'm a Professor, and I Carry a Gun on Campus: Here's Why." Federalist, August 16. https://thefederalist.com/2019/08/16/im-professor-carry-gun-campus-heres/

Hutchens, Neal, & Melear, Kerry, 2017. "More States Are Allowing Guns on College Campuses." The Conversation, August 17. https://theconversation.com/more-states-are-allowing-guns-on-college-campuses-81791

Kopel, David, 2015. "Guns on University Campuses: The Colorado Experience." *Washington Post*, April 20. https://www.washingtonpost.com/news/volokh-conspiracy/wp/2015/04/20/guns-on-university-campuses-the-colorado-experience/

Lee, Timothy, 2018. "CDC Admission: Guns Used Far More Often in Self-Defense than Crime." CFIF, April 26. https://cfif.org/v/index.php/commentary/54/4038-cdc-admission-guns-used-far-more-often-in-self-defense-than-crime

Pelosi, Andy, & Johnson, John, 2014. "The Important Work of Keeping Guns Off Campus." Public Purpose, Spring. https://www.aascu.org/WorkArea/DownloadAsset.aspx?id=8726

Polumbo, Brad, 2019. "Myth Busted: Campus Carry Never Caused That Increase in Violence Liberals Predicted." *Washington Examiner*, December 13. https://www.washingtonexaminer.com/opinion/myth-busted-campus-carry-never-caused-that-increase-in-gun-violence-liberals-predicted

Price, Autumn, 2017. "Prof Quits Tenured Job to Protest Kansas Campus Carry Law." Campus Reform, May 9. www.campusreform.org/?id=9159

Torreano, Jennifer, & Merkle, H. Bart, 2019. "Guns on College Campuses: A Clash of Perspectives." ScholarWorks @GVSU, January. https://scholarworks.gvsu.edu/coe_otherpubs/1/

Valentine, Matt, 2019. "The Growing Crisis of Guns on Campus." *New Republic*, March 22. https://newrepublic.com/article/153356/growing-crisis-guns-campus

Warta, Joseph, 2018. "The Success of Concealed Carry Texas Public Colleges." Martin Center, October 12. https://www.jamesgmartin.center/2018/10/the-success-of-concealed-carry-at-texas-public-colleges/

Q22. ARE CURRENT GUN REGULATIONS EFFECTIVE IN PREVENTING SCHOOL SHOOTINGS?

Answer: Many gun control proponents maintain that "common sense" laws rigorously regulating the sale and possession of firearms (and thus keeping guns out of the hands of individuals who should not have them) are essential for protecting schoolchildren and curbing school violence. For example, prominent among the National Education Association's approach to enhancing school safety is a call for limiting the possession of assault-style weapons and high-capacity magazines—which the association considers weapons of war—to military units and police officers (NEA, n.d.).

Teachers themselves strongly agree that tough gun regulation would aid in preventing school shootings. A 2018 Gallup poll of 497 kindergarten through 12th-grade teachers (weighted to represent U.S. teachers nationwide) revealed that teachers considered restrictions on gun ownership the best way to prevent school shootings. In particular, they endorsed bans on certain types of firearms and stricter background checks on people seeking to buy firearms (Jones, 2018). Other proponents of gun control also have argued that firearm regulation reduces gun violence in schools. They assert that federal and state laws making schools "gun free zones" have significantly increased school safety (Giffords Law Center, 2018).

Further, some research at least indirectly supports the efficacy of gun regulation in making schools safer. In an analysis of student survey data collected over a 16-year period by the Centers for Disease Control and Prevention, investigators found that high school students reported fewer gun-related threats or injuries in states where gun laws were strengthened relative to states where such laws were relaxed over the same period. Additionally, strengthening gun laws correlated with adolescents reporting fewer missed school days due to feeling unsafe; and fewer claims of carrying a weapon (Ghiani, Hawkins, & Baum, 2019). As the researchers note, various biases (such as social desirability) may have influenced the teens' self-reported responses, so interpreting the findings requires caution.

Other survey evidence suggests that universal background checks (UBCs) may reduce adolescent gun carrying. Examining National Youth

Risk Behavior Survey data from 1993 to 2017, investigators discovered that 5.8 percent of about 180,000 respondents reported carrying a gun. However, a significant division existed within the gun-carrying cohort: 83 percent lived in states without UBCs, while only 17 percent lived in UBC states. Further, UBCs, together with the National Instant Background Check System (NICS), appeared to reduce adolescent gun carrying by 25 percent (Timsina et al., 2020). Again, as with all self-reported data, interpreting these findings requires caution; and the overall impact of such a reduction in gun carrying on potential school shootings is unknown. Nonetheless, these results and those above suggest that current gun regulations make students feel safer, and may diminish school violence.

On the other hand, gun rights proponents are generally skeptical about the effectiveness of gun regulations for reducing school shootings. They claim that the country's enactment of assault weapon and high-capacity magazine bans in the 1990s had little or no impact on gun violence trends in America (e.g., Gius, 2014; Koper, Woods, & Roth, 2004; Smart, 2018). Similarly, they see calls for even more stringent background checks—presumably "universal" or "private seller" background checks—as likely ineffective, arguing that even hardened criminals seldom obtain their firearms from private sellers (Alper & Glaze, 2019; Miller, Hepburn, & Azrael, 2017), much less underaged school shooters. Instead of focusing on gun regulations to deter school shootings, gun rights advocates propose strategies that "harden" school infrastructure (e.g., buildings having a single point of entry; interior windows made of ballistic glass), together with the presence of trained, armed teachers, administrators, and resource officers willing to confront school shooters (Shaw, 2018).

Overall, the effectiveness of current gun regulations for preventing school shootings appears limited. As gun rights proponents note, the gun regulations most often examined—gun bans, background checks, gun free designations—have had only modest success in reducing gun violence generally, and these approaches are unlikely to fare any better as school safety strategies. Gun control advocates contend, however, that such regulations are not enforced adequately or have big loopholes, greatly reducing their efficacy.

While untested, gun rights advocates believe that other strategies not focused on gun regulation may prove more fruitful. These strategies include efforts to develop emergency plans and create threat assessment programs (Everytown for Gun Safety, 2019), provide additional resources for counseling and mental health care (Jones, 2018), and offer firearms training support for school volunteers willing to challenge threats (Shaw, 2018).

The Facts: Individuals are fiercely divided over the role that firearms play (or should play) in making schools safe. On the one hand, supporters of gun control restrictions and regulations assert that firearms lie at the heart of the problem. They argue that strong gun laws—requiring background checks for all gun sales and not just gun dealer sales; banning the sale of AR-15 rifles and other semiautomatic "assault" weapons; banning mechanisms that convert "ordinary" firearms into automatic weapons; raising the purchasing age for certain guns; encouraging responsible firearms storage; passing "red flag" laws, and so on—are the most effective way to prevent school shootings (Everytown for Gun Safety, 2019; Jones, 2018). Going further, they assert that "guns have no place in our nation's schools" and suggest that even allowing legally permitted individuals to carry concealed weapons on school grounds (as some "gun free" school laws do) is dangerous and can "threaten the safety of children" (Giffords Law Center, 2018).

On the other hand, pro-gun factions argue that firearms—in trained hands—are a more likely solution to school shootings. For example, the National Rifle Association (NRA) has responded to the tragedies caused by deranged school shooters by calling for armed security in schools. In defending this approach, Oliver North, former president of the NRA, noted, "After all, we protect our banks, sport stadiums and office buildings with armed guards. Surely our children are more important and deserve at least that level of protection" (North, 2019). Further, many senior conservative politicians at both the state and federal levels endorse arming trained teachers and school staff (Litvinov, 2019; Horsley, 2018).

Modest evidence evaluating these two divergent approaches to school safety is available. As noted previously, a large majority of teachers at least believe that strong gun laws can prevent school shootings (Jones, 2018), and some findings suggest that such laws make students feel safer (Ghiani et al., 2019). Still other findings suggest that universal background checks may reduce gun carrying in the small percentage of adolescents prone to carry guns (CNN Wire, 2019). Additionally, proponents suggest that strengthening current gun regulations may further enhance their effectiveness. They argue that banning assault-style rifles, raising the firearms purchasing age, mandating background checks on private gun sales, and so on, can also limit shootings.

Gun rights proponents dismiss this gun-focused approach as simply a general response to gun violence and not specifically school-centric. The effectiveness of these measures for reducing *school* shootings, if achieved at all, is only achieved indirectly, from expected reductions in overall gun violence. However, gun control advocates suggest coupling these measures with additional actions believed useful for reducing school shootings. These actions include requiring schools to assess school climate and maintain physically and emotionally safe conditions; increase mental health services; train threat assessment teams; and share information across involved agencies (e.g., educational, mental health, law enforcement) when a student has threatened violence (Everytown for Gun Safety, 2019; Interdisciplinary Group on Preventing School and Community Violence, 2018). These proponents staunchly *oppose* arming school teachers and staff, arguing that teachers are not trained law enforcement officers and that "there is no reason to believe [arming staff] will help curb those rare instances of gun violence at school" (Giffords Law Center, 2018).

In contrast, arming teachers and staff is typically a central component of the approach advocated by gun rights proponents for preventing school shootings. The NRA is probably the most prominent champion of this strategy. For example, following the attack at Sandy Hook Elementary School, the association began a "School Shield" program in 2012. Typically conducted by certified NRA police instructors, the weeklong program offers specialized training for school resource officers, law enforcement officials, and other personnel having direct responsibility for school security. Coverage includes threat assessment procedures, building security considerations, emergency response protocols, relevant emerging technologies, and so forth (A1F Staff, 2019).

While the School Shield program focuses on already-armed law enforcement personnel and not unarmed teachers, a primary element of the program's philosophy nevertheless is armed security. Wayne LaPierre, NRA CEO, in describing the Shield program, noted the importance of building design, access control, and student/teacher preparedness for keeping schools safe, but sharply stressed armed defense (Mencimer, 2018). These same priorities were echoed by President Donald Trump in the aftermath of the Marjory Stoneman Douglas High School massacre in Parkland, Florida, in February 2018 (e.g., Rucker, 2018). Thus, Shield proponents advocate revising state laws that prohibit firearms in the classroom and strongly support arming appropriately trained teachers and administrators. For instance, proponents applauded the decision of 30 Utah educators to get tactical training from police instructors on ways to best respond to active shooters. The training was not limited to static target shooting. With cardboard props used to simulate hostages and assailants, participants navigated a school-like maze and, on encountering a student or teacher being held hostage, had to shoot the assailant without harming the hostage (Luebbert, 2019).

As gun control advocates (e.g., Giffords Law Center, 2018) have suggested, this type of armed-teacher response involves substantial risk both to the teacher and the hostages, because of possible cross fires, shooting inaccuracies, and even negligent discharges. Nonetheless, Sheila Brantley, NRA School Shield program director, argues that such risk is justified: "When a threat occurs, a quick and timely response by law enforcement professionals is what everyone hopes for. However, when time is clearly of the essence, the NRA strongly believes that trained school personnel can also serve a vital role" (Luebbert, 2019).

As with the gun control approach to preventing school shootings, evidence assessing the effectiveness of the school-centric approach is also limited. A primary reason for this lack of clear evidence is that schools actually are—and remain, in spite of the headlines—extremely safe environments (Giffords Law Center, 2018). Thus, it is difficult to gauge the effectiveness of policies aimed at preventing incidents that happen only rarely, even if each happening is individually tragic (Bump, 2018). In this light, it may be unreasonable to expect *any* approach—whether gun regulation or "hardening" schools—to prevent these horrible but uncommon events.

FURTHER READING

A1F Staff, 2019. "NRA School Shield Helps Schools with Safety Training." America's 1st Freedom, May 6. https://www.americas1stfreedom.org/articles/2019/5/6/nra-school-shield-helps-schools-with-safety-training

Alper, Mariel, & Glaze, Lauren, 2019. "Source and Use of Firearms Involved in Crimes: Survey of Prison Inmates, 2016." Bureau of Justice Statistics, Special Report, January 9. https://www.bjs.gov/index.cfm?ty=pbdetail&iid=6486

Bump, Philip, 2018. "The NRA's Solution to School Shootings: Making Schools Battle-Ready." *Washington Post*, February 23. https://www.washingtonpost.com/news/politics/wp/2018/02/23/the-nras-solution-for-school-shootings-making-schools-battle-ready/

CNN Wire, 2019. "Youth in States Requiring Universal Background Checks Are Less Likely to Carry Guns to School, Study Says." CBS 6, December 2. https://www.wtvr.com/2019/12/02/youth-in-states-requiring-universal-background-checks-are-less-likely-to-carry-guns-to-school-study-says/

Everytown for Gun Safety, 2019. "Keeping Our Schools Safe: A Plan for Preventing Mass Shootings and Ending All Gun Violence in American Schools." Everytown for Gun Safety, February 11. https://

everytownresearch.org/reports/keeping-schools-safe-plan-stop-mass-shootings-end-gun-violence-american-schools/

Ghiani, Marco, Hawkins, Summer, & Baum, Christopher, 2019. "Gun Laws and School Safety." *Journal of Epidemiology and Community Health*, 73(6), 509–515. https://jech.bmj.com/content/73/6/509

Giffords Law Center, 2018. "Guns in Schools." https://lawcenter.giffords.org/gun-laws/policy-areas/guns-in-public/guns-in-schools/

Gius, Mark, 2014. "An Examination of the Effects of Concealed Weapons Laws and Assault Weapons Bans on State-Level Murder Rates." *Applied Economic Letters*, 21(4), 265–267. https://www.tandfonline.com/doi/abs/10.1080/13504851.2013.854294

Horsley, Scott, 2018. "Renewing Call to Arm Teachers, Trump Tells Governors the NRA Is 'On Our Side.'" NPR, February 26. https://www.npr.org/2018/02/26/588865775/renewing-call-to-arm-teachers-trump-tells-governors-the-nra-is-on-our-side

Interdisciplinary Group on Preventing School and Community Violence, 2018. "Call for Action to Prevent Gun Violence in the United States of America." Youth Violence Project, February 28. https://curry.virginia.edu/prevent-gun-violence

Jones, Jeffrey, 2018. "U.S. Teachers Prioritize Gun Control to Prevent Mass Shootings." Gallup, March 22. https://news.gallup.com/poll/231224/teachers-prioritize-gun-control-prevent-shootings.aspx

Koper, Christopher, Woods, Daniel, & Roth, Jeffrey, 2004. "Updated Assessment of the Federal Assault Weapons Ban: Impacts on Gun Markets and Gun Violence, 1994–2003." Report to the National Institute of Justice, July. https://www.ncjrs.gov/pdffiles1/nij/grants/204431.pdf

Litvinov, Amanda, 2019. "Lawmakers in These 6 States Are Pushing to Arm Teachers." Education Votes, April 25. educationvotes.nea.org/2019/04/25/lawmakers-in-these-6-states-are-pushing-to-arm-teachers/

Luebbert, L. A., 2019. "Firearm Training Preps Utah Teachers." America's 1st Freedom, July 17. https://www.americas1stfreedom.org/articles/2019/7/17/firearm-training-preps-utah-teachers/

Mencimer, Stephanie, 2018. "After Sandy Hook, the NRA Made Big Promises about a New School Safety Program. It Hasn't Done Much." *Mother Jones*, February 26. https://www.motherjones.com/politics/2018/02/after-sandy-hook-the-nra-made-big-promises-about-a-new-school-safety-program-it-hasnt-done-much/

Miller, Matthew, Hepburn, Lisa, & Azrael, Deborah, 2017. "Firearm Acquisition without Background Checks: Results of a National Survey." *Annals of Internal Medicine*, 166(4), 233–239. https://www.annals.org

/aim/fullarticle/2595892/firearm-acquisition-without-background-checks-results-national-survey

NEA (National Education Association), n.d. "Three Keys to School Safety and Gun Violence Prevention." Accessed December, 2019. www.nea.org/home/54092.htm (URL no longer active).

North, Oliver, 2019. "President's Column | Arming School Staff Offers Stronger Protection for Our Students." America's 1st Freedom, March 19. https://www.americas1stfreedom.org/articles/2019/3/19/president-s-column-arming-school-staff-offers-stronger-protection-for-our-students/

Rucker, Philip, 2018. "White House Vows to Help Arm Teachers and Backs Off Raising Age for Buying Guns." *Washington Post*, March 12. https://www.washingtonpost.com/politics/white-house-vows-to-help-arm-teachers-and-backs-off-raising-age-for-buying-guns/2018/03/11/14da0c8e-253a-11e8-bc72-077aa4dab93f_story.html

Shaw, Jerry, 2018. "7 School Safety Tips from the NRA." Newsmax, March 20. https://www.newsmax.com/fastfeatures/school-safety-tips-nra/2018/03/20/id/849650

Smart, Rosanna, 2018. "Effects of Assault Weapon and High-Capacity Magazine Bans on Mass Shootings." RAND Corporation, April 22. https://www.rand.org/research/gun-policy/analysis/ban-assault-weapons/mass-shootings.html

Timsina, Lava, Qiao, Nan, Mongalo, Alejandro, Vetor, Ashley, Carroll, Aaron, & Bell, Teresa, 2020. "National Instant Criminal Background Check and Youth Gun Carrying." *Pediatrics*, 145(1), 1–9. https://pubmed.ncbi.nlm.nih.gov/31792166/

Q23. DOES DESIGNATING SCHOOLS AS "GUN FREE" ZONES INCREASE SCHOOL SAFETY?

Answer: Congress in 1990 passed the Gun-Free Schools Zone Act (GFSZA). With certain exceptions, this federal law prohibits guns in all public, private, and parochial elementary schools and high schools; and makes it illegal for unauthorized individuals to possess a loaded or unsecured firearm within 1,000 feet of a school (Shaw, 2017). Proponents of GFSZA assert that the law's impact enhances school safety. They claim that by removing (or at least reducing) the possibility of firearm injuries associated with escalating student conflicts, careless gun handling, and criminal behavior, GFSZA shields students from the type of gun violence commonly occurring elsewhere. These advocates further point to a general drop in the number of students reporting that they carried weapons to school, and a decrease in student homicide rates in the years following GFSZA's enactment, as indicative of its effectiveness (Giffords Law Center, 2018).

In contrast, critics of GFSZA—and gun free zones (GFZs) overall—are convinced that, instead of making schools safer, GFSZA simply makes them a more inviting target for potential mass shooters. For unbalanced shooters seeking to inflict maximum harm, GFZs (disparagingly referred to as "unarmed-victim zones" by opponents) are attractive because they are unlikely to house armed defenders. To buttress this argument, critics cite the manifestos, diaries, online postings, and conversations of various mass killers, where they explicitly highlight the "benefits" of targeting gun free locales.

For example, Patrick Crusius, the accused assailant in the 2019 El Paso, Texas, Walmart shooting that left 22 people dead and another 24 injured, wrote a "manifesto" to other shooters contemplating similar massacres. In it, he noted, "Don't attack heavily guarded areas. . . . Attack low security targets. . . . Do not throw away your life on an unnecessarily dangerous target." Similarly, Elliot Rodger, the mass murderer who targeted the University of California at Santa Barbara for a killing spree in 2014, explained in his "manifesto" that the absence of armed resistance in the area was a factor in his decision to attack there. Other considered locations might have had individuals with guns to cut short his attack. Likewise, the diary of the 2012 Aurora, Colorado, theater killer revealed that an airport's substantial security discouraged an assault at that location. Instead, he chose the one movie theater (out of seven nearby) with posted "gun free zone" declarations for his atrocity. Other mass shooters have displayed a comparable affinity for soft targets, leading opponents of GFZs to suggest that "however well-intentioned, gun-free zones do not work" (Parry, 2019).

Defenders of gun free zones dismiss the examples discussed above as misleading anecdotes. They label the notion that mass killers target GFZs "a lie that's been pushed for years by the National Rifle Association and other staunch opponents of gun safety laws" and cite an investigative report that examined 62 mass shootings over 30 years where "not a single case includes evidence that the killer chose to target a place because it banned guns" (Follman, 2018).

In an effort to resolve such conflicting claims, the RAND Corporation (2018) undertook an analysis of research examining the effects of GFZs on such outcomes as mass shootings, unintentional injuries and death, and violent crime. RAND found no qualifying studies that indicated GFZs increased or decreased any of these three outcomes. In explaining these inconclusive results, RAND suggested that the available data were neither detailed enough nor methodologically consistent enough to allow meaningful interpretation.

In the absence of rigorous research evidence, it is difficult to determine with confidence whether GFZs increase school safety as its supporters argue, or whether GFZs decrease safety as its critics contend. However, informal indicators suggest that many political conservatives have concluded that GFZs likely decrease school safety. This is indicated in the promise of President Donald Trump—and in the ongoing efforts of Congressional Republicans (e.g., Fearnow, 2019)—to eliminate GFZs (Jacobson, 2018). It is also reflected in the endeavors of Wyoming (NRA-ILA, 2019) and other state legislatures (e.g., Clark, 2017; Zercoe, 2017) to repeal such restrictions. Further, numerous commentaries typically penned by conservative pundits and pro-gun rights scholars (e.g., Hawkins, 2019; Knighton, 2019; Lott, 2018; Parry, 2019; Pratt, 2018; Schmidt, 2018; and others) have fiercely asserted that GFZs decrease rather than enhance safety, and should be eliminated. While gun rights partisans have penned many of these articles, even some sources typically favorable to firearms restriction such as *Salon* (e.g., Tesfaye, 2017) and the *Trace* (e.g., Shaw, 2017) acknowledge growing skepticism—presumably misplaced—about GFZs' effectiveness.

Nonetheless, these arguments have not convinced supporters of GFZs that such zones actually decrease safety. They maintain that GFZs effectively prevent gun violence by eliminating the possibility that gun owners might accidentally shoot themselves or other staff and students. Further, they argue that GFZs also insure that well-intentioned but untrained individuals do not intervene and inadvertently wound or kill an innocent person during a school shooting.

The Facts: No standard definition of a "gun free zone" exists. While the phrase generally refers to areas where a "typical" person cannot legally carry a firearm, each state independently specifies areas where firearms are prohibited (i.e., GFZs); and designates the classes of individuals (e.g., no one, law enforcement officers, licensed concealed carry holders, etc.) exempted from the prohibition. Airports, post offices, court buildings, stadiums, and other public offices are frequently GFZs. Further, business establishments such as restaurants and retail stores may also declare their premises gun free areas if they choose to do so (Shaw, 2017).

Additionally, Congress enacted two federal laws in the 1990s that specifically made kindergarten to 12th-grade schools gun free locations. The first was GFSZA. As discussed above, this act barred firearms not only on school grounds but also within 1,000 feet of the school. Individuals licensed by the state or locality to possess a firearm, such as concealed carry holders or school-contracted security personnel, were exempted. The second law, passed in 1994, was the Gun-Free Schools Act (GFSA). Aimed expressly at students, this legislation attempted to deter students from carrying guns to school. The act mandates a minimum yearlong expulsion for any student found in possession of a gun on school grounds. States failing to enact appropriate expulsion regulations forfeit certain federal education funds (Giffords Law Center, 2018).

Determining the GFZ's effectiveness for enhancing school safety is problematic, since students aren't allowed to have guns on campus anyway. Because schools are exceptionally safe environments normally, experiencing relatively few incidents of gun violence (Giffords Law Center, 2018), attempting to gauge the additional safety impact of GFZs is difficult and potentially misleading. Examining small numbers of relatively rare occurrences severely limits the statistical reliability of any findings produced. Thus, analysts have typically investigated GFZs across a broad spectrum of gun free locations. While this approach makes sense—if GFZs increase safety generally, it is reasonable to infer that they also increase school safety—it loses the benefit of GFSZA's explicit definition of a "gun free zone," and opens the door for researchers and organizations to adopt idiosyncratic notions of what constitutes a gun free location. Consequently, using different definitions of GFZs, investigations have generated noticeably contradictory results and conclusions.

For example, John Lott's Crime Prevention Research Center (noted for its gun rights perspective) examined mass shootings from 1950 to 2018 and concluded that 98 percent of the attacks occurred in GFZs. In contrast, Everytown for Gun Safety (noted for its gun control perspective) asserts that, from 2009 to 2016, only 10 percent of mass shootings took place in GFZs. These stark differences in findings result from substantial differences in the organizations' definitions of "gun free zones" and "mass shootings."

Everytown defines gun free zones quite narrowly, as "areas where civilians are prohibited from carrying firearms *and* there is not a regular armed law enforcement presence." The CPRC defines GFZs more broadly, as "places where it is illegal to carry a permitted concealed handgun, places that are posted as not allowing a permitted concealed handgun, places where 'general citizens' are not allowed to obtain permits . . . or [are issued] to only a very tiny selective segment" (Kelly, 2018). Pragmatically, CPRC's notion of a GFZ is inclusive, and considers even states without a right-to-carry or a concealed-carry law as GFZs. Everytown's GFZ notion is exclusive, omitting even schools if armed school resource officers are present (Sherfinski, 2018). Reflecting these GFZ definitional differences, CPRC classified 24 mass shootings as happening in GFZs between 2009 and 2016, while Everytown categorized just 16 incidents as occurring in GFZs during this time.

Similarly, the two organizations define mass shootings differently. While both agree that a "mass shooting" is any incident at one locale where four or more individuals (excluding the assailant) are fatally shot, CPRC specifically focuses on mass *public* shootings, that is, incidents occurring at commercial areas, school campuses, open spaces, government settings, religious houses, hospital/health care facilities, and so forth. CPRC explicitly omits incidents that happen in private residences, or that occur during the commission of a crime, or that result from gang- or drug-related violence (Kelly, 2018). The rationale here is that mass *public* shootings are typically uniquely motivated—killing as an end in itself—distinct from mass shootings where killing is merely instrumental to a more primary purpose (e.g., turf dominance, personal revenge, robbery, etc.).

Everytown does not make these distinctions. The organization's analysis of the 2009 to 2016 period found that the majority—63 percent—of mass shootings took place in private homes, usually linked to domestic violence. Consequently, Everytown's analysis for this period contains 156 mass shooting incidents, while CPRC's analysis includes only 28 (Kelly, 2018). These organizational differences in classifying both mass shooting incidents and gun free zones account for the startling discrepancy in the two organizations' conclusions.

Of course, neither of these analyses indicate that GFZs make schools—or any other locations—*safer*. Both really just gauge the degree to which crazed and unbalanced shooters might find GFZs attractive: perhaps only a little (Everytown) or perhaps quite a bit (CPRC). As noted earlier, the RAND Corporation (2018) investigated the evidence assessing the efficacy of GFZs, and concluded that the available data were simply insufficient to determine whether GFZs heighten or diminish safety. Nonetheless, logical considerations regarding the likely attractiveness of gun free zones to deranged killers seeking high body counts appears to have convinced many conservative politicians (Fearnow, 2019), state legislatures (Clark, 2017), academic researchers (Lott & Mauser, 2016), and average citizens (Bektesh, 2019) that GFZs decrease safety, despite assertions to the contrary by supporters of such zones (e.g., Giffords Law Center, 2018; Follman, 2018).

FURTHER READING

Bektesh, Alycin, 2019. "Without Conclusive Data, One City Grapples with Gun-Free Zones." WAMU 88.5, December 9. https://wamu.org/story/19/12/09/without-conclusive-data-one-city-grapples-with-gun-free-zones/

Clark, Kristen, 2017. "No More 'Gun-Free Zones' in Florida? Lawmakers Float Plan to End Them." *Miami Herald*, February 15. https://miamiherald.com/news/politics-government/state-politics/article132817159.html

Fearnow, Benjamin, 2019. "House Republicans Reintroduce Bill Eliminating All Gun-Free School Zones across U.S." *Newsweek*, June 13. https://www.newsweek.com/gun-free-school-zones-repeal-house-republicans-thomas-massie-1443921

Follman, Mark, 2018. "No, Mass Shooters Do Not Target 'Gun Free Zones.'" *Mother Jones*, March 1. https://www.motherjones.com/politics/2018/03/no-mass-shooters-do-not-target-gun-free-zones/

Giffords Law Center, 2018. "Guns in Schools." https://lawcenter.giffords.org/gun-laws/policy-areas/guns-in-public/guns-in-schools/

Hawkins, AWR, 2019. "Study: 89% of 21st Century Mass Shootings Occurred in Gun-Free Zones." Breitbart, July 31. https://www.breitbart.com/politics/2019/07/31/study-89-of-21st-century-mass-shootings-occurred-in-gun-free-zones/

Jacobson, Louis, 2018. "Bill That Would Ease Gun-Carrying Rights in Schools Passed House in December." PolitiFact, February 15. https://www.politifact.com/truth-o-meter/promises/trumpometer/promise/1356/eliminate-gun-free-zones-schools-and-military-base/

Kelly, Meg, 2018. "Do 98 Percent of Mass Public Shootings Happen in Gun Free Zones?" *Washington Post*, May 10. https://www.washingtonpost.com/news/fact-checker/wp/2018/05/10/do-98-percent-of-mass-public-shootings-happen-in-gun-free-zones/

Knighton, Tom, 2019. "Gun-Free Zones, Mass Shootings, and the Leftist Media Attempt to Hide Reality." Bearing Arms, August 1. https://bearingarms.com/tom-k/2019/08/01/gun-free-zones-mass-shootings-and-the-leftist-medias-attempt-to-hide-reality/

Lott, John, 2018. "How Gun-Free Zones Invite Mass Shootings." *Chicago Tribune*, November 20. https://www.chicagotribune.com/opinion/commentary/ct-perspec-mass-shooters-russia-public-shootings-thousand-oaks-mercy-hospital-chicago-1121-story.html

Lott, John, & Mauser, Gary, 2016. "Researcher Perceptions of Lawful, Concealed Carry of Handguns." *Regulation*, 39(2), 26–30. https://www.cato.org/sites/cato.org/files/serials/files/regulation/2016/6/regulation-v39n2-3.pdf

NRA-ILA, 2019. "Wyoming: Legislation Introduced to Repeal Gun-Free Zones." NRA-ILA, January 17. https://www.nraila.org/articles/20190117/wyoming-legislation-introduced-to-repeal-gun-free-zones

Parry, George, 2019. "Mass Shootings in Gun-Free Zones." *American Spectator*, August 7. https://spectator.org/mass-shootings-in-gun-free-zones/

Pratt, Erich, 2018. "Repeal Gun-Free Zones." *USA Today*, February 15. https://www.usatoday.com/story/opinion/2018/02/15/repeal-gun-free-zoneserich-pratt-editorials-debates/110464412/

RAND Corporation, 2018. "The Effects of Gun Free Zones." RAND Corporation, March 2. https://www.rand.org/research/gun-policy/analysis/gun-free-zones.html

Schmidt, Tim, 2018. "Why 'Gun-Free' Zones Don't Work and How to Survive Them." *Washington Examiner*, December 4. https://www.washingtonexaminer.com/opinion/op-eds/why-gun-free-zones-dont-work-and-how-to-survive-them

Shaw, Kerry, 2017. "What Is a 'Gun-Free Zone,' and What's behind the Movement to Get Rid of Them?" The Trace, March 16. https://www.thetrace.org/2017/03/gun-free-zone-facts/

Sherfinski, David, 2018. "Data Duel: Are Gun-Free Zones Really Safer?" *Washington Times*, August 19. https://www.washingtontimes.com/news/2018/aug/19/gun-free-zones-school-safety-tough-debate-settle/

Tesfaye, Sophia, 2017. "Armed for 2017: New State Gun Laws Shrink 'Gun-Free Zones,' Expand Access to Concealed Carry without Training or Permit." Salon, January 4. https://www.salon.com/2017/01/04/armed-for-2017-new-state-gun-laws-shrink-gun-free-zones-expand-access-to-concealed-carry-without-training-or-permit/

Zercoe, Cole, 2017. "5 Things to Know about Gun-Free Zones." PoliceOne.Com, February 24. police1.com/active-shooter/articles/5-things-to-know-about-gun-free-zones-ljkb8W6Vzyd5r9ac/

Q24. DOES ARMING WILLING TEACHERS AND SCHOOL STAFF INCREASE SCHOOL SAFETY?

Answer: The idea of arming teachers willing to use a firearm to defend students against deranged murderers has generated fierce controversy. Some opponents of the idea claim that the tactic is simply ineffective. For example, Adam Winkler, a UCLA School of Law professor specializing in gun control and Second Amendment issues, asserts that "there is no evidence to show that arming teachers will see a reduction of mass shootings—we've seen them occur on campuses where there are armed security personnel" (Rosenblatt, 2018).

Other opponents denounce the idea as too risky, noting that teachers are not trained law enforcement officers and that "an armed teacher is much more likely to shoot a student bystander or be shot by responding law enforcement" than to stop an active shooter. They also fear that students may acquire teachers' firearms, either by theft or unintentional misplacement, thus greatly increasing the risk of possible shootings and accidental discharges (Everytown for Gun Safety, n.d.).

Additionally, opponents note that the country's two major teachers' associations—the National Education Association (NEA) and the American Federation of Teachers (AFT)—are against the idea. Becky Pringle, vice president of the NEA, expressed her organization's opposition this way: "This idea of putting guns in the hands of educators: just no. Just no." Similarly, Randi Weingarten, president of the AFT, argued that "the one thing we do know doesn't work is . . . simply a reflex to . . . arm people" (Camera, 2019). A majority of teachers (73 percent) also oppose arming teachers, with only 7 percent endorsing this tactic as a likely solution to school shootings, according to one survey (Brenan, 2018; Jones, 2018). As one new teacher put it, "I'd feel as comfortable carrying a gun into a classroom as I would a bottle of bourbon. A weapon in the classroom destroys the environment I have to work so hard to create and cultivate. Guns have no place here" (Lucier, 2018).

On the other hand, some high-level conservative politicians and appointees (such as former U.S. President Donald Trump and former U.S. Secretary of Education Betsy DeVos) keenly believe that armed teachers already on the scene have a better chance of protecting endangered students from active shooters than police officers who have yet to arrive (Education Week, 2018; Montanaro, 2018). Similarly, several Republican state legislatures also think that arming teachers makes sense, and are considering loosening statutes that prevent teachers and staff from carrying guns in school (Litvinov, 2019).

Along these lines, the chairman of the Marjory Stoneman Douglas High School Public Safety Commission, Pinellas County Sheriff Bob Gualtieri, also supports allowing trained teachers to have guns on campus to defend against unbalanced assailants. Although he long believed that only law enforcement officers should carry guns at school, his investigation of the Stoneman Douglas attack changed his mind, convincing him that "if someone else in that school had a gun it could have saved kids' lives" (Associated Press, 2018). Of course, the school resource officer, Scot Peterson, was on-site and armed during the shooting at Lakeland, but he remained outside the building.

Without objective evidence, it is difficult to determine whether arming teachers is especially perilous, or whether it offers enhanced protection for vulnerable student populations. In this case, some empirical evidence exists. While limited to just one investigation, the findings nonetheless are straightforward. Using data covering all K–12 school shootings from January 2000 to August 2018, the prominent but controversial gun rights scholar John Lott found that schools allowing teachers and staff to be armed were safer than those that did not (Lott, 2019). The average rate of death or injury from a shooting during these years was 0.039 per 100,000 students across all schools versus 0.000 in schools with armed staff. Further, the study uncovered no incidents of students accessing teachers' guns, and only one accidental discharge outside of school hours.

The Facts: Calls for arming teachers to bolster school security began shortly after Eric Harris and Dylan Klebold carried out their ghastly attack on Columbine High School in 1999, and the idea gained further traction after the 2012 Sandy Hook Elementary School shooting (Rosenblatt, 2018). However, a number of important stakeholder organizations (e.g., the Major Cities [Police] Chiefs Association and the National Association of School Resource Officers)—as well as a majority of teachers themselves—have opposed the idea (Everytown for Gun Safety, n.d.).

Additionally, polling evidence from Florida—a state that allows teachers to carry firearms—suggests that the average individual is ambivalent about the movement to arm teachers: about half of the respondents opposed the idea (Newborn, 2019). Identical results were obtained in an online poll of over 500 parents of school-aged children, conducted by PDK International, a professional association of educators. The poll found that half the participants were against allowing armed teachers and staff, even if they had 80 hours of training and approval by the school board and local law enforcement (Blad, 2018).

Opposition to arming teachers and staff centers on several overlapping concerns. From a law enforcement perspective, armed teachers put responding officers in a problematic situation. As J. Thomas Manger, president of the Major Cities Chiefs Association, said, "A cop shows up and there's people with guns in their hands. We don't know who's the good guy, who's the bad guy. That's very dangerous. . . ." (Patterson, 2018). Mo Canady, the executive director of the National Association of School Resource Officers, echoes this fear of mistaken identity. He also asserted that without the extensive training sworn officers receive, teachers will have neither the mental and emotional preparation required for taking a life (especially the life of a student assailant); nor the physiological and fine motor skills required for accurate shooting. Further, observing that shooting in a crowded room or confined hallway invariably involves a high probability of hitting guiltless students or staff members, Canady also expressed concern that teachers will not assess shooting risks appropriately, and may fire even when the risks are too high (Canady, 2018b).

For their part, many teachers object to having new and radically different job expectations—for which they say they are woefully unprepared—thrust upon them. A nationally representative online Gallup Panel survey of almost 500 teachers revealed that 73 percent of respondents not only opposed suggestions that certain teachers and staff receive training to carry guns in school, but that 82 percent also asserted they would forego applying for such training, even if offered. Further, 71 percent of respondents did not think arming teachers would reduce the number of casualties were a shooting incident to occur; and 58 percent thought schools would be less safe if teachers and staff members were armed (Brenan, 2018).

Other opponents of arming teachers emphasize their belief that there would be an increased likelihood of accidents and unintentional discharges as the number of school-based firearms expands. Citing incidents where teachers and authorized individuals left their guns in bathrooms, locker rooms, and stadiums, these critics also worry that some misplaced firearms could find their way into the hands of students—with potentially disastrous results (Everytown for Gun Safety, n.d.). Further, in addition to the various life-threatening liabilities potentially associated with arming teachers, financial liabilities also arise. It is not certain that a school's insurer would indemnify the school against monetary claims should school policies or a teacher's action inadvertently fall afoul of state or federal law. Indeed, at least one insurance company (EMC Insurance of Kansas), alluding to the heightened liability risks created by firearms on school premises, has chosen not to insure schools that allow employees to carry concealed handguns. Similarly, Oregon's major liability insurance consortium surcharges school districts for each armed civilian employee (Hiltzik, 2018).

Proponents of arming school teachers argue that appropriate procedures exist that can minimize these concerns. For example, they have suggested that teachers who are going to carry guns in school receive practical, hands-on training not only in firing accurately in high-stress situations but also in rapidly evaluating whether firing is appropriate (i.e., based on the risks of injuring innocent others). The training would emphasize adopting a "defensive mode" in the classroom, whereby teachers understand that they only fire their weapons for the immediate protection of their students—that is, they should not leave their classroom or students to hunt down an active shooter (Canady, 2018a).

Further, despite the reluctance of most teachers to take up arms, almost one in five have indicated a willingness to do so, assuming school policy allowed it and special training was provided. Two-thirds of these individuals are "very confident" that they could effectively handle a gun in actual shooting situations, presumably because they already own or have experience with firearms (Brenan, 2018). Additionally, the reservations of police chiefs and other law enforcement officials notwithstanding (e.g., Patterson, 2018; Canady, 2018a; 2018b), patrol officers overwhelmingly believe (80 percent of more than 14,000 police respondents in one 2013 online poll of law enforcement) that legally armed citizens (which would include teachers) can reduce active-shooter casualties. Contrary to the fears expressed by critics of arming teachers—that cross fires and misses will cost innocent lives—less than 6 percent of the police respondents think that an active gunfight is likely to result in greater student casualties (PoliceOne.com, 2013).

Proponents of arming teachers also recognize that some teachers and parents believe that just the simple proliferation of guns on campus makes schools less safe, through inevitable misplacements, thefts, accidental discharges, and other carelessness. Addressing these concerns, they point to a possible compromise approach, whereby authorized teachers and staff would not carry firearms on their person, but rather access guns distributed throughout the school (like fire extinguishers) in sophisticated, tamper-proof metal safes.

One such system—the Active Shooter Response System—insets safes into corridor walls, and allows access only to those individuals who pass a dual authentication procedure (e.g., an RFID code card and a fingerprint/face scan). The system can also record the individual accessing the safe, send out a notification of access to a central control, and notify law enforcement regarding who accessed the firearm and where it was accessed (ASRS, 2019).

Of course, such systems are expensive, and even if employed, they may not fully relieve the anxiety of those parents and teachers fearing that guns in school are likely to do more harm than good. Further, as one observer noted, "it remains to be seen whether . . . teachers who oppose [arming teachers] would agree to teach in a school" where firearms are present (Brenan, 2018). Nonetheless, at least one incident (i.e., Aguilera, Gunia, & Law, 2019) has demonstrated that a highly trained civilian volunteer can succeed in stopping a shooting attack even in a crowded environment. Proponents thus emphasize the potential for highly trained volunteer teachers to do the same in school settings.

FURTHER READING

Aguilera, Jasmine, Gunia, Amy, & Law, Tara, 2019. "Parishioner Who Volunteered for Texas Church's Security Team Killed Gunman in Shooting. Here's What to Know." *Time*, December 30. https://time.com/5756485/white-settlement-church-texas-shooting/

ASRS, 2019. "Should Teachers Be Armed?" ASRS, July 31. https://asrs.io/should-teachers-be-armed/

Associated Press, 2018. "Florida Sheriff Supports Armed Teachers in Schools to Stop Shooters." Fox News, November 22. https://www.foxnews.com/us/florida-sheriff-supports-armed-teachers-in-schools-to-stop-shooters

Blad, Evie, 2018. "One Third of Parents Fear for Their Child's Safety at School." *Education Week*, July 17. edweek.org/leadership/one-third-of-parents-fear-for-their-childs-safety-at-school/2018/07

Brenan, Megan, 2018. "Most U.S. Teachers Oppose Carrying Guns in Schools." Gallup, March 16. https://news.gallup.com/poll/229808/teachers-oppose-carrying-guns-schools.aspx

Camera, Lauren, 2019. "Educators Endorse Safety Measures—Not Arming Teachers." *U.S. News & World Reports*, February 11. usnews.com/news/education-news/articles/2019-02-11/educators-endorse-safety-measures-not-arming-teachers

Canady, Mo, 2018a. "NASRO Expands upon Recommendation on Arming Teachers." NASRO, March 1. https://www.nasro.org/news/2018/03/01/news-releases/nasro-expands-upon-recommendation-on-arming-teachers/

Canady, Mo, 2018b. "NASRO Opposes Arming Teachers." NASRO, February 22. https://www.nasro.org/news/2018/02/22/news-releases/nasro-opposes-arming-teachers/

Education Week, 2018. "Should Teachers Carry Guns? The Debate, Explained." *Education Week*, November 28. https://edweek.org/leadership/should-teachers-carry-guns-the-debate-explained/2018/08

Everytown for Gun Safety, n.d. "Arming Teachers Introduces New Risks into Schools." https://everytownresearch.org/arming-teachers-introduces-new-risks-into-schools/

Hiltzik, Michael, 2018. "Column: One Big Problem with the Idea of Arming Teachers: Insurance Companies Won't Play Along, and for Good Reason." *L.A. Times*, February 26. https://www.latimes.com/business/hiltzik/la-fi-hiltzik-arming-teachers-20180226-story.html

Jones, Jeffrey. 2018. "U.S. Teachers Prioritize Gun Control to Prevent Shootings." Gallup, March 22. https:// news.gallup.com/poll/231224/teachers-prioritize-gun-control-prevent-shootings.aspx

Litvinov, Amanda, 2019. "Lawmakers in These Six States Are Pushing to Arm Teachers." Education Votes, April 25. https://educationvotes.nea.org/2019/04/25/lawmakers-in-these-6-states-are-pushing-to-arm-teachers/

Lott, John, 2019. "Schools That Allow Teachers to Carry Guns Are Extremely Safe: Data on the Rate of Shootings and Accidents in Schools That Allow Teachers to Carry." Crime Prevention Research Center, April 25. https://papers.ssrn.com/sol3/papers.cfm?abstract_id=3377801

Lucier, Peter, 2018. "Arming Teachers Is a Dangerous Back-to-School Accessory." Task & Purpose, September 6. https://taskandpurpose.com/opinion/arming-teachers-back-school

Montanaro, Domenico, 2018. "Who Wants to Arm Teachers? Republican Men." NPR, March 2. https://npr.org/2018/03/02/590308832/who-wants-to-arm-teachers-republican-men

Newborn, Steve, 2019. "Poll: Floridians Sharply Divided on Arming School Teachers." WGCU, December 27. https://news.wgcu.org/post/poll-floridians-sharply-divided-arming-school-teachers

Patterson, Brandon, 2018. "America's Police Chiefs Call BS on Arming Teachers." *Mother Jones,* March 8. https://www.motherjones.com/politics/2018/03/police-chiefs-call-bullshit-on-arming-teachers-sandy-hook-parkland-columbine/

PoliceOne.com, 2013. "Gun Policy & Law Enforcement: Survey Results." https://media.cdn.lexipol.com/p1_gunsurveysummary_2013.pdf

Rosenblatt, Kalhan, 2018. "Teachers and Guns: Inside a Firearm Training Where Educators Learn to Take Down Shooters." NBC News, June 19. https://www.nbcnews.com/news/us-news/i-want-be-able-protect-them-after-parkland—some-teachers-n882261

5

Guns and the Law

Almost from the country's beginnings, two great interwoven forces have fashioned Americans' relationship with firearms: the U.S. Constitution, acknowledging and endorsing a right for citizens to "keep and bear arms"; and a body of laws passed over the course of decades regulating and limiting that right in the furtherance of the common good. In modern times—starting with New York's Sullivan Laws in 1911, through federal gun regulation in the 1930s and 1960s, and continuing with additional federal and state legislation in the 1980s and 1990s—America has sought to craft gun laws that effectively keep firearms out of the hands of the lawless, the unhinged, and the irresponsible, while simultaneously not excessively impeding law-abiding individuals' rightful access to guns.

Americans frequently clash—often vigorously—in their assessments of how successful the country has been in achieving this conflicting balance. Some are convinced that current gun laws are inadequate, fall far short of preventing the "wrong" people from acquiring firearms, and therefore require additional strengthening to succeed. Others are equally convinced that gun laws are typically ill-conceived, inherently limited in their ability to stop gun crime, and continually infringe on a constitutionally enumerated right.

The five questions in this chapter touch on this divide. Two questions examine whether simple "tweaks" to the country's present approach to gun regulation might improve the system's overall effectiveness in separating firearms and unsuitable individuals. The first assesses whether current firearm laws are simply not enforced rigorously; and the second analyzes the likely impact that harsher illegal gun possession penalties would have on violent crime. Both ideas perennially surface whenever new gun laws are debated, often garnering bipartisan endorsement.

The next three questions explore constitutional limits imposed on gun regulation, and the impact these limits have on gun violence. The first of these questions evaluates whether the *Heller* view of the Second Amendment—that keeping and bearing arms is an individual right divorced from any militia requirement—makes the country more gun-prone and less safe. The second question focuses on government "watch list" individuals, and whether their continued ability to purchase and possess firearms (despite being prohibited from flying) contributes to violent crime. The last question investigates whether the strategy of numerous American cities and counties to declare themselves "Second Amendment sanctuaries"—and thereby nullify gun laws they consider unconstitutional—heightens the country's susceptibility to gun violence.

Q25. ARE AMERICAN GUN LAWS LAXLY ENFORCED?

Answer: A recurring assertion that invariably arises during debates about new gun control restrictions is that the country already has enough gun regulations to combat gun violence—and that the real problem is the poor enforcement of current laws. Further, both pro-gun (e.g., Keane, 2019) and anti-gun (Lopez, 2017) proponents appear to share this complaint, with both sides asserting that better state and federal enforcement of existing firearms regulations could prevent gun tragedies and limit gun violence.

The laxity these critics protest takes multiple forms. Problems encompass legislative carelessness in crafting enforceable gun laws; prosecutorial unwillingness to invoke available gun trafficking statutes; public agencies' neglect to follow prescribed criminal and mental health reporting regulations; authorities' failure to pursue background check violations; and police willingness to overlook blatant violations of firearm transfer laws.

An illustrative example of legislative laxity is the State of Nevada's passage of a private-seller criminal background check law in 2016. *After* passage of the law, a dispute arose over the database the background check would use—the FBI's NICS or Nevada's central records repository. When the FBI eventually declined to do the checks, the state's attorney general deemed the law unenforceable, and excused Nevadans from compliance. As Adam Skaggs, chief counsel of the Law Center to Prevent Gun Violence, noted:

"Had there been more communication . . . before the drafting process . . . this impasse could have been avoided" (Beckett, 2017b).

While legislative laxity in drafting implementable firearm regulations usually reflects simple carelessness, other lax enforcement issues have more complicated origins, and more severe societal costs. For instance, in the absence of a federal statute against gun trafficking, many states have passed state laws prohibiting trafficking (i.e., the purchase or sale of a gun with the intent to transfer it illegally) and gunrunning (i.e., the illegal transfer of three or more guns). These statutes typically have more severe penalties than simple illegal gun possession statutes.

The State of Illinois has all three prohibitions. Yet, despite making more than 27,000 arrests for illegal gun possession during one 10-year period, Chicago police made *no* arrests for either gun trafficking or gunrunning. Similarly, Cook County prosecutors pursued almost 10,000 illegal gun possession cases during one 4-year period, but only pursued 12 gunrunning cases, and no gun trafficking cases. Because trafficking and gunrunning laws impose a high burden of proof for conviction, district attorneys are unwilling to commit investigative resources to such uncertain prosecutions (Dumke, 2017).

Violations of background check regulations also receive scant enforcement attention. Purchasing a handgun from a federally licensed firearms dealer requires all buyers to complete ATF Form 4473, a questionnaire form used to identify "prohibited" individuals (such as convicted felons) who are not legally permitted to buy or possess a firearm. Penalties for lying on Form 4473 are potentially severe—up to 10 years imprisonment and a quarter-million dollar fine. Nonetheless, an FBI review in 2017 uncovered 112,000 instances in which individuals seeking firearms lied on Form 4473.

Despite having the names and addresses of these violators—information listed on the form—only 12 of those 112,000 individuals were prosecuted. Nor is such lax enforcement limited to just the federal government. Ten of 13 states that conduct their own background checks neither investigate nor prosecute individuals who lie while attempting to purchase a gun. California alone annually declines to prosecute about 10,000 individuals who attempt a "lie-and-try" gun purchase despite having some of the strictest gun laws in the country (*USA Today* Editorial Board, 2018).

Prosecutors similarly give low enforcement prioritization to a related violation of the background check system—"straw purchases." A straw purchase involves a nonprohibited individual (i.e., a person who can buy and possess a gun legally) purchasing a firearm for a prohibited individual (i.e., a person legally disqualified from buying or possessing a gun). Straw buyers incur the same potential penalties as "lie-and-try" violators, but these individuals also are rarely prosecuted. As Lawrence Keane of the National Shooting Sports Foundation, notes, "The law says that [straw buyers] could go to jail for up to ten years. . . . Why that doesn't happen more often is a question for . . . the federal judiciary and the Department of Justice" (Wang, 2015).

Other instances of problematic enforcement involve the military and other public agencies ignoring federal guidelines for reporting criminal and mental health adjudications to the National Criminal Information Center (e.g., *USA Today* Editorial Board, 2019; Lopez, 2017); and police willingness at times to ignore noncompliant gun owners who break the law (e.g., Beckett, 2017). Overall, given the current evidence, a conclusion that some prominent American gun laws are laxly enforced appears justified.

The Facts: For at least 55 years, politicians and gun rights proponents have refuted calls for additional gun regulation with the argument that America already has "over 20,000 laws governing the sale, distribution, and use of firearms." Representative John Dingell of Michigan first made this observation in a Senate subcommittee meeting in 1965, and it has been frequently repeated since then to suggest that current gun laws are sufficient to minimize gun violence—if they only were properly implemented and enforced (Kessler, 2013).

While the claim of "20,000 gun laws" is likely colorful hyperbole that gained credence through unquestioned repetition, the contention that proper enforcement of current gun statutes would eliminate the need for additional laws is a significant assertion. It implies that societal efforts to control gun violence put too much emphasis on passing laws and restrictions, and too little emphasis on implementation and enforcement. As one gun rights advocate has observed, the country seems better at passing gun laws than in employing them (Keane, 2019).

On the other hand, a simple focus on the *number* of gun laws—whether that number is 20,000 or 20—is potentially misleading. Most gun laws do not regulate the actual sale or possession of guns but rather deal with related peripheral issues (e.g., gun store zoning regulations, concealed carry restrictions, transport and discharge rules within municipal boundaries, etc.). These gun laws have little relevance to violent crime or to stopping malignant individuals from obtaining guns (Violence Policy Center, n.d.). Indeed, rejecting the assertion that current gun laws are sufficient to stop gun violence, some analysts have noted that the perpetrators of the Gilroy, California, El Paso, Texas, and Dayton, Ohio, mass shootings all used legally purchased firearms (Irby & Cadei, 2019).

Nonetheless, despite this disagreement about the sufficiency or insufficiency of current gun regulations, there exists a widespread consensus that important gun laws specifically tailored to keep guns from dangerous individuals are generally poorly enforced. Perhaps the most egregious example of lax enforcement are violations of the criminal background check regulations. As noted earlier, these nationwide regulations are designed to prevent "prohibited" individuals (including convicted felons, drug addicts, mental patients, domestic abusers, fugitives, and undocumented/illegal aliens) from purchasing firearms. Anyone wanting to buy a firearm from a federally licensed gun dealer (an FFL holder) must submit to this background check and complete ATF Form 4473; it is one of the country's primary tools for keeping guns out of the "wrong" hands.

Despite the ostensible importance of the background check system for limiting dangerous individuals' access to firearms, however, "lie-and-try" violations are rarely prosecuted. Some licensed gun dealers even compound this problem by knowingly making sales to prohibited buyers, even when the prohibited buyer answers the disqualifying questions on Form 4473 honestly, and clearly should be denied. Avery Gardiner, co-president of the Brady Campaign to Prevent Gun Violence, contends that the Bureau of Alcohol, Tobacco, Firearms, and Explosives (BATFE)—the agency charged with enforcing gun laws—has identified numerous dealers engaging in these illegal sales, but allows them to keep their FFL certificates. She notes, "Not only have these gun dealers evaded prosecution . . . but they remain in business profiting from illegal gun sales. . . . If it's official DOJ policy to enforce existing gun laws, why isn't the government following its own policy?" (Davidson, 2018).

Similarly, straw buyers also violate criminal background check regulations by falsely indicating on Form 4473 that they are the "true" buyers of the firearm when in reality they are purchasing the gun for someone else. They too are rarely charged. Despite straw purchases contributing significantly to the flow of illegally trafficked guns, U.S. Attorneys seldom pursue this crime because proving a straw purchase violation is difficult, and judges rarely impose severe sentences anyway. As one former ATF special agent observed, "Most federal judges look at [straw purchase cases] as a waste of their time" (Yablon, 2015).

Cassandra Crifasi, a gun control researcher at the Johns Hopkins Center for Gun Policy and Research, echoes these conclusions. She argues that "Prosecutors' decisions to bring charges . . . are going to be influenced by the magnitude of the penalty or the ease of getting a conviction . . . stronger penalties for violations increase the incentive for prosecutors to build cases against individuals suspected of engaging in multiple straw purchases" (Samuels, 2018).

Perceived difficulty in obtaining convictions is also the rationale typically used to explain failures to pursue gun trafficking and gunrunning violations (e.g., Dumke, 2017). Such convictions are difficult—requiring clear evidence that defendants knowingly transferred a firearm to a prohibited person, or knowingly transferred the gun for illegal purposes—and meeting this burden puts significant time and resource demands on the prosecutor's office. Given inadequate budgets and limited investigative hours, prosecutors do not want to waste effort on gun crimes particularly hard to prove. Nonetheless, critics argue that poor enforcement of gun trafficking and gunrunning laws is precisely why illicit gun markets continue to thrive.

While much agreement exists that authorities are lax in enforcing important gun regulations (e.g., Beckett, 2017a; Kopan, 2016; Lopez, 2017; MacBradaigh, 2013), the role of gun politics (e.g., Campbell, 2019) in creating at least some of this laxity is fiercely disputed. For example, in responding to political opponents' complaints about poor gun law enforcement, President Barack Obama observed, "those very same members of Congress then cut [BATFE's] budgets to make it impossible to enforce the law." Further elaborating on this idea, Sarah Trumble, senior policy counsel at the national think tank Third Way, asserted that "it is true that gun laws are vastly under-enforced, but . . . not because . . . law enforcement has failed; it's because they're written in a way that makes them impossible to enforce—intentionally. They're too vague to prosecute, the standards are too high to meet, [and] the penalties are too low to be a deterrent." Many gun control proponents emphatically agree, characterizing the underfunding of agencies (such as BATFE) and the legal ambiguity of some regulations as deliberate gun lobby strategies to prevent the enforcement of gun laws (Kopan, 2016). Gun rights proponents strongly reject such assertions, though. They reference the comment of Avery Gardiner (of the Brady Campaign to Prevent Gun Violence) about lax enforcement: "None of the gun rights supporters that I speak to think that felons should have easy access to guns" (Davidson, 2018).

Regardless of the underlying reasons for lax enforcement, the evidence confirms that poor enforcement of important gun regulations is a serious issue, and one that contributes to the country's gun violence problem. Authorities at both the federal (e.g., Department of Justice, 2019) and state level (e.g., Illinois State Police, 2019) have initiated policies to correct this situation, and these efforts may at some future point resolve the practical problems currently preventing the laws' effective implementation.

FURTHER READING

Beckett, Lois, 2017a. "Gun Laws That Cost Millions Had Little Effect because They Weren't Enforced." *The Guardian*, October 13. https://www.theguardian.com/us-news/2017/oct/13/gun-laws-that-cost-two-state-lawmakers-their-seats-had-little-effect-study-finds

Beckett, Lois, 2017b. "Nevada Voters Approve a New Gun Control Law—So Why Was It Not Enforced?" *The Guardian*, October 3. https://www.theguardian.com/us-news/2017/oct/03/nevada-gun-control-law-las-vegas-shooting

Campbell, Donald, 2019. *America's Gun Wars: A Cultural History of Gun Control in the United States*. Santa Barbara, CA: Praeger.

Davidson, Joe, 2018. "Lying to Buy a Gun? Don't Worry about the Feds." *Washington Post*, September 11. https://www.washingtonpost.com/politics/2018/09/11/lying-buy-gun-fear-not-feds/

Department of Justice, 2019. "Attorney General William P. Barr Announces Launch of Project Guardian—a Nationwide Strategic Plan to Reduce Gun Violence." Justice News, November 13. justice.gov/opa/pr/attorney-general-william-p-barr-announces-launch-project-guardian-nationwide-strategic-plan

Dumke, Mick, 2017. "Why (Almost) No One Is Charged with Gun Trafficking in Illinois." Pro Publica Illinois, October 13. https://www.propublica.org/article/gun-trafficking-charges-illinois

Illinois State Police, 2019. "Illinois State Police: We Are Improving Gun Law Enforcement." *USA Today*, March 6. usatoday.com/story/opinion/2019/03/06/illinois-state-police-we-improving-gun-law-enforcement-editorials-debates-3085716002/

Irby, Kate, & Cadei, Emily, 2019. "Fact Check: Were Existing Gun Laws Enough to Prevent Gilroy, El Paso and Dayton Shootings?" *Sacramento Bee*, August 5. https://www.sacbee.com/news/politics-government/article233541837.html

Keane, Larry, 2019. "It's Not about New Laws; It's about Enforcing the Ones We Have." Ammoland, February 19. https://www.ammoland.com/2019/02/no-new-laws-enforcing-ones-we-have/

Kessler, Glenn, 2013. "The NRA's Fuzzy, Decades-Old Claim of '20,000' Gun Laws." *Washington Post*, February 5. https://www.washingtonpost.com/blogs/fact-checker/post/the-nras-fuzzy-decades-old-claim-of-20000-gun-laws/2013/02/04/4a7892c0-6f23-11e2-ac36-3d8d9dcaa2e2_blog.html

Kopan, Tal, 2016. "Why Even the Gun Laws That Exist Don't Always Get Enforced." *CNN Politics*, January 9. https://www.cnn.com/2016/01/09/politics/Obama-executive-orders-gun-control-enforcement-gap/index.html

Lopez, German, 2017. "America's Poor Enforcement of Its Gun Laws Keeps Contributing to Mass Shootings." Vox, November 7.

MacBradaigh, Matt, 2013. "Gun Control Facts: Existing Gun Laws Would Reduce Crime, but These Are Not Enforced." Mic, January 14. https://www.mic.com/articles/22802/gun-control-facts-existing-gun-laws-would-reduce-crime-but-these-are-not-enforced

Samuels, Alicia, 2018. "Prosecuting Background Check and Straw Purchase Violations Depends on State Laws." Johns Hopkins News, January 23. https://www.jhsph.edu/news/news-releases/2018/prosecuting-background-check-and-straw-purchase-violations-depends-on-state-laws.html

USA Today Editorial Board, 2018. "When Gun Buyers Are Caught in 'Lie-And-Try,' How Many Are Prosecuted? 12." USA Today, September 19. https://www.usatoday.com/story/opinion/2018/09/19/gun-buyers-lie-and-try-only-12-prosecuted-editorials-debates/1288699002

USA Today Editorial Board, 2019. "New Gun Control Laws Can Save Lives, but So Can Enforcing Old Gun Control Laws." USA Today, March 6. https://www.usatoday.com/story/opinion/2019/03/06/enforce-existing-gun-control-laws-save-lives-editorials-debates/3065809002

Violence Policy Center, n.d. "A Brief History of Firearms Law." https://vpc.org/publications/cease-fire-a-comprehensive-strategy-to-reduce-firearms-violence/a-brief-history-of-firearms-law/

Wang, Hansi Lo, 2015. "'Straw Buyers' of Guns Break the Law—and Often Get Away with It." NPR, December 9. https://www.npr.org/2015/12/09/459053141/straw-buyers-of-guns-break-the-law-and-often-get-away-with-it

Yablon, Alex, 2015. "Amid Dearth of Federal Action on Straw Buyers, States Forge Ahead on Their Own." The Trace, August 21. https://www.thetrace.org/2015/08/straw-purchases-law-atf-gun/

Q26. DO HARSHER SENTENCING PENALTIES REDUCE GUN VIOLENCE?

Answer: Imposing tougher sentencing penalties is frequently suggested as a judicious response to gun crime. The approach targets individuals who repeatedly violate gun possession laws (e.g., felon-in-possession violations), and researchers (e.g., Kessler & Levitt, 1998; Owens, 2009) indicate that stiffer sentences reduce gun violence in two ways. First, lengthier prison terms insure that criminals using guns are "off the streets" for longer periods, and during this time, they obviously cannot engage in gun violence—the "incapacitation" effect of harsher sentences. Second, lengthier prison sentences can impact a criminal's cost/benefit calculations, with the risk of an extended prison stay outweighing the benefits of carrying a firearm during criminal activity—the "deterrence" effect.

Police and politicians often support harsh penalties for firearms violations. For example, over 90 percent of more than 14,000 law enforcement professionals responding to an online police association poll endorsed stiff, mandatory sentences with no plea bargains for individuals perpetrating a crime using a firearm; and almost 60 percent of them believe that increasing the severity of punishments for gun trafficking and straw buyers would reduce gun crime (PoliceOne.com, 2013). Similarly, politicians in Illinois have periodically proposed bills that increase the sentencing range on gun crimes in the hopes of reducing Chicago's notorious levels of gun violence (Pfeifer, 2017). In Baltimore, the mayor, the state's attorney, and the police commissioner have all in the past advocated for statewide mandatory minimum sentences in an attempt to hold gun criminals more accountable for their actions (Cohen, 2017).

Some empirical evidence indicates that both incapacitation and deterrence can diminish the level of gun crime experienced in a community. For example, in the late 1990s, researchers examined the impact of California's Proposition 8—a law lengthening the penalties for repeat offenses of several crimes, including aggravated assault with a firearm. They found that those crimes fell about 8 percent within three years, and were down 20 percent seven years later. Similar crimes (e.g., aggravated assault without a firearm) not targeted by Proposition 8 showed no such reduction (Kessler & Levitt, 1998).

Noting that the early 8 percent decrease could not be due to incapacitation—criminals impacted by the law would have been imprisoned anyway, even without an enhanced sentence—the researchers attributed this decline to deterrence. They concluded that other criminals, wary of the stiffer penalties, reduced their illegal gun activity. The investigators further attributed the continuing decrease in gun crime over time to incapacitation. Because convicted criminals were serving longer sentences and still locked away, they were not on the streets committing gun crimes (Francis, 1998). Other researchers have found that deterrence depends on several influencing factors (age, education, crime type, etc.) but primarily on how an individual values future occurrences. Harsh penalties are less likely to deter criminals who heavily "discount" future events (Mastrobuoni & Rivers, 2016).

Critics of enhanced sentencing question its overall effectiveness in deterring gun crime (Cohen, 2017; Okeke & Sakala, 2019; Yablon, 2015). They argue that research (e.g., Nagin, 2013) shows that the probability of being caught is a substantially greater deterrent than even draconian prison sentences; and that increasing the severity of punishment is ineffective because criminals are frequently unaware of the relevant sanctions for specific crimes (National Institute of Justice, 2016). Further, because such sentences are usually attached to crimes (e.g., drug and gun possession) that are heavily charged against minority members (Gaille, 2018), enhanced sentencing impacts Black communities disproportionately, and are often opposed by Black legislators as discriminatory in their effect (Pfeifer, 2017). Finally, some critics argue that incarceration is incredibly expensive, and lengthy prison sentences steal financial resources from alternative strategies likely to have a greater impact. As one skeptic put it, "It may be a better investment to put more squad cars on street corners than to jack up sentences" (Cohen, 2017).

As with most other approaches to controlling gun violence, determining the effectiveness of harsh sentencing for discouraging illegal gun use is primarily a judgment call. The evidence indicates that lengthy prison sentences certainly can lessen violence, gun crimes, and murders through both incapacitation and deterrence. But the drawbacks of this approach—financial and sociological—are high, and substantial controversy swirls around whether the benefits gained justify the costs involved. The empirical evidence is not yet sufficient to resolve this cost/benefit dispute.

The Facts: The rationale underlying sentence enhancement laws—sometimes called determinate sentencing laws, repeat-offender enhancements, "three strike" laws, and so forth—is that stiffer punishment for violent gun crimes gets dangerous individuals locked up and out of the community longer; and the lengthier sentences serve to discourage potential offenders from carrying firearms. The most extreme form of enhanced sentencing—mandatory minimum sentences for firearm offenses—dates back on the federal level to 1984 with the passage of the Armed Career Criminal Act. Addressing gun crimes committed in the course of another crime (e.g., an assault or drug trafficking), the act adds from 5 to 30 years to a felon's sentence, depending on the individual's prior convictions and the type of firearm used (Yablon, 2015).

Even before the passage of this federal law, other jurisdictions had enacted mandatory minimums for gun violations. For example, Massachusetts in 1974 imposed a one-year minimum sentence for carrying a handgun without a license. Similarly, New York passed a state law in 1980 imposing a one-year mandatory sentence on individuals convicted of carrying a loaded, illegal gun on the street, increasing the penalty to 3.5 years in 2006 (Yablon, 2015). Currently, virtually all states use some form of sentence enhancement as a way to fight gun violence (Francis, 1998; Restore Justice, n.d.), and the approach has support across a wide spectrum of constituencies—Republicans and Democrats, gun control advocates and gun rights proponents, conservatives and liberals (Denvir, 2013).

Despite such general support, sentence enhancement remains controversial. As noted, while harsher sentences for gun crimes may reduce gun violence by deterrence and incapacitation, opponents argue that this reduction comes at too high a price. They note that such sentences are typically imposed *after* a crime has occurred, and thus are inherently limited in their ability to reduce violence relative to strategies that increase potential offenders' expectations of being caught (e.g., through increased police patrols in the neighborhood); or through community-based solutions that attempt to alleviate gun violence by involving people in closest proximity to that violence. Citing programs like Safe Streets Baltimore (which treats gun violence as a public health problem and uses ex-offenders as mediators in neighborhood disputes), these critics (e.g., Cohen, 2017) see longer prison sentences as inferior to approaches that are financially much less costly and much less socially disruptive to impoverished families and poorer communities (Okeke & Sakala, 2019).

The issue is further complicated because sentence enhancement has racial implications, in that crimes with enhancements disproportionately impact Black offenders more than any other racial group (United States Sentencing Commission, 2018). For example, although designed to get violent gun criminals—hardened "evildoers" in Mayor Bill de Blasio's words—off the streets, New York's 2013 SAFE Act (Secure Ammunition and Firearms Enforcement Act) has primarily impacted young Black teenagers, almost all them charged with simple gun possession—not firing a gun, or pointing a gun, just having a gun. In about 70 percent of 200 cases examined, the defendants had no previous felony convictions. The defendants also typically claimed they needed the firearm for self-protection because they lived in gang-infested, dangerous neighborhoods (Bazelon, 2019). The argument is that people carry guns because they feel unsafe, but many of the very individuals most likely to fall prey to gun violence cannot carry firearms legally (Pfeifer, 2017). Regardless, under the SAFE Act, illegal possession of a loaded gun carries a minimum prison sentence of 3.5 years and a maximum of 15 years. For many critics in communities of color, the SAFE Act does not represent a targeted attack on gun violence as much as a targeted attack on young Black men (Bazelon, 2019).

Dayvon Love, director of public policy for a Baltimore nonprofit opposed to mandatory minimums, echoes a similar sentiment and raises a related concern, "They couldn't care less if this [enhanced sentencing] bill [has] the possibility of destroying the lives of black people who become more prone to violent activity because they were sucked into the criminal justice system" (Cohen, 2017). Love's concerns are not just speculation. Some limited research calls into question the belief that long prison sentences make offenders less likely to commit future crimes. To the contrary, prisons may "school" offenders in new criminal activities and exacerbate recidivism (National Institute of Justice, 2016).

Ironically, one oft-claimed benefit of mandatory minimums is that such sentences make punishment more consistent and fairer across offender groups by limiting sentencing discretion. In actuality, because district attorneys have wide latitude in the cases they choose to bring to trial, the potential for biases (racial or otherwise) to impact sentencing merely shifts from judges to prosecutors (Yablon, 2015). Further, even when potentially sympathetic judges have some leeway to modify an enhanced sentence—based on extenuating circumstances or potential for rehabilitation—the disproportionate impact on minority offenders insidiously remains. Minority offenders (just like majority offenders) are likely to accept an offer of a reduced sentence simply to avoid the risk of extended prison time—even if they might otherwise have beaten the original charge (Pfeifer, 2017).

While acknowledging that enhanced sentencing is a limited and imperfect solution to gun violence, supporters of the approach defend it as necessary and appropriate. They frame these measures as society's attempt to make a clear declaration about crimes that are simply intolerable. Further, pointing to substantial decreases in nationwide crime following a push for enhanced sentencing in the 1990s, proponents argue that, even with all its problems, the approach works (Yablon, 2015). Baltimore Police Commissioner Kevin Davis, for example, declared that the use of mandatory minimums "isn't about mass incarceration or locking up more people. It's about holding the right people accountable" (Cohen, 2017).

Two contrasting assertions succinctly summarize the dispute over enhanced sentencing for limiting gun violence. Opposing this approach as ineffective, Jeremy Haile of the Sentencing Project argues that "these penalties are limited because they address severity of punishment, not certainty. Because most people engaged in criminal activity do not expect to get caught, few think about the penalties they will face if convicted." Advocating for the approach, and defending New York City's enhanced sentencing model, then-mayor Michael Bloomberg asserted, "The NRA believes—rightly—that enforcing the law means prosecuting criminals to the fullest extent" (Denvir, 2013). In the absence of compelling empirical evidence, the determination of whether the societal benefits of enhanced sentencing justify its societal costs necessarily remains an individual value judgment.

FURTHER READING

Bazelon, Emily, 2019. "Charged." *Slate*, April 17. slate.com/news-and-politics/2019/04/slate-presents-charged-podcast-emily-bazelon-new-york-gun-court.html

Cohen, Rachel, 2017. "Reeling from a Murder Spike, Baltimore Grasps at a Gun Bill." Citylab, September 22. https://www.citylab.com/equity/2017/09/reeling-from-a-murder-spike-baltimore-grasps-at-a-gun-bill/540813/

Denvir, Daniel, 2013. "The Worst Gun Control Idea Has Bipartisan Support." *New Republic*, May 1. https://newrepublic.com/article/113088/gun-control-and-mandatory-minimum-sentences-chigo-and-philadelphi

Francis, David, 1998. "—David R. Francis." National Bureau of Economic Research, October. nber.org/digest/oct98/david-r-francis

Gaille, Louise, 2018. "11 Mandatory Minimum Sentences Pros and Cons." Vittana, February 27. https://vittana.org/11-mandatory-minimum-sentences-pros-and-cons

Kessler, Daniel, & Levitt, Steven, 1998. "Using Sentence Enhancements to Distinguish between Deterrence and Incapacitation." NBER Working Paper Series, # 6484, March. https://www.nber.org/system/files/working_papers/w6484/w6484.pdf

Mastrobuoni, Giovanni, & Rivers, David, 2016. "Criminal Discount Factors and Deterrence." I Z A Discussion Paper, No. 9769, February 12. papers.ssrn.com/sol3/papers.cfm?abstract_id=2742557&download=yes

Nagin, Daniel, 2013. "Deterrence in the Twenty-First Century." *Crime and Justice*, 42(1), 199–264. journals.uchicago.edu/doi/full/10/1086/670398

National Institute of Justice, 2016. "Five Things about Deterrence." https://nij.ojp.gov/topics/articles/five-things-about-deterrence

Okeke, Cameron, & Sakala, Leah, 2019. "Harsher Penalties Won't Stop Gun Violence in DC." Urban Institute, March 29. greaterdc.urban.org/blog/harsher-penalties-wont-stop-gun-violence-dc

Owens, Emily, 2009. "More Time, Less Crime? Estimating the Incapacitative Effect of Sentence Enhancements." *Journal of Law & Economics*, 52(3), 551–579. https://www.jstor.org/stable/10.1086/593141?read-now=1&seq=1#page_scan_tab_contents

Pfeifer, Jamison, 2017. "Lawmakers Propose Harsher Gun Sentences, Tiptoe around 'Mandatory Minimums.'" *Chicago*, February 1. https://www.chicagomag.com/city-life/January-2017/IL-Repeat-Offender-Law/

PoliceOne.com, 2013. "Gun Policy & Law Enforcement: Survey Results." https://media.cdn.lexipol.com/p1_gunsurveysummary_2013.pdf

Restore Justice, n.d. "Know More: Firearm Sentence Enhancements." Restore Justice. https://restorejustice.org/about-us/resources/know-more/know-more-firearm-sentence-enhancements/

United States Sentencing Commission, 2018. "Mandatory Minimum Penalties for Firearms Offenses in the Federal System." https://www.ussc.gov/research/research-reports/mandatory-minimum-penalties-firearms-offenses-federal-system

Yablon, Alex, 2015. "Mandatory Minimums: Can Tougher Sentences Curb Gun Violence?" The Trace, August 5. https://www.thetrace.org/2015/08/mandatory-minimum-gun-violence-policy/

Q27. DOES THE *HELLER* INTERPRETATION OF THE SECOND AMENDMENT MAKE THE COUNTRY LESS SAFE?

Answer: Because the U.S. Supreme Court's landmark 2008 decision in *District of Columbia v. Heller* made gun possession easier—it affirmed an individual's constitutional right to possess firearms in the home, unconnected from any militia service requirement—many commentators favoring strong gun control argued that the ruling made the country less safe. For example, shortly after the Court announced its decision overturning the District of Columbia's handgun ban and firearms storage requirements, Adrian Fenty, the District's mayor, remarked, "I'm disappointed in the Court's ruling and believe introducing more handguns into the District will mean more handgun violence."

Similarly, Senator Dianne Feinstein of California stated, "I believe the people of this great country will be less safe because of [the *Heller* decision]" (Temple-Raston, 2008). Further, even years after the ruling, other pundits continued to assert that the *Heller* decision made the country more dangerous. Dorothy Samuels, a columnist for *The Nation* and a former member of the *New York Times* editorial board, argued in 2015 that "By upending the well-established meaning of the Second Amendment, the Court made the country less safe and less free" (Samuels, 2015).

The implicit argument underlying these assertions is that the *Heller* ruling, by supporting gun ownership as a fundamental, constitutional right, makes the enactment of reasonable gun regulations more difficult. Assuming that such regulations typically make the community safer—the avowed aim of gun control—then the *Heller* ruling necessarily makes the country more dangerous and less secure. Further, particularly in terms of making gun control laws more difficult to pass and defend against legal challenges, some indicators clearly support this belief. For example, gun rights proponents immediately cheered the decision, and the National Rifle Association (NRA) promptly filed lawsuits challenging (and dismantling) similar handgun restrictions in other cities (Temple-Raston, 2008).

Additionally, gun control advocates—presumably wary of the long-term implications of the *Heller* decision on gun safety reforms—have actually begun to argue for repeal of the Second Amendment. After noting that the *Heller* decision "provided the N.R.A. with a propaganda weapon of immense power," former Supreme Court Justice John Paul Stevens wrote that "Overturning that [*Heller*] decision via a constitutional amendment to get rid of the Second Amendment would . . . do more to weaken the N.R.A.'s ability to stymie legislative debate . . . and make our schoolchildren safer than they have been since 2008" (Stevens, 2018). Other like-minded individuals have endorsed Stevens's call (e.g., Lopez, 2019; Mystal, 2019; Wedler & Miltimore, 2019).

Despite Stevens's assurance that repeal "would be simple," however, few gun control proponents believe repeal is probable (Berman, 2018). Further, while the *Heller* decision surely imposes limitations on gun regulation, these limitations are likely less severe than many critics fear. As other commentators have suggested, the Second Amendment—like all constitutional rights—is not an "all-or-nothing" proposition (West, 2015). The *Heller* decision itself explicitly notes that Congress still can enact reasonable gun regulations, with the expectation that future court cases will evolve and clarify the meaning of "reasonable" over time (Blocher & Rubin, 2018; Shelley, 2019; Toobin, 2012).

In terms of making the country less safe, the limited evidence is less clear. One analysis has indicated that the country's gun death rate increased 17 percent since the *Heller* decision, rising from 10.21 per 100,000 in 2009 (the year after *Heller*) to 11.96 per 100,000 in 2016 (Martinelli, 2018). However, these figures aggregate suicides, homicides, and accidents, and do not break out justifiable homicides. Thus they offer only limited insight into violent crime, presumably the primary dimension for assessing community safety.

Further, an analysis of the *Heller* decision's impact on gun homicides in the District of Columbia—the banning locale—suggested that lifting handgun restrictions had virtually no effect. Although the number of gun homicides dropped substantially after the 2008 ruling, the drop simply reflected an overall downward trend that started in 2002 and continued through 2012 before starting to rise again. Noting that homicide rates abruptly decreased nationwide in large cities after 2008, Daniel Webster, an investigator with the Johns Hopkins Center for Gun Policy and

Research, rejected the notion that the District of Columbia's decrease was due to *Heller* (Barton, 2017). Given that a whole array of broad social, economic, and political factors impact crime trends, it is perhaps not surprising that isolating the impact of *Heller* on violent crime is especially unclear and difficult.

Overall, the evidence indicates that the *Heller* decision has neither upended reasonable gun control regulations nor has it made the country noticeably more unsafe. While the ruling expanded gun rights, its judicial impact has been modest (Campbell, 2019: 125–126); and by legalizing individuals' ready access to handguns in the home—presumably discouraging break-ins and home invasions—supporters assert that *Heller*'s long-term impact may serve to increase rather than decrease community safety (Barton, 2017).

The Facts: Prior to the *Heller* decision, considerable ambiguity surrounded the "appropriate" interpretation of the Second Amendment. Proponents of gun regulation typically emphasized the amendment's introductory clause—"A well-regulated Militia, being necessary to the security of a free State . . ." as a clear indication that the amendment was explicitly about militia service, and simply granted Americans a *collective* right to an armed militia (Bogus, 2000). In contrast, gun rights proponents emphasized the follow-up clause of the Second Amendment: "the right of the people to keep and bear Arms shall not be infringed." They asserted that this follow-up clause represented the heart of the amendment, and demonstrated an *individual* right to possess and use firearms "outside of, or even notwithstanding, governmental regulation" (Bogus, 2000).

Despite advocates' claims that the "collective rights" model represented "a settled legal consensus for many decades" (e.g., Samuels, 2015), the *Heller* ruling questioned such assertions. Justice Antonin Scalia, writing for the majority, argued that an earlier Supreme Court case often cited as presenting convincing support for the collective model—*United States v Miller*—offered at most only a cursory analysis of the Second Amendment. In his examination of *Miller*, Scalia noted that the government's brief was quite short (two pages); provided little discussion of the amendment's history; and acknowledged that past court cases showed various interpretations of the amendment's meaning. Further, Scalia pointed out that the Court had heard no counterarguments or analysis, since one defendant had died and the other had disappeared. Finally, remarking on judges who possibly relied on *Miller* in adjudicating past Second Amendment cases, Scalia observed, "If [they did] so, they over-read *Miller*. And their erroneous reliance upon an uncontested and virtually unreasoned case cannot nullify . . . the true meaning of the right to keep and bear arms" (Campbell, 2019: 120–122).

While *Heller* supported the individual model over the collective model—much to the delight of gun rights proponents who saw the decision as a restoration of the amendment's pre-20th-century meaning (Cooke, 2018)—the ruling is not nearly as radical or as extreme as gun control proponents painted it (e.g., Lopez, 2019; Mystal, 2019; Samuels, 2015; Toobin, 2019). Scalia's majority opinion made clear that Congress still could impose reasonable prohibitions on the Second Amendment, even as an individual right. Further, some empirical evidence indicates that *Heller*'s practical impact on firearms cases has been modest.

For instance, researchers examined over 1,000 lower court cases since *Heller* where a litigant challenged a gun regulation as unconstitutional. Findings showed that only 9 percent (108 cases) succeeded, with the majority of unsuccessful cases failing because of "long-standing prohibitions" explicitly noted as permissible in *Heller* (e.g., felon-in-possession laws). More generally, about three out of four challenges involved defendants facing substantial prison time. These individuals had strong motivations to make whatever defense they could—including objections to the constitutionality of the gun laws they violated. Courts upheld only 6 percent of these Second Amendment claims (Blocher & Ruben, 2018). Thus, while *Heller* did make gun control more difficult—it tightened the judicial standard used for determining the constitutional acceptability of firearms restrictions (Law Center to Prevent Gun Violence, 2017)—it did not make regulation unduly onerous.

Has *Heller* made the country less safe, as critics suggested it would? This assessment is more difficult to judge. If we accept the assertion from gun control organizations, for example, that *Heller* has at least increased the number of guns criminals can steal from newly armed citizens (e.g., Barton, 2017), it could be argued that *Heller* has made the country more dangerous. But in the District of Columbia, for example, very few new guns were registered in the aftermath of the *Heller* decision (Barton, 2017). Further, even if law-abiding residents had acquired a significant number of new pistols and revolvers, proponents of the decisions contended that the decreased safety posed by potentially stolen firearms might be offset by the increased safety provided by readily accessible guns deterring (and defending against) violent crime (Barton, 2017).

More broadly, the empirical evidence regarding *Heller*'s impact on safety is limited. As noted, gun violence—as measured by homicides—decreased in the District of Columbia after *Heller*, but that decrease was part of a larger trend that had started long before the ruling, so its relevance is questionable. The other evidence—a 17 percent increase in the country's gun death rate since *Heller*—is also difficult to interpret. During the eight-year period examined (2009—2016), many economic, political, and legal influences, in addition to *Heller*, likely impacted the gun death rate, and isolating that part of the change attributable to Heller is impossible.

Similarly, the specific data used in the analysis are not nuanced enough to determine the primary factor driving the noted gun death increase. Is the increase due to a rise in criminal homicides? Did the percentage of justifiable homicides increase over the period examined? What part did suicides and gun accidents play in the increase? Without this information, drawing conclusions about increases or decreases in community safety is simply speculative. Thus, overall, despite its legal significance in America's gun culture wars, a reasonable assessment of *Heller* is that the ruling has had limited practical impact in shaping gun regulations, and has not made the country noticeably less—or more—safe.

FURTHER READING

Barton, Ethan, 2017. "Eliminating DC's Handgun Ban Had No Effect on Homicides." Daily Caller, April 17. https://dailycallernewsfoundation.org/2017/04/17/eliminating-dcs-handgun-ban-had-no-effect-on-homicides/

Berman, Russell, 2018. "Where the Gun-Control Movement Goes Silent." *Atlantic*, March 1. https://www.theatlantic.com/politics/archive/2018/03/gun-second-amendment-repeal/554540/

Blocher, Joseph, & Ruben, Eric, 2018. "The Second Amendment Allows for More Gun Control than You Think." Vox, June 14. https://www.vox.com/the-big-idea/2018/5/23/17383644/second-2nd-amendment-gun-control-debate-santa-fe-parkland-heller-anniversary-constitution

Bogus, Carl, 2000. "The History and Politics of Second Amendment Scholarship: A Primer." *Chicago-Kent Law Review*, 76(3), 1–25. https://scholarship.kentlaw.iit.edu/cgi/viewcontent.cgi?article=3286&context=cklawreview

Campbell, Donald, 2019. *America's Gun Wars: A Cultural History of Gun Control in the United States.* Santa Barbara, CA: Praeger.

Cooke, Charles, 2018. "The Truth about the Second Amendment." *National Review*, August 9. https://www.nationalreview.com/magazine/2018/08/27/the-truth-about-the-second-amendment/

Law Center to Prevent Gun Violence, 2017. "Post-*Heller* Litigation Summary." Law Center to Prevent Gun Violence, April. https://giffords.org/lawcenter/gun-laws/litigation/post-heller-litigation-summary/

Lopez, German, 2019. "Democrats Have Been Discussing the Same Ideas on Guns for 25 Years. It's Time to Change That." Vox, October 2. https://www.vox.com/policy-and-politics/2019/7/1/18683860/democrats-2020-gun-control-mass-shootings

Martinelli, Sally, 2018. "U.S. Gun Death Rate Jumps 17 Percent since 2008 Supreme Court *District of Columbia v. Heller* Decision Affirming Right to Own a Handgun for Self-Defense." Violence Policy Center, January 17. vpc.org/press/u-s-gun-death-rate-jumps-17-percent-since-2008-supreme-court-district-of-columbia-v-heller-decision-affirming-right-to-own-a-handgun-for-self-defense/

Mystal, Elie, 2019. "It's Time to Repeal—and Replace—the Second Amendment." *The Nation*, August 7. https://www.thenation.com/article/archive/repeal-second-amendment-gun-control/

Samuels, Dorothy, 2015. "The Second Amendment Was Never Meant to Protect an Individual's Right to a Gun." *The Nation*, September 23. https://www.thenation.com/article/archive/how-the-roberts-court-undermined-sensible-gun-control/

Shelley, Susan, 2019. "The U.S. Supreme Court and the Second Amendment." *Orange County Register*, February 11. https://www.ocregister.com/2019/02/09/the-u-s-supreme-court-and-the-second-amendment/

Stevens, John Paul, 2018. "John Paul Stevens: Repeal the Second Amendment." *New York Times*, March 27. https://www.nytimes.com/2018/03/27/opinion/john-paul-stevens-repeal-second-amendment.html

Temple-Raston, Dina, 2008. "Supreme Court: Individuals Have Right to Bear Arms." NPR, June 26. https://www.npr.org/templates/story/story.php?storyid=91911807

Toobin, Jeffrey, 2012. "So You Think You Know the Second Amendment?" *New Yorker*, December 17. https://www.newyorker.com/news/daily-comment/so-you-think-you-know-the-second-amendment

Toobin, Jeffrey, 2019. "Politics Changed the Reading of the Second Amendment—and Can Change It Again." *New Yorker*, August 5. https://www.newyorker.com/news/daily-comment/politics-changed-the-reading-of-the-second-amendmentand-can-change-it-again

Wedler, Carey, & Miltimore, Jon, 2019. "Lawmakers in Hawaii Propose Repealing Second Amendment." Foundation for Economic Education, March 7. https://fee.org/articles/lawmakers-in-hawaii-propose-repealing-second-amendment/

West, Sonja, 2015. "The Second Amendment Is Not Absolute." *Slate*, December 7. https://slate.com/news-and-politics/2015/12/second-amendment-allows-for-gun-control.html

Q28. DOES ALLOWING "WATCH LIST" INDIVIDUALS TO BUY GUNS REDUCE GENERAL SAFETY?

Answer: Managed by the Federal Bureau of Investigation and commonly known as "the watch list," the Terrorist Screening Database (TSDB) is a single central database containing the identities and other details of individuals "known or reasonably suspected of being involved in terrorist activity" (Terrorist Screening Center, n.d.). In turn, various government agencies use the TSDB to create focused screening systems and watch lists, such as the Department of Homeland Security's Selectee List (targeting selected air passengers for additional inspection) and its No Fly List (identifying individuals prohibited from commercial air travel into, out of, or within the United States).

Politically, the TSDB—and the No Fly List in particular—has been controversial. Many prominent politicians, including Senator Dianne Feinstein, former secretary of state Hillary Clinton, and former president Barack Obama, have suggested using the No Fly List to ban listed individuals from purchasing firearms. In an Oval Office televised address, President Obama asked, "What could possibly be the argument for allowing a terrorist suspect to buy a semiautomatic weapon?" (*L.A. Times* Editorial Board, 2015). On another occasion, he tweeted, "Closing the No-Fly loophole is a no-brainer" (Smith, 2015). Similarly, Hillary Clinton observed, "If you are too dangerous to get on a plane, you are too dangerous to buy a gun in America" (Stern, 2016).

In 2015, Democratic senator Dianne Feinstein of California reintroduced legislation in 2015 to ban not only those on the No Fly List from buying guns, but everyone listed in the broader TSDB (Lesniewski, 2016). As Feinstein put it, "I'd like to try again. . . . The ease with which a potential terrorist can buy a weapon in this country is frightening" (Stern, 2016). While this legislative effort did not succeed, the idea continues to have widespread appeal. In 2018, U.S. senators Susan Collins from Maine and Heidi Heitkamp from North Dakota introduced a similar but narrower bill focused on just the No Fly and Selectee lists. Collins asserted that "This bill is a sensible step . . . [to] close the loophole that allows known and suspected terrorists to legally purchase firearms," a sentiment her cosponsors all echoed (Collins, 2018).

Three factors made these efforts controversial. First, the No Fly List, as well as the broader TSDB, is not especially accurate in identifying suspected terrorists. Detractors of the lists have variously described them as "mistake-ridden" and "notoriously inaccurate" (Stern, 2016); "opaque" and "arbitrary"

(Codrea, 2019); and "error-prone" and "unreliable" (Kassem, 2016). In one egregious no-fly blunder, an airline prevented an 18-month-old child from flying because her name was on the list. In another widely publicized mistake, Senator Edward Kennedy was stopped and questioned on several occasions at different airports because terrorist suspects apparently used "T. Kennedy" as an alias. Problems of mistaken identity—confusing people with similar names—have plagued the lists (Smith, 2015).

Second, because the lists' basic dimensions (e.g., the number of individuals included, the criteria for inclusion, etc.) are classified, critics argue that the lists' lack of transparency compromise constitutional guarantees of due process. Noting that inclusion on the list does not require concrete facts but merely "a reasonable suspicion" of some connection to terrorism, one commentator observed that "reasonable suspicion is the low standard by which your rights are trampled if you have the misfortune of [being nonwhite or Muslim]" (Kassem, 2016).

Finally, along similar due process lines, opponents object to using the terrorist lists to bar individuals from gun purchases because citizens only *suspected* of terrorism are still considered innocent, and still retain their constitutional rights—including the right to keep and bear firearms. As the Editorial Board of the *L.A. Times* argued, "citizens would be barred from exercising a constitutional right . . . we find it dangerous to let the government restrict the exercise of a right based on mere suspicion." Further, indirect empirical evidence suggests that upholding this gun right does *not* come at the cost of reduced general safety. More than 2,000 people on the No Fly List passed background requirements and legally purchased firearms between 2004 and 2014. No evidence indicates that any of these guns were used in a crime, much less in an act of terrorism (*L.A. Times* Editorial Board, 2015).

The Facts: Established in 2003, the FBI's Terrorist Screening Center consolidated about a dozen lists of known or suspected terrorists that various federal agencies had been using into a single integrated database known as the TSDB (Fram, 2016). With the creation of the TSDB, the different agencies were able to use the database to tailor more comprehensive watch lists that still centered on their own particular security responsibilities. Additionally, the National Counterterrorism Center (NCTC) also maintains a terrorist database—the Terrorist Identities Datamart Environment (TIDE)—dedicated specifically to international terrorists.

Thus, "terrorist watch list" is an imprecise designation that may refer to any number of terrorist lists. This, together with the secrecy that surrounds all the lists—the government neither confirms nor denies any information on federal watch lists (Kassem, 2016)—means that different sources offer different estimates for the number of people included on watch lists. But whatever the actual number, the estimates all agree that the numbers have ballooned over time. For example, the *L.A. Times* suggested that the TSDB contained about 480,000 names in 2011, swelling to 1.1 million in 2015 (*L.A. Times* Editorial Board, 2015). Other sources (Fram, 2016; Giffords Law Center, n.d.; Smith, 2015) provided lower estimates, but still placed the count at 700,000 or 800,000 for the 2014/2015 period.

Similarly, the No Fly List, which contained only 16 names on September 11, 2001, when the United States suffered its worst-ever terrorist attack, had expanded to 81,000 by 2016 (Kassem, 2016). Another source reported that in the two-year period between September 2011 and August 2013, the size of the list almost tripled, from 16,000 to 47,000 (Smith, 2015); and by 2014, the list had about 64,000 names (Fram, 2016). Although the vast majority of people on the No Fly List and in the broader TSDB database are foreigners (and thus already barred from purchasing guns in the United States), the lists still impact a significant number of Americans—about 1,300 individuals on the No Fly List (Fram, 2016) and about 10,000 in the TSDB (*L.A. Times* Editorial Board, 2015) in the mid-2010s. The lists' critics argue that the inclusion standards are vague, overbroad, and unduly inflate the size of lists—and inevitably lead to identity mix-ups that hamper the effectiveness of the lists (Smith, 2015).

As noted earlier, the lists' constitutional problems center on these inclusion standards. The lists use "predictive assessments" about potential threats to determine who gets subject to further scrutiny or stopped from flying—not records of past demonstrated offenses. In essence, individuals are targeted based on what the government *thinks* they might do rather than on what they have already done. For example, actually engaging in terrorism is not a requirement for an individual's inclusion on the list. A tenuous connection to merely a *suspected* terrorist—if it arouses "reasonable" suspicion—is enough. Thus, business associates, siblings, parents, and other relatives of the suspected individual may also land on the list. As one federal prosecutor noted, "These lists are horribly imprecise. They are based on rumor and innuendo, and it's incredibly easy to get on the list and incredibly difficult to get off the list. There's no due process for getting off the list" (Zetter, 2016).

While the government asserts that revealing the kinds of information used for placing individuals on watch lists would put "highly sensitive national security information directly in the hands of terrorist organizations and other adversaries" (Ackerman, 2015), civil libertarians counter that governmental "guesses or hunches, or the reporting of suspicious activity alone, are not sufficient to establish [even] reasonable suspicion," let alone probable cause (Ackerman, 2015).

Because of these due process issues with terrorist watch lists, even some normally "anti-gun" advocates have questioned the wisdom of using the lists for gun prohibition. *Slate*'s Mark Stern is representative: "If the government can revoke your rights to access firearms simply because it has decided to place you on a secret, notoriously inaccurate list, it could presumably restrict your other rights. . . . You could be forbidden from advocating for causes you believe in. . . . And you would have no recourse: The government could simply declare that, as a name on a covert list, you are owed no due process at all" (Stern, 2016).

Nonetheless, despite these due process concerns, other gun control proponents (e.g., Everytown for Gun Safety, 2015) appear to believe the increase in safety possibly gained by banning watched individuals from gun purchases (and gun possession) warrants the curtailment of these citizens' constitutional rights. Noting that the perpetrators involved in mass shootings at Fort Hood, Texas (2009) and Orlando, Florida (2016) had been on watchlists as potential terrorists, they question why such individuals were nevertheless still able buy guns (Giffords Law Center, n.d.). To remedy the problem, they point to New Jersey's "Terror Gap" law—which simply added a new "prohibited" background check category for any person named in the TSDB—as a potential model for federal legislation (Giffords Law Center, 2018).

How serious a threat to general safety are terrorist-watched individuals? Certainly, some of the 40,000 Americans in the TSDB (Ingraham, 2016) are truly a threat. For example, Omar Mateen, the American mass murderer responsible for the Pulse nightclub massacre, had been on the FBI's terrorist watch list for almost a year, and had been interviewed three times by federal agents, prior to his attack. Yet, since he did not fall into any of the gun-buying background check prohibited categories, he remained legally qualified to purchase firearms (Lichtblau & Apuzzo, 2016).

Between 2004 and 2015, about 2,477 terrorist-watched Americans attempted to purchase firearms legally, and underwent the firearms background check system. More than 90 percent of these individuals (2,265 purchasers) passed the background check and qualified to buy a gun (Ingraham, 2016). Gun control advocates (e.g., Everytown for Gun Safety, 2015; Giffords Law Center, 2018) view these figures with alarm. However, an alternative interpretation is available. Taking into account the limitations of the "predictive assessment" procedures the government uses to populate the terrorist lists—based on no scientifically validated process (Ackerman, 2015)—and the noticeable rates of mistaken identity, it is possible that the high background check pass rate simply indicates the individuals involved were just law-abiding citizens who wanted a gun rather than terrorists.

This is the interpretation that was presumably favored by the *L.A. Times* Editorial Board in 2015 when it noted that none of the 2,265 terrorist-watched purchasers—or their firearms—ever subsequently made the news for a terrorist act, or even for a gun crime. Of course, the editorial appeared before the 2016 Pulse nightclub mass shooting in Orlando, which was carried out by an individual who *was* on the terrorist watch list; perhaps that incident might have changed the *L.A. Times'* position. Nonetheless, the empirical numbers cited by the *Times* suggest that the vast majority of watch-listed individuals do not pose a significant threat to general safety. Prohibiting them from gun purchases is thus regarded by critics as an unconstitutional infringement of constitutional rights that would have little if any impact on overall societal violence.

FURTHER READING

Ackerman, Spencer, 2015. "No-Fly List Uses 'Predictive Assessments' Instead of Hard Evidence, US Admits." *The Guardian*, August 10. https://www.theguardian.com/us-news/2015/aug/10/us-no-fly-list-predictive-assessments

Codrea, David, 2019. "Terror Watch List Ruling Can Help Expose Gun Prohibitionist Tyranny." Ammoland, September 12. https://www.ammoland.com/2019/09/terror-watch-list-ruling-can-help-expose-gun-prohibitionist-tyranny/#axzz6DDN4iM3n

Collins, Susan, 2018. "Bipartisan Group of Senators Introduce Proposal to Keep Guns from Terrorists." *Press Releases*, February 27. https://www.collins.senate.gov/newsroom/bipartisan-group-senators-introduce-proposal-keep-guns-terrorists

Everytown for Gun Safety, 2015. "Closing the Terror Gap in Gun Background Checks." Everytown for Gun Safety. Accessed February 2020. everytownresearch.org/documents/09/closing-terror-gap-gun-background-checks.pdf/ (URL no longer active).

Fram, Alan, 2016. "Why Can People on the Terrorist Watch List Buy Guns, and Other FAQs." *PBS News Hour*, June 14. https://www.pbs.org/newshour/nation/why-can-people-on-the-terrorist-watch-list-buy-guns-and-other-faqs

Giffords Law Center, n.d. "Terrorist Watchlist." https://lawcenter.giffords.org/gun-laws/policy-areas/who-can-have-a-gun/terrorist-watchlist/

Giffords Law Center, 2018. "Closing the Terror Gap." Giffords Law Center. Accessed February 2020. lawcenter.giffords.org/wp-content/uploads/2018/01/Terror-Gap-Factsheet-GLC.pdf (URL no longer active).

Ingraham, Christopher, 2016. "Every Two Days a Suspected Terrorist Buys a Gun in the U.S." *Washington Post*, June 17. https://www.washingtonpost.com/news/wonk/wp/2016/06/17/every-two-days-a-suspected-terrorist-buys-a-gun-in-the-u-s/

Kassem, Ramzi, 2016. "I Help Innocent People Get Off Terrorism Watch Lists. As a Gun Control Tool, They're Useless." *Washington Post*, June 28. https://www.washingtonpost.com/posteverything/wp/2016/06/28/i-help-innocent-people-get-off-terror-watch-lists-as-a-gun-control-tool-theyre-useless/

L.A. Times Editorial Board, 2015. "Editorial: Should People on the No-Fly List Be Able to Buy Guns? Yes." *Los Angeles Times*, December 7. https://www.latimes.com/opinion/editorials/la-ed-terrorist-watch-list-20151207-story.html

Lesniewski, Niels, 2016. "Senate Democrats Renew Push to Keep Terror Suspects from Buying Guns." Roll Call, June 13. https://rollcall.com/2016/06/13/senate-democrats-renew-push-to-keep-terror-suspects-from-buying-guns/

Lichtblau, Eric, & Apuzzo, Matt, 2016. "Orlando Gunman Was on Terror Watchlist, F.B.I. Director Says." *New York Times*, June 13. https://www.nytimes.com/2016/06/14/us/omar-mateen-fbi.html

Smith, David, 2015. "'The Illusion of Security': No-Fly List Draws Scrutiny from Left and Right." *The Guardian*, December 9. https://www.theguardian.com/us-news/2015/dec/09/no-fly-list-errors-gun-control-obama

Stern, Mark, 2016. "Don't Tie Gun Control to the Terrorist Watch List." *Slate*, June 13. https://slate.com/news-and-politics/2016/06/hillary-clinton-is-wrong-about-the-terror-watch-list.html

Terrorist Screening Center, n.d. https://www.fbi.gov/about/leadership-and-structure/national-security-branch/tsc

Zetter, Kim, 2016. "How Does the FBI Watch List Work? And Could It Have Prevented Orlando?" *Wired*, June 17. https://www.wired.com/2016/06/fbi-watch-list-prevented-orlando-heres-works/

Q29. DOES THE SECOND AMENDMENT SANCTUARY MOVEMENT INCREASE GUN VIOLENCE?

Answer: "Second Amendment sanctuaries" are states, counties, cities, and other jurisdictions that have passed resolutions indicating that they will not enforce gun control laws that they perceive as unconstitutional. Adapted from the "sanctuary city" movement, in which municipal authorities refuse to assist in enforcing federal immigration laws, Second Amendment sanctuaries specify that they will not enforce gun laws they consider questionable or clearly in conflict with Second Amendment rights. Gun control measures that have been subjected to this treatment include "red flag" laws, private-seller background check requirements, federal gun licensing procedures, magazine bans, and bans on semiautomatic firearms (Shepardson, 2019).

Gun control proponents argue that the Second Amendment Sanctuary movement is dangerous and disturbing. They note that the movement has generated anti-government rhetoric on blogs and gun message boards, inciting (and perhaps encouraging) speculation about armed insurrectionism (Horwitz, 2019; Galuszka, 2020). Mary McCord, the legal director of Georgetown University Law Center's Institute for Constitutional Advocacy and Protection and a former acting assistant director for national security, has voiced similar concerns: "[Second Amendment Sanctuary resolutions have] spurred extremists who want to stand up local militias to engage in armed rebellion against the state—action that isn't just dangerous but that also runs counter to the Constitution" (Edwards, 2020b).

Additionally, critics have suggested that Second Amendment sanctuaries foster increased gun violence indirectly. Because many county sheriffs have endorsed Second Amendment sanctuary resolutions and have indicated they will abide by such local ordinances, opponents fear that, by disregarding legal tools designed to limit gun violence, law enforcement neglect will actually heighten such violence (Schneider, 2019). Similarly, opponents have asserted that the movement "threatens the safety of communities nationwide by fostering distrust in law enforcement and may deter people from reporting individuals" likely to hurt themselves or others (Everytown for Gun Safety, 2019). Other opponents, focusing specifically on suicides and the movement's characteristic rejection of "red flag"/extreme risk protection orders (i.e., laws allowing judges to order the immediate, temporary removal of firearms from individuals deemed a risk to themselves or others), contend that Second Amendment sanctuaries endanger "the most vulnerable among us" (Giffords Law Center, n.d.).

Proponents of the movement reject these fears as unfounded, painting them as "just the latest attempt to demonize gun owners and Second Amendment supporters" (Edwards, 2020a). While acknowledging that some extreme advocates have used anti-government language, defenders assert that it is average citizens peaceably defending rights they see as under attack who promote Second Amendment Sanctuary initiatives. They describe sanctuary resolutions as an understandable and legitimate response to state authorities contemplating additional firearms restrictions that flout Second Amendment rights.

For example, after Democrats took control of the Virginia state legislature and moved forward with new gun regulations (i.e., universal background checks, an "assault weapons" ban, a red flag law), many Virginia counties passed Second Amendment sanctuary resolutions declaring that their police would not enforce gun laws in violation of the Second Amendment. In response, Virginia state representative Donald McEachin noted that Governor Ralph Northam "may have to nationalize the National Guard to enforce the law.... I don't know how serious these counties are.... But that's obviously an option he has" (Picket, 2019). Gary Soltis, a military law professor at Georgetown University, confirmed that the governor would have the authority to do so. "Until nationalized, it's a creature of the state [and] yes, the governor can activate the National Guard to enforce even a state law" (Read, 2019). For its part, Northam's administration never indicated that it would even entertain the idea of using the Guard in such a fashion, but a confiscation scenario involving the state National Guard nonetheless went "viral" in the online gun community. Supporters suggest that, in this light, it is not surprising that gun owners might choose a highly dramatic way to convey their concerns to their state representatives (Edwards, 2020a).

Other supporters have also rebuffed the idea that the movement implicitly promotes gun violence, emphasizing instead the symbolic and communicative characteristics of the undertaking. Erich Pratt, senior vice president of Gun Owners of America and a leader in the sanctuary movement, argues that "Sanctuary resolutions are important because they provide the best way for local officials to inform [state authorities] that if they rush forward to create new felony crimes to jail law-abiding [citizens]— just for exercising their most fundamental and natural right of self-defense—then they cannot expect localities to enforce such unjust laws. What these sanctuary jurisdictions are doing is not resistance but noncooperation—a principal . . . dating from colonial America" (Bedard, 2020).

These two divergent interpretations of the sanctuary movement—law-abiding individuals peacefully non-cooperating with unconstitutional regulations versus armed fanatics defying legally enacted gun laws— suggest that a dual evaluation of the movement's impact on gun violence is appropriate. The first assessment—its current impact—is clear. No evidence indicates that the Second Amendment sanctuary resolutions have produced aggressive confrontations, much less actual gun violence, as of late 2020. The areas declaring themselves sanctuaries invariably emphasize that supporters will use all *lawful* methods to defend their perceived constitutional rights, including court challenges.

The second assessment—the movement's potential for creating gun violence—is less clear. Given the high probability that sympathetic sheriffs in these districts will place little priority on enforcing new gun regulations they regard as objectionable (e.g., Pearce, 2019), a determined state governor could conceivably employ outside forces under his authority to compel compliance (Read, 2019). This scenario, unlikely though it might be, might perhaps result in armed confrontations and gun violence. Further, as sanctuary opponents have argued, just the police's lack of enforcement of newly enacted gun laws (such as "extreme risk"/"red flag" orders) may increase gun violence indirectly, for example, by failures to remove firearms in preventable gun suicide or domestic abuse situations.

The Facts: Although several states as early as 2009 had enacted measures indicating they would ignore federal gun laws seen as unconstitutional, the real flash point for the Second Amendment Sanctuary movement occurred a decade later, when voters elected Democratic governors and sent Democratic majorities to the legislatures of both Illinois and Virginia. Democrats in both legislatures subsequently announced sweeping gun reform measures. Officials in Effingham County in Illinois responded to these measures by passing a resolution in 2018 declaring all of the Democrats' gun proposals unconstitutional. The Second Amendment Sanctuary movement rapidly spread from there (Shepardson, 2019).

Opponents of the movement have faulted it on legal, ethical, and safety grounds. Legally, sanctuary resolutions do not appear to have any lawful force behind them. As Jason Darnell, Kentucky's Marshall County Attorney, notes, "We have no authority to declare a state statute or a federal statute null and void.... You can put it in writing but it has no legal effect" (Edward, 2019b). Commenting on Virginia's sanctuary resolutions, Mary McCord, the former acting assistant attorney general, made the same point: "Virginia state law prohibits local governments from enacting ordinances or resolutions that are inconsistent with state laws and, more directly, specifically prohibits local governments from regulating firearms" (Edwards, 2020b).

Adversaries of the movement also question its ethical foundations, suggesting that the undertaking has philosophical roots in racist ideology. Howard Graves, a senior analyst at the Southern Poverty Law Center, maintains that "the current push for 'Second Amendment sanctuaries' is predicated on a belief system that was pioneered by white supremacists in the early 1970s and has been implicated in antigovernment and racially motivated violence" (Edward, 2019a). Others have argued that the movement conjures up the "disturbing nullification movements of the past three centuries in Virginia [suggesting] that the states have the right to ignore federal laws they consider unconstitutional. That thinking was applied to proslavery movements, leading to the Civil War and the fight over integration in the 1950s and 1960s" (Galuszka, 2020).

Regarding safety, opponents observe that armed individuals, defying legitimate laws and holding impassioned views about gun rights, spark legitimate fears about real and potential violence. They note instances of threats toward Ralph Northam, the governor who championed new gun control legislation in Virginia after assuming office in January 2018; and the presence of out-of-state, militia-oriented groups—Oath Keepers from Nevada, Three Percent Security Force from Georgia, and so forth—arriving in Richmond for protest rallies. Often viewed as part of the sanctuary movement, these groups typically hold anti-government attitudes and orientations. Given their extreme views, and especially in light of the sanctuary movement's apparent willingness to ignore laws, critics see such developments as a prelude to eventual bloodshed (Schneider & Vozzella, 2020).

Proponents of the movement have a much different view of the legal, ethical, and safety issues critics have raised. Most sanctuary supporters do not see the movement as inciting unlawful defiance of government authority. They view the resolutions as exercises in free speech, not in need of any legal standing; and they see their practical impact deriving not from their own statutory authority, but from the enforcement discretion of sympathetic sheriffs, prosecutors, and local authorities. Defenders argue further that such discretion is not unique to gun laws, pointing to local prosecutors who in the past have declined to pursue marijuana drug violations, or states' attorney generals who declined to defend bans on gay marriage. Finally, they note that almost all sanctuary resolutions explicitly call for challenging questionable gun laws legally, in court (Edwards, 2020b).

Sanctuary advocates also reject opponents' assertions that the movement has racist roots because of its nullification overtones. They point out that the legal theory of nullification long preceded the Civil War; and that such luminaries as Thomas Jefferson and James Madison argued that states have the right to ignore federal laws they deemed unconstitutional (Galuszka, 2020). Further, while racists may have endorsed nullification for abhorrent purposes, the principle was also used for more worthy purposes—for example, by antislavery proponents to undermine the Fugitive Slave Act and protect defendants who assisted runaway slaves (Bedard, 2020). Proponents also note that, judging by past statistics and historical trends, the gun control laws that the sanctuary movement opposes will likely send proportionally many more young Black men to prison for nonviolent gun crimes than white men (Edwards, 2019a).

Further, at least one militia group that supports sanctuary resolutions—the Three Percenters—have explicitly disavowed racism and alignment with white supremacists. The group has emphasized that while the Three Percenters "support and defend everyone's right to free speech, we will not align ourselves with any type of racist group. We strongly reject and denounce anyone who calls themselves a patriot or a Three Percenter that has attended or is planning on attending . . . white supremacist and Nazi groups" (MacNab, 2017).

Regarding concerns about heightened gun violence, sanctuary advocates argue that these fears are completely speculative. As one commentator has noted, far from fostering distrust in law enforcement, the movement has done the opposite, with local residents cheering sheriffs for refusing to enforce "unconstitutional" gun laws (Edwards, 2019a)—an orientation also shared by 62 percent of over 14,000 police professionals who in an online poll sponsored by a major police association indicated they would not enforce more restrictive gun laws (PoliceOne.com, 2013). Of course, these findings must be viewed cautiously. The survey was internally developed and administered, and various unknown respondent biases may have influenced the results. Other analyses suggest that while sheriffs and law enforcement officials in smaller departments tend to support gun rights, police chiefs and administrators in major U.S. cities tend to favor more stringent gun laws (Glenza & Beckett, 2016).

Sanctuary proponents also point to numerous meetings across multiple states associated with the sanctuary movement, and assert that at virtually all these gatherings, the crowds—though passionate about gun rights—have been peaceable (Edwards, 2020a). Nonetheless, opponents of the movement argue that many residents are likely frightened of potentially angering those members of their community carrying high-powered firearms.

This is not to say that the sanctuary movement's impact on gun violence is completely benign, or that future circumstances will not arise that provoke some type of armed response from sanctuary supporters. As noted previously, opponents' concerns about the indirect effects of nonenforcement of gun laws—for example, domestic abuse gun violence that might have been prevented had a sheriff enforced an extreme risk protection order—are valid considerations. Similarly, should unlikely scenarios occur—for example, where state authorities attempt to forcibly confiscate common firearms in everyday use—the likelihood of violence increases. But such possibilities are again completely speculative, and sanctuary advocates counter-speculate that unenforced gun laws will likely keep more guns in the hands of law-abiding individuals. Thus, they assert that the Second Amendment Sanctuary movement enhances the possibility of self-defense, increases personal and family safety (Bedard 2020), and actually reduces criminals' attraction to armed assault.

In weighing all these arguments, the Second Amendment Sanctuary movement appears to be, at its core, primarily a symbolic communicative undertaking by the gun rights community. As its detractors suggest, under peculiar circumstances, the movement has the potential to devolve into aggressive confrontations and perhaps even violence. But as of 2020, there have been no documented cases of actual violence *directly* attributable to the movement despite its presence in more than 400 municipalities across 20 states (Mascia, 2020).

FURTHER READING

Bedard, Pual, 2020. "Gun 'Sanctuaries' Compared to Slavery, 'Dangerous,' 'Ugly,' 'Disturbing.'" *Washington Examiner*, January 5. https://www.washingtonexaminer.com/washington-secrets/gun-sanctuaries-compared-to-slavery-dangerous-ugly-disturbing

Edwards, Cam, 2019a. "Everytown Demands Sheriffs, Police Denounce 2A Sanctuary Movement." Bearing Arms, December 20. https://bearingarms.com/cam-e/2019/12/20/everytown-demands-sheriffs-police-denounce-2a-sanctuary-movement/

Edwards, Cam, 2019b. "Kentucky County Facing Pushback Over 2A Sanctuary Ordinance." Bearing Arms, December 24. https://bearingarms.com/cam-e/2019/12/24/kentucky-county-facing-pushback-over-2a-sanctuary-ordinance/

Edwards, Cam, 2020a. "The Push Is On to Demonize Second Amendment Sanctuaries as 'Dangerous.'" Bearing Arms, January 2. https://bearingarms.com/cam-e/2020/01/02/the-push-is-on-to-demonize-second-amendment-sanctuaries-as-dangerous/

Edwards, Cam, 2020b. "Washington Post Launches Another Attack on 2A Sanctuaries." Bearing Arms, January 8. https://bearingarms.com/cam-e/2020/01/08/wapo-another-attack-2a-sanctuaries/

Everytown for Gun Safety, 2019. "Everytown for Gun Safety Support Fund and Moms Demand Action Urge Sheriff's Association, Association of Counties, Others to Condemn 'Second Amendment Sanctuary' Resolutions." Everytown for Gun Safety, December 19. https://everytown.org/press/everytown-for-gun-safety-support-fund-and-moms-demand-action-urge-sheriffs-association-association-of-counties-others-to-condemn-second-amendment-sanctuary-resolutions/

Galuszka, Peter, 2020. "The Disturbing 'Second Amendment Sanctuary' Trend in Virginia." *Washington Post*, January 3. https://www.washingtonpost.com/opinions/local-opinions/the-disturbing-second-amendment-sanctuary-trend-in-virginia/2020/01/03/21a442b2-2c0f-11ea-bcb3-ac6482c4a92f_story.html

Giffords Law Center, n.d. "How 'Second Amendment Sanctuaries' Are Threatening Lifesaving Gun Laws." lawcenter.giffords.org/how-second-amendment-sanctuaries-are-threatening-lifesaving-gun-laws/

Glenza, Jessica, & Beckett, Lois, 2016. "Gun Control Still 'Not the Issue' for Law Enforcement Despite Police Attacks." *The Guardian*, July 19. https://www.theguardian.com/us-news/2016/jul/19/gun-control-police-open-carry-law

Horwitz, Josh, 2019. "Josh Horwitz Column: The Rhetoric of 'Second Amendment Sanctuaries' Becomes Increasingly Dangerous." *Richmond

Times-Dispatch, December 30. https://richmond.com/josh-horwitz-column-the-rhetoric-of-second-amendment-sanctuaries-becomes-increasingly-dangerous/article_38777b36-9f59-508b-98ed-bd2a317366ff.html

MacNab, JJ, 2017. "The Three Percenters Official Statement Regarding the Violent Protests in Charlottesville." Twitter, August 13. https://twitter.com/jjmacnab/status/896927138397405185

Mascia, Jennifer, 2020. "Second Amendment Sanctuaries, Explained." The Trace, January 14. https://www.thetrace.org/2020/01/second-amendment-sanctuary-movement/

Pearce, Tim, 2019. "Sheriff Promises to 'Deputize Thousands' If His State Passes Gun Control." *Washington Examiner*, December 10. https://www.washingtonexaminer.com/news/sheriff-promises-to-deputize-thousands-if-his-state-passes-gun-control

Picket, Kerry, 2019. "'The Law Is the Law': Virginia Democrats Float Prosecution and National Guard Deployment if Police Don't Enforce Gun Control." *Washington Examiner*, December 11. https://www.washingtonexaminer.com/news/the-law-is-the-law-virginia-democrats-float-prosecution-national-guard-deployment-if-police-dont-enforce-gun-control

PoliceOne.com, 2013. "Gun Policy & Law Enforcement: Survey Results." https://media.cdn.lexipol.com/p1_gunsurveysummary_2013.pdf

Read, Russ, 2019. "Yes, Virginia, the Governor Really Can Use the National Guard to Enforce Gun Control." *Washington Examiner*, December 14. https://www.washingtonexaminer.com/policy/defense-national-security/yes-virginia-the-governor-really-can-use-the-national-guard-to-enforce-gun-control

Schneider, Gregory, 2019. "In Virginia, and Elsewhere, Gun Supporters Prepare to Defy New Laws." *Washington Post*, November 23. https://www.washingtonpost.com/local/virginia-politics/in-virginia-and-elsewhere-gun-supporters-prepare-to-defy-new-laws/2019/11/23/4a95fcc2-0c86-11ea-bd9d-c628fd48b3a0_story.html

Schneider, Gregory, & Vozzella, Laura, 2020. "Prospect of Gun Control in Virginia Draws Threats, Promise of Armed Protest." *Washington Post*, January 5. https://www.washingtonpost.com/local/virginia-politics/prospect-of-gun-control-in-virginia-draws-threats-promise-of-armed-protest/2020/01/05/7e9b230c-2e38-11ea-bcd4-24597950008f_story.html

Shepardson, Noah, 2019. "America's Second Amendment Sanctuary Movement Is Alive and Well." *Reason*, November 21. https://reason.com/2019/11/21/americas-second-amendment-sanctuary-movement-is-alive-and-well/

6

Guns, Drugs, and Mental Illness

The Firearms Transaction Form (ATF 4473) is the federal background check questionnaire that every potential gun purchaser must complete if buying a firearm from a federally licensed dealer. The questionnaire lists 10 categories of individuals prohibited from firearms possession or ownership. For a number of the categories, such as felony convictions, domestic violence crimes, or being a fugitive from justice, the connection between the categories and potential gun violence is simple and straightforward. But for two of the categories—drug use and mental illness—the connections are more involved and complicated.

For example, while unlawful use of depressants or stimulants disqualifies an individual from buying firearms, the prescribed use of the same substances for treating certain mental afflictions does not—despite the drugs' capacity to sometimes induce violent thoughts and behavior (Gorvett, 2020; Hohmann, 2015). Complicating matters further, mental illness severe enough to require institutionalization also serves as a bar to buying or owning firearms, but the majority of mentally ill individuals are no more prone to violence than the average individual (Beckett, 2015; McDonald, 2019), particularly if they are receiving psychological treatment (including drug treatment).

Additionally, from an entirely different perspective, drugs are also a core commodity in major criminal enterprises in the United States. Illegal drugs fuel significant episodes of gun violence among competing dealers, rival gangs vying to maintain (or expand) their turf, and drug addicts engaging in armed assaults for quick cash. Thus, intricate links connect drugs, mental health, and gun violence. This chapter examines four significant issues in this arena—two primarily related to drugs and gun violence, and two related to mental illness and gun violence.

The first question is community oriented, and explores the impact of the "war on drugs" on gun violence. A debate has long raged in America about whether modifying current drug laws could substantially decrease gang violence, particularly in the urban areas where such violence is endemic. This initial question assesses the evidence for this claim. The second question is individually oriented, and explores the role psychotropic drugs play in creating crazed shooters. Some gun rights proponents have pointed to a startling commonality in the backgrounds of many mass shooters: a substantial majority were on—or had been on—psychotropic drug medications before their rampages. The question examines the evidence indicating that the drugs, presumably prescribed to alleviate mental issues, exacerbate individuals' violent tendencies.

The third question examines the connections between mental illness and gun violence generally, and assesses whether banning the mentally ill (however that term is defined) from firearms possession would significantly lessen such violence. The chapter's final question examines a specific purchasing restriction often proposed by gun control proponents: waiting periods. The typical rationale for such periods assumes that they provide time for the transient emotional states of disturbed individuals to subside. Thus, waiting periods can lessen the gun suicides and impulse killings these temporarily unbalanced persons might otherwise inflict. The question explores whether the evidence supports such a belief.

FURTHER READING

Beckett, Lois, 2015. "Myth vs. Fact: Violence and Mental Health." ProPublica, June 18. https://www.propublica.org/article/myth-vs-fact-violence-and-mental-health

Gorvett, Zaria, 2020. "The Medications That Change Who We Are." BBC Future, January 8. https://www.bbc.com/future/article/20200108-the-medications-that-change-who-we-are

Hohmann, Leo, 2015. "Big List of Drug-Induced Killers." WND, June 18. https://www.wnd.com/2015/06/big-list-of-drug-induced-killers/

McDonald, Jessica, 2019. "The Facts on Mental Illness and Mass Shootings." FactCheck.Org, October 18. https://www.factcheck.org/2019/10/the-facts-on-mental-illness-and-mass-shootings/

Q30. WOULD RELAXING CURRENT DRUG LAWS REDUCE GANG-RELATED GUN VIOLENCE?

Answer: Gang-related gun violence has plagued the country for decades, and while gangs engage in a spectrum of illegal activity—armed robbery, people smuggling, auto theft, extortion, home invasions, gunrunning, and so forth—drug trafficking substantially underwrites such violence. Analysts estimate that Americans spend about $100 billion annually on illegal drugs, and as one commentator noted, "You just can't move $100 billion worth of illegal product without a lot of assault and homicide" (Allen, 2015). Criminologists and law enforcement personnel examining trends in murder and other violent crimes typically attribute increases to drug-related gang activity.

Because of this link between gang violence and drug trafficking, a number of commentators have argued that legalizing currently prohibited drugs or reducing sentences for various drug offenses offers a likely method for reducing gun violence. Drug enforcement efforts, by curbing supply, raise the price of illegal drugs, and make "turf wars" (to maintain a local drug supply monopoly) worth waging (Smith, 2012). Drug legalization would negate this incentive, and substantially curtail the primary funding source of many gangs (Eckert, 2017). Further, the illegality of the drug trade obviously precludes the use of the courts and law enforcement for dispute resolution. Thus, gang members can only rely on "private enforcement"—usually violence—to resolve conflicts. Some observers believe that drug legalization and regulation would also dampen this violence dynamic (Fryklund, 2016).

While these arguments have an evident reasonableness to them, in the absence of actual legalization, there is little empirical evidence to assess the objective impact that drug decriminalization would have on gun violence. Investigations of the impact of marijuana legalization have generally supported arguments that decriminalization reduces violent crime. One 2018 analysis that specifically examined the legalization of medical marijuana found significant reductions in both property and violent crimes, as well as reductions in crime throughout the supply chain—that is, the production, distribution, sale, and possession of marijuana. The researchers compared crime data before and after legalization within states, as well as with states that had not legalized marijuana. They discovered a clear decline in both violent crime and theft—the two types of crime investigated—particularly in legalized states that shared a border with

Mexico (Gavrilova, Kamada, & Zoutman, 2017; Morris, 2018). Whether similar outcomes would occur with other illegal drugs is unknown.

Significantly, the idea of legalizing and regulating prohibited drugs to decrease gang gun violence has received little or no attention among organizations and advocates prominently concerned about such violence, suggesting that drug legalization as a strategy for reducing gun violence is viewed as infeasible politically (e.g., Morgan, 2008) and pragmatically (e.g., Drug Enforcement Administration, 2003). For instance, the Department of Justice's comprehensive approach to curbing gang violence emphasizes prevention, intervention, and suppression, but does not mention relaxing drug laws (Office of Juvenile Justice and Delinquency Prevention, n.d.). Similarly, the gang prevention program developed by the National League of Cities stresses the development of "strategic partnerships" across various stakeholder groups, as well as operating street outreach programs, but does not explore the potential ramifications of modifying drug laws (National League of Cities Institute for Youth, Education, and Families, 2015).

Even researchers and academics using a public health framework to understand and limit gang violence (e.g., Brzenchek, 2018) have given little consideration to the possible usefulness of modifying drug laws. Asserting that most targets of gun violence and gun homicides are young minority men typically considered "perpetrators" or "suspects," these analysts argue that this "criminal" frame is itself a major obstacle in creating effective violence prevention programs. Instead of a criminal frame that frightens people, they recommend an approach that focuses on individuals as victims and treats gang violence as an epidemic involving behaviors, norms, and transmission mechanisms that require social and behavioral adjustments (NPR Staff, 2017). However, the potential costs and benefits that drug law relaxation might have on gang and gun violence have not been a primary research focus.

Overall, then, logical reasons exist to expect that decriminalizing currently prohibited drugs and imposing a legal regulatory framework for their manufacture, sale, and use would likely decrease gun violence. Further, empirical evidence with the decriminalization of medical marijuana also suggests that drug legalization might reduce gun violence. Nonetheless, major societal stakeholders in gun violence reduction (e.g., Congress, Department of Justice, etc.) have not pursued this potential solution because of the belief that such a course of action does not have sufficient public or political support.

The Facts: Academic research on gang violence dates at least as far back as the 1960s (e.g., Miller, 1966), and such violence received considerable political and popular attention in the 1970s with President Richard Nixon's "War on Drugs" initiative. Measuring the magnitude of gang violence is difficult—little agreement exists on the defining "characteristics" of gang-related crime—but FBI analyses suggest that at least 785,000 gang members belonging to over 25,000 gangs were dispersed throughout the country in 2008 (Kingsbury, 2008). Another survey of gangs in the United States published by the Department of Justice in 2011 estimated a U.S. population of 731,000 gang members and more than 28,000 gangs (Egley & Howell, 2011). The common element across most of these gangs are drug dealing and gun violence.

Since the illegal drug trade is essentially a business with producers, importers, distributors, and retailers, initial efforts to control gang violence heavily emphasized various drug interdiction efforts (to interfere with producers and importers outside the country) and arrest and incarceration (for distributors and retailers inside the country). Later efforts modified this primary law-enforcement-and-punishment approach by enlisting the aid of neighborhood community organizations, social work agencies, and local leaders to help dampen gang violence stemming from the illegal drug trade (e.g., Kingsbury, 2008; Office of National Drug Control Policy, n.d.).

Despite this broadened perspective, official policy continues to stress prohibition and treatment-oriented incarceration for illegal drug activities. As the Office of National Drug Control Policy (n.d.) notes, "individuals should be held responsible for breaking the law. Policies and programs such as injection rooms, drug distribution efforts and drug legalization should be opposed because they tolerate drug use and allow . . . addiction to continue untreated." While official assessments of the country's current drug strategy (e.g., Office of National Drug Control Policy, 2016) indicate progress in disrupting violent drug-trafficking gangs and cartels, other evaluations remain much more negative (e.g., Coyne & Hall, 2017). Observing that drug-related gun violence still afflicts many of America's urban centers, with illegal drug use common all across the country, some observers have concluded that current drug policies do not work and issued calls for drug decriminalization.

Writing for the *Atlantic* in 2012, Noah Smith—a professor of finance at Stony Brook University and staunch gun control supporter—argued that, short of universal gun confiscation (which he considered politically impossible), even the most stringent gun regulations would not appreciably reduce gun-linked violence. For example, given the durability of firearms, and the number of guns already in individuals' hands, even a total ban on firearms sales would take decades before impacting gun violence. He noted that even this outcome was uncertain: Brazil at the time had a murder rate more than quadruple that of the United States, yet had less than a tenth of America's gun ownership. Asserting that most gun deaths result not from mass shootings but from more mundane incidents—gang wars, personal quarrels, drive-by shootings, and so forth—Smith contended that "if we really cared about those [many] souls who are shot to death each year, there is an extremely effective policy we could enact right now that would probably save many of them. I'm talking about ending the drug war" (Smith, 2012).

Smith's belief in the efficacy of drug decriminalization for reducing gun violence rests primarily on logical considerations: decriminalization would lessen gangs fighting over drug territories, suppliers resolving disputes by shooting each other, addicts assaulting the unwary to obtain the cost of a "fix," and so on. As he stated, "Ending the drug war would involve reducing all of these incentives to murder" (Smith, 2012). Another commentator, labeling the war on drugs as Prohibition 2.0, and noting that estimates of drug-related homicides sometimes go as high as half the total homicides in the country, reached similar conclusions about the causes of gun violence and how to reduce it. "If concerned citizens want to get serious about reducing gun violence, they should ... focus more on ending our failed ... trillion-dollar battle against narcotics. .... The war on drugs is ... a slow-killing, institutionalized type of violence" (Stooksberry, 2016). Others have contended that since the war on drugs has produced a far greater number of casualties than every mass shooting in America combined, ending the drug war would significantly decrease gun fatalities across the board (Eckert, 2017).

The empirical evidence most relevant to these decriminalization arguments centers on the country's experience with marijuana legalization. This experience is generally supportive of arguments that drug decriminalization could result in less gun violence. For instance, one study that examined 16 years of state panel data found that the legalization of medical marijuana did not appear to exacerbate drug offenses, and seemed to correlate with a reduction in homicide and assault rates (Morris et al., 2014). A second study using data from the FBI's Uniform Crime Reports was more definitive. Findings showed that decriminalization of medical marijuana resulted in an almost 13 percent decrease in violent crime (i.e., homicides, assaults and robberies) in states bordering Mexico (Gavrilova et al., 2017).

Critics of legalization are not convinced that drug decriminalization would actually decrease violent crime. They assert that gun violence is not just limited to the *trafficking* of drugs. It is endemic to the *use* of drugs, with significantly more homicides committed by individuals *on* drugs relative to individuals looking to *buy* drugs; and they argue that decriminalization would increase both drug use and addiction. Additionally, while legalization might reduce the black market in illegal drugs, it would not eliminate it—a market would exist for anyone under the established legal age (e.g., 18 or 21). With drug consumption most prevalent among teens and young adults, drug-trafficking gangs would still retain a ready customer base (DEA, 2003).

Opponents also maintain that it is an oversimplification to infer that marijuana legalization has decreased crime. They argue that the statistics used are sometimes incomplete and unrepresentative of overall crime (e.g., Sabet, 2014); and that gun violence is still prevalent as would-be thieves now attempt to steal both the legal crop and the cash it generates. As sheriffs in California's Emerald Triangle put it, "People are getting shot over this plant. We're seeing more robberies and more gun violence. All legalization did was create a safe haven for criminals" (Chun, 2019).

On balance, both the logical arguments for drug decriminalization and the academic evidence regarding marijuana legalization seem sufficient to justify the conclusion that relaxing drug laws could have an overall positive effect on gang and gun violence. However, the contrary evidence—DEA's assessments, sheriffs' observational impressions, and so forth—suggest that the decrease in potential violence is unlikely to be as great as proponents imply. In any case, as noted earlier, revising current drug laws to reduce gang and gun violence remains a politically infeasible solution.

FURTHER READING

Allen, Danielle, 2015. "How the War on Drugs Creates Violence." *Washington Post*, October 16. https://www.washingtonpost.com/opinions/how-the-war-on-drugs-creates- violence/2015/10/16/6de57a76-72b7-11e5-9cbb-790369643cf9_story.html

Brzenchek, Robert, 2018. "Why Gang Violence Should Be Treated as a Public Health Issue." Public Safety, July 10. inpublicsafety.com/2018/07/why-gang-violence-should-be-treated-as-a-public-health-issue/

Chun, Rene, 2019. "Ending Weed Prohibition Hasn't Stopped Drug Crimes." *Atlantic*, January/February. https://www.theatlantic.com/magazine/archive/2019/01/California-marijuana-crime/576391/

Coyne, Christopher, & Hall, Abigail, 2017. "Four Decades and Counting: The Continued Failure of the War on Drugs." Cato Institute Policy Analysis, April 12. https://www.cato.org/publications/policy-analysis/four-decades-counting-continued-failure-war-drugs?gclid=CjwKCAiA7t3yBRADEiwA4GFII9z9P2_sMfk3gxpdNHOp_16yig

Drug Enforcement Administration (DEA), 2003. "Speaking Out against Drug Legalization." web.archive.org/web/20060627082607/http://www.usdoj.gov/dea/demand/speakout/speaking_out-may03.pdf

Eckert, Thomas, 2017. "To End Gun Violence, Abandon the War on Drugs." *Newsweek*, October 20. https://www.newsweek.com/end-gun-violence-abandon-war-drugs-689459

Egley, A., Jr., & Howell, J. C., 2011. *Highlights of the 2009 National Youth Gang Survey. Fact Sheet.* Washington, DC: U.S. Department of Justice, Office of Justice Programs, Office of Juvenile Justice and Delinquency Prevention. https://www.ncjrs.gov/pdffiles1/ojjdp/233581.pdf

Fryklund, Inge, 2016. "The Link between Drugs and Violence." HuffPost, July 27. https://www.huffpost.com/entry/the-link-between-drugs-an_b_11095430

Gavrilova, Evelina, Kamada, Takuma, & Zoutman, Floris, 2017. "Is Legal Pot Crippling Mexican Drug Trafficking Organizations? The Effects of Medical Marijuana Laws on US Crime." *Economics Journal*, 129(617), 375–407. https://academic.oup.com/ej/article-abstract/129/617/375/5237193

Kingsbury, Alex, 2008. "Inside the Feds' War on Gang Violence." *U.S. News & World Report*, December 10. https://www.usnews.com/news/national/articles/2008/12/10/inside-the-feds-war-on-gang-violence?page=3

Miller, Walter, 1966. "Violent Crimes in City Gangs." *Annals of the American Academy of Political and Social Science*, 364(1), 96–112. journals.sagepub.com/doi/abs/10.1177/000271626636400110

Morgan, Scott, 2008. "Rule #1 of Drug Legalization Is Don't Talk about Drug Legalization." https://stopthedrugwar.org/speakeasy/2008/feb/18/rule_1_drug_legalization_dont_ta

Morris, Julian, 2018. "Does Legalizing Marijuana Reduce Crime?" *Reason*, September. reason.org/wp-content/uploads/does-legalizing-marijuana-reduce-crime.pdf

Morris, Robert, TenEyck, Michael, Barnes, J. C., & Kovandzic, Tomislav, 2014. "The Effects of Medical Marijuana Laws on Crime: Evidence from State Panel Data, 1990–2006." *PloS One*, March 26. https://journals.plos.org./plosone/article?id=10.1371/journal.pone.0092816#pone.0092816-Pedersen1

National League of Cities Institute for Youth, Education, and Families, 2015. "Preventing Gang Violence and Building Communities Where Young People Thrive." yvppolicyportal.safestates.org/wp-content/uploads/2015/09/NLC-Preventing-Gang-Violence.pdf

NPR Staff, 2017. "Researchers Begin to Look at Gun Violence as Public Health Issue." NPR, January 7. https://www.npr.org/2017/01/07/508722484/researchers-begin-to-look-at-gun-violence-as-public-health-issue

Office of Juvenile Justice and Delinquency Prevention, n.d. "Gang Violence Prevention." https://ojjdp.ojp.gov/programs/gang-violence-prevention

Office of National Drug Control Policy, n.d. "Principles of Modern Drug Policy." https://obamawhitehouse.archives.gov/ondcp/policy-and-research/principles-of-modern-drug-policy

Office of National Drug Control Policy, 2016. "National Drug Control Strategy." https://obamawhitehouse.archives.gov/sites/default/files/ondcp/policy-and-research/prs_2016.pdf

Ryan, Jason, 2009. "Gangs Blamed for 80 Percent of U.S. Crimes." ABC News, January 30. https://abcnews.go.com/TheLaw/FedCrimes/story?id=6773423&page=1

Sabet, Kevin, 2014. "Crime Is Up in Colorado: What That Tells Us about Pot Legalization and, Perhaps More Importantly, Lazy Reporting." HuffPost, October 11. https://www.huffpost.com/entry/crime-is-up-in-colorado-w_b_5663046

Smith, Noah, 2012. "The Single Best Anti-Gun-Death Policy? Ending the Drug War." *Atlantic*, December 21. https://www.theatlantic.com/business/archive/2012/12/the-single-best-anti-gun-death-policy-ending-the-drug-war/266505

Stooksberry, Jay, 2016. "Want to Reduce Gun Violence? Halt the War on Drugs." *Newsweek*, August 16. https://www.newsweek.com/want-reduce-gun-violence-halt-war-on-drugs-488879

Q31. DO PSYCHOTROPIC DRUGS INCREASE THE LIKELIHOOD OF GUN VIOLENCE?

Answer: Because of the inexplicable nature of mass shootings—what could conceivably propel individuals to gun down multiple victims, often chosen at random and without purpose?—possible explanations have received prominent attention in social media and the popular press. One conjecture has focused on the potential role psychiatric drugs play in such shootings. For example, several on-line internet sources provide lists of mass killers believed to have been on psychotropic medications prior to, or during, their murderous sprees. While these sources (e.g., Citizens Commission on Human Rights International, 2018; Goldman & Moore, 2019; Hohmann, 2015) are not medically authoritative and their claims are typically dismissed by mainstream mental health experts, gun rights commentators, such as the National Rifle Association's Dana Loesch, give some credence to the speculation that these drugs induce violence (Hargis, 2019).

As noted, many mental health professionals and other critics disparage such speculation. For example, one columnist dismissed Loesch's reference to the possible influence of psychotropic drugs on mass shooters as "a right-wing myth pushed by conspiracy theory sites like Infowars," noting that drugs are a response to a mental problem, not the cause of it (Hargis, 2019). Other authorities and media voices (e.g., Fast, 2018) also suggest that blaming psychiatric drugs for spree killings gets the causal relationship backwards. Dr. Gwen Adshead, a forensic psychotherapist and an expert on the psychology of violent behavior, notes that "Most people who commit these kinds of acts of severe violence are only on prescribed medication because of their horrible thoughts, moods, and ideas." Similarly, Dr. James Knoll, director of forensic psychiatry at SUNY Upstate Medical University, argues that psychological autopsies of public mass shooters indicate that the murderers' violent feelings were present before taking medication (Kruzel, 2019).

Additionally, medical experts point to the *lack* of connection (in the general population) between increased uses of psychotropic drugs and increased violence as evidence that the drugs do not trigger mass shootings. For example, given that 42 million Americans have taken antidepressants—a drug allegedly linked to violence—skeptics argue that the country should have experienced a great deal more violence and many more mass shootings than it has. Further, since women and individuals over 60 are prescribed antidepressant medications at higher rates than the general population, increased violent behavior should characterize those cohorts—but it does not (Kruzel, 2019).

Other analysts have made the same point more generally. Dr. Peter Langman, a counseling psychologist and an authority on school shooters, maintains that the use of psychiatric medications has grown significantly in America since the 1980s. Ritalin (a psycho-stimulant) increased about fourfold between 1987 and 1996; and the use of antidepressants increased 75 percent between 1996 and 2005. Yet, during this period, violent crime actually decreased substantially, including dramatic decreases in the overall murder rate, as well as homicides committed by youths (Langman, 2016).

Proponents believing that the drugs cause violence claim that the refutations outlined above miss the point. They argue that these widely prescribed drugs may well benefit a majority of medicated individuals, and still adversely affect a small percentage of patients—inducing or exacerbating violent thoughts and behaviors, and perhaps prompting school shootings. They point to warnings provided by the pharmaceutical companies themselves, as well as warnings generated by regulatory agencies such as the Food and Drug Administration (FDA). For instance, Novartis Pharmaceutical Company (the manufacturer of Ritalin) and Eli Lily & Company (the manufacturer of Prozac) both mention uncommon but serious side effects associated with these drugs. For Ritalin, the possible effects for up to 1 percent of users include altered mood and mood swings, hallucinations, anger, and suicidal ideation (Drugs.com, n.d.a). For Prozac, up to 1 percent of users may experience anxiety, nervousness, paranoid reactions, and suicidal thoughts or behavior. For about one user in a thousand, Prozac symptoms may include aggression, antisocial reactions, delusions, and hallucinations (Drugs.com, n.d.b).

The Physician's Desk Reference Manual also notes that virtually *all* psychiatric medications have the potential to produce a wide range of abnormal behaviors, including psychosis, violence, and suicidal or homicidal thoughts (Stolzer, 2013). These possible side effects are so dangerous that the FDA requires the drug industry to prominently include severe warnings on package inserts (Mental Health Rights, 2015). Additionally, because the medical establishment and the scientific community are uncertain regarding how the drugs actually work—drug labels typically indicate the "mechanism of action" is unknown or is "presumed to be" or "hypothesized to be"—proponents argue that potential miscalculations in appropriate drug dosages, or changes in dosages, or in drug types, or adding/subtracting new medications may alter the drugs' influence, converting beneficial effects into harmful outcomes (Goldman & Moore, 2019).

In assessing these competing arguments relative to the drugs' likely impact on gun violence, a reasonable conclusion is that the drugs are unlikely to trigger violence in the vast majority of users. As the data indicate, substantially more people have taken psychotropic medications in the past quarter-century than in earlier periods, but the level of societal violence—including gun violence—has *decreased* over the same period. This would not be the case if the drugs induced violent behavior in most individuals. On the other hand, from a statistical perspective and given the drugs' unknown influences on brain function, the data also indicate that psychotropic drugs likely induce violence in a small percentage of users—from about one in a hundred to one in a thousand users, depending on the drug (Drugs.com, n.d.a; Drugs.com, n.d.b). Whether the potential violence-dampening effects in the vast majority of users offset the potential violence-exacerbating effects in the remaining users is impossible to calculate.

The Facts: While many social and psychological factors presumably converge in individuals who perpetrate senseless acts of gun violence, speculative explanations for such violence frequently center on whether such shooters appear to have been on or have taken psychiatric medications or other mind-altering drugs. For example, one source (i.e., Citizens Commission on Human Rights International, 2018) highlights and briefly discusses over 70 cases where psychiatric drugs were linked to acts of violence, including 20 attacks involving fatalities. Another source (i.e., Hohmann, 2015) discusses 25 assailants on psychotropic drugs who were responsible for horrific gun massacres or gun violence. Still another source (i.e., Goldman & Moore, 2019) asserts that "The list of school shooters under the influence of psychiatric drugs at the time of their rampage is a long one" and then proceeds to discuss several well-known incidents. Proponents of this theory contend that, while it is possible that the drug/violence link in some of these cases is unfounded, unless *all* such claims are unsupported, the conjecture that psychotropic drugs may induce violent behavior warrants further study. They contend that "research has shown that psychiatric drugs can make people manic, psychotic, aggressive, suicidal, and homicidal. These . . . drug reactions . . . often disappear when the drug is withdrawn . . . and reappear when the drug is resumed." Further, such reactions do not occur just in the mentally ill, but also in otherwise healthy volunteers participating in drug testing (Goldman & Moore, 2019).

Other observers and researchers, however, emphasize that psychotropic drugs are regularly associated with mass and spree killers simply because, almost by definition, something is wrong with their brains (Fast, 2018). Citing research that examined the relationship between homicides and psychotic illness (i.e., Nielssen & Large, 2010), they assert that 39 percent of such homicides occur in individuals with psychoses *before* they have ever been treated—a rate 22 times higher than the rate in individuals who had been treated (Torrey, n.d.). They conclude that the real issue is not psychiatric drugs, but "mental illness" (Fast, 2018) or "access to firearms" (Hargis, 2019).

Further, because the etiology behind many mass shootings remains largely unknown, some defenders of psychotropic drugs (e.g., Hargis, 2019) see any discussion of the role of psychotropic drugs in mass violence as a ploy to divert attention from the role of firearms in such shootings. The staunch defenses that gun rights groups (such as the National Rifle

Association) typically mount when gun rights are threatened makes such suspicions understandable.

However, concerns about the negative effects of psychiatric drugs are not limited to gun rights proponents. Patient-advocate organizations have also asserted that such drugs can have dangerous, violence-inducing side effects. Noting that a diagnosis of mental illness is often fairly subjective—typically based on a patient-completed questionnaire and not objective medical tests—they emphasize that these drugs can cause paranoia, thoughts about suicide and dying, and aggressive or violent behavior, among a host of other less-severe effects (Mental Health Rights, 2015). Additionally, because of the widespread use of these drugs—psychiatric diagnoses "skyrocketed" in the United States after passage of the Americans with Disabilities Act (ADA) in 1990 (Stolzer, 2013)—even if these negative effects impact only a small percentage of total users, the number of affected individuals is still substantial (Gorvett, 2020).

Critics of the burgeoning use of psychotropic drugs further defend their concerns by noting that economic incentives exist for overprescribing these medications. Under the ADA, negative life experiences and conduct (such as anxiety, behavioral disorders, oppositional defiance actions, etc.) are legitimate psychiatric disorders that make schools eligible for additional federal monies for each child so diagnosed (Stolzer, 2013). These critics assert that about 98 percent of all pediatric referrals for psychiatric diagnoses originate in the public school system (Baughman, 2006); and because of the financial enticement, many more schoolchildren (85 to 90 percent of them male) are now diagnosed and treated as mentally troubled for stresses and behaviors considered normal in the past (Stolzer, 2013). Other researchers, associated with the University of New England College of Osteopathic Medicine, note in a review article that people with diagnosed mental illnesses account for only about 3 to 5 percent of violent crime, and also acknowledge that psychiatric medication can induce murder and suicide (Marvasti & Friel, 2019).

Overall, these seemingly contradictory arguments concerning the violence-inducing properties of psychiatric drugs may be more apparent than real. As many proponents of psychiatric drugs have pointed out, the increasingly widespread use of psychotropic medications by individuals with mental illness—without a correspondingly proportional increase in societal violence—certainly demonstrates that, for the great majority of patients, the drugs are not violence-inducing (Kruzel, 2019).

But proponents of a linkage between acts of violence and use of psychotropic medications emphasize that the drugs' action mechanisms are unknown, that they are likely overprescribed (Stolzer, 2013), and that both drug manufacturers and the FDA have acknowledged potentially severe side effects that include violent thoughts and behavior in a small percentage of users. For this small group of individuals, the medications can induce various abnormal behaviors, including—if juries adjudicating cases of psychiatric drug–related violence are to be believed (e.g., Marvasti & Friel, 2019)—gun violence. As noted earlier, whether the potential violence tempered by these drugs in the overwhelming majority of users offsets the potential violence induced by the drugs in a small minority of individuals is impossible to determine.

FURTHER READING

Baughman, Fred, 2006. *The ADHD Fraud: How Psychiatry Makes "Patients" of Normal Children.* Oxford, England: Trafford Publishing.

Citizens Commission on Human Rights International, 2018. "Psychiatric Drugs Create Violence & Suicide." Citizens Commission on Human Rights International, March. https://www.cchrint.org/pdfs/violence-report.pdf

Drugs.com, n.d.a. "Ritalin Side Effects." https://www.drugs.com/sfx/ritalin-side-effects.html

Drugs.com, n.d.b. "Prozac Side Effects." https://www.drugs.com/sfx/prozac-side-effects.html

Fast, Julie, 2018. "Why Psychiatric Drugs Don't Cause Mass Shootings." *Psychology Today*, May 21. psychologytoday.com/us/blog/take-charge-bipolar-disorder/201805/why-psychiatric-drugs-dont-cause-mass-shootings

Goldman, Ronald, & Moore, Diane, 2019. "Medication-Induced Violence: Do Psychiatric Drugs Play a Role in Mass Shootings?" https://www.baumhedlundlaw.com/medication-induced-violence/

Gorvett, Zaria, 2020. "The Medications That Change Who We Are." *BBC Future*, January 8. https://www.bbc.com/future/article/20200108-the-medications-that-change-who-we-are

Hargis, Cydney, 2019. "NRA Spokesperson Dana Loesch Says 'Psychotropic Drugs' May Be to Blame for School Shootings." Mediamatters, May 9. https://www.mediamatters.org/national-rifle-association/nra-spokesperson-dana-loesch-says-psychotropic-drugs-may-be-blame-school

Hohmann, Leo, 2015. "Big List of Drug-Induced Killers." WND, June 18. wnd.com/2015/06/big-list-of-drug-induced-killers/

Kruzel, John, 2019. "What's behind the Dubious Claim That Psychiatric Drugs Fuel Mass Shootings?" PolitiFact, August 16. https://www

.politifact.com/article/2019/aug/16/whats-behind-dubious-claim-psychiatric-drugs-fuel-/

Langman, Peter, 2016. "Psychiatric Medications and School Shootings." Langman Psychological Associates, February. https://www.researchgate.net/publication/308220517_Psychiatric_Medications_and_School_Shootings

Marvasti, Jamshid, & Friel, Shelby, 2019. "Psychiatric Diagnoses and Medications: Do They Cause Gun Violence?" *Connecticut Medicine*, 83(3), 113–121. https://forensicpsychology.org/MarvastiHandout2019.pdf

Mental Health Rights, 2015. "Psychotropic Drugs Side Effects." MHR, April 14. Accessed July 2020. mentalhealthrights.org/psychotropic-drugs-side-effects/ (URL no longer active).

Moore, Thomas J., Glenmullen, Joseph, & Furberg, Curt D., 2010. "Prescription Drugs Associated with Reports of Violence toward Others." *PLoS ONE*, December 15. https://doi.org/10.1371/journal.pone.0015337

Nielssen, Olav, & Large, Matthew, 2010. "Rates of Homicide during the First Episode of Psychosis and after Treatment: A Systematic Review and Meta-Analysis." *Schizophrenia Bulletin*, 36(4), 702–712. https://www.ncbi.nlm.nih.gov/pmc/articles/PMC2894594/

Stolzer, Jeanne, 2013. "The Systematic Correlation between Psychiatric Medications and Unprovoked Mass Murder in America." *New Male Studies: An International Journal*, 2(2), 9–23. psychrights.org/Research/Digest/Misc/PsychDrugsMassMurderCorrelationJStolzer2013.pdf

Tiihonen, Jari, Lehti, Martti, Aaltonen, Mikko, Kivivuori, Janne, Kautiainen, Hannu, Virta, Lauri, & Hoti, Fabian, et al. 2015. "Psychotropic Drugs and Homicide: A Prospective Cohort Study from Finland." *World Psychiatry*, 14(2), 245–247.

Torrey, E. Fuller, n.d. "Antipsychotics Don't Cause Homicide." https://mentalillnesspolicy.org/consequences/suicideantipscyhotics.html

Q32. WOULD PROHIBITING THE MENTALLY ILL FROM OWNING GUNS REDUCE GUN VIOLENCE?

Answer: A fair answer to this question necessitates distinguishing between *individuals* who are mentally ill, and *mental illness*—an umbrella term that encompasses a wide variety of emotional and behavioral problems, ranging from anxieties and depressions up to psychiatric disorders such as paranoia, schizophrenia, and psychosis (Mayo Clinic Staff, n.d.; BU Center for Psychiatric Rehabilitation, n.d.). In the case of individuals with severe mental illness (SMI)—particularly schizophrenia, major depression, and bipolar disorder—empirical evidence suggests that an increased risk of violent behavior relative to the general population does exist. However, heightened risk of violence generally does *not* characterize individuals suffering from milder forms of mental illness (McDonald, 2019).

For example, the risk factors for mentally unbalanced individuals likely to carry out a mass shooting—young, isolated, alienated, and male—describe thousands of troubled young men for whom gun violence will never be an issue. Experts such as Professor Jeffery Swanson, a leading researcher in mental health and violence at the Duke University School of Medicine, have asserted that while people with serious mental illness are several times more likely to be violent than individuals without such illnesses, the vast majority of mentally ill individuals are not violent "and never will be" (Beckett, 2015)

Nevertheless, misconceptions of the mentally ill as especially dangerous—as "ticking time bombs ready to explode into violence"—are deeply ingrained in society (Knoll & Annas, 2015). In the nineteenth and early twentieth centuries, the mentally ill were often demonized or institutionalized and forgotten. Understanding of mental illness has greatly improved since that time, but research suggests that fears of the potential for violence among people clearly grappling with mental illness has actually increased since the 1950s (Knoll & Annas, 2015). Contributing to these misconceptions is the prominent attention mass shootings receive in the mass media. Although such shootings constitute only a small fraction of societal gun violence, their frequent association with individuals suffering with SMI (Duwe & Rocque, 2018) has contributed to the false impression that *all* (or at least an alarming percentage of) mentally troubled individuals are violent.

Further, explanations for gun violence by prominent Republican officials with pro-gun rights orientations have strengthened the public's perceived linkage between violence and general mental illness. For example, in attempting to make sense of two mass shootings that occurred in August, 2019, in El Paso, Texas, and Dayton, Ohio, Republican president Donald Trump suggested that mental derangement—and not lack of gun control regulations—was the precipitating cause of the violence: "Mental illness and hatred pulls the trigger, not the gun" (McDonald, 2019). By issuing such a broad statement about mental illness in general, critics said that Trump's remarks inadvertently supported stereotypical linkages between mental illness and violence.

However, in considering just individuals with severe mental illness, experts do see a fairly strong connection between mental abnormality and violence. For example, Dr. Michael Stone, a forensic psychiatrist at Columbia University, asserts that severe mental illness—psychotic or delusional thinking—characterizes only about 1 percent of the general population, but is found in about 20 percent of mass murderers. Further, depression and antisocial traits characterize another 15 percent (Carey, 2017). Other investigators have also linked SMI to violence, finding that about 60 percent of public mass shootings were perpetrated by individuals demonstrating signs of SMI—a rate 15 times higher than the rate of SMI in the general population (Duwe & Rocque, 2018).

Because of their statistical infrequency, mass shootings may provide an incomplete or distorted picture of mental illness and violence. Swanson's analysis of the National Institute of Mental Health's Epidemiological Catchment Area survey found that 12 percent of all people with SMI were violent. This rate fell to 7 percent when limited to individuals *only* with SMI and no substance abuse problems. Overall, the analysis suggested that, while the absolute risk of violence is low, mental illness alone approximately triples the probability of some form of violence. Additionally, in apportioning the percentage of total violence due to mental illness, the study concluded that mental illness alone accounts for about 3 to 5 percent of all violence. In other words, if society could somehow completely eliminate mental illness, about 96 percent of societal violence would still occur (McDonald, 2019; Matthews, 2019).

So, overall, the evidence (e.g., Duwe & Rocque, 2018; Knoll & Annas, 2015; Carey, 2017) supports the conclusion that gun prohibitions on individuals with severe mental illness would only marginally reduce gun violence. In fact, many of these individuals *are* prohibited from owning or possessing firearms, either because of involuntary commitments for psychiatric treatment, or because of disqualifying criminal records (Beckett, 2015). For Americans diagnosed with less severe forms of mental illness—about 47 million U.S. adults (19 percent of the total adult population) had some type of mental illness in 2018 (McDonald, 2019)—blanket gun prohibitions would have even less impact on gun violence. Gun rights advocates contend that such prohibitions might modestly decrease gun violence, but only by potentially banning firearm ownership for as many as one in five Americans who have been diagnosed with mental illness.

The Facts: The belief that mentally ill individuals are more dangerous than people without mental illness has a long history, regularly reinforced by popular media. Not only are the mentally ill portrayed as dangerous, but, as some psychiatric experts note, common periodicals frequently make presumptive associations between mental illness, criminality, and derangement—associations the lay public needs little persuasion to accept (Knoll & Annas, 2015). But as suggested above, such associations are too broad, stigmatizing the vast majority of mentally troubled individuals with qualities characteristic only of those with severe mental illness.

Further, while individuals with SMI are three to four times more likely to be violent than "normal" individuals (Beckett, 2015), these individuals frequently are already barred from possessing firearms. For example, one of the disqualifying questions on ATF Form 4473—the background check form completed by every potential purchaser of a firearm when buying from a federally licensed gun dealer—specifically targets for rejection individuals who ever were committed to a mental institution. While this bar is less effective than in the past—social policy beginning in the 1960s shifted much treatment of the mentally ill from psychiatric institutions to outpatient community health centers, reducing the question's relevancy—other bars keep individuals with SMI from legally owning a gun. Professor Jeffrey Swanson analyzed the records of over 23,000 individuals with SMI in the state of Connecticut. His analysis showed that while mental health records disqualified about 7 percent of them from gun ownership, 35 percent had a disqualifying criminal record (Beckett, 2015). Other sources indicate that about 16 percent of all jail and prison inmates—over 350,000 individuals—are severely mentally ill (Amadeo, 2020). Most of these individuals, as convicted felons, cannot legally own or possess a firearm.

Another consideration relevant in examining mental illness and gun violence is the nature of the violence involved. Discussions of the severely mentally ill typically focus on the violence they inflict on others—for example, mass shootings and spree killings. However, Swanson asserts that most of the lethal gun violence perpetrated by the mentally ill is harm to *self*. As he puts it, "If you were to back out all the risk associated with mental illness that's contributing to the 300,000 people killed by gunshot wounds in the last ten years, you could probably reduce deaths by about 100,000 people. Ninety-five percent of the reduction would be from suicide. Only 5 percent would be from reducing homicide" (Beckett, 2015). Thus, while placing firearm restrictions on the mentally ill could have limited impact in reducing *homicidal* gun violence, without additional mental health interventions, such restrictions are unlikely to deter the seriously suicidal from using other means to inflict self-harm.

Along related lines, some psychiatric experts (e.g., Knoll & Annas, 2015) more generally question the likely effectiveness of gun prohibition laws aimed at the mentally ill. Noting that gun violence is relatively rare even among the seriously mentally ill, they see an emphasis on gun laws to resolve the violence issue as "grasping a problem by the wrong handle."

Given that gun violence is hard to anticipate and avert, they argue that a better strategy is to encourage family members and social acquaintances of potentially troubled individuals to watch for "leaked" intent of violence in verbal communications, on social media postings, and so on—and then to step in if necessary to ensure that the individual receives evaluation and treatment (Knoll & Annas, 2015). Other investigators examining low-frequency/high-intensity events such as mass shootings (e.g., Meloy et al., 2012) have identified "warning behaviors" that indicate when a potentially at-risk individual poses a threat. They have argued that specialized threat assessment teams can use these warning behaviors to proactively intervene and prevent violence in schools and workplaces.

Another influential group of societal stakeholders—state legislators—have provided a further alternative to imposing a complete gun prohibition on the mentally ill. Recognizing that life stressors may sometimes provoke mental disturbances in normally healthy individuals, a significant number of state legislatures have passed "red flag" laws that allow for the temporary seizure of a person's firearms if that individual is (or appears to be) in a crisis state. When the crisis subsides, the law provides for the return of the individual's guns. While these laws have notable constitutional and practical difficulties (e.g., Edwards, 2020), they implicitly recognize that much mental illness—like much physical illness—is not usually a lifelong affliction; and that individuals who perhaps had a suicidal mental health crisis in the past may no longer be at risk in the present.

These alternatives to simple gun prohibition for the mentally ill appear to reflect an underlying assumption. If violence prevention efforts are to succeed, the complexities of determining an individual's mental state (whether healthy or ill) and the unpredictable nature of gun violence mean that multiple approaches—and not just blanket gun prohibitions—are needed. Some people contend, for example, that a blanket prohibition on gun ownership for individuals with SMI may be appropriate. In fact, one online poll of law enforcement found that about 20 percent of police professionals see aggressive institutionalization of the severely mentally ill as the most effective strategy for preventing large-scale public shootings (PoliceOne.com, 2013).

But for most mentally ill individuals, who are likely never to be violent (Beckett, 2015), critics see a blanket gun prohibition as unnecessarily punitive. They claim that a general ban would deprive millions of Americans of an enumerated constitutional right, do little to address the mental health issues potentially underlying gun violence (e.g., Follman, 2012), and would result only in an uncertain—and probably minimal—reduction in such violence. Determining whether this anticipated reduction justifies its associated costs is primarily a matter of subjective judgment.

FURTHER READING

Amadeo, Kimberly, 2020. "Deinstitutionalization, Its Causes, Effects, Pros, and Cons." The Balance, February 17. https://www.thebalance.com/deinstitutionalization-3306067

Beckett, Lois, 2015. "Myth vs. Fact: Violence and Mental Health." ProPublica, June 18. propublica.org/article/myth-vs-fact-violence-and-mental-health

BU Center for Psychiatric Rehabilitation, n.d. "What Is Psychiatric Disability and Mental Illness?" Accessed July 2020. cpr.bu.edu/resources/reasonable-accomodations/what-is-psychiatric-disability-and-mental-illness/ (URL no longer active).

Carey, Benedict, 2017. "Are Mass Murderers Insane? Usually Not, Researchers Say." *New York Times*, November 8. https://www.nytimes.com/2017/11/08/health/mass-murderers-mental-illness.html

Duwe, Grant, & Rocque, Michael, 2018. "Op-Ed: Actually, There Is a Clear Link between Mass Shootings and Mental Illness." *Los Angeles Times*, February 23. https://www.latimes.com/opinion/op-ed/la-oe-duwe-rocque-mass-shootings-mental-illness-20180223-story.html

Edwards, Cam, 2020. "Colorado's 'Red Flag' Gun Seizure Law Now in Effect." Bearing Arms, January 1. https://bearingarms.com/cam-e/2020/01/01/colorados-red-flag-gun-seizure-law-now-in-effect/

Follman, Mark, 2012. "Mass Shootings: Maybe What We Need Is a Better Mental-Health Policy." *Mother Jones*, November 9. https://www.motherjones.com/politics/2012/11/jared-loughner-mass-shootings-mental-illness/

Knoll, James, & Annas, George, 2015. "Mass Shootings and Mental Illness." https://www.researchgate.net/publication/284156856_Mass_Shootings_and_Mental_Illness

Matthews, Dylan, 2019. "Stop Blaming Mental Illness for Mass Shootings." Vox, August 5. vox.com/policy-and-politics/2017/11/9/16618472/mental-illness-gun-homicide-mass-shootings

Mayo Clinic Staff, n.d. "Mental Illness: Symptoms and Causes." https://www.mayoclinic.org/diseases-conditions/mental-illness/syc-20374968

McDonald, Jessica, 2019. "The Facts on Mental Illness and Mass Shootings." FactCheck.Org, October 18. factcheck.org/2019/10/the-facts-on-mental-illness-and-mass-shootings/

Meloy, John, Hoffmann, Jens, Guldimann, Angela, & James, David, 2012. "The Role of Warning Behaviors in Threat Assessment: An Exploration and Suggested Typology." *Behavioral Sciences & the Law*, 30(3), 256–279. https://www.researchgate.net/publication/224897312_The_Role

_of_Warning_Behaviors_in_Threat_Assessment_An_Exploration
_and_Suggested_Typology
PoliceOne.com, 2013. "Gun Policy & Law Enforcement: Survey Results."
https://media.cdn.lexipol.com/p1_gunsurveysummary_2013.pdf

Q33. DO PURCHASE WAITING PERIODS REDUCE GUN SUICIDES AND IMPULSE KILLINGS?

Answer: Waiting periods (WPs) stop gun buyers from taking possession of a purchased firearm immediately. They interpose a certain number of days—the specific number varies by state—between the date the purchaser buys the gun and the date on which the individual actually acquires the firearm. The primary idea behind WPs is that such delays may inhibit impulsive acts of gun violence—gun homicides and, particularly, gun suicides.

Gun control organizations and lawmakers are supportive of WPs. The Giffords Law Center, for example, stated that people often act on temporary emotional states. It noted that suicide attempts are frequently "impulsive, singular episodes that involve little planning . . . [and that] some of the factors that incite violence against others, such as anger and rage, can be short-lived" (Giffords Law Center, n.d.). Proponents say that by creating a time buffer between the purchase and acquisition of a firearm, WPs give individuals a chance to calm down, think more clearly, and reconsider their contemplated actions. Further, supporters of waiting periods assert that empirical evidence supports these expectations, citing studies showing that WPs appear to reduce suicide rates by as much as 11 percent, and homicide rates by about 17 percent (Giffords Law Center, n.d.).

Opponents of WPs regard these claims skeptically, arguing that only anecdotal evidence supports the notion that guns are frequently used impulsively or in crimes of passion (Chestnut, 2015). For example, Bureau of Alcohol, Tobacco, Firearms, & Explosives (BATFE) time-to-crime trace data show an average of almost *nine years* from purchase to criminal use—hardly suggesting impulsive criminal usage; and guns used in suicides are not routinely traced. Further, these opponents assert that the majority of prior research examining the effects of WPs on gun suicides and homicides has found mixed or inconclusive results; and more recent investigations (e.g., Luca, Malhotra, & Poliquin, 2017; Edwards et al., 2015) showing beneficial effects frequently appear to have methodological or analytical flaws limiting the reliability of their findings. The National Rifle Association

(NRA), the most prominent and powerful gun rights organization in the United States, asserts that WPs "are arbitrary impositions with no effect on crime or suicide, introduce no additional investigative avenues, and only burden law-abiding gun owners" (NRA-ILA, 2019).

The nonpartisan RAND Corporation assessed the effectiveness of WPs for reducing suicides, violent crime, and mass shootings. Those analyses indicated that the empirical evidence shows uncertain and inconsistent effects of WPs on mass shootings, and is thus inconclusive regarding their impact in this area. However, for suicide, RAND concluded that two studies met the methodological criteria needed for reliable interpretation. Both studies (i.e., Edwards et al., 2015; Luca et al., 2017) found that WPs were associated with statistically significant decreases in gun suicides, with the Luca et al. (2017) study additionally finding that WPs were also associated with a statistically significant decrease in total suicides. Based on these two studies, RAND concluded "limited" evidence indicates that WPs may reduce total suicides; and that "moderate" evidence indicates that WPs may reduce gun suicides (Smart, 2020).

Similarly, RAND identified several qualifying studies that examined the effects of waiting periods on both overall homicide rates and firearm homicide rates. One study (Edwards et al., 2015) found that WPs had no effect on total homicide rates but did appear to reduce gun homicides. A second investigation (Luca et al., 2017) found that WPs appeared to reduce both total homicides and firearm homicides. However, two other studies found that WPs either had no significant effect on homicides (Hepburn et al., 2004) or WPs had uncertain effects on police officer homicides (Mustard, 2001). A fifth study (Roberts, 2009) indicated the WPs between two and seven days seemed to reduce total intimate partner homicides, as well as firearm-involved intimate partner homicides. However, this finding did not hold for WPs that were shorter or longer. Based on these studies, RAND concluded "limited" evidence indicates that WPs may reduce gun homicides, and that "moderate" evidence indicates that WPs may reduce total homicides (Morral, 2020).

The supporting evidence for these generally positive assessments of the effectiveness of WPs for reducing suicides and homicides is primarily derived from the findings of the Edwards et al. (2015) and the Luca et al. (2017) investigations. Despite RAND's evaluation, as noted earlier, gun rights proponents dismiss these results, asserting that the studies have methodological and analytical limitations that make their conclusions suspect.

As the RAND analysis suggests, evaluating the effectiveness of WPs on suicide (or homicide) requires examining their impact on both *gun* suicides and *total* suicides (Michaels, 2018), For instance, if WPs decrease gun suicides but not total suicides (presumably because suicidal individuals unable to access firearms simply turn to other methods), their effectiveness in saving such lives would be questionable. Further, at least one investigation has encountered this complication. Professors Jens Ludwig of Georgetown University and Philip Cook of Duke University analyzed United States' vital statistics data from 1985 through 1987 and found that the Brady Act-imposed waiting period appeared to reduce gun suicides among individuals 55 years and older, but with no reduction in the nation's overall suicide rate. They attributed this result to a likely offsetting increase in non-gun suicides (Ludwig & Cook, 2000). Noting the impact of the waiting period on just gun suicides without examining total suicides would have resulted in misleading conclusions.

Another complication is identifying the length of time needed for a waiting period to achieve the "cooling off" effect required to reduce impulsivity (Lewiecki & Miller, 2013). In the absence of a federal mandate, states have instituted waiting periods ranging from a low of 3 days to a high of 14 days. Too short a time period may result in research findings that suggest WPs are ineffective, but too long a period may unnecessarily delay the acquisition of a firearm urgently needed for protection (Smart, 2020). John Lott, a prominent but controversial gun rights proponent and founder of the Crime Prevention Research Center, asserts that longer waiting periods may actually have a pernicious effect. He states, "There's some evidence that once you get past three days . . . you'll see slight increases in rape rates. A woman may have a . . . serious stalker [and] even a delay of a few days can make a difference" (Michaels, 2018).

Thus, despite the immediate intuitive logic of waiting periods for decreasing an individual's potentially lethal impulses, the mixed nature of current empirical evidence—as well as noted complicating considerations—makes WPs' effectiveness for limiting suicides and impulse homicides a subject of continued fierce debate.

The Facts: Initially, before implementation of the National Instant Criminal Background Check System (NICS) in 1998, a waiting period functioned to give federally licensed gun dealers time to run background checks on prospective firearms purchasers. With NICS implementation, almost instant verification of an individual's firearms purchase eligibility became possible, and eliminated the need for the background check waiting period. While waiting period proponents (e.g., Giffords Law Center, n.d.; Kertscher, 2015) still suggest that WPs are useful for giving law enforcement agencies more time to investigate questionable purchasers—a claim opponents strongly dispute (e.g., NRA-ILA, n.d.)—the primary justification for WPs is that they may reduce impulsive gun suicides and homicides. As proponents of WPs note, while guns do not represent the most common suicide method—comprising only 6 percent of all suicide attempts—they are the most fatal, making up 54 percent of all lethal attempts (Shaw, 2019). Thus, advocates of WPs claim that limiting gun suicide attempts could save a substantial number of lives.

The empirical evidence examining the efficacy of WPs for reducing impulse lethality has generally shown mixed or inconclusive results. For example, the Centers for Disease Control (CDC) in 2003 evaluated the effectiveness of WPs for reducing suicides and impulsive violence, and concluded that the small number of studies, inconsistent findings, and methodological limitations made determining the effectiveness of WPs impossible (CDC Morbidity and Mortality Weekly Report, 2003). In contrast, the RAND Corporation's assessment of waiting periods in 2020 is more positive regarding WP effectiveness (e.g., Morral, 2020; Smart, 2020).

For example, a team of Harvard Business School researchers published a study in 2017 indicating that handgun waiting periods *are* effective, impressively so (Luca et al., 2017). The Harvard researchers found a 17 percent reduction in gun homicides (equivalent to about 39 fewer homicides per year for the average state); a 6 percent reduction in gun suicides (about 17 fewer suicides per year for the average state); and no evidence of a method substitution effect. These results were stronger than an earlier study (i.e., Edwards et al., 2015) that found a waiting period had no impact on homicides, but did reduce suicides by 3 percent with no evidence of method substitution effects. Proponents of WPs (e.g., Giffords Law Center, n.d.) and the popular media (e.g., Gerdeman, 2017; Kruzel, 2018; Jones, 2019; Heintz, 2020) have heavily emphasized the findings of the 2017 Harvard investigation.

However, this study has engendered suspicion among gun rights proponents (e.g., Michaels, 2018) and has received significant criticism from other pro-gun analysts. Methodologically, these critics fault the study for its failure to incorporate control variables (i.e., educational attainment, crime rates, police resources, etc.) normally used in firearm policy investigations. More substantively, they also question the study's several counterintuitive and improbable findings. These include results indicating that background checks *increase* homicides; that poverty *decreases* firearms-related homicides; and that poverty, urban areas, and younger-aged cohorts are *not* associated with total homicides (NRA-ILA, 2019). Given such results, pro-gun critics contend that the research model used is likely incorrectly specified, making the reliability of *all* the findings suspect.

Nonetheless, the RAND Corporation found the study's results credible (Morral, 2020; Smart, 2020).

Aside from equivocal empirical evidence, logical considerations suggest that the efficacy of WPs for reducing suicides and homicides is obviously limited to those households that currently do not possess a gun. For example, about 42 percent of households already contain a firearm, and 66 percent of gun owners own more than one firearm (Parker et al., 2017). For these individuals who already have access to guns, waiting periods are irrelevant. For non-gun-owning households, however, WPs may have some utility. Further, as noted earlier, the length of a waiting period can influence their efficacy (Lewiecki & Miller, 2013; Roberts, 2009). While at least one study found a significant negative association between waiting period length and firearm suicides—the longer the waiting period, the fewer the suicides (Anestis & Anestis, 2015)—little is generally known about the most appropriate time delay. Thus, policy makers are sometimes reluctant to enact a WP for fear it may have unintended negative consequences, such as possibly delaying the acquisition of a firearm for self-defense by an endangered individual.

To that end, in June 2019 Republican Governor Phil Scott of Vermont vetoed a bill providing for a 24-hour WP for handgun purchases at least in part because no data demonstrated the usefulness of a mere 24-hour delay (Heintz, 2020). Additionally, studies have found that individuals are more likely to commit suicide within a week after purchasing a gun, but even with a 15-day waiting period, the risk of suicide during the first week of taking possession is still often elevated (Michael, 2018). Complicating matters further, WPs involve Second Amendment considerations, and determining a legally "reasonable" length for a waiting period is likely to become a constitutional question. Associate Supreme Court Justice Clarence Thomas implied this in questioning California's 10-day gun purchase WP in 2018. He pointed out that more liberal members of the Court might object to waiting periods imposed for other hotly debated rights: "I suspect that four members of this court would review a 10-day waiting period for abortion, notwithstanding a state's purported interest in creating a 'cooling off' period" (Marcus, 2018).

Limited empirical findings do provide support for arguments that WPs can reduce suicides and impulse killings. However, critics of WPs say that additional factors should also be weighed, including inconsistent research results; clashes over what constitutes an "appropriate" waiting period length; concerns that a purchase delay may endanger some applicants (such as individuals seeking protection from stalkers or abusive relationship partners); the possibility of suicide even after a lengthy waiting period; and potential constitutional issues.

FURTHER READING

Anestis, Michael, & Anestis, Joyce, 2015. "Suicide Rates and State Laws Regulating Access and Exposure to Handguns." *American Journal of Public Health,* 105(10), 2049–2058. https://ajph.aphapublications.org/doi/full/10.2105/AJPH.2015.302753

CDC Morbidity and Mortality Weekly Report, 2003. "First Reports Evaluating the Effectiveness of Strategies for Preventing Violence: Early Childhood Home Visitation and Firearm Laws." MMWR, 52, No. RR-14, October 3. https://www.cdc.gov/mmwr/PDF/rr/rr5214.pdf

Chestnut, Mark, 2015. "What's Wrong with Waiting Periods." America's First Freedom, May 7. https://www.americas1stfreedom.org/articles/2015/5/8/whats-wrong-with-waiting-periods/

Edwards, Griffin, Nesson, Erik, Robinson, Joshua, & Vars, Fredrick, 2015. "Looking Down the Barrel of a Loaded Gun: The Effect of Mandatory Handgun Purchase Delays on Homicide and Suicide." *Economics Journal,* September. https://www.researchgate.net/publication/281649738_Looking_Down_the_Barrel_of_a_Loaded_Gun_The_Effects_of_Mandatory_Handun_Purchase_Delays_on_Homicide_and_Suicide

Gerdeman, Dina, 2017. "Handgun Waiting Periods Prevent Hundreds of Homicides Each Year." *Forbes,* November 9. https://www.forbes.com/sites/hbsworkingknowledge/2017/11/09/handgun-waiting-periods-prevent-hundreds-of-homicides-each-year/#45dc4d314ee9

Giffords Law Center, n.d. "Waiting Periods." https://lawcenter.giffords.org/gun-laws/policy-areas/substitution/gun-laws/policy-areas/gun-sales/waiting-periods/

Heintz, Paul, 2020. "Vermont Senate Seeks to Revive Vetoed Gun Waiting Period Bill." Seven Days, January 23. https://www.sevendaysvt.com/OffMessage/archives/2020/01/23/Vermont-senate-seeks-to-revive-vetoed-gun-waiting-period-bill

Hepburn, Lisa, Miller, Matthew, Azrael, Deborah, & Hemenway, David, 2004. "The Effect of Nondiscretionary Concealed Weapon Carrying Laws on Homicide." *Journal of Trauma: Injury, Infection, and Critical Care,* 56(3), 676–681. https://journals.lww.com/jtrauma/Abstract/2004/03000/The_Effects_of_Nondiscretionary_Concealed_Weapon.30.aspx

Jones, Megan, 2019. "Legislators in Aurora Hope National Cooling-Off Period for Handgun Purchases Will Save Lives." *Beacon-News,* April 8. https://www.chicagotribune.com/suburbs/aurora-beacon-news/ct-abn-legislators-cool-off-act-0409-story-html

Kertscher, Tom, 2015. "No Statistical Evidence That a Waiting Period for Handgun Purchases Reduces Violence, Lawmaker Says." PolitiFact,

April 27. politifact.com/factchecks/2015/apr/27/van-wanggaard/no-evidence-waiting-period-handgun-purchases-reduc/

Kruzel, John, 2018. "Yes, Waiting Periods on Gun Purchases Have Been Linked to Suicide Reduction." PolitiFact, March 24. https://www.politifact.com/factchecks/2018/mar/24/doug-jones/yes-waiting-periods-gun-purchases-have-been-linked/

Lewiecki, E. Michael, & Miller, Sara, 2013. "Suicide, Guns, and Public Policy." *American Journal of Public Health*, 103(1), 27–31. https://www.deepdyve.com/lp/American-public-health-association/suicide-guns-and-public-policy-MthvwWzCcc

Luca, Michael, Malhotra, Deepak, & Poliquin, Christopher, 2017. "Handgun Waiting Periods Reduce Gun Deaths." *Proceedings of the Academy of Sciences*, 114(46), 12162–12165. https://www.pnas.org/content/pnas/early/2017/10/11/1619896114.full.pdf

Ludwig, Jens, & Cook, Philip, 2000. "Homicide and Suicide Rates Associated with Implementation of the Brady Handgun Violence Protection Act." *Journal of the American Medical Association*, 284(5), 585–591. https://jamanetwork.com/journals/jama/fullarticle/192946?appld=scweb

Marcus, Josh, 2018. "Supreme Court Lets California's 10-Day Waiting Period for Gun Purchases Survive." Vice News, February 20. https://www.vice.com/en_us/article/a34nkb/californias-10-day-waiting-period-for-gun-purchases-survives-after-supreme-court-ruling

Michaels, Jordan, 2018. "Exclusive: Not Worth the Wait. The Inconclusive, Contradictory Research on Waiting Period Laws." Guns America Digest, July 25. https://www.gunsamerica.com/digest/waiting-period-laws/

Morral, Andrew, 2020. "Effects of Waiting Periods on Violent Crime." RAND Corporation, April 22. https://www.rand.org/research/gun-policy/analysis/waiting-periods/violent-crime.html

Mustard, David, 2001. "The Impact of Gun Laws on Police Deaths." *Journal of Law & Economics*, 44(S2), 635–657. https://www.journals.uchicago.edu/doi/10.1086/323312

NRA-ILA, 2019. "Waiting Periods." NRA-ILA, September. https://www.nraila.org/get-the-facts/waiting-periods/

Parker, Kim, Horowitz, Juliana, Igielnik, Ruth, Oliphant, J. Baxter, & Brown, Anna, 2017. "The Demographics of Gun Ownership." Pew Research Center, June 22. https://www.pewsocialtrends.org/2017/06/22/the-demographics-of-gun-ownership/

Roberts, Darryl, 2009. "Intimate Partner Homicide: Relationships to Alcohol and Firearms." *Journal of Contemporary Criminal Justice*, 25(1), 67–88. https://journals.sagepub.com/doi/10.1177/1043986208329771

Shaw, Kerry, 2019. "10 Essential Facts about Guns and Suicide." The Trace, April 4. https://www.thetrace.org/2016/09/10-essential-facts-guns-suicide/

Smart, Rosanna, 2020. "Effects of Waiting Periods on Suicides." RAND Corporation, April 22. https://www.rand.org/research/gun-policy/analysis/waiting-periods/suicide.html

7

Guns and Civil Societies: Acceptable Social Contracts

Of the unique characteristics that distinguish America from other nations, the country's ongoing embrace of guns and gun culture is especially notable, acknowledged not just by Americans but by the rest of the world as well. Within America, gun culture has divided society for at least a hundred years into passionate pro- and anti-gun factions; and outside America, the country's gun culture has fascinated and bewildered foreigners for just as long. A clash of fundamental values appears to underlie the divisiveness that gun culture has created, with the values of self-reliance and rugged individualism upholding firearms on the one hand, and the values of peaceful communitarianism and cooperation rejecting them on the other (Campbell, 2019).

It seems only appropriate, then, to conclude this analysis of guns in America with an examination of four questions that encapsulate the influence guns have had on American society—values reciprocally shaping and being shaped by that society. The opening inquiry explores the possible societal cost inherent in accepting a "gun culture." This question assesses the evidential strength undergirding an oft-heard assertion that American gun values and the country's concomitant loose regulation of firearms have resulted in much more violent crime than in Western democracies with stricter gun regulations. Has America's gun culture made the United States less safe than other developed countries?

The second question looks at how American society itself may inadvertently encourage violent behavior. The question weighs the evidence that

Americans' fascination with gun violence—as captured and glorified in films, television, digital video games, and other entertainment media—potentially contributes to actual gun violence.

The third question, focusing on the country's growing political, racial, and ethnic divisions and the resurgence of violence-oriented fringe organizations, evaluates the evidence that these divisions and fringe groups contribute disproportionately to gun violence. The chapter's final question addresses a theme common in many popular accounts of American society—that the country has become an increasingly dangerous and violent place. Thus, this last inquiry investigates whether modern America is actually more violent now than American society has been in past years.

FURTHER READING

Campbell, Donald, 2019. *America's Gun Wars: A Cultural History of Gun Control in the United States*. Santa Barbara, CA: Praeger.

Q34. DO WESTERN DEMOCRACIES WITH STRICT GUN CONTROL REGULATIONS HAVE LESS VIOLENT CRIME?

Answer: Proponents of strong firearms laws frequently point to nations economically similar to the United States—but with much more stringent gun regulations—and assert that these countries have significantly less violent crime precisely because firearms are so rigorously regulated. U.S. politicians and policy makers favoring stronger gun regulation often reference such comparisons to support their legislative agenda. For example, former Texas representative Beto O'Rourke, a 2020 Democratic presidential hopeful, lamented the restraining influence of the National Rifle Association on firearms regulation by declaring, "How else can we explain that we lose nearly 40,000 people in this country to gun violence, a number that no other country comes even close to . . . ?" (Mekelburg, 2019).

While O'Rourke engaged in a bit of hyperbole—more than a dozen countries have higher gun deaths per capita than the United States (Aizenman, 2018)—his implication that the country's firearms death rate is a significant outlier relative to other economically developed nations (i.e., "peer" nations) is substantially correct. With the exception of Mexico, the United States has a gun death rate higher (frequently many *multiples* higher) than the rate of every other member country of the Organization for Economic Cooperation and Development (OECD)—the 36 countries typically used for making "apples-to-apples" socioeconomic comparisons (e.g., Grinshteyn & Hemenway, 2016; Mekelburg, 2019).

For example, in 2017, the United States had a gun death rate of 4.43 gun deaths per 100,000 individuals, which was nine times Canada's rate (0.47/100,000) and 29 times higher than Denmark's rate (0.15/100,000), both OECD members. Indeed, 10 countries—not all of them even OECD members—had gun death rates smaller than 0.10/ per 100,000 persons in 2017 (Aizenman, 2018). For gun control proponents, the implications of such findings are clear. The comparatively lax gun regulation in the United States makes the country more dangerous and less safe than its peer nations. As one gun violence researcher—Dr. Erin Grinshteyn, assistant professor in the School of Community Health at the University of Nevada-Reno—put it, "These results are consistent with the hypothesis that our firearms are killing us rather than protecting us" (Preidt, 2016).

Gun rights proponents question the relevance of these findings for drawing meaningful conclusions about the impact of gun regulation on societal safety. They argue that limiting gun death rate comparisons only to OECD nations is actually not as justified as it initially appears; and that by doing so, the comparisons provide a skewed perspective both on the relative usefulness of gun control for limiting violent crime, and for judging the safety of the United States relative to other nations. These critics cite individuals (e.g., Rosling, 2006) who suggest that dividing the world into just two categories—"developed" and "undeveloped" countries—is no longer justified. While such a division may have been accurate and useful in the 1950s and '60s, developmental data show that this separation is now largely artificial. No bright lines exist on the developmental spectrum of nations, and only graduated changes across multiple dimensions truly distinguish nations from one another (Rosling, 2006).

Gun rights advocates contend that if this is the case—that most countries nowadays actually group together in the middle of the developmental spectrum—then restricting comparisons of gun murder rates to only OECD nations has little empirical justification. Further, doing so prevents comparisons with countries whose per capita GDP may be less than the United States, but whose history, size, ethnic diversity, and demographics may make them better candidates for comparison. For example, when the U.S. gun murder rate is viewed against an expanded list of countries using human development index (HDI) numbers, a much different picture emerges. The HDI is a statistical index of life expectancy, education level, and standard of living compiled by the United Nations Development Programme. Many of these nations—Argentina, Bahamas, Belarus, Costa Rica, Cuba, Estonia, Latvia, Lithuania, Russia, Uruguay, and

Venezuela—have HDI evaluations similar to some OECD members (e.g., Chile, Mexico, and Turkey). These HDI countries also have restrictive gun regulations but higher gun murder rates than the United States, with some rates multiples of the U.S. rate (McMaken, 2015). Nonetheless, gun control proponents assert that the generally higher rates of poverty, lower rates of education, and the prevalence of weak legal and policing institutions in many of these nations make comparisons with the United States too questionable to be useful.

Still, gun rights advocates insist that evaluating violent crime (as measured by gun murder rates) using only Western democracies with tight gun control regulations is not compelling. They assert that other measures of national development (such as the country's HDI number) can easily generate alternative sets of comparison countries demonstrating that severe gun control results in violent crime and gun murder rates much higher than in the United States. Thus, any conclusions about gun regulation and violent crime based solely on OECD comparisons have to be drawn cautiously, and may not be completely reliable.

The Facts: Investigators examining American gun violence commonly restrict cross-national comparisons to a select set of countries—typically to the "world's most developed nations" (Masters, 2019), to "other high-income countries" (Mekelburg, 2019; Preidt, 2016), to "countries with the top indicators of socioeconomic success" (Aizenman, 2018), to "20 developed countries" (Beauchamp, 2018), and so forth. The justification for this restriction is usually assumed to be self-evident, but one investigator, Erin Grinshteyn, has offered an explicit rationale. She suggests that these countries provide an "apples-to-apples" comparison, noting that "countries that are less developed are not similar to the United States in many ways, and would not typically be used as a comparison on other health indicators" (Mekelburg, 2019).

While such a rationale is meaningful if gun violence is framed as a public health problem (e.g., Novella, 2018), some observers believe that it is less persuasive if violent gun crime is framed as a societal or cultural issue (e.g., Campbell, 2019; Dorell, 2012). They assert that if gun violence is cultural, selecting countries with similarities to U.S. culture needs to incorporate considerations beyond GDP and economic development. The HDI (Human Development Index) metric offers developmental rankings that align reasonably well with OECD rankings, but are more comprehensive, specifically taking into account life expectancy, education, and per capita income (Stanton, 2007).

Gun rights proponents contend that this metric enlarges the pool of appropriate comparison countries for judging U.S. gun violence. They point to an oft-cited study (i.e., Grinshteyn & Hemenway, 2016) that examined 22 OECD countries, finding that the U.S. gun-related murder rate was an astounding 25 times higher than in these "high-income nations" (Preidt, 2016). However, the set of OECD countries included Belgium, Czech Republic, Denmark, Finland, Hungary, Japan, Korea, Norway, Slovakia, and Switzerland. The authors of the study contended that the small size, cultural history, ethnic homogeneity, or geographic features of these nations substantially limit their relevance as comparison nations to the United States (McMaken, 2015). These gun rights proponents argue that HDI numbers allow for a wider selection of countries having more in common with the United States (at least in terms of size, history, ethnic diversity, etc.) but that are still comparable to OECD countries having low to mid-range HDI scores.

For example, the HDI ratings of OECD members Chile, Mexico, and Turkey are 0.843, 0.774, and 0.791 respectively (World Population Review, 2020a). While Argentina (0.825), Venezuela (0.761), and Russia (0.816) are not OECD members, gun proponents note that the HDI ratings of these three nonmember countries are similar to the three member states above. They contend that these countries provide gun violence comparisons to the United States that are at least as legitimate as the OECD comparison mentioned earlier, but generate substantially different results.

Using World Population Review data (2020b), such comparisons reveal that Argentina's homicide rate (5.94 per 100,000 people) is slightly higher than the U.S. rate (5.35/100,000), while Russia's homicide rate (10.82/100,000) is twice the American figure. Venezuela's homicide rate, at 56.33/100,000, is a spectacular 10 times the U.S. rate. Further, even Mexico, an OECD member, has a substantial homicide rate—19.26/100.000—almost four times higher than the American figure. Stringent gun regulations are characteristic of all these nations. Consequently, gun rights proponents dismiss gun violence comparisons using only "developed" countries (i.e., OECD members) as "cherry-picked" data offering little insight into gun control's usefulness for reducing violent crime (e.g., McMaken, 2015). As noted earlier, however, gun control proponents argue that drug gangs and drug murders are rampant in many Latin American nations, and law enforcement is often overwhelmed or corrupt. In contrast, socioeconomically advanced nations are generally able to enforce the laws they pass with some degree of effectiveness. Because less advanced nations frequently struggle with enforcement, gun control advocates see efforts to expand comparisons to developing nations as suspect and unconvincing.

Gun control proponents (e.g., Zimring, 2012) have also analyzed the gap between American and OECD members' murder rates using a "crime" perspective, hypothesizing that murder rate differences may result from America simply being a more crime-prone society in general (Beauchamp, 2018). One 1997 study undertaken along these lines by scholars Franklin Zimring—a noted professor of law at UC Berkeley—with his colleague Gordon Hawkins found that while the United States had a nonviolent crime rate comparable to rates in many other Western (i.e., OECD) nations, its lethal violence rate was substantially higher (Zimring & Hawkins, 1997). Based on these findings, Zimring concluded that the country's proliferation of guns—and not criminality per se—created America's high level of lethal violence (Beauchamp, 2018).

Other investigators have questioned whether gun proliferation adequately accounts for the country's gun homicide rate. For example, Centers for Disease Control figures show that the number of firearms in America almost doubled during the 20-year period examined, growing from 185 million in 1993 to 357 million in 2013. During this same period, gun-related homicides *declined* almost 50 percent, from about 7 per 100,000 individuals in 1993 to 3.6/100,000 in 2013 (Perry, 2015). With current gun-growth and gun-violence figures showing a similar pattern, it is unlikely that the mere proliferation of firearms explains the country's gun homicide rate.

Other commentators have also suggested that the large number of guns in America contribute to its firearms-related homicides. These observers note that while gun restrictions have greatly decreased violent *gun* crime in the countries of England and Wales, the *total* number of violent crimes is more than double that of the United States on a per capita basis. In effect, a person in Britain and Wales has a much smaller chance of experiencing violent gun crime relative to an individual in the United States, but a much higher chance of experiencing other forms of violent crime (e.g., knives, clubs, bottles, etc.).

For example, Louis Jacobson, a fact-checker for PolitiFact, investigated an internet claim that the United Kingdom had a violent crime rate more than five times greater than the United States: 2,000+ crimes per 100,000 individuals versus 466 violent crimes per 100,000 in the United States. While he dismissed this claim as false—arguing that differences in crime data classification and recording across the two nations made "a truly valid" comparison impossible—he nevertheless attempted to adjust the available data to account for such classification differences. His analysis obtained a rate of 775 violent crimes per 100,000 individuals versus the U.S. rate of 383 violent crimes per 100,000 (Jacobson, 2013). This is about a 2:1 ratio, in line with the conclusion that the United States has half the violent crime of the United Kingdom.

As Jacobson indicates, given the need for adjusting crime classifications (a procedure frequently required even when comparing crime statistics across different American states, counties, and cities), such results must be viewed cautiously. Nonetheless, while the data do not support the internet claim of a fivefold difference between the two countries, Jacobson's analysis does suggest that while an American has a greater chance of being the victim of a violent crime *involving a gun* relative to his British counterpart, the American has a much smaller chance (i.e., by about half) of experiencing a violent crime *in general*.

Regardless of possible explanations for why the United States has a higher gun murder rate than other Western democracies (i.e., OECD member states), the empirical evidence clearly shows that this is the case. However, drawing inferences that go beyond simply noting this rate difference is perilous. Despite the presumption that comparisons to OCED nations are particularly appropriate because of the nations' common economic success, significant historical, cultural, demographic, and geographic differences distinguish many OECD nations from the United States.

Further, pro-gun rights voices emphasize that when the pool of nations includes countries justified as comparisons by their size, diversity, history, and HDI numbers, the U.S. gun murder rate ceases to be an outlier and is simply average. Many of these nations have strong restrictions on firearms (similar to OECD members) but much higher gun murder rates than the typical OECD member (similar to the United States). Nonetheless, gun control advocates contend that expanding the pool of comparison countries to include nations having much weaker judicial and law enforcement traditions (relative to OECD members) is simply inappropriate. Further, because empirical findings depend so heavily on the subset of countries selected for examination, determining whether a particular country is a suitable comparison nation is an essential requirement for gauging whether strict gun regulations reduce violent crime. In the absence of such agreement, the use of country-level comparisons to draw conclusions about the effectiveness of gun regulations for limiting gun violence remains open to interpretation.

FURTHER READING

Aizenman, Nurith, 2018. "Deaths from Gun Violence: How the U.S. Compares with the Rest of the World." NPR, November 9. https://www.npr.org/sections/goatsandsoda/2018/11/09/666209430/death-from-gun-violence-how-the-u-s-compares-with-the-rest-of-the-world

Beauchamp, Zach, 2018. "America Doesn't Have More Crime than Other Rich Countries. It Just Has More Guns." Vox, February 15. https://www.vox.com/2015/8/27/9217163/america-guns-europe

Campbell, Donald, 2019. *America's Gun Wars: A Cultural History of Gun Control in the United States*. Santa Barbara, CA: Praeger.

Criminal Justice Degree Hub, n.d. "Violent Crime: The US and Abroad." https://www.criminaljusticedegreehub.com/violent-crime-us-abroad/

Dorell, Oren, 2012. "In Europe, Fewer Mass Killings Due to Culture Not Guns." *USA Today*, December 17. https://www.usatoday.com/story/news/world/2012/12/17/guns-mass-killings-worldwide/1776191/

Grinshteyn, Erin, & Hemenway, David, 2016. "Violent Death Rates: The US Compared with Other High Income OECD Countries, 2010." *American Journal of Medicine*, 129(3), 266–273. https://pubmed.ncbi.nlm.nih.gov/26551975/

Jacobson, Louis, 2013. "Social Media Post Says U.K. Has Far Higher Violent Crime Rate than U.S. Does." PolitiFact, June 24. https://www.politifact.com/factchecks/2013/jun/24/blog-posting/social-media-post-says-uk-has-far-higher-violent-c/

Masters, Jonathan, 2019. "U.S. Gun Policy: Global Comparisons." Council on Foreign Relations, August 6. https://www.cfr.org/backgrounder/us-gun-policy-global-comparisons

McMaken, Ryan, 2015. "The Mistake of Only Comparing US Murder Rates to Developed Nations." Mises Institute, October 12. https://mises.org/wire/mistake-only-comparing-us-murder-rates-developed-countries

Mekelburg, Madlin, 2019. "Are There More Gun Deaths in the United States than Any Other Country?" PolitiFact, August 2. https://www.politifact.com/factchecks/2019/aug/02/beto-orourke/are-there-more-gun-deaths-united-states-any-other-/

Novella, Steven, 2018. "Gun Violence as a Public Health Issue." Science-Based Medicine, February 21. https://sciencebasedmedicine.org/gun-violence-as-a-public-health-issue/

Perry, Mark, 2015. "Chart of the Day: More Guns, Less Gun Violence between 1993 and 2013." American Enterprise Institute, December 4. aei.org/carpe-diem/chart-of-the-day-more-guns-less-gun-violence-between-1993-and-2013/

Preidt, Robert, 2016. "How U.S. Gun Deaths Compare to Other Countries." CBS News, February 3. https://www.cbsnews.com/news/how-u-s-gun-deaths-compare-to-other-countries/

Rosling, Hans, 2006. "Debunking Myths about the Third World." Gapminder. https://www.gapminder.org/videos/hans-rosling-ted-2006-debunking-myths-about-the-third-world/

Stanton, Elizabeth, 2007. "The Human Development Index: A History." Political Economy Research Institute, February. https://scholarworks.umass.edu/cgi/viewcontent.cgi?article=1101&context=peri_workingpapers

World Population Review, 2020a. "Human Development Index (HDI) by Country 2020." https://worldpopulationreview.com/countries/hdi-by-country

World Population Review, 2020b. "Violent Crime Rate by Country 2020." https://worldpopulationreview.com/countries/violent-crime-rates-by-country

Zimring, Franklin, 2012. "The Politics of Gun Control." SFGate, July 27. https://www.sfgate.com/opinion/article/The-politics-of-gun-control-3741623.php

Zimring, Franklin, & Hawkins, Gordon, 1997. *Crime Is Not the Problem: Lethal Violence in America.* New York: Oxford University Press.

Q35. DOES MODERN ENTERTAINMENT CONTRIBUTE TO SOCIETAL GUN VIOLENCE?

Answer: In attempting to understand otherwise incomprehensible assaults and murders, individuals frequently look to the assailants' social milieu for answers. Especially with highly publicized mass killings and school shootings, politicians and commentators have speculated about the cultural factors in the larger society that may have contributed to the carnage. They often suggest that the violence portrayed in the country's mass entertainment media is a likely culprit.

For instance, after the El Paso, Texas, mass shooting in 2019, President Donald Trump observed, "We must stop the glorification of violence in our society. This includes the gruesome and grisly video games that are now commonplace." Commenting on that same shooting, Republican House minority leader Kevin McCarthy stated, "The idea of these video games to dehumanize individuals, to have a game of shooting individuals and others—I've always felt that it's a problem for future generations" (Limbong, 2019).

Concerns about the potentially brutalizing effects of such games are not new. In 1976, a member of the National Safety Council, reflecting on the goal of a video game called *Death Race*—to mow down as many pedestrians as possible—commented, "I shudder to think what will come next if this is encouraged. It will be pretty gory." Indeed, *Death Race* was an early precursor of the even more violent (and extraordinarily popular) *Grand Theft Auto* video game 30 years later (Kain, 2013).

Unease about the dehumanizing consequences of violent entertainment is not limited to video games. Long before their advent, psychologists and other social scientists worried about the accumulative effects of observed violence in both Hollywood films and in television programming. The bases for their concern were investigations that clearly suggested observed violence in movies and TV led to increased aggression in "real life." For example, in the 1970s, Professor Leonard Eron, a noted research psychologist at the University of Illinois at Chicago Circle, examined a group of youngsters at 8, and then again at 18. He found that "the best single predictor we had on how aggressive these people were at 18 was the violence in the programs they viewed at age 8. Furthermore, the more violent the programs, the more aggressive the children became" (Bennetts, 1981).

Not all behavioral scientists even in the 1970s and 1980s thought that violence in entertainment media was a significant factor in actual societal violence. Professor Seymour Feshback, chair of UCLA's Psychology Department during that time, argued that the effects of observed violence depended on several other factors—for example, the age of the viewer, the degree of realism and centrality of the violence, and so forth (Bennetts, 1981). Nonetheless, until recently, the prevailing view among behavioral and medical scientists was that exposure to media violence generally desensitizes individuals to actual violence, and increases aggressive thoughts and behaviors (e.g., American Psychological Association [APA], 2015; American Academy of Family Physicians [AAFP], 2016; American Academy of Pediatrics [AAP], 2009; Anderson et al., 2010).

Beginning around 2005 or so, however, some investigators began to dispute the validity of these generally accepted conclusions. In 2007, Christopher Ferguson, a prominent researcher in this area, conducted a meta-analysis of studies examining the effects of violent video games on aggression. His analysis did not support the conclusion that such games contribute to aggressive behavior (Ferguson, 2007). In a later study, he and a colleague compared trends in movie violence against trends in societal violence (e.g., homicides and youth violence) and found the two were unrelated (Ferguson & Markey, 2019). Other investigators (e.g., Przybylski & Weinstein, 2019; Burroughs, 2019) have also questioned the accepted link between entertainment violence and actual violence. In 2013, an international group of more than 200 academics published an open letter to the APA Task Force on Violent Media that objected to its conclusions regarding the impact of entertainment violence on society (Bornstein & Miller, 2015).

Nevertheless, for several reasons, the weight of the empirical evidence favors the established view that entertainment violence influences actual violence. First, the accumulated research demonstrating such a connection is particularly convincing (Strasburger & Wilson, 2016); and it includes several longitudinal investigations (e.g., Eron et al., 1972; Huesmann et al., 2003; Robertson, McAnally, & Hancox et al., 2013). Methodologically, longitudinal studies allow researchers to draw much stronger conclusions from their data—including causal relationships—than do more typical cross-sectional research investigations (Schipani, 2018). Additionally, these studies frequently included strong operationalizations of "aggression," examining not only subjective measures (e.g., questionnaire reports) but also objective indicators (e.g., criminal and violent convictions).

Second, the methodological and definitional problems marring some studies in this body of research (e.g., Benen, 2018; Bump, 2018; Burroughs, 2019; Ferguson, 2017) are not flaws in all the studies, and are not compelling enough to reject the entire body of decades of investigations. Finally, a well-developed and highly regarded psychological framework—social learning and social cognitive theories (Bandura, 1977, 1986)—offers a logical rationale and a cognitive explanation for why observed violence links to actual violence.

The Facts: The controversy surrounding the potential impact of violent entertainment on actual violence reflects two dimensions: a) a dispute over what the relevant research actually demonstrates; and b) a disagreement regarding the importance of possible limitations of that research. Regarding the first dimension—determining what the research actually shows—the argument centers both on inconsistencies in findings and on the different measures investigators have used to gauge aggression. Critics of the claim that media violence contributes to actual violence argue that investigators have conducted dozens of studies on violent video games since the 1980s, and while some studies show aggression effects, others show a "calming" effect, and even cooperation effects with some games. Commenting on these contradictory findings, Christopher Ferguson, professor of psychology and criminal justice at Texas A&M International University, concluded, "anybody who tells you that there's any kind of consistency to the aggression research is lying . . . my impression is that . . . [the research] is not strong enough to draw . . . even really correlational links between video game violence and aggression" (Kain, 2013).

Ferguson and others have also suggested that at least some of the supporting evidence for aggression effects relies on questionable, transient aggression measures—"annoying behavior" in the words of one scholar (Limbong, 2019)—that is not representative of real-world violence. Benjamin Burroughs, professor of emerging media at the University of Nevada,

Las Vegas, argues that some studies may show angry thoughts and feelings, and perhaps increased shouting and brief verbal exchanges, after playing video games, "but nothing that rises to the level of violence," and "certainly there is no linkage to gun violence" (Burroughs, 2019).

Even when researchers generally agree that entertainment violence influences actual violence, they may disagree regarding its overall significance. Psychology professor Seymour Feshbach, who studied linkages between television and aggression, conceded that while media violence might stimulate real violence under certain limited conditions, media violence generally plays only a minor part in criminal behavior (Bennetts, 1981). Along these lines, Patrick Markey, a Villanova University researcher focusing on video games, asserts "people who play video games right after might be a little hopped up and jerky, but it doesn't fundamentally alter who they are" (Burroughs, 2019). Further, given the immense popularity of video games both in the United States and other countries, some observers contend that societal violence levels would be much higher if media violence and actual violence (e.g., gun death murders) were actually linked (Benen, 2018; Bump, 2018).

Controversy about the meaning and significance of empirical findings is not unusual. Any complex research domain producing multiple hundreds of publications will have some conflicting and contradictory findings, with different researchers championing their preferred interpretation. In resolving such conflicts, investigators typically rely on the overall "weight of the evidence"—that is, the general pattern of findings in the total body of relevant research. Thus, faced with conflicting conclusions in a specific research area (e.g., Anderson et al., 2010 versus Ferguson, 2007), analysts assess the findings using the whole pattern of results in that area.

For the current controversy, most analysts—for example, the American Psychological Association (2015); the American Academy of Family Physicians (2016); the American Academy of Pediatrics (2010)—agree the weight of the evidence supports the conclusion that media violence encourages both aggression and, sometimes, actual violence. As Victor Strasburger, a media effects expert and Distinguished Professor of Pediatrics at the University of New Mexico, notes, "there is a great deal of evidence linking media violence to aggression. Experimental studies have established a cause-and-effect relationship . . . ; surveys have documented this pattern . . . ; longitudinal studies show that early exposure is predictive of increases in aggression . . . ; and meta-analyses . . . show a consistent link between exposure . . . and aggressive behavior. . . ." (Strasburger & Wilson, 2016).

The second dimension of the controversy centers on the various limitations of prior investigations. For instance, if a substantial number of prior investigations have severe methodological or conceptual limitations, regardless of the weight of the evidence, erroneous conclusions about the likely link between media and actual violence may result. Some investigators have argued that this is precisely the case with media violence. These critics have questioned the appropriateness of the statistical procedures used in conducting prior meta-analyses; as well as the "ad hoc" and unstandardized measures of aggression used in many laboratory investigations (Ferguson, 2013).

While such research flaws may characterize and discredit some supporting studies, these limitations do not characterize the whole body of research. Reputable academic journals use a peer-review process to insure that published findings meet stringent professional standards, including the methodological procedures used in obtaining the findings. Poorly conceptualized or executed studies may sometimes slip through, but these are exceptional cases. Thus, while a critic may fault some studies for using weak measures of aggression—for example, self-reports of wanting to slap an opponent—such criticism is not relevant to other studies using much stronger aggression measures, such as pushing another person, hitting a spouse, or having violent criminal convictions (e.g., Robertson et al., 2013; Schipani, 2018).

Further, if aggression and violence are conceptualized as a continuum—aggressive feelings and thoughts evolving into aggressive behaviors and actions, evolving into serious physical violence—then even research using weak measures of aggression inform our understanding of violent media effects. This is especially so if, as some analysts have implied (e.g., Media Education Foundation, 2005), it is the *accumulative* exposure to entertainment violence that eventually sparks episodes of physical aggression and violence. The argument implied here is that, even as just one "contributing" factor among several others, media violence's influence on actual violence grows with increased exposure—and in America, that exposure is substantial. By age 18, according to one 2005 estimate tabulated by Media Education Foundation, a nonprofit organization devoted to studying the impact of mass media on American society, the typical child has seen about 200,000 acts of media violence, including 16,000 murders (Media Education Foundation, 2005).

As a final consideration, a persuasive conceptual and theoretical framework offers a compelling psychological reason for believing entertainment violence contributes to real violence. Albert Bandura, an eminent social psychologist, outlined a learning theory directly relevant to media violence in the 1970s. This research-based theory—social learning theory—proposes that people not only learn effective behaviors by experiencing the rewarding or punishing consequences of their own actions, but that they also learn "vicariously"—by watching similar others and noting the behavioral consequences that befall their actions. Were those actions rewarded or punished (Bandura, 1977, 1986)? Observers then integrate others' rewarded actions into their own behavioral repertoire, avoiding behaviors that were punished. Further, as one commentator has observed, the dominant perpetrators of media violence are typically struggling, imperfect, morally flawed individuals—perhaps "antiheroes" but people we nonetheless identify with—and the violence they mete out is invariably rewarded (Boorman, 2017). Thus, in addition to empirical evidence, theoretical considerations (i.e., vicarious learning) also provide a reason for supposing entertainment violence influences actual violence.

While neither the research evidence nor social learning theory can conclusively demonstrate that media violence directly causes *gun* violence, both factors justify concluding that media violence influences actual aggression and violence. Thus, it appears reasonable—if aggression and violence form a continuum as suggested earlier—to also conclude that modern entertainment at least indirectly contributes to societal gun violence.

FURTHER READING

American Academy of Family Physicians (AAFP), 2016. "Violence in the Media and Entertainment (Position Paper)." https://www.aafp.org/about/policies/all/violence-media-entertainment.html

American Academy of Pediatrics (AAP), 2009. "Media Violence." *Pediatrics*, 124(5), 1495–1503. https://pediatrics.aapublications.org/content/124/5/1495

American Psychological Association (APA), 2015. "APA Task Force on Violent Media." https://www.apa.org/pi/families/violent-media

Anderson, Craig, Shibuya, Akiko, Ihori, Nobuko, Swing, Edward, Bushman, Brad, Sakamoto, Akira, Rothstein, Hannah, et al., 2010. "Violent Video Game Effects on Aggression, Empathy, and Prosocial Behavior in Eastern and Western Countries: A Meta-Analytic Review." *Psychological Bulletin*, 136(2), 151–173. https://www.apa.org/pubs/journals/releases/bul-136-2-151.pdf

Bandura, Albert, 1977. *Social Learning Theory*. New York, NY: Prentice-Hall.

Bandura, Albert, 1986. *Social Foundations of Thought and Action: A Social Cognitive Theory*. Englewood Cliffs, NJ: Prentice-Hall.

Benen, Steve, 2018. "Why Blaming Gun Violence on Video Games Doesn't Make Sense." MSNBC, February 22. https://www.msnbc.com/rachel-maddow-show/why-blaming-gun-violence-video-games-doesnt-make-sense-msna1071166

Bennetts, Leslie, 1981. "Do the Arts Inspire Violence in Real Life?" *New York Times*, April 26. https://www.nytimes.com/1981/04/26/movies/do-the-arts-inspire-violence-in-real-life.html

Boorman, Georgi, 2017. "Why Our Obsession with TV Antiheroes Is Destroying Our Souls." Federalist, September 14. https://thefederalist.com/2017/09/14/obsession-tv-antiheroes-destroying-souls/

Bornstein, Brian, & Miller, Monica, 2015. "Media Violence and the Real World." *Psychology Today*, August 19. https://www.psychologytoday.com/us/blog/sound-science-sound-policy/201508/media-violence-and-the-real-world

Bump, Philip, 2018. "If Video Games Spur Gun Violence, It's Only in the United States." *Washington Post*, March 8. https://www.washingtonpost.com/news/politics/wp/2018/02/22/if-video-games-spur-gun-violence-its-only-in-the-united-states/

Burroughs, Benjamin, 2019. "No, There's Still No Link between Video Games and Violence." *Los Angeles Times*, August 6. At latimes.com/world-nation/story/2019-08-06/video-games-violence-studies

Eron, Leonard, Huesmann, Rowell, Lefkowitz, Monroe, & Walder, Leopold, 1972. "Does Television Violence Cause Aggression?" *American Psychologist*, 27(4), 253–263. https://psycnet.apa.org/record/1973-09034-001

Ferguson, Christopher, 2007. "The Good, the Bad, and the Ugly: A Meta-Analytic Review of Positive and Negative Effects of Violent Video Games." *Psychiatric Quarterly*, 78, 309–316. https://link.springer.com/article/10.1007/s11126-007-9056-9

Ferguson, Christopher, 2013. "Letter to APA on Policy Statement on Violent Media." Stetson University Today, October 7. https://www.stetson.edu/today/2013/10/letter-to-apa-on-policy-statement-on-violent-media/

Ferguson, Christopher, 2017. "Why Fictional Media Violence Doesn't Desensitize Us to Real-Life Violence." HuffPost, April 9. https://www.huffpost.com/entry/why-fictional-media-doesn_b_9645614?guccounter=1&guce_referrer=aHR0cHM6Ly93d3cuZ29vZ2xlLmNvbS8&

Ferguson, Christopher, & Markey, Patrick, 2019. "PG-13 Rated Movie Violence and Societal Violence: Is There a Link?" *Psychiatric Quarterly*, 90, 395–403. https://link.springer.com/article/10.1007/s11126-018-9615-2

Huesmann, Rowell, Moise-Titus, Jessica, Podolski, Cheryl-Lynn, & Eron, Leonard, 2003. "Longitudinal Relations between Children's Exposure to TV Violence and Their Aggressive and Violent Behavior in Young

Adulthood: 1977–1992." *Developmental Psychology*, 39(2), 202–221. https://www.apa.org/pubs/journals/releases/dev-392201.pdf

Kain, Erik, 2013. "The Truth about Video Games and Gun Violence." *Mother Jones*, June 11. https://www.motherjones.com/politics/2013/06/video-games-violence-guns-explainer/

Limbong, Andrew, 2019. "Video Games Are Still Blamed for Gun Violence despite Studies Showing No Connection." NPR, August 5. https://www.npr.org/2019/08/05/748387407/video-games-are-still-blamed-for-gun-violence-despite-studies-showing-no-connect

Media Education Foundation, 2005. "Media Violence: Facts & Statistics." https://www.mediaed.org/handouts/ChildrenMedia.pdf

Przybylski, Andrew, & Weinstein, Netta, 2019. "Violent Video Game Engagement Is Not Associated with Adolescents' Aggressive Behavior: Evidence from a Registered Report." Royal Society Open Science, February 13. https://royalsocietypublishing.org/doi/10.1098/rsos.171474

Robertson, Lindsay, McAnally, Helena, & Hancox, Robert, 2013. "Childhood and Adolescent Television Viewing and Antisocial Behavior in Early Adulthood." *Pediatrics*, 131(3), 439–446. https://www.researchgate.net/publication/235659510_Childhood_and_Adolescent_Television_Viewing_and_Antisocial_Behavior_in_Early_Adulthood

Schipani, Vanessa, 2018. "The Facts on Media Violence." FactCheck.Org, March 8. https://www.factcheck.org/2018/03/facts-media-violence/

Strasburger, Victor, & Wilson, Barbara, 2016. "Television Violence: 60 Years of Research." In Gentile, Douglas, ed., *Media Violence and Children*. https://www.researchgate.net/publication/307970395_Media_Violence_Strasburger_Wilson_Gentile_book_2016

Q36. DO POLITICAL, RACIAL, AND ETHNIC EXTREMISTS CONTRIBUTE DISPROPORTIONATELY TO GUN VIOLENCE?

Answer: With terror attacks providing horrifying demonstrations of the perils of extremist beliefs, commentators have raised questions about the dangers of domestic extremists—that is, home-grown, fanatical groups championing racial superiority, religious bigotry, or anti-government activities (Perlstein, 2017; Wiles, 2017). Periodic reports of lethal attacks in popular media—including racially oriented murders in a Pittsburgh synagogue in 2018, a lethal clash at a white nationalist rally in Virginia in 2017, a deadly shooting in a Charleston church in 2015, and killings in a Wisconsin Sikh temple in 2012 (Pegues, 2019)—implicitly suggest that extremist ideology is an outsized contributor to societal gun violence. This belief is further reinforced by the Federal Bureau of Investigation's (FBI) assertion that racially motivated extremists are a national threat, and pose as great a danger as ISIS and other foreign terrorist organizations (Donaghue, 2020).

The idea that extremists are a lethal threat and provoke gun violence has empirical backing. The Anti-Defamation League (ADL), in its analysis of murder and extremism in the United States for 2018, notes that "firearms remain the weapon of choice for extremists who kill. Guns were responsible for 42 of the 50 deaths . . ." (ADL, 2019). Its 2019 report further asserts, "For the eighth year in a row, domestic extremists overwhelmingly used firearms to commit mass killings. Almost half of the people killed by extremists in the past 10 years were killed in mass murders, all but one of which involved the use of firearms" (ADL, 2020). James Zogby, president of the Arab American Institute, also notes a connection between extremism and guns: "By any measure, racist hate groups and gun violence are the gravest threats we face today" (Zogby, 2016).

More generally, much evidence supports the idea that domestic adherents to extremist ideologies see gun violence as an acceptable means to a desired end. For example, before being apprehended, members of a right-wing white supremacist group called The Base planned to use gun violence at a Virginia gun rights rally to precipitate a civil war (Kunzelman, 2020). A left-wing extremist carried out a shooting attack on a congressional representative in 2017, and fears of gun violence marked Antifa (for "antifascist") clashes with right-wing college groups in Berkeley, Portland, and Olympia (Kaste, 2017). Additionally, Black extremists have engaged in premeditated lethal violence against law enforcement officers (FBI Intelligence Assessment, 2017); and Islamist extremists, the majority of them American citizens or U.S. legal residents, have executed deadly firearm attacks against civilians (Valverde, 2017).

Nonetheless, not everyone concurs that extremist gun violence is a significant societal threat. Reacting to a *New York Times* editorial focused on the 387 extremist-related fatalities that occurred over a 10-year period in the United States, one commentator noted that the *annual* average fatality rate was actually less than annual deaths from wasp and bee stings (Catron, 2019). Further, data from the Anti-Defamation League's (ADL) Center on Extremism notes that the country experienced 17 extremist incidents in 2019, resulting in 42 fatalities. The 42 fatalities represented a decrease from 2018 (53 extremist-related killings), but an increase from 2017 (41 killings). On average, from 2010 through 2019, extremist-related killings have totaled less than 45 deaths annually (ADL, 2020).

Researchers with the Center for Strategic and International Studies also examined domestic terrorism. They analyzed an original data set of 893 terrorist plots and attacks in the United States covering about a quarter-century, from January 1994 through May 2020. Their analysis indicated that right-wing extremists perpetrated 57 percent of the 893 attacks, with left-wing extremists responsible for 25 percent, and religious extremists for 15 percent. Ethno-nationalist extremists accounted for 3 percent.

The analysis also indicated that, over this period, extremist attacks resulted in 3,448 fatalities (about 138 per year). However, this figure included the 2,977 deaths resulting from the September 11, 2001, attack. Excluding this singular event, extremist attacks accounted for about 19 fatalities per year, with 109 fatalities attributable to religious extremism, 335 to right-wing extremism, 22 to left-wing extremism, and 5 to ethno-nationalist extremism. Overall, extremists engaged in about 36 attacks a year (Jones, Doxsee, & Harrington, 2020).

Given these figures, despite the horror and fear generated by each particular violent act, extremist incidents comprise a small percentage of overall gun violence in America. With gun murders in the United States averaging over 10,000 annually, the small number of firearms-related extremist murders—although tragic and despicable—is not a major contributor to the country's gun violence.

The Facts: Defining violent extremism as "encouraging, condoning, justifying, or supporting the commission of a violent act to achieve political, ideological, religious, social or economic goals," the Federal Bureau of Investigation (FBI) has identified about a half-dozen domestic groups as having violent ideologies. The FBI's categorization includes abortion extremists, anarchist extremists, animal rights and environmental extremists, militia extremists, sovereign citizen extremists, and white supremacy extremists (FBI, n.d.).

Of these groups, popular media appear to pay particular attention to right-wing extremists—for example, white supremacists, militia extremists, sovereign citizens, and so on—that have been identified as responsible for the majority of domestic terrorism attacks since the mid-1990s (Jones, Doxsee, & Harrington, 2020). Often these media accounts present these radical extremists as a counterpoint to Islamist extremists. For example, a *Newsweek* report in 2016 notes that right-wing militants have killed more people in the United States than jihadists, with the Islamists launching nine attacks and killing 45, "while the right-wing extremists struck 18 times, leaving 48 dead." The same article emphasizes that law enforcement agencies regard anti-government extremists (e.g., sovereign citizens) as a greater violence threat than radicalized Muslims (Eichenwald, 2016). Similarly, an article in *The Atlantic*, citing ADL statistics, notes that right-wing extremists committed about 73 percent of extremist killings from 2009 to 2018, "compared with 23 percent for Islamists" (Serwer, 2019). The extremist research conducted by the Center for Strategic and International Studies reached comparable conclusions about the relative prevalence of right-wing extremism (Jones, Doxsee, & Harrington, 2020). Other periodicals (e.g., Wiles, 2017) also see right-wing gun violence likely emerging from various militia organizations and anti-government groups.

Along racial/anti-government lines, Black extremists have also endorsed violent methods. As noted earlier, an internal FBI report linked six acts of premeditated gun violence against police to "Black Identity Extremists (BIEs)," including a 2016 shooting of 11 police officers in Dallas. The report speculated that these extremists would continue to engage in lethal retaliatory violence against law enforcement officers, using perceptions of police brutality against African Americans to justify such attacks (FBI Intelligence Assessment, 2017). Some former government officials and legal experts have questioned the accuracy of the BIE designation, suggesting that six examples hardly constitute a violent movement, and that the term represents a politically motivated attempt to create an equivalent to white supremacists (Winter & Weinberger, 2017). The FBI later incorporated the BIE category into the broader designation of "racially motivated violent extremism" (Tau, 2019).

To a lesser degree, the media have also scrutinized the violence of left-wing radicals, but analysts assert that their numbers are smaller and their violence proclivities muted. Aside from the 2017 shooting of Republican representative Steve Scalise and three others by a left-wing radical extremist, and the aggressive encounters Antifa extremists have had with conservative groups, far-left violence (much less gun violence) has been minimal. Mark Pitcavage, a senior research fellow at ADL's Center on Extremism, suggests that the last big cycle of far-left violence occurred in the 1970s, and leftist extremist groups have not been especially violent since. Nevertheless, the Center for Strategic and International Studies (Jones, Doxsee, & Harrington, 2020) notes that left-wing extremism is becoming more active, and Pitcavage has expressed fears that extremists on both sides see firearms and political violence as an increasingly attractive option (Kaste, 2017).

J. J. MacNab, an expert on domestic extremist organizations and a Fellow in George Washington University's Program on Extremism, believes that left-wing extremist violence from groups like Antifa is inevitable. She argues, "This is a dangerous game [that Antifa is playing]; people are going to die. No one's died yet, but it's just a matter of time" (Kaste, 2017). Other analysts have reached similar conclusions about the potential for Antifa violence. Mark Bray, a Rutgers University history lecturer with expertise in political extremism, has noted that many Antifa members justify using violence to disrupt fascist and racist groups in order to protect marginalized communities from the future violence they anticipate such groups will inflict (Bogel-Burroughs & Garcia, 2020). Further, researchers at the Center for Strategic and International Studies speculated that the November 2020 Presidential election might spark extremist violence, likely provoked by left-wing extremists (such as Antifa) if Donald Trump were re-elected, or by right-wing extremists (such as white supremacists) if he were not (Jones, Doxsee, & Harrington, 2020). The swarming of the U.S. Capitol Building on January 6, 2021, by groups of rioters and protestors (*USA Today*, 2021) confirmed the accuracy of such speculation.

While the analysis above can establish that violent extremism unsurprisingly mirrors the political, racial, and ethnic divisions of American society, it cannot establish that extremist violence has a disproportionate impact on the country's level of gun violence. Statistics contained in the U.S. Extremist Crime Database are useful here. The Government Accounting Office (GAO) found that between September 12, 2001, and December 31, 2016, extremists carried out 85 deadly attacks in the United States. Far-right extremists perpetrated most of the attacks (i.e., 62 vs. 23), but jihadist extremists killed more people (i.e., 119 vs. 106). In total, extremist attacks resulted in 225 fatalities (GAO Report, 2017).

Additionally, the think tank New America examined the number of deaths associated with different extremist ideologies. Through August 2017, New America noted 95 deaths by jihadists; 68 by far-right extremists; and 8 by Black extremists (Valverde, 2017). By 2020, attributions increased to 107, 110, and 12, respectively (New America, n.d.). In total, the New America analysis indicates 229 victims of extremist violence.

An ADL (2020) analysis of domestic extremist killings, covering the 10-year period from 2010 to 2019, revealed a total of 435 fatalities in the United States. And, as noted earlier, the Center for Strategic and International Studies analysis found that, over a quarter-century period, extremist attacks resulted in 3448 fatalities, including the 2,977 deaths resulting from the singular September 11, 2001, attack (Jones, Doxsee, & Harrington, 2020). Using this last figure—the largest of the four estimates—the average number of extremist-related fatalities is less than 140 deaths annually. Further, the 140 estimate includes deaths caused by *all* lethal methods (e.g., planes, knives, cars, bombs, etc.), not just firearms. Thus, the number of deaths attributable to gun violence is even less.

For 2017, the Centers for Disease Control (CDC) indicated that *total* gun deaths in the United States reached a record high of almost 40,000 individuals. Of these, about 24,000 were suicides and about 16,000 were homicides (Charlton, 2019). Based on the above estimates (i.e., 140/16,000), extremist violence accounts for less than 1 percent of annual U.S. gun homicides. Thus, despite the headline-grabbing attention they receive, domestic extremist violence actually generates massively fewer gun deaths and casualties than common run-of-the-mill criminality.

FURTHER READING

ADL, 2019. "Murder and Extremism in the United States in 2018." Center on Extremism, January. https://www.adl.org/murder-and-extremism-2018

ADL, 2020. "Murder and Extremism in the United States in 2019." Center on Extremism, February. At https://www.adl.org/murder-and-extremism-2019

Bogel-Burroughs, Nicholas, & Garcia, Sandra, 2020. "What Is Antifa, the Movement Trump Wants to Declare a Terror Group?" *New York Times*, September 28. https://www.nytimes.com/article/what-antifa-trump.html?

Catron, David, 2019. "The Mythical Rise in White Supremacist Violence." *American Spectator*, February 25. https://spectator.org/the-mythical-rise-in-white-supremacist-violence/

Charlton, Emma, 2019. "US Gun Deaths Are at Their Highest Rate in 40 Years." World Economic Forum, January 3. https://www.weforum.org/agenda/2019/01/chart-of-the-day-us-gun-deaths-skyrocket-driven-by-a-rise-in-suicides/

Donaghue, Erin, 2020. "Racially-Motivated Violent Extremists Elevated to 'National Threat Priority,' FBI Director Says." CBS News, February 5. https://www.cbsnews.com/news/racially-motivated-violent-extremism-isis-national-threat-priority-fbi-director-christopher-wray/

Eichenwald, Kurt, 2016. "Right-Wing Extremist Are a Bigger Threat to America than ISIS." *Newsweek*, February 4. https://www.Newsweek.com/2016/02/12/right-wing-extremists-militants-bigger-threat-america-isis-jihadists-422743.html

FBI, n.d. "What Are Known Violent Extremist Groups?" https://cve.fbi.gov/whatare/?state=domestic

FBI Intelligence Assessment, 2017. "(U//FOUO) Black Identity Extremists Likely Motivated to Target Law Enforcement Officers." Intelligence Assessment, August 3. https://assets.documentcloud.org/documents/4067711/BIE-Redacted.pdf

GAO Report, 2017. "Countering Violent Extremism: Actions Needed to Define Strategy and Assess Progress of Federal Efforts." April. https://www.gao.gov/assets/690/683984.pdf

Jones, Seth, Doxsee, Catrina, & Harrington, Nicholas, 2020. "The Escalating Terrorism Problem in the United States." Center for Strategic and International Studies, June. https://www.csis.org/analysis/escalating-terrorism-problem-united-states

Kaste, Martin, 2017. "Fact Check: Is Left-Wing Violence Rising?" NPR, June 16. https://www.npr.org/2017/06/16/533255619/fact-check-is-left-wing-violence-rising

Kunzelman, Michael, 2020. "Documents: Extremist Group Wanted Rally to Start Civil War." *U.S. News & World Report*, January 21. https://www.usnews.com/news/us/articles/2020-01-21/feds-white-supremacists-hoped-rally-would-start-civil-war

New America, n.d. "Terrorism in America after 9/11: Part IV. What Is the Threat to the United States Today?" https://www.newamerica.org/in-depth/terrorism-in-america/what-threat-united-states-today/

Pegues, Jeff, 2019. "U.S. Sees Steady Rise in Violence by White Supremacists." *CBS Evening News*, March 15. https://www.cbsnews.com/news/new-zealand-shooting-highlights-rise-violence-linked-to-white-supremacy-2019-03-15

Perlstein, Rick, 2017. "Guns, Extremism, and Threats of Escalation." *Washington Spectator*, April 14. https://washingtonspectator.org/trump-guns-extremism-perlstein/

Serwer, Adam, 2019. "The Terrorism That Doesn't Spark a Panic." *Atlantic*, January 28. https://www.theatlantic.com/ideas/archive/2019/01/homegrown-terrorists-2018-were-almost-all-right-wing/581284/

Tau, Byron, 2019. "FBI Abandons Use of Term 'Black Identity Extremism.'" *Wall Street Journal*, July 23. https://www.wsj.com/articles/fbi-abandons-use-of-terms-black-identity-extremism-11563921355

USA Today, 2021. "Rioters Storm into U.S. Capitol." January 11. https://www.usatoday.com/picture-gallery/news/politics/2021/01/06/protesters-storm-into-u-s-capitol/6568847002/

Valverde, Miriam, 2017. "A Look at the Data on Domestic Terrorism and Who's behind It." PolitiFact, August 16. https://www.politifact.com/article/2017/aug/16/look-data-domestic-terrorism-and-whos-behind-it/

Wiles, Tay, 2017. "Meet Your Local Anti-Government Extremist Groups." High Country News, September 27. https://www.hcn.org/articles/politics-anti-government-groups-in-the-west-right-now

Winter, Jana, & Weinberger, Sharon, 2017. "The FBI's New U.S. Terrorist Threat: 'Black Identity Extremists.'" *Foreign Policy*, October 6. https://

foreignpolicy.com/2017/10/06/the-fbi-has-identified-a-new-domestic-terrorist-threat-and-its-black-identity-extremists/

Zogby, James, 2016. "Racism and Gun Violence Are Killing Us, Literally." HuffPost, June 20. https://www.huffpost.com/entry/racism-and-gun-violence-a_b_7627318

Q37. IS MODERN AMERICA MORE VIOLENT THAN AMERICA IN PAST YEARS?

Answer: In 2018, reacting to a shooting in a country-western bar in Southern California where a dozen people were massacred, the *Washington Post* reposted an article that had originally appeared a year earlier. The title of the piece: "America Is a Violent Country" (Healy, 2018). In 2019, the *Washington Times* published an analysis entitled, "America Is a Violent Country, with or without Guns" (Epstein, 2019). *Fast Company* also saw America as a disturbingly (and increasingly) violent society, "How the U.S. Is Getting More Violent, by the Numbers" (Diaz, 2018).

News outlets are not the only sources that have suggested the country is becoming increasingly violent and dangerous. In testimony to Congress in 2017, Attorney General Jeff Sessions testified that "the violent crime rate has risen, and the homicide rate has risen by more than 20 percent in just two years" (Kaplan, 2017). Noting the particularly vitriolic political anger and violence characteristic of modern America, then House Minority Leader Nancy Pelosi lamented, "It didn't used to be this way" (Heer, 2017). On the campaign trail in 2016, Republican nominee Donald Trump asserted that modern America has become more violent than in past eras, tweeting "Crime is out of control and rapidly getting worse" (McGill, 2016), a theme he later reiterated at his inauguration.

Not surprisingly, then, the majority of Americans—60 percent—believe that crime and violence is worsening in America (Gallup, 2018). This belief—that crime and violence is on the rise and worsening—has been a consistent finding in Gallup surveys for decades. For example, 17 Gallup surveys conducted since the early 1990s indicate that at least 6 in 10 respondents believed that more crime occurred in the current year than in the previous year. Yet Pew Research Center statistics indicate that violent crime rates actually *peaked* in the early 1990s, and have substantially decreased over the next three decades. According to FBI figures, the crime rate declined almost by half (i.e., 48 percent) in 25 years; and Bureau of Justice statistics (based on their annual surveys) suggested that the crime rate fell even further—almost 75 percent—during the same time period

(Perfas, 2018). Presented slightly differently, the national violent crime rate in 1991 was about 770 cases per 100,000 persons, and the murder rate was almost 10 murders per 100,000. In 2017, violent crime had fallen to about 370 cases per 100,000 and murders had dropped to about 5.5 per 100,000 (Statista Research, 2020; Routley, 2019).

Thus, in spite of the common perception that America is more violent now than ever before, the objective data paint a much different picture. While almost half of America (48 percent) continues to rate the problem of crime as "very" or "extremely serious" (Gallup, 2018), the reality is that the country is actually safer now than it has been in decades (Perfas, 2018). As New York University's Brennan Center for Justice noted in 2015, "Although headlines suggesting a coming crime wave make good copy, a look at the available data shows there is no evidence to support that claim. The average person . . . is safer walking down the street today than he or she would have been at almost any time in the past 30 years" (Grawert & Cullen, 2015). Accordingly, it seems reasonable to conclude that modern America is really no more violent—and (judging by crime statistics) likely much less violent—than the United States of past eras.

The Facts: The general belief that the United States is an increasingly violent country is perhaps understandable. Media reports of assaults, burglaries, high-speed chases, mass shootings, and severe acts of violence receive extensive airtime, and—if the incident is particularly gruesome—people are assailed with images and accounts of the crime multiple times, often for weeks (Brown, 2015). Some commentators argue that both national and local media overreport violent crime, substantially influencing the public's misperception of societal violence, and feeding fear and anxiety over potential victimization (Sun, 2018).

This is not to suggest that media exaggeration is completely misleading. The country clearly has a considerable level of violent crime—drug war murders, mass shootings, gang killings, armed assaults, intimate partner attacks, and so forth. Gun violence especially is a particular American scourge. But even discounting gun murders, the United States would still have a non-gun murder rate (i.e., 1.5 homicides per 100,000 people) higher than 70 other countries (Epstein, 2019). Thus, while some justification exists for considering the United States a "violent" country (e.g., Diaz, 2018; Healy, 2018; Heer, 2017), the country is much safer and less violent than in previous decades. Robberies, burglaries, aggravated assaults, thefts, murders, and so forth all show the same pattern: a continuing sharp decline from the 1990s through the late 2010s (Routley, 2019).

The same decrease is evident even in schools. Federal data show that bullying, violence, crime, and drugs have noticeably decreased in the 20 years since the Columbine High School shooting. For example, only 20 percent of students (ages 12–18) experienced bullying at school in the 2016–17 school year, the lowest level of reported bullying since the government started collecting this data in 2005. Similarly, only 6 percent of students (grades 9–12) were threatened or injured with a weapon on school grounds in 2016–17, down from 9 percent in 2000–01. Students reporting a fear of being attacked or harmed at school also decreased during this same period, from 6 percent of students to 4 percent (Camera, 2019). Nonetheless, in a poll conducted by the Associated Press-NORC Center for Public Affairs Research, 67 percent of respondents believed that schools were less safe than 20 years ago (AP-NORC, 2019). Similarly, a 2016 survey conducted by the market research and public opinion firm Ipsos found that 65 percent of Americans believed that youth today were less safe from crime and harm than their parents had been (Routley, 2019).

As noted earlier, the typical explanation for the misalignment of Americans' perception of violence and crime and objective reality is media influence and effects (e.g., Brown, 2015; Perfas, 2018; Sun, 2018). News outlets, television entertainment, and other media overemphasize incidents of crime and violence presumably because, as the Brennan report suggests, such incidents "make good copy" and attract readers and viewers. Whatever the reasons for such sensationalization, the misperceptions generated create serious societal issues. Not only do overreports of criminal violence generate unnecessary fear and anxiety, they also feed unfair racial and ethnic biases about those responsible. For example, despite homicide being a largely intraracial crime, overreporting of less common incidents of Black-on-white homicide stokes fear of Black people and worsens racial tensions (Sun, 2018).

Another commentator reflecting on the overreporting of violence observes that in actuality women are *less* likely to become a crime victim than men (although they are at much greater risk of being a victim of certain types of crimes, such as sexual assault). Further, because the media typically portray women as victims, women then become the focus of crime prevention campaigns that offer advice that assumes that they are at greatest risk of victimization from strangers—for example, "don't go out late at night," "don't go out without your friends," and so forth. Yet, rather than this implied "stranger-danger," crime statistics indicate that women are much more likely to be harmed by someone they know—a friend, relationship partner, or other acquaintance—rather than a random unknown assailant. Thus, media-created misperceptions result in crime-prevention tips that often do not focus on the greatest sources of risk to them (Perfas, 2018).

Aside from the media's impact on the country's distorted assessment of violence, another factor—the politicization of violence perceptions—also contributes to the distortion. In the ongoing cultural and political wars between pro-gun and anti-gun factions, both sides emphasize that the country is a violent and dangerous place. For example, one gun control proponent—Kieran Healy, a professor of sociology at Duke University—observed that "Even as overall rates of violent death decline, the horrific, high-visibility mass shooting appears to have become more common in the United States in recent years. It is by now well institutionalized as a mode of violence. For as long as powerful firearms remain easily available to private citizens, the United States is likely to remain well above the OECD [Organization for Economic Cooperation and Development] average when it comes to violent death" (Healy, 2018).

In a similar vein, gun control organizations typically present alarming graphics about gun violence in America. Everytown for Gun Safety (2020) provides an illustration: "Every day, more than 100 Americans are killed with guns and 200 more are shot and wounded . . . gun violence shapes the lives of millions of Americans. . . ." While the statistics presented are arguably accurate snapshots, they don't reflect the decades-long decline in gun murders and gun violence.

Gun rights organizations also have a vested interest in emphasizing societal violence. For example, the National Rifle Association's flagship publication, *American Rifleman*, has a monthly feature entitled "The Armed Citizen." The column always contains about a half-dozen vignettes taken from news sources around the country, each describing how a law-abiding individual used a firearm to ward off an assailant or to stop a home invasion. Further, the theme of many of the advertisements carried in the publication is the need to guard against violence—for example, "HK Heckler & Koch Pistol: *Better to Have It and Not Need It, than to Need It and Not Have It*" "M&P Shield Pistol: *Protection Made Easy*"; "Norma MHP (Monolithic Hollow Point) Cartridges: *Ultimate Self Defense Ammunition*"; "Sneaky Pete Carry Faithfully Holsters: *Sometimes Even in the Most Sacred Places It's Not as Safe as It Should Be*" (see American Rifleman, 2020). Again, the content of the column and the focus of the ads are not false or deceptive, but both imply a society that is more violent than objective reality warrants.

For instance, in 2014 and using murders as a metric of violence, more than half the counties (54 percent) in the United States saw no murders at all. Further, 51 percent of all murders in the country occurred in just

2 percent of U.S. counties. The majority of violence in America is highly concentrated, typically occurring in the troubled areas of big cities (Epstein, 2019). From this perspective, not only is violence decreasing in America, but for a substantial majority of Americans, violence has never been an issue to begin with. In any case, despite perceptions to the contrary, the objective evidence is clear: modern America is no more violent—and probably much less violent—than America in past eras.

FURTHER READING

American Rifleman, 2020. Advertisements. May, 168(5), pp. 7, 23, 29, 63.

AP-NORC, 2019. "School Safety and Shootings." Associated Press-NORC Center for Public Affairs Research, March. https://apnorc.org/projects/Pages/School-Safety-And-Shootings

Brown, Brittni, 2015. "Is the Media Altering Our Perceptions of Crime?" *International Policy Digest*, March 11. https://intpolicydigest.org/2015/03/11/is-the-media-altering-our-perceptions-of-crime/

Camera, Lauren, 2019. "Federal Data Show Decreasing Rates of Bullying and Violence in Schools." *U.S. News & World Report*, April 17. https://www.usnews.com/news/education-news/articles/2019-04-17/20-years-after-columbine-shooting-federal-data-show-bullying-violence-and-crime-in-schools-is-down

Diaz, Jesus, 2018. "How the U.S. Is Getting More Violent, by the Numbers." Fast Company, August 3. https://www.fastcompany.com/90212938/the-u-s-is-getting-more-violent-by-the-numbers

Epstein, Ethan, 2019. "America Is a Violent Country, with or without Guns." *Washington Times*, August 8. https://www.washingtontimes.com/news/2019/aug/8/america-is-a-violent-country-with-or-without-guns

Everytown for Gun Safety, 2020. "Gun Violence in America." Everytown for Gun Safety, February 20. https://everytownresearch.org/gun-violence-in-america/

Gallup, 2018. "Americans' Concerns about National Crime Abating." Gallup, November 7. https://news.gallup.com/poll/244394/americans-concerns-national-crime-abating.aspx

Grawert, Ames, & Cullen, James, 2015. "Crime in 2015: A Final Analysis." Brennan Center for Justice. https://www.brennancenter.org/sites/default/files/analysis/Crime_in_2015_A_Final_Analysis.pdf

Healy, Kieran, 2018. "America Is a Violent Country." *Washington Post*, November 8. https://www.washingtonpost.com/news/monkey-cage/wp/2017/10/03/america-is-a-violent-country/

Heer, Jeet, 2017. "America Has Always Been Angry and Violent." *New Republic*, June 15. https://newrepublic.com/article/143361/America-always-angry-violent

Kaplan, Sophie, 2017. "The Violent Crime Rate Has Risen, and the Homicide Rate Has Risen by More than 20 Percent in Just Two Years, Really after 30 Years of Decline in Violent Crime." PolitiFact, December 4. https://www.politifact.com/factchecks/2017/dec/04/jeff-sessions/violent-crime-some-still-well-historical-highs/

McGill, Andrew, 2016. "Is Violence in America Going Up or Down?" *Atlantic*, July 15. https://www.theatlantic.com/politics/archive/2016/07/is-violence-in-america-going-up-or-down/491384

Perfas, Samantha, 2018. "Episode 1: High Crime and Misperceptions." *Christian Science Monitor*, October 15. https://www.csmonitor.com/USA/Justice/2018/1015/Episode-1-High-Crime-and-Misperceptions

Routley, Nick, 2019. "The Crime Rate Perception Gap." Visual Capitalist, February 5. visualcapitalist.com/crime-rate-perception-gap/

Statista Research, 2020. "Reported Violent Crime Rate in the U.S. from 1990 to 2019." https://www.statista.com/statistics/191219/reported-violent-crime-rate-in-the-usa-since-1990/

Sun, Elizabeth, 2018. "The Dangerous Radicalization of Crime in U.S. News Media." Center for American Progress, August 29. https://www.americanprogress.org/issues/criminal-justice/news/2018/08/29/455313/dangerous-radicalization-crime-u-s-news-media/

Index

ABC World News Tonight, 124
Active Shooter Response System (ASRS), 152–153
Adshead, Gwen, 196
Alper, Mariel, 8, 10, 11, 12, 13, 14, 16, 17, 35, 38, 137, 140
American Academy of Family Physicians (AAFP), 224, 228
American Academy of Pediatrics (AAP), 224, 228
American Civil Liberties Union of Rhode Island (ACLU-RI), 69, 70
American Federation of Teachers (AFT), 149
American Psychological Association (APA), 224, 228, 229
American Rifleman, 240, 241
Americans with Disabilities Act (ADA), 199
America's Rifle, 36
Anti-Defamation League (ADL), 231, 233, 234, 235; Center on Extremism, 231, 233
Antifa, 231, 233, 234, 235
Arab American Institute, 231

Armalite Rifle/AR-15, 11, 32–36, 38, 39, 82, 97, 138
Armed Career Criminal Act, 164
Armed citizens, 5, 74, 79, 80, 82, 83, 131, 134, 152, 171; teachers, 137, 149, 150, 153
Armed Citizens Legal Defense Network, 105
Assault rifles, 11, 32, 33, 36, 37, 38. *See also* Armalite Rifle/AR-15
Assault weapons ban, 12, 33, 35–39, 93, 95, 97, 141, 180
Assessment of evidence, 4, 6, 7, 16–17, 20–23, 29, 33, 35, 37, 46, 48–49, 53, 80, 188–190, 192–194, 208, 216, 238, 241. *See also* Nature of evidence; Weight of evidence
Associated Press-NORC Center for Public Affairs Research, 239, 241
Association of American Educators, 51
ATF Form 4473, 157, 159, 187, 204
Atlantic, 129, 172, 191, 193, 195, 233, 236, 242

Aurora, Colorado shooting, 127, 143, 212
Automatic weapon, 25, 32–35, 92, 93, 96, 100, 138. *See also* Semi-automatic weapon
Azrael, Deborah, 13, 16, 18, 54, 56, 58, 59, 92, 137, 141, 212

Background checks, 5, 13–19, 80–81, 85, 100, 136–138, 141–142, 175–178, 187, 204; private transaction, 101; universal, 17–18, 101, 103, 136–138, 140, 180; violations, 156–159, 162; waiting period, 209. *See also* Private seller checks
Ballistic fingerprinting, 2, 7, 25–32
Bandura, Albert, 126, 128, 225, 227, 228
Baxley, Dennis, 63, 65
Bell, Larry, 5, 6
Black Armed Guard, 112
Black Panthers, 112
Black rifle, 34. *See also* Armalite Rifle/AR-15
Blau, Benjamin, 37, 38
Bloomberg, Michael, 166
Bloomberg News, 58, 59
Booker, Cory, 100, 103
Boss, Stephen, 132
Boston Police Department, 27, 31
Bradford, E. J., 113
Brady Campaign to Prevent Gun Violence, 28, 100, 159–160
Brady Handgun Violence Prevention Act (Brady Bill), 15, 18, 209, 213
Brantley, Sheila, 140
Bray, Mark, 234
Brennan Center for Justice, 238, 241
Brookings Institution, 111, 115
Bump stocks, 74, 92–96
Bureau of Alcohol, Tobacco, Firearms, and Explosives (BATFE), 159, 160, 207

Bureau of Justice Statistics, 9, 10, 12, 13, 17, 38, 140, 237
Burroughs, Benjamin, 224, 225, 226
Bush, George W., 81

California Department of Justice, 28, 32
Campus carry, 130–135
Canady, Mo, 150–153
Castile, Philando, 113
CBS News, 70, 76, 78, 79, 105, 107, 109, 222, 235
Center for Research in Crime and Justice, 20
Center for Strategic and International Studies, 232–234, 236
Centers for Disease Control and Prevention (CDC), 103, 135, 212; gun deaths, 74–75, 78–79, 235; licensing and registration, 99, 102; research ban, 4; waiting periods, 210
Chicago Police, 9, 21, 24, 157
Child access prevention (CAP) laws, 51, 55–59
Cleaver, Eldridge, 112
Clinton, Hillary, 16, 174, 179
Clinton administration, 33
Coalition to Stop Gun Violence (CSGV), 27, 28, 29, 30, 31
Collective right, 170, 171. *See also* Individual Right
Collins, Susan, 174, 178
Colt firearms, 9, 33, 90
Columbine High School shooting, 111, 117, 118, 121, 122, 126, 127, 150, 154, 239, 241
Communitarianism, 215. *See also* Rugged individualism
Concealed carry, 6, 80–82, 84–85, 111, 113, 131–133, 136, 144–148, 158. *See also* Open carry
Concealed handguns, 80, 81, 84, 151
Constitutional/permitless carry, 82–85

Contagion effects, 124–129
Cook, Philip, 2, 6, 15, 18, 209, 213
Copy-cat shootings, 125
Crifasi, Cassandra, 22, 25, 86, 88, 89, 90, 159
Crime Prevention Research Center (CPRC), 63, 65, 68, 79, 81, 83, 84, 145, 154, 209
Crusius, Patrick, 143

Darnell, Jason, 182
Davis, Kevin, 166
Davis, Nezida, 112
de Blasio, Bill, 165
Defensive gun uses (DGUs), 42–45, 46, 47, 66
Denver Post, 68, 72
Department of Homeland Security, 174
Department of Justice, 4, 5, 51, 158, 160, 161, 190, 191, 194
Deterrence effect, 163–165, 167
Dickey, Jay, 4; amendment, 4
DiMaggio, Charles, 37, 38, 39
Dingell, John, 158
Drug legalization, 189–195. *See also* Marijuana legalization
Drugs, 187–189, 192, 239; illegal, 132, 190, 193; psychiatric/psychotropic, 195–201; war on, 188, 191–195
Due process, 67–70, 175–177
Duty to retreat, 60, 61, 63, 106

Eddie Eagle program, 49, 51–53
El Paso Walmart shooting, 143, 158, 161, 202, 223
Eli Lily & Company, 197
Enhanced sentencing, 163–168; Proposition 8, 163. *See also* Mandatory minimum sentence
Epidemiological approach, 45, 46, 124
Epidemiological Catchment Area Survey, 203

Eron, Leonard, 224, 225, 229
Everytown for Gun Safety, 67, 68, 71, 74, 78, 83, 84, 93, 96, 119, 120, 122, 123, 130–132, 134, 137–140, 145–146, 149, 150, 151, 153, 177–178, 180, 185, 240, 241
Extreme Risk Protection Orders (ERPOs), 67–70. *See also* Red flag laws
Extremists, 180, 230–237

Fast Company, 237, 241
Federal Bureau of Investigation (FBI), 4, 11, 35, 44, 75, 77, 85, 179, 191, 237; intelligence assessment, 175, 177, 231–233, 235–237; NICS checks, 100, 156–157, supplemental homicide reports, 10, 65; uniform crime reports, 192
Federal firearms license (FFL), 14, 159
Feinstein, Dianne, xiii, xvi, 96, 168, 174
Felon-in-possession violation, 10, 162, 171
Fenty, Adrian, 168
Ferguson, Christopher, 121, 123, 224–227, 229
Feshback, Seymour, 224
Fifer, Michael, 94
Firearm Owners Protection Act (FOPA), 14, 15, 99, 100
Follman, Mark, 127, 128, 143, 146, 147, 205, 206
Food and Drug Administration (FDA), 197, 200
Forbes, 5, 6, 53, 109, 212
Fort Hood, Texas shooting, 177
Fox, James Allen, 36, 39, 119, 121, 122
Fox News, 27–28, 31, 104, 114, 153
Frank, Robert, 107
Fugitive Slave Act, 183

Gang violence, 188–191, 193–195
Gardiner, Avery, 159, 160

Giffords, Gabby, 16, 81, 93
Giffords Law Center to Prevent Gun Violence, 16, 18, 20, 22–24, 27, 31, 43, 47, 53, 55–57, 59–61, 64, 65, 81, 83, 84, 92, 95, 96, 98, 101, 103, 130, 134, 135, 136, 138–141, 143, 145–147, 172, 176–178, 180, 185, 207, 209, 210, 212
Gius, Mark, 11, 12, 37, 39, 137, 141
Glaze, Lauren, 8, 10–14, 16, 17, 35, 38, 137, 140
Glock firearms, 9
Graham, Lindsey, 68, 71
Graves, Howard, 182
Grinshteyn, Erin, 217–219, 222
Gualtieri, Bob, 149
Gun Control Act (GCA), 14, 19, 24, 100
Gun culture, 7, 117, 172, 215
Gun deaths, xv, 50, 56, 67, 75–79, 91, 111, 114, 130, 192, 213, 216, 217, 222, 235
Gun Free Schools Act (GFSA), 145
Gun Free Schools Zone Act (GFSZA), 142, 143, 145
Gun free zones, 118, 136, 142–144, 146, 147
Gun homicides, 3, 5, 13, 17, 22, 23, 37, 60, 62, 99, 110, 111, 169, 190, 207, 208, 210, 220, 235. *See also* Homicides
Gun liability insurance, 74, 104, 105–110, 151
Gun licensing, 22, 104
Gun Owners of America (GOA), 27, 28, 31, 69, 181
Gun politics, 11, 12, 17, 63, 81, 160
Gun registration/registry, 1, 19, 20, 22, 23, 73, 98–104, 110. *See also* National registry
Gun regulation, xiv, xvi, 77, 113, 136, 137, 140, 155, 156, 158, 169, 170, 171, 216–218
Gun running, 157, 160, 189

Gun safety, 48–54, 56, 58, 86, 92, 96, 143, 169; training, 42, 48–51, 53, 85
Gun sales, 1, 5, 6, 7, 13, 14, 15, 18, 19, 20, 21, 25, 74, 138, 159
Gun show loophole, xiii, 1, 13–16, 19. *See also* Private seller loophole
Gun suicides, 42, 49, 50, 67, 120, 188, 207–210; proxy estimate, 3. *See also* Gun homicides
Gun tracing, 21, 26
Gun trafficking, 21, 24, 101, 156, 157, 160, 161, 163
Guns Down, 105

Haile, Jeremy, 166
Hammer, Marion, 63
Hammond, Michael, 69
Handgun Control, Inc., 11
Harris, Eric, 150
Harvard School of Public Health, 58
Hawkins, Gordon, 220, 223
Healy, Kieran, 237, 238, 240, 241
Heitkamp, Heidi, 174
Heller decision, 156, 162, 168–173
Hemenway, David, 42–45, 47, 59, 77, 78, 212, 217, 219, 222
Hepburn, Lisa, 13, 16, 18, 20, 22, 25, 98, 104, 137, 141, 208, 212
Heritage Foundation, 4, 7, 45, 79, 97, 133
Hi Point firearms, 240
Holmes, Oliver Wendell, 63
Homicides, xv, 4, 10, 11, 17, 23, 25, 35, 45, 66, 79, 87, 111, 126, 171, 192, 196, 198, 208–212, 224, 235, 238; intimate partner, 3, 21, 24, 25, 67, 208; justifiable, 3, 48, 60, 64, 65, 169, 172; rate, 21, 22, 62, 63, 74–77, 219, 220, 237, 242. *See also* Gun homicides
Huffington Post, 4, 7
Humphreys, David, 62, 63, 65

Human Development Index (HDI), 217–219, 221, 223
Hunter safety, 52, 54

Illegal gun sales/possession, 20, 156, 157, 159, 163, 164
Impulse killings/impulse suicides, 86, 188, 207, 209–211
Imitation, 125, 126, 129
Incapacitation effect, 162–165, 167
Independence Institute, 35, 68
Individual right, 156, 170, 171. *See also* Collective right
Institute for Constitutional Advocacy and Protection, 180
Ingraham, Christopher, 11, 12, 177, 178
Insurance Law Center, 107
Ipsos polls, 94, 97, 239
Ivey, Amy, 133

Jack the Ripper, 125
Jacobs, James, 20, 21, 23, 24
Jacobson, Louis, 144, 147, 220–222
Jefferson, Thomas, 183
Jetter, Michael, 125, 126, 129
Johns Hopkins Bloomberg School of Public Health, 86
Johns Hopkins Center for Gun Policy and Research, 159, 162, 169
Johnson, Lyndon, 100
Junk science, 43

Kaine, Timothy, 16, 18
Keane, Lawrence, 86, 88, 90, 156, 158, 161
Kellermann, Arthur, 43, 45, 47, 48, 54
Kelly, Mark, 16, 19, 81, 84
Kennedy, Edward, 175
Klebold, Dylan, 150
Kleck, Gary, 3, 4, 7, 15, 20, 22, 24, 42, 43, 44, 46, 47
Knoll, James, 196, 202–205, 206

Kochenburger, Peter, 107
Kollmorgen, Sarah, 9, 11, 13
Kopel, David, 35, 39, 57, 59, 68, 130, 132, 133, 135

L.A. Times, 153, 174–178, 179
Laney, General, 112
Langman, Peter, 196, 201
LaPierre, Wayne, 139
Law Center to Prevent Gun Violence, 43, 156, 171, 172
Legislative laxity, 156, 157, 160
Libresco, Leah, xv, xvi
Lie-and-try violations, 157, 159, 162
Loesch, Dana, 105, 196, 200
Loomis, Steve, 82
Lott, John, 5–7, 26, 28, 31, 37, 39, 55, 56, 59, 63, 67, 68, 71, 79, 84, 111, 113, 114, 144, 146, 147, 150, 154, 209
Love, Dayvon, 165, 166
Ludwig, Jens, 15, 18, 209, 213

MacNab, J. J., 183, 186, 233
Madison, James, 183
Magazines (LCMs), 33, 73, 74, 92–96, 97, 136
Major Cities Chiefs Association, 150
Malcolm, John, 4, 6, 7, 75, 79, 93, 97
Mandatory minimum sentence, 164–168. *See also* Enhanced sentencing
Manger, J. Thomas, 150
Marijuana legalization, 189, 192, 193. *See also* Drug legalization
Marjory Stoneman Douglas High School shooting, 139, 149. *See also* Parkland, Florida shooting
Markey, Patrick, 224, 226, 229
Martin, Trayvon, 61, 106
Maryland State Police, 28
Massie, Thomas, 94, 97, 147
Mateen, Omar, 177, 179
Mayors Against Illegal Guns, 22, 24

McAuliffe, Terry, 16, 18
McCarthy, Kevin, 223
McCord, Mary, 180, 182
McDonald, Otis, 111
McEachin, Donald, 181
Measures/measurement, xv, 2, 22, 11, 20–23, 35, 94, 102, 121, 122, 138, 139, 153, 179, 218; of aggression, 225, 227; limitations of, 2, 227; reliable, 33, 37
Media Education Foundation, 227, 230
Mental illness, 187, 188, 198, 199, 201, 202–206; severe, 202–204
Meyer, Chris, 131
Microstamping, 2, 25–27, 29–32
Military-style rifle, 2, 11. *See also* Armalite Rifle/AR-15
Militia, 232, 233, 156, 168, 170, 183
Miller, Matthew, 18, 54, 56, 58, 59, 92, 137, 141
Miller case, 170
Minority communities, 74, 110–114, 164, 166, 190
Modeling effects, 52, 124, 126, 127. *See also* Social learning
Mortenson, Catherine, 130
Mother Jones, 76, 97, 127, 128, 141, 147, 154, 206, 230
Mulford Act, 112
Mullen, Paul, 125

Nation, 168, 173
National Academy of Sciences, 6
National African American Gun Association (NAAGA), 112, 113
National Association of Chiefs of Police, 80, 82, 84
National Association of School Resource Officers, 150
National Black Sportsman's Association, 112
National Center for Health, 51, 129

National Counterterrorism Center (NCTC), 175
National Crime Victimization Survey, 9, 44
National Criminal Information Center, 158
National Education Association (NEA), 136, 141, 142, 149, 154
National Firearms Act (NFA), 100
National Instant Criminal Background Check System (NICS), 13, 15, 16, 19, 24, 81, 85, 100, 137, 156, 209
National Institute of Standards and Technology (NIST), 29, 32
National Integrated Ballistics Identification Network (NIBIN), 26, 27, 31
National League of Cities, 190, 194
National registry, 16, 98–102. *See also* Gun registration/registry
National Research Council (NRC), 20, 24, 25, 28, 29, 32
National Rifle Association (NRA), 4, 17, 26, 28, 36, 43, 46, 48–51, 54–56, 59, 62, 63, 66, 78, 89–91, 105, 106, 109, 114, 130, 138–142, 166, 169, 200, 208
National Rifle Association-Institute for Legislative Action (NRA-ILA), 11, 13–19, 21, 24, 26, 28, 30, 32, 35, 40, 51, 54, 64, 104, 148, 208, 210, 213
National Safety Council, 223
National Sheriffs' Association, 51
National Shooting Sports Foundation (NSSF), 36, 86, 89, 91, 158
National Trace Center, 100
National Youth Risk Behavior Survey, 136
Natural right, 130, 181. *See also* Self-defense/self-protection

Nature of evidence, xiv, xvi, 69, 70.
See also Assessment of evidence;
Weight of evidence
New American, 85
New Jersey Childproof Handgun Law,
89, 90
New York Daily News, 128
New York Times, 30, 38, 67, 71, 84, 85,
104, 118, 122, 128, 173, 179, 206,
229, 235; editorial, 26, 28, 32, 81,
84, 85, 130, 168, 231
Nixon, Richard, 191
No Fly List, 174–176, 178, 179
North, Oliver, 138, 142
Northam, Ralph, 181, 183
Novartis Pharmaceutical
Company, 197
Nullification, 182, 183

Oath Keepers, 183
Obama, Barack, 17, 32, 34, 39, 81, 160,
161, 174, 179, 195
Open carry, 82–84, 112, 114. See also
Concealed carry
Organization for Economic
Cooperation and Development
(OECD), 76, 216–222, 240
Orlando, Florida shooting, 34, 177,
178, 179. See also Pulse night club
shooting
O'Rourke, Beto, 100, 216

Paddock, Stephen, 92
Parkland, Florida shooting, 16, 34, 111,
116, 122, 139, 154, 172. See also
Marjory Stoneman Douglas High
School shooting
PDK International poll, 150
Pelosi, Nancy, 134, 237
Permits, 22, 106, 145; concealed carry,
6, 79, 80, 81, 83, 84, 111, 113;
open carry, 83; permitless carry,
84, 85; shall-issue, 6
Peterson, Jillian, 120, 122, 125

Peterson, Scot, 149
Pew Research Center, 5, 73, 74,
84, 112, 113, 115, 118, 123,
213, 237
Phillips, David, 125
Pitcavage, Mark, 233
PolitiFact, 18, 19, 39, 65, 147, 200, 201,
212, 213, 220, 222, 236, 242
Polls, 5, 42, 68, 86, 99; Gallup, 41, 136;
Ipsos, 94; NBC/*Wall Street
Journal*, 41, 44; online, 82, 99,
150, 152, 184, 205; Pew, 73
Pratt, Erich, 144, 148, 181
Predictive assessments, 176–178
President's Council of Advisors on
Science and Technology, 26,
29, 32
Pringle, Becky, 149
Private seller checks, 13, 15–17, 101,
137, 138, 156, 179; exemption, 15.
See also Background checks
Private seller loophole, 15, 17. See also
Gun show loophole
Prohibited person, 14, 87, 160
Prozac, 197, 200
Psychiatric/psychotropic drugs, 188,
195–201. See also Drugs
Pulse night club shooting, 177, 178. See
also Orlando, Florida shooting

Racial disparities, 64–65, 111, 165,
166, 216, 230, 233, 234, 239
Rand, Kristen, 81
RAND Corporation, 7, 17, 18, 20, 21,
23–25, 55, 56, 58, 60, 66, 79,
142–144, 146, 148, 208, 210, 211,
213, 214
Reagan, Ronald, 112
Reasonable prohibitions, 171
Red flag laws, 42, 66–72, 138, 179, 180,
182, 205, 206. See also Extreme
Risk Protection Orders (ERPOs)
Replacement effect, 68. See also
Substitution effect

RFID technology, 86, 88, 89, 152
Risk warrants, 66. *See also* Extreme Risk Protection Orders (ERPOs)
Ritalin, 196, 197, 200
Rodger, Elliot, 143
Rolling Stone, 35, 38
Rossi, Peter, 8–13
Ruger, William, 94
Ruger/Sturm, Ruger & Co. firearms, 9, 30, 90, 94
Rugged individualism, xiii, 215. *See also* Communitarianism
Rutherford Institute, 99

Safe storage, 42, 47, 50, 54–59, 88
Salon, 123, 144, 148
Samuels, Dorothy, 168, 170, 171, 173
Sanders, Bernie, 16
Sandia National Laboratories, 88
Sandy Hook Elementary School shooting, 34, 111, 118, 122, 126, 139, 141, 150, 154
Santa Fe shooting, 111
Saturday night specials, 8
Scalia, Antonin, 170, 171
Scalise, Steve, 233
Schildkraut, Jaclyn, 122
School resource officers, 122, 139, 146, 149, 150
School Shield program, 139, 140
School shootings, 12, 117–127, 129, 132, 134, 136–140, 142, 148–150, 197, 200, 201, 223
Schovanec, Lawrence, 131
Schumer, Charles, 28
Schwarzenegger, Arnold, 29
Scott, Phil, 211
Second Amendment, 64, 65, 67, 78, 83, 99, 102, 108, 109, 148, 156, 168–173, 179–181, 211
Second Amendment sanctuary movement, 70, 71, 156, 179–182, 184–186
Secure Ammunition and Firearms Enforcement (SAFE) Act, 165

Selectee List, 174
Self-defense/self-protection, 8, 11, 41–45, 46–48, 50, 55, 57, 60, 61, 63–66, 81, 85, 105–109, 112, 113, 132, 135, 165, 173, 184, 211, 240; natural right, 130, 181. *See also* Stand your ground (SYG) laws
Semi-automatic weapon, xiii, 9, 11, 27, 32–35, 37, 38, 96, 138, 174, 180. *See also* Automatic weapon
Sentencing Project, 166
Sessions, Jeff, 237, 242
Siegel, Michael, 93
Skaggs, Adam, 156
Slate, 97, 114, 167, 173, 179
Smart guns, 86–92
Smith, Noah, 191, 192, 195
Smith, Philip, 112, 113
Smith & Wesson firearms, 9, 30, 90
Social learning, 126–128, 225, 227, 228. *See also* Modeling effects
Soltis, Gary, 181
Southern Poverty Law Center, 182
Stand your ground (SYG) laws, 42, 60–66, 106, 107. *See also* Self-defense
Stern, Mark, 174, 177, 179
Stevens, John Paul, 169, 173
Stone, Michael, 203
Stoner, Eugene, 33
Strasburger, Victor, 225, 226, 230
Straw purchase, 14, 87, 157–160, 162, 163
Students for Concealed Carry on Campus, 132
Sturm, Ruger & Co. firearms. *See* Ruger/Sturm, Ruger & Co. firearms
Substitution effect, 2, 210, 212. *See also* Replacement effect
Sugarmann, Josh, 11, 13, 34, 35, 40
Suicides, xv, 45–51, 53–59, 67, 68, 74, 75, 78, 111, 169, 172, 207–211, 214, 235; child, 67, 56; impulse, 86, 188; and media, 125–127; and red flag laws, 67, 68, 70, 72, 180;

smart guns, 87. *See also* Gun suicides
Sullivan law, xiii, 155
Surrender of weapons orders, 24, 102,
Swanson, Jeffery, 68, 70, 72, 202, 204
Swearer, Amy, 4, 6, 7, 45, 48, 75, 79, 93, 97, 98, 133

Tarde, Gabriel, 125
Taurus firearms, 9
Terrorist Identities Datamart Environment (TIDE), 175
Terrorist Screening Center, 174, 175, 179
Terrorist Screening Database (TSDB), 174–177
The Base, 231
Third Way, 160
Thomas, Clarence, 211
Threat assessment programs, 137, 139, 205–207
Three Percent Security Force, 183, 186
Three strike laws, 164
Trace, 12, 13, 42, 47, 59, 103, 109, 129, 135, 144, 148, 162, 168, 186, 214
Trigger locks, 54, 87, 110
Trumble, Sarah, 160
Trump, Donald, 19, 96, 114, 139, 141, 144, 149, 202, 223, 234, 235–237
Twain, Mark, 41

Umpqua Community College shooting, 131
Underground market, 10, 11
Universal gun registration, 1
Unregulated market, 13, 14, 16
U.S. Concealed Carry Association, 105, 106
U.S. Extremist Crime Database, 234
U.S. Law Shield, 105

Values, xiii, xiv, 67, 77, 215
Vermont carry, 83
Vernick, Jon, 20, 22, 25, 98, 194

Vicarious learning, 228. *See also* Social learning
Violence Policy Center (VPC), 13, 40, 48, 54, 81, 85, 87, 92, 162, 173
Violence Project, 125, 141
Violent Crime Control and Law Enforcement Act (Assault Weapons Ban Act), 95. *See also* Assault weapons ban
Virginia Tech shooting, 16, 93, 126, 132
Volsky, Igor, 105

Waiting periods (WPs), 207–211
Walker, Jay, 125, 126, 129
Wall Street Journal, 41, 44, 123, 129, 236
Washington Post, xvi, 12, 24, 31, 48, 59, 84, 96, 123, 124, 135, 140, 142, 147, 161, 178, 179, 185, 186, 193, 229, 237, 241
Washington Times, 98, 148, 237, 241
Watch lists, 156, 174–179
Watts, Shannon, 17, 19
Webster, Daniel, 20–23, 25, 90, 98, 104, 169
Weight of evidence, xiv, 20, 83, 224, 226–227. *See also* Assessment of evidence; Nature of evidence
Weingarten, Randi, 149
Weisser, Mike, 4, 5, 7
White supremacy, 182, 183, 231–236
Whitehead, John, 99
Williams, Robert, 112
Winkler, Adam, 5, 32, 56, 59, 68, 72, 148
Wolfers, Justin, 107
Wright, James, 8–13

Zawitz, Marianne, 8–10, 13
Zimring, Franklin, 5, 7, 14, 15, 19, 219, 220, 223
Zimmerman, George, 61
Zogby, James, 231, 237

About the Author

Donald J. Campbell, PhD, is professor emeritus of leadership and management at the U.S. Military Academy at West Point, New York. He received his graduate degrees in psychology from Purdue University, West Lafayette, Indiana.

www.ingramcontent.com/pod-product-compliance
Lightning Source LLC
Chambersburg PA
CBHW070244230426
43664CB00014B/2402